Right at the Centre

Cecil Parkinson

Right at the Centre

an autobiography

Weidenfeld and Nicolson
London

First published in Great Britain in 1992 by
George Weidenfeld & Nicolson Limited
Orion House,
5 Upper St Martin's Lane,
London WC2H 9EA

British Library Cataloguing-in-Publication Data
is available on request

Typeset by Selwood Systems, Midsomer Norton
Printed and bound in Great Britain by
Butler & Tanner Ltd, Frome and London

Contents

Acknowledgements vi

List of Illustrations vii

Prologue 1

1 A Dragon in Shallow Waters 5

2 Diffidence and Deference 51

3 The Imaginative and the Contrived 65

4 Laying Foundations 78

5 Just Another Useful Vote 92

6 Joining the Whips 107

7 The Statutory Female Aggravator 129

8 Bosses and Buses 146

9 A Very Straightforward Job 173

10 'That's a Hell of a Tough Lady' 193

11 In the Hands of the Electorate 214

12 The Big Decisions Are Taken Here 234

13 Megavars and Motorways 257

Epilogue 301

Index 306

Acknowledgements

To Michael Simmonds for his research, help and encouragement,

To Mary Carson and Patricia Gray for deciphering my handwriting and hours of typing,

To Hilary Laurie, my Editor, for her quiet insistence,

To Gina Thomas for reading large parts of the text and eliminating unnecessary words,

To Pamela Norris for her copy editing,

To Dr Gell, assistant archivist at Emmanuel College for her help with the Cambridge years,

My thanks.

Illustrations

Between pages 152 and 153

Schoolboy, aged 14
Graduating from Cambridge, 1955
Receiving Victor Ludorum, 1948
Training at Fenners, 1954
Mary 10, Emma 8 and Joanna 6 watching production of the *Northampton Chronicle and Echo* (*Northampton Chronicle and Echo*)
Family skiing holiday, January 1970
Election Night, Northampton, June 1970 (*Northampton Chronicle and Echo*)
Arriving to take seat in the House of Commons, December 1970 (*The Times*)
European Parliamentary Ski Race, March 1972
As Minister of Trade with Norman Lamont and British Ambassador to the Soviet Union, October 1979
With Vice Premier Yu Qiuli of China at Fiddler's Ferry power station, 1979
Meeting President Videla of Argentina, 8 August 1980 (Argentine Government)
Presenting English language laboratory to University of Cameroon, Yaoundé, 1981
Trade promotion visit to Saudi Arabia, 1981
Breakfast with Ann and Joanna the day after becoming Party Chairman, September 1981
Accompanying the Queen on a visit to the Duchy of Lancaster estates in Staffordshire, June 1982
Running in Battersea Park, September 1982 (*Evening Standard*)
Meeting with President Reagan, March 1983 (*White House*)
Celebrating election victory Borehamwood, June 1987 (*Borehamwood Post*)
Visit to Morcambe Bay gas platform as Energy Secretary, October 1987 (*British Gas*)
Landing in 'Hong Kong' in flight simulator as Transport Secretary, May 1990 (British Airways)
With Mrs Thatcher, July 1991 (Billett Potter)

Every effort has been made to trace the source of photographs. When a source is not given, the pictures come from the author's collection.

To my wife, Ann

Prologue

Thursday 22 November 1990 At about 7.0 a.m. the telephone rang in my London flat. I was surprised to hear the voice of Chris Chope, one of my junior ministers at the Department of Transport. He had some appalling news for me. Margaret Thatcher was almost certain to announce that she would not be a candidate in the second ballot for the leadership of the Conservative Party and would be resigning as Prime Minister. He was telephoning to ask me to make a last-minute appeal to her to change her mind. I was stunned. I had seen her the previous evening at about 6.0 p.m. At that time she was full of enthusiasm and determined to win on the second ballot. I therefore went out to dinner with my wife and a group of friends feeling sure that with the full and active support of the Cabinet, and with better organization than in the first ballot, she would win well.

We had a very relaxed dinner and got home at about midnight. I went straight to bed, and was soon in such a deep sleep that I did not hear the telephone when it rang at about 12.45 a.m. My wife answered. It was Trevor Kavanagh, the Political Editor of *The Sun*. He had heard a strong rumour that Margaret was resigning and he wanted to talk to me about it. Ann said that I was asleep, needed the rest and she would not disturb me. She told me about this the next morning after my conversation with Chris Chope.

By 7.10 a.m. I was on the telephone to Number 10 and asked to speak to the Prime Minister. The operator asked me to wait. She came back on the line to tell me that the PM was at that moment under the hair dryer and suggested that I telephone again in about half an hour.

I then rang Norman Tebbit to find out what he knew. As usual, he knew a lot. He had been with her until late the night before, working on her speech for the Censure Debate that afternoon, and he was sure that she would be resigning. We agreed that it would be pointless for me to telephone her again.

I left for the office where I was due to meet my ministerial colleagues in Transport for one of our regular early morning prayers. We held them on Tuesdays and Thursdays. Tuesday was 'departmental' and included the Permanent Secretary. Thursday was political and only ministers, my special adviser, Elizabeth Buchanan, and the desk officer from Conservative Research Department, Perry Miller, attended. We met at 8.30, but before that Chris Chope and Elizabeth Buchanan came in and we pieced together a clear picture of the events of the previous evening and discussed the likely outcome of Cabinet. We were a sombre group.

As a departmental team we had been totally committed to Margaret Thatcher and we were still unanimous in wishing her to carry on as leader. By then, it was becoming clear that a group of younger Cabinet ministers had played a decisive role in persuading her to change her mind. For my part, I did not feel that they were particularly well qualified to interpret the mood of either the parliamentary party or the party in the country to her.

Cabinet had been called for 9.0 a.m. and we adjourned our meeting at about 8.50 so that I could get there. We arranged to meet again at 10.30 so that I could report back to them the outcome of Cabinet.

I left Marsham Street with Elizabeth Buchanan. She was on her way to the meeting of special advisers which took place each week at the same time as Cabinet. It was jokingly called the Shadow Cabinet and those present liked to think that the standard of discussion was of a higher quality, possibly than the Cabinet, and certainly than the other Shadow Cabinet.

We were both in a gloomy and angry frame of mind. I arrived at Number 10 unusually early, to find that a number of Cabinet colleagues were already waiting in the anteroom outside the Cabinet room. Most of them were looking grim and saying little. Ken Clarke was the exception. He was telling anybody who cared to listen that if the PM did not resign he would resign before noon that day. He was adamant that she had to go. James Mackay, the Lord Chancellor, was quiet and looked preoccupied. The reason for that became clear a few minutes later.

It was not unusual for Cabinet to start a few minutes late and it did that day. The waiting on this occasion was almost unbearable and the atmosphere became more tense by the minute. At about 9.10 the door of the Cabinet room was opened and we went in. The Prime Minister was already there, sitting in her usual place, with Sir Robin

Butler, the Cabinet Secretary next to her. She had been crying, her eyes were red and swollen and she looked deeply distressed. As we came in I noticed that a carton of tissues had been placed next to her on the Cabinet table. She picked one from the box and wiped away the tears which had welled up into her eyes. There was a deathly silence in the room. In a halting voice she said that she wished to make a statement, following which we would return to normal Cabinet business. She started to read but broke down after a few words. She started a second time and again she broke down. At this point I spoke, saying 'For God's sake, James, you read it.' This broke the tension. Various colleagues disagreed with me, and in the few seconds this took, the Prime Minister regained her composure and read out the statement. It was the one that was made public a little later.

As she was reading her statement I glanced at my colleagues. Most of them could not bring themselves to look at her. They sat staring at the Cabinet table so intently that they looked as if they were trying to drill holes in it with their eyes. Two or three were in tears. I felt deep anger and bitterness that the Prime Minister who had led us to three election victories, and who had only two days earlier been a pivotal figure at a great international conference in Paris to mark the end of the Cold War, should have been treated so shabbily by her parliamentary colleagues.

James Mackay had obviously been warned in advance and had prepared a statement of his own in which he thanked the Prime Minister on behalf of the Cabinet for her outstanding service to the nation over such a long period. One or two other people added their own tributes, but the Prime Minister brought this phase to an early halt with a characteristic remark that she found business easier to cope with than sympathy. By this time she was totally in control of herself and the Cabinet, and we moved on to our normal weekly business.

Cabinet business was despatched quickly that morning and by ten o'clock we had finished. We all realized that this would probably be the last Cabinet over which she would preside, and nobody wanted to be the first to leave. She clearly wanted to talk and suggested that we have coffee. Officials then left the Cabinet room and a rather desultory conversation began. I remember very little of what was said but three things stuck in my mind. The first was a general agreement that the next leader must come from the Cabinet. It should not be Michael Heseltine. The second was that the Cabinet felt both John

Major and Douglas Hurd should be put up as candidates in the second ballot since it was not possible to know with any degree of certainty, nor was it possible to find out in the time available, which of them was the preferred candidate. The third and most memorable moment came when a colleague said, 'We are going to pin regicide on Heseltine.' The Prime Minister looked puzzled for a moment, and then came the devastating riposte: 'Oh no, it wasn't Heseltine, it was the Cabinet.' It was all the more telling because it was said without the slightest rancour. It was, to her, a simple statement of fact.

1 A Dragon in Shallow Waters

One of Margaret Thatcher's favourite sayings is that 'the unexpected always happens'. She likes to call it Thatcher's law. Certainly, in October 1990 as the Conservative Party met in Bournemouth for its 107th annual Conference all seemed set fair for her. After a number of difficult months her standing and that of the party was improving. Indeed, on Monday 8 October, the day before the Conference began, *The Times* reported that Labour's lead over the Conservatives had shrunk by five per cent over the previous quarter, and Mrs Thatcher's personal rating had improved by six per cent. The next day, the same paper in its leader column argued that, 'The Tory Party remains Mrs Thatcher's Party. On no other conceivable basis could it hope to win the next election'. As Conservative constituency activists gathered in Bournemouth one would have been hard-pressed to find many to disagree with this assessment.

The first day of the Conference got off to a slow start and much of the next day's press focused on fringe meetings which had been held away from the main conference hall. The speakers who attracted most attention could hardly have provided a greater contrast, or have better illustrated the differences within the Conservative Party on Britain's future role within the European Community. Michael Heseltine, the glamorous and ambitious self-made man, who had stormed out of Mrs Thatcher's Cabinet nearly five years earlier, was addressing the Tory Reform Group on the need for a more 'positive' position on Europe. In a nearby room Nicholas Ridley, an uncompromising supporter of Mrs Thatcher who had little regard for the usual political skills of presentation and tact, and whose outspoken and ill-judged remarks about the European Commission in a magazine interview the previous July had led to his resignation from the Cabinet, outlined a rather different vision to the Young Conservatives. Nick Ridley's meeting was better attended, and a number of journalists commented to me that Michael Heseltine's grip on the party's affections seemed to be slipping. For the first time since 1968 he appeared to be a peripheral figure at a party Conference.

John Major and Douglas Hurd made good speeches and were warmly received by a crowded Conference. It was clear to all that the Prime Minister had particular confidence in John, and many present, including me, felt that she regarded him as heir apparent, indeed a number of newspapers said so. On the Friday Margaret Thatcher made her sixteenth speech to the Conference as leader and her twelfth as Prime Minister. It contained a lot of humour, was well delivered and the Conference loved it. Her dismissal of the Labour Party's claim to be a government in waiting was masterful: 'Beneath its contrived self-confidence lies a growing certainty that the world and history has passed it by and that if Britain rejects it as I believe it will, socialism must return forever to its proper place – the reading room of the British Library where Karl Marx found it: section, history of ideas; sub-section, nineteenth century; status, archaic'.

Margaret Thatcher found the traditional standing ovations for the leader at the end of his or her speech to the Conference an embarrassment, and over the years those in the chair tried various ruses to shorten them. They all failed. In 1989 Willie Whitelaw actually prolonged the applause, by roaring at the audience to stop in a performance that reduced the platform and half the audience to a state of helpless laughter. Nineteen ninety was no exception. The applause went on for more than nine minutes, at the end of which Margaret Thatcher left the hall to a resounding chorus of 'Land of Hope and Glory'.

One of the saddest and most poignant moments I remember at any conference came when Jane Gow, the widow of Ian, the MP for Eastbourne, appeared on the platform. Ian had been murdered by the IRA only a few weeks earlier. In the days and weeks following his death she had shown tremendous courage and defiance of the IRA. The Conference rose spontaneously to cheer her as she pointed to Ian's watch and signet ring which she had had repaired, and which she wears every day in his memory. The by-election caused by Ian's murder was due to take place the following Thursday, and some warped minds saw her appearance as a publicity stunt. It was the party's opportunity to share Jane's grief and to show her that she had its affection and support, and that was the only reason for it.

The next day, Saturday, was Margaret Thatcher's birthday and she invited a small group of what she described over dinner as her very oldest and closest friends to dinner at Chequers. It was a very enjoyable and optimistic gathering. The government seemed to be coming out of a difficult patch. After a scratchy start the Conference had ended on an excellent note. Margaret Thatcher was looking forward to the next session of parliament. We had a good programme to be outlined in the Queen's Speech and we were building up to the next election, although this was not discussed in any depth at all. Kenneth Baker, the Party Chairman, and his wife, Mary, were there, and one felt that Mrs Thatcher had developed confidence in him as the man to organize her fourth general election campaign. They seemed to be evolving a good way of working together, and Denis said he had the feeling that the next election was going to be like the '83 one and not the '87 where unnecessary friction and controversy marred what turned out to be a very satisfactory result.

Only forty days later this apparently unassailable leader had resigned. Anyone predicting this at the end of the Conference would have been treated as mad. Yet it happened. It should not, with the benefit of hindsight, have been a surprise. In July I had said to my wife that if there had been a vote in Cabinet on the simple question, 'Would you prefer to work for Margaret Thatcher or Douglas Hurd as Prime Minister?' I reckoned she would have been lucky to receive three votes. That was probably an underestimate, but not by much. She was supposed to be domineering and intolerant of the views of her Cabinet and Shadow Cabinet. In fact she had in her Cabinet, for the majority of the time she led the Conservative Party, a minority of people who shared her views. Therein lies the first extraordinary feature of Margaret Thatcher's term as Prime Minister.

After she announced her first Shadow Cabinet in 1975, following her election as leader, *The Times* said, 'Mrs Thatcher's shadow cabinet does credit to Mrs Thatcher herself. This shadow cabinet is not notably to the right of the previous one. Indeed, if anything, it gives stronger positions of influence to the conservatism of compassion'. One of Margaret Thatcher's main weaknesses was that she constantly gave too much opportunity to those who did not share her views and too little to those who did. Yet the popular myth was that she did the opposite.

Just after Christmas, in December 1990, she came to lunch at my home in Hertfordshire and we discussed what had gone wrong. I reminded her of a remark once made by Harry Truman, the former American President, who has always been one of my favourite politicians. Truman had an extraordinary political career, winning elections against the predictions of all the expert political commentators. In his battle to retain his seat in the Senate in 1940 he faced a particularly difficult challenge for the Democratic nomination. Although Truman was considered the outsider he soon became confident of victory. Recalling Plutarch's description of the Roman Emperor Nero, Truman was sure that his opponent's troubles originated 'when he began to take his friends for granted and started to buy his enemies'. This is what happened to Margaret Thatcher.

Any new leader, especially a newly elected first woman leader, needs to unite the party behind him or her, and Margaret Thatcher was no exception. What one expected was that over a period the new leader would gradually introduce new people into the team who shared her sense of purpose and commitment. She recognized that this was necessary in an interview she gave to Kenneth Harris in February 1979. 'As Prime Minister I couldn't waste time having any internal arguments ... When the time comes to form a real Cabinet, I do think that I've got to have a Cabinet with equal unity of purpose, and a sense of dedication to it. It must be a Cabinet that works on something much more than pragmatism, or consensus. It must be a "conviction" Government.' Yet having identified the need she failed to meet it. The solid central core of the Cabinet – Carrington, Soames, Pym, Prior, Walker, Heseltine – tolerated her views, they did not share them. Of the leading figures in the Cabinet only Geoffrey Howe and Keith Joseph met the 'conviction' criterion. Willie Whitelaw was in a special category of his own. Whether he shared her convictions, I do not know. But he saw it as his duty to give her his total loyalty and support, and this he did to such a degree that he forfeited in part the friendship of some of his colleagues and natural allies. They felt he had let them down. He believed he owed it to the party and the country to support the person who had beaten him in the contest for the leadership and who had subsequently won, not just one, but three general elections. He was unswerving in his support and she benefited enormously from this. Time after time, even after 1981, when she finally got a majority in her own Cabinet, Willie's interventions eased the doubts of those who had them, and united the Cabinet. In those early years when she was in a minority his support must have been priceless. Although she never felt at ease with what she called the grandees, Willie was a grandee whom she did trust.

Some colleagues never became comfortable with the idea of a woman leader, let alone one who was as assertive and determined as she. Over a period remarks made by colleagues during lunches in the City and elsewhere were reported back to Margaret Thatcher at Number 10. 'The Conservative Party is a cavalry regiment led by a WRAC corporal' was one such remark. It was Willie who acted as bridge between her and them. The fact that the majority only tolerated her views did not matter as long as they did tolerate them. In opposition, all were united by the desire to get back into government and disagreements were surpressed more or less willingly. For the first two years after our victory in 1979, people felt that having led us to victory she was entitled to implement the policies on which she had been elected, and with varying degrees of enthusiasm they went along with her views. Rising unemployment, and the recession of which it was the consequence, soon began to put a strain on the loyalty of a number of the Cabinet.

One of the features of almost all British governments since the war had been their inability to carry through the policies which they had put to the electorate. Both Labour and Conservative governments consistently changed direction once in office. At the four general elections since 1950 which saw them elected to government, the Labour Party supported a policy of growth and employment. Under Labour, the theory was, government and unions would work well together. The economy would be planned and would grow steadily; the end result would be an expansion of the economy, more jobs, and greater prosperity which would fund better public services and higher social spending. In practice, within about two years after the election the economy would be in a mess, the International Monetary Fund would move in, the policies on which the government had been elected would be abandoned and a severe package of public expenditure cuts and other measures implemented. Sound money and the control of inflation would become the order of the day. This was the case in 1966, 1968 and 1976. It would almost certainly be the case were another Labour government to be elected.

Conservative governments, on the other hand, were always elected on a basic policy of sound money. Control of inflation was to be the number one priority and control of public spending was to be a vital part of a sound money economy. The Conservative manifesto of 1955, for example, referred to the 'constant danger of inflation' and pledged the continued use of 'sound monetary and fiscal policies'.

In his much misquoted 'never had it so good' speech in 1957, Harold Macmillan called the control of inflation 'the problem of our time'. In spite of the fact that by comparison with the 1970s, the 1950s saw low inflation (inflation rose above five per cent in only twenty-seven months throughout the 1950s, whereas it was above five per cent for all but two months in the 1970s), Conservative concern over its effects did not begin in 1979. Every Conservative government since the war has been elected on a promise to tackle inflation. As well as being opposed to inflation and in favour of strict control of public spending, the Conservative election manifestos committed the Tory government from 1951 to 1964 to a programme of reduced state control and abandonment of planning. Yet, gradually the platform was abandoned. In 1956 *The Daily Telegraph* castigated Anthony Eden's government for 'its changes of mind ... half measures, and the postponement of decisions' and called for 'the smack of firm government'. By 1958 Peter Thorneycroft, the Chancellor of the Exchequer, had resigned from Harold Macmillan's government warning that the failure to tackle underlying economic problems and the failure to take sufficient action against inflation meant that Britain was on 'the road to ruin'. The 1959 budget reversed the trend of the previous seven years, and saw an increase in planned public expenditure as a proportion of national income. By 1962 the government was experimenting with economic planning.

Ted Heath's 1970 government was a classic example of the genre. Elected in 1970 on a radical sound money policy, by 1972, with unemployment rising and uncertainty in the Middle East, it decided to make a dash for growth and accept the inflationary consequence as part of the price of winning the next election. Labour, the growth party in opposition, unwillingly became the sound money party in government. Conservatives, the sound money party on election, became the growth party in government. This almost institutionalized volte-face was dubbed 'the U-turn', and seemed to be more and more accepted as an inevitable feature of British politics.

It was no surprise, therefore, that in 1981, two years after our election victory, with unemployment rising, the traditional pressure for the U-turn should manifest itself at the July meeting of Cabinet at which the public expenditure plans for the next financial year beginning April 1982 were discussed in general terms. The Cabinet refused to endorse the Treasury views. It became clear to the Prime Minister that if the matter were forced to a conclusion then the decision would favour an increase in public spending to a figure beyond that which she and her Chancellor, Sir Geoffrey Howe, felt the economy could stand. More serious than that it would be a signal that sound money policies were to be abandoned and that the promises on which she had been elected were to be ditched. What actually happened was the turning point in Margaret Thatcher's premiership and the basis of her next two election victories. Unlike her predecessors she decided that what was needed was not a change of policy but a number of changes in the Cabinet. Out went Gilmour, Soames, Carlisle, in came Tebbit, Lawson, Janet Young and myself. I replaced Lord Thorneycroft as Party Chairman, with a seat in the Cabinet. After being leader of her party for six-and-a-half years, two of them as Prime Minister, Margaret Thatcher finally had a majority in her Cabinet who shared her convictions especially on the central issue of the economy. She also underlined a principle which had been virtually abandoned in British politics since the election of 1945, namely that election manifestoes were a commitment to a course of action and the outline of a programme of work, and not a set of promises designed to get a party elected into government, only to be subsequently abandoned. Not since Clement Attlee had a Prime Minister been so committed to a programme and to changing society.

By the time of the leadership election in 1990 Margaret Thatcher was once again in a minority in her Cabinet, and had been for some time. Some of her most trusted allies, Keith Joseph and Norman Tebbit, had retired from Cabinet. Willie Whitelaw had left because of ill health. Nigel Lawson and Geoffrey Howe had become disaffected and resigned. This quintet had been the dominant group in the Cabinet in the middle years of her government and, as they and others such as Lord Young and Nicholas Ridley left, their replacements were of a noticeably more pragmatic inclination. She was aware of this but she faced a problem. The most promising members of the 1974 and 1979 intake into the Conservative parliamentary party had been predominantly on the left and centre left. Prominent amongst the newcomers in the 1974 parliament were Douglas Hurd and David Hunt (who entered the Commons following a by-election in 1976). Some of those elected in 1979 – including future ministers like Robert Atkins, Tristan Garel-Jones, Douglas Hogg, Chris and John Patten, and William Waldegrave – formed a dining club which soon became known as the 'Blue Chip' Club. Although the nature of the group later changed, in these early days the 'Blue Chips' were certainly not Thatcherites.

By contrast, the 1983 intake contained a substantial number of extremely able people from the centre right, among them Chris Chope, Michael Forsyth, Peter Lilley, Francis Maude and Michael Portillo, who formed the 'No Turning Back Group' and produced a number of pamphlets urging the case for more of the free market policies which had been the hallmark of the first Thatcher government. These natural Thatcherites were put on what Mrs Thatcher called 'the fast track'. They were given accelerated promotion, but they had several years to catch up on the earlier group. By the time of the leadership election only one of them, Peter Lilley, had actually joined the Cabinet. Two of the original 'Blue Chip' members, on the other hand, had already joined Douglas Hurd and David Hunt around the Cabinet table. One of Mrs Thatcher's aims was to stay as leader until the balance of the Cabinet could be restored or, even better, tilted back in favour of the conviction group.

Whatever her plans, the plain fact was that at the time of the leadership election there were many more pragmatists in the Cabinet than conviction politicians, to use her 1979 definition. It was to this group that she turned for advice on that fateful Wednesday evening in November 1990.

The key appointment which Margaret Thatcher had had to make upon her election as leader of the opposition was that of Shadow Chancellor. She was determined that her election should see a change in the economic policy of the party and it was crucial that she should have someone she could trust to handle that policy. Instead of turning to Sir Keith Joseph, the man who more than anyone else had shaped the party's new economic thinking, she appointed Sir Geoffrey Howe. In view of her particular concern about economic policy, it was a compliment to him and a measure of her confidence in him. Although Geoffrey Howe had played a leading role in the Heath government, first as Solicitor-General, and later as Minister of Trade and Consumer Affairs, he had accepted the new policies and became their most determined exponent.

They presented quite a contrast in temperament, style and personality. Margaret Thatcher is volatile and, once she has heard all sides of an argument, quick to take decisions. Geoffrey Howe is placid and very easy-going. He positively enjoys the process of arriving at a decision by carefully considering all aspects of a problem beforehand. He is very patient, she can be extremely impatient. In spite of these differences, they worked very well together, first of all in opposition and then in government. He was an excellent Chancellor from 1979 to 1983, and his dogged ability to resist pressure was a vital asset to the government especially in the years from 1979 to 1982. At a time of great economic difficulty he kept his nerve and rightly stood firm against demands from industry, the opposition and a substantial number of our own party for the relaxation of his tough policies. He pressed steadily on.

To the growing frustration of his critics and the delight of his friends Geoffrey Howe's policies began to pay off. Inflation was reduced from a peak of 21.9 per cent in May of 1980 to 3.7 per cent in May and June of 1983, public spending was brought under control and productivity improved dramatically. The previously unattainable goal of a competitive Britain became a distinct possibility. I have always believed that the success of our economic policies far more than the Falklands factor was the reason for our election victory in 1983. Geoffrey deserved great credit for this.

After the 1983 election Mrs Thatcher rewarded him by making him Foreign Secretary, and they continued to work well together for most of the next six years. Although close colleagues, they never seemed to me to be great friends. During his period as Foreign Secretary and especially after the 1987 election there were times when they scarcely seemed to be friends at all. After the Madrid Summit in June 1989 when, following pressure and threats of resignation from Geoffrey Howe and Nigel Lawson, the Prime Minister reluctantly spelled out the conditions for our entry into the Exchange Rate Mechanism, Geoffrey's days as Foreign Secretary were distinctly numbered.

The question of British membership of the Exchange Rate Mechanism of the European Monetary System had been before the government ever since its election in 1979. In those early days we had all been convinced that fixed exchange rates (or the 'managed' fixed system of the ERM) would not help our central task of reducing inflation through the control of the rate of monetary growth in the economy. Fixed exchange rates would also have made abolition of exchange controls almost impossible. As Nigel Lawson told the House of Commons in November 1980, '... if we had been in the EMS, it would have disrupted our monetary policy'.

However, gradually, and particularly after 1983, Nigel Lawson, who had succeeded Geoffrey as Chancellor, and Howe himself became more and more attracted to UK membership of the ERM. They were encouraged in this view by, in particular, the CBI who argued that industry would benefit from the removal of uncertainty in the foreign exchange markets which ERM membership would provide. It was argued that the ERM would, by effectively pegging the pound to the German Deutschmark, provide a guarantee against inflation. This view was anathema to Margaret Thatcher who believed such an approach to be a counsel of despair. It struck me as a strange switch in policy since our success against inflation in the early 1980s had been achieved by, in Geoffrey Howe's words in 1982, allowing the exchange rate 'to be regulated by market forces'. If we had pegged our exchange rate in 1979, it is unlikely that we would have been able to sustain the tight monetary squeeze which brought such economic benefits in the mid-1980s.

When in October 1990 Mrs Thatcher was persuaded by John Major to allow Britain to enter the ERM she only did so on the basis that the pound would be allowed to float within a range of six per cent above or below the agreed parity and, as she told me subsequently, with the belief that it might be necessary to revalue if domestic monetary conditions demanded it.

But that was in the future. By early 1989 Mrs Thatcher had decided to move Sir Geoffrey Howe.

In the reshuffle in July 1989, he was moved from the Foreign Office and the relationship came to an abrupt and complete end. By this time the Prime Minister felt he had lost his touch while Howe was increasingly exasperated by her attitude to the European Economic Community and to him. In my view, she would have been wise, feeling as she did, to have dropped him from the government. Although popular, he had few troops and nobody would have resigned with him.

The concept of 'with or without troops' marks a fundamental distinction between politicians. I was introduced to it by John Nott during a debate in late 1977. In a typical speech full of jokes and a rather casual viciousness, he contrasted the then Prime Minister, Jim Callaghan, with his recently appointed Foreign Secretary, David Owen: 'If we talk about troops, the Prime Minister certainly has them, in a political sense. I do not think that the Foreign Secretary has many – he arrived by patronage and will depart hastily into oblivion. Some politicians have troops and some do not.' John's remarks showed particular prescience. Although for a short while David Owen had troops as leader of the Social Democratic Party, he has now returned to the position described by John Nott.

Although Geoffrey Howe did not have a group of backbenchers to lead a revolt against Margaret Thatcher, she did not drop him but gave him a job as leader of the House of Commons and Lord President which he quite clearly did not want. To make it palatable to him, he was given the title of Deputy Prime Minister and, after some wrangling, the use of a country house, Dorneywood. The next day to counter wild press speculation it was explained by Bernard Ingham, the Number 10 Press Secretary, that the title Deputy Prime Minister was of little consequence. It also emerged that Geoffrey had been told that he could have had Douglas Hurd's job at the Home Office but that Mrs Thatcher knew that he did not want it, and that Nigel Lawson, who had been using Dorneywood, had lost it without being consulted. At a stroke the Prime Minister had upset her three principal colleagues, her Deputy, her Chancellor and her Home Secretary. In another astonishing move which further alienated Geoffrey, she appointed John Major, who openly admitted to having no real knowledge of foreign affairs, as his successor.

All this upset Geoffrey, but it infuriated his wife, Elspeth, the doyenne of protective, committed ministerial wives. It was not a skilful performance by the Prime Minister and those who advised her. It was a mistake which was subsequently to cost her dear.

From that time, until his resignation, Geoffrey harboured a deep resentment, whilst Margaret found it increasingly difficult to disguise her lack of respect for him. At that time Geoffrey still maintained hopes of succeeding her. It was clear that he would never be her nominee, and he therefore had every reason to start to distance himself from her politically. He made a number of speeches in which he set out his political agenda. Although these built on the achievements of the Thatcher years there were some notable differences in emphasis – particularly over Europe, but also at home. His arguments about the importance of manufacturing to the British economy, for example, were interpreted by many as a veiled criticism of the policies being conducted by the Department of Trade and Industry.

In his new role Geoffrey was allowed no opportunity of addressing the party Conference in 1989 and 1990. He resented this and was reduced to speaking at fringe meetings. His speech on Economic and

Monetary Union in 1990 to a Bow Group meeting was easily his most outspoken to date. In a scarcely disguised attack on Mrs Thatcher's attitude towards the European Community, he said : 'The next European train is about to leave, for a still undefined destination, but certainly in the direction of some form of EMU. Shall Britain be in the driver's cab this time or in the rear carriage ?' Personally I have always preferred to know where a train is going before I board it, but Geoffrey's message was clear. The Deputy Prime Minister was openly questioning the Prime Minister's European policy.

On the Thursday of the week after the party Conference the Eastbourne by-election took place. I spoke at a public meeting in support of the candidate Richard Hickmet on the Monday evening. It was well attended, and both the candidate and the local party workers felt that they were on course for a win, albeit by a narrow margin. There was some criticism of the candidate, but I thought that he was perfectly adequate. He had won a very difficult seat in 1983, which he had very narrowly lost in 1987, and had been well regarded in the House. Having been elected myself in a by-election, I had a fellow feeling for Richard Hickmet in what is at best a lonely and exposed position.

The result, a Liberal Democratic victory by the good margin of 4,550, came as a shock. Having been Party Chairman when we lost the even safer Crosby seat at a by-election by an even larger margin, I was disappointed but not dismayed. I realized that there would be a renewed outbreak of introspection and criticism of the Prime Minister and I was not surprised when two papers, *The Observer* and *The Independent on Sunday*, called on her to resign. Coming from these two newspapers, both distrusted by most Conservative supporters, I felt this would help rather than damage Mrs Thatcher.

On the Tuesday, Labour chose to debate the government's recent decision to join the Exchange Rate Mechanism of the European Monetary System. They hoped that the Conservative Party, depressed by the result at Eastbourne, would be split on this issue and further confound what they hoped would be its own confusion. This did not happen, but Nigel Lawson, increasingly and understandably resentful at being blamed for the country's economic problems, gave the opposition a bonus by speaking in the debate. The former Chancellor declared it was a 'real tragedy' that the decision to join the ERM had been so long delayed. The implication was clear, the Prime Minister had not taken his advice and staying out of the ERM was a substantial contributor to our current difficulties, if not the main cause of them.

The rest of the week passed off reasonably peacefully and Mrs Thatcher left on Friday evening for the Rome Summit. The negotiations to amend the General Agreement on Tariffs and Trade were in deep trouble, and many of us felt that it was vital for the future of world trade that the EEC should soften the hard protectionist line it was taking. It came as a surprise to Mrs Thatcher that the GATT talks were not even on the agenda. It must have seemed to her all too typical of some of her European colleagues that they should ignore the pressing issue of the moment and prefer to concentrate on an issue, Economic and Monetary Union, which, in her view, was a grandiose, if not dangerous, dream. As a result she found herself totally isolated and for once outflanked.

On the Sunday, Geoffrey Howe appeared on the Walden programme on London Weekend Television. He was, by his own careful standards, extremely outspoken. He said that Mrs Thatcher did not believe in a single currency and was 'never going to have it'. But he went on to hint that that might not matter. He said that both he and Nigel Lawson had originally shared Mrs Thatcher's views on the ERM, putting all their faith in monetary policy. As he and Mr Lawson had been to IMF meetings and spoken to their European colleagues they had become convinced that ERM entry was sensible 'and that has now become the view of the entire government'. He made it clear that Mrs Thatcher would be forced to accept whatever approach the Deputy Prime Minister and the Chancellor agreed.

Within less than a week the Conservative Party had seen the damaging sight of two former Chancellors critical of the Prime Minister, and telling the world that they had effectively overruled her on a central issue and that the same thing might have to happen again. The cat was away, and the mice were certainly playing. The next day *The Times*, which only two weeks earlier had told us, 'she is under no threat any more within her own party', carried a report headed 'Thatcher may face challenge as leader'.

On Tuesday Mrs Thatcher reported to the House on the outcome of the Rome Summit. She was in fighting mood, and her statement made the government's position on Europe, and in particular on European Economic and Monetary Union, crystal clear: 'I again emphasized that we would not be prepared to have a single currency imposed upon us, nor to surrender the use of the pound sterling as our currency'. In retrospect, it was her unscripted responses to questions that caused trouble. Her forthright attack on the President of the European Commission attracted most attention: 'The President of the Commission, M. Delors, said at a press conference the other day that he wanted the European parliament to be the democratic body of the Community, he wanted the Commission to be the Executive and he wanted the Council of Ministers to be the Senate. No. No. No.' During the whole of the statement and the question and answer session which followed it, Geoffrey Howe sat looking grim and disapproving. But he was a member of a small minority. She cheered up the backbenchers and her critics seemed tiny in number and isolated.

The House was still tidying up the last bills of the session's legislative programme. We had had a particularly busy parliamentary year and in the spillover period after the party Conferences literally hundreds of amendments had had to be pushed through both chambers. It was not a satisfactory state of affairs. Everybody realized, especially Geoffrey Howe as leader of the House of Commons, that if we were to keep open the option of a June 1991 election we must have a smaller, better-prepared legislative programme for the coming session.

One of the difficulties which had arisen from the long overspill was that parliamentary draftsmen, who should have been working on the bills for the next session, had been bogged down in tidying up and drafting amendments for the current session's bills. This meant that a number of the bills which should have been ready for introduction early in the next session were still incomplete. My own department, the Department of Transport, had not had a major bill since 1986, but was to have four major bills in the new session. Although the department had issued instructions detailing the purpose of the bills they were in varying degrees of readiness. However, the key draftsman was now making good progress with the outstanding work. We faced a dilemma: we could produce a more finished bill, which would need fewer changes in committee, but it was not possible to do so in time for the beginning of the session. If we produced a bill prematurely, it would need more changes as it went through the Lords and Commons and could cause the next session to overrun. Geoffrey Howe had made tremendous efforts to make sure that the legislation to be introduced was well prepared and that the programme remained of a manageable size. The fact that the 1990–1 session went very smoothly suggests that he handed over to John MacGregor, his successor, a tidy legacy.

Nevertheless, at the Thursday Cabinet, when the subject of the future legislative programme was discussed, the Prime Minister gave Geoffrey a very rough ride. He clearly felt it was unjustified and unnecessary. The atmosphere was distinctly cool between them but not noticeably more so than usual. It was agreed that Geoffrey would investigate the position with the parliamentary draftsmen and the ministers concerned to see if faster progress could be made.

After Cabinet I went back to my office in Marsham Street for a working lunch, and a series of meetings. At about 4.40 that afternoon, Geoffrey telephoned me. He had had meetings with the parliamentary draftsmen, and although it would not be perfect there would be a bill ready for introduction into the House of Lords at the start of the next session the following week. The bill was the New Roads and Street Works Bill which we would have preferred to introduce into the Commons, because it was politically popular and we wanted to get the maximum exposure for it, but Geoffrey and I agreed that the balance of advantage lay in getting it started in the Lords. It was a long and detailed conversation and I had to break it off because I was expecting the Prime Minister to arrive at the department at 5.0 p.m. As I put down the telephone I had no inkling of the dramatic events Geoffrey was about to set in motion. The Prime Minister was coming to visit a part of the department whose workload had been increased substantially by the Iraqi invasion of Kuwait, and to thank the staff for their efforts. She seemed relaxed, took a great interest in the people and their work and the visit was much appreciated. I had been told that she had to be back at Number 10 by 6.0 p.m. and by the combined efforts of myself and Charles Powell, her trusted Private Secretary, we managed to get her to her car at about ten minutes to six. Walking back to the car she mentioned that she was going back to meet Geoffrey who had asked to see her. She seemed to think it was a routine business meeting. Twenty-five minutes after the Prime Minister left, my Private Secretary came into my room looking stunned. He told me, 'Sir Geoffrey Howe has resigned.'

Only sixteen months earlier, at the first Cabinet meeting following the July 1989 reshuffle, the Prime Minister had said, 'This is the team which will fight the next election.' Since that time Nigel Lawson, Norman Fowler, Peter Walker and Nicholas Ridley had resigned, and now Geoffrey had left. The reasons for the resignations were different in each case, but the cumulative effect was devastating, and the public was left with the impression of a government falling apart at the seams and deeply divided on the issue of Europe.

The Prime Minister acted quickly to limit the damage, John Mac-Gregor, a very capable and popular minister, took Geoffrey's job as leader of the House, Ken Clarke replaced John MacGregor at Education and William Waldegrave, a founder member of the 'Blue Chip' Club, joined the Cabinet as Health Secretary.

It has been suggested that the roughing-up he received in Cabinet that morning was the last straw for Geoffrey, but I believe he had decided to resign some time before. The Prime Minister's treatment of him earlier in the day can only have reinforced his resolve, it did not provoke his departure. In his typically thorough way he chose to go on the last day of the 1989–90 session and after trying to leave the preparation of the next session's programme in the best possible order. In his letter of resignation Geoffrey made it clear that he was leaving because of differences with the Prime Minister and the majority of the Cabinet over Europe. He argued that Mrs Thatcher's performance at the Rome Summit and in the House of Commons two days earlier had made it 'more difficult for Britain to hold and retain a position of influence' in the debate on the Community's future. He continued, 'The need to find and maintain common ground on the European issue within our own party will be crucial to our electoral success and the future of the nation. In all honesty I now find myself unable to share your views of the right approach to this question. On that basis, I do not believe that I can any longer serve with honour as a member of your government'. Geoffrey's resignation was clearly a blow to the government. It was far from clear how much of a blow it was to be to Mrs Thatcher.

The next morning I flew up to the North West to do a press conference at a by-election in the safe Labour seat of Bootle and spent the rest of the day speaking at meetings in a number of other constituencies. The press conference at Bootle was packed, but there was scarcely a question about the election campaign. Almost all the questions were about Sir Geoffrey Howe and the leadership. I stuck to the line used by Kenneth Baker, the Party Chairman, the night before, that this was a dispute about style rather than substance and not about policy. I still believe that it was more about personalities than policy. What I did not realize at the time was that Geoffrey did not intend his resignation to be the end of the matter. He had given up his leadership ambitions, but he intended to play a part in promoting a change of leader.

Having resigned, he developed some form of throat infection which genuinely but conveniently silenced him, and for the next few days he said nothing. Michael Heseltine, however, saw this as an opportunity that was too good to miss. He was due to leave Britain for a four-day tour of Jordan and Israel, but before he went he resorted to the time-honoured method used by those who want to say something but haven't a readily available occasion on which to say it, of writing a letter to his constituency Chairman and releasing it to the press.

Not to put too fine a point on it, Michael detested Mrs Thatcher. He disagreed with her policies and had made no secret of his antipathy for a long time, even before his resignation over Westland. His letter to his Chairman attacked the government, its policies, its style, but above all its leader and her style of leadership. Michael Heseltine was particularly critical of Mrs Thatcher's attitude over Europe. In his letter he called for a collectively agreed European policy and echoed Geoffrey Howe's belief that Mrs Thatcher was an obstacle to this. He wrote: '[S]killed political leadership demands judgement as to where to strike the balance. I believe the collective wisdom of the Cabinet can find exactly that balanced judgement which is the great strength of the Tory Party. If decisions continue to be taken or imposed that do not carry this collective endorsement the stresses will continue to show and could be our undoing'.

The *Daily Mail* headlined its front-page report of the Heseltine letter, 'Does he have the Courage?', and in its Comment column argued that 'Mr Heseltine now has a duty to "put up or shut up"'. Just in case anybody had missed the point a Number 10 source was widely quoted as saying that the letter was being treated with contempt and disdain.

A Member's letter to his Chairman is usually a one-way correspondence, no answer is expected or received. This time it was different. While Michael was appearing on our television screens meeting King Hussein and other Middle Eastern leaders, his constituency officers met to consider his letter and to draft a response. With the advice of the area Central Office agent a short reply was formulated. The letter declared:

We have considered your letter dated November 2 at an Association Officers meeting and reiterated the following. Number One: This Association supports the leadership of the party.

Number Two: We agree that the issues facing Britain in the events unfolding in Europe are momentous for this country. They need discussion and debate so that they can be better understood by the electorate before commitment to irrevocable steps.

Number Three: We shall continue to direct our energy to exposing the brittle veneer of Labour Party policies so as to make absolutely clear to the nation the importance of returning a Conservative government at the next election.

This unprecedented public reply was treated by the press as a rebuke for Heseltine and an endorsement of Mrs Thatcher and her government's policies. The pressure on Michael was building.

At this stage, I felt that the main objective should be to avoid having a leadership election. I felt that Mrs Thatcher would win but that she would be damaged, and we would have up to two weeks of speculation and campaigning at a time when we should be focusing the electorate's attention on the prospect of economic recovery and on the new legislative programme. I am sure that at this stage Michael Heseltine had not finally decided to challenge Mrs Thatcher, but it seemed as if her advisers in Number 10 were trying to provoke him. We already had reason to know that he was a volatile, headstrong character, but we also knew that he could only make one bid and that if that was unsuccessful, he would probably never get another chance. Michael wanted to get rid of Mrs Thatcher but not so that someone else could succeed her. He was not at all sure that he could beat her. He is also a proud man, and using terms like 'disdain' and 'contempt' when referring to his letter was bound to infuriate him.

On the same day as the *Daily Mail* headline challenging Michael Heseltine, Monday 5 November, Mrs Thatcher agreed to bring forward the date for a possible leadership election in order to 'flush out challengers'. Nominations were to open on the eighth and close on 15 November. The Prime Minister announced that she would be a candidate and that Douglas Hurd and John Major would sign her nomination forms. Voting would be on 20 November. The aim was to put an end to uncertainty as quickly as possible, and the fact that Mrs Thatcher had an impossibly crammed diary in the five days between the final nomination day and voting, including being in Paris for the last two days, was accepted as a price worth paying for an end to damaging speculation and an early result. Not only was the Prime Minister going to be away, but her proposer and seconder would be unavailable. Douglas Hurd was to be with her in Paris, and John Major was due to have a delayed, necessary and very painful operation on his jaw. None of this seemed particularly important at the time.

On the Thursday, the day after the State Opening, we did badly in yet another by-election in Bradford North, where our candidate was pushed from a close second place at the 1987 election to a poor third. The result was not unexpected but it gave rise to another bout of speculation about Mrs Thatcher's leadership. By then, the media scented the possibility of a real challenge and were doing their best to promote one. The weekend press was dominated by the subject.

Mrs Thatcher spent the weekend at Chequers preparing her annual speech for the Lord Mayor's Banquet, which she was due to make on the Monday evening. It was a combative speech with the Prime Minister making it clear that she was ready to take on all comers at home and abroad. She used an amusing if slightly strained cricketing analogy: 'I am still at the crease, although the bowling has been pretty hostile of late. And in case anyone doubted it, can I assure you there will be no ducking the bouncers, no stonewalling, no playing for time. The bowling's going to get hit all round the ground. That's my style.'

Geoffrey Howe had let it be known that he would be speaking in the debate on the Queen's Speech probably on the Tuesday. Most of us expected him to make an interesting contribution but not one of any great political significance. We could not have been more wrong. It was easily the most effective speech he had ever made, and disproved completely Denis Healey's much-quoted remark that being attacked by Geoffrey was like being savaged by a dead sheep. Margaret Thatcher was there to hear it. Her expression as the speech progressed was well described in the next day's newspapers. As Matthew Parris, who had been Mrs Thatcher's Political Secretary in opposition and a Member of Parliament from 1979 to 1986 when he had resigned to replace Brian Walden as the presenter of LWT's *Weekend World* programme, wrote in *The Times*: 'Mrs Thatcher started with a look of tense composure and a faint smile. The composure held, the tension grew, and the smile disappeared.' There was a look of bewilderment and hurt on Mrs Thatcher's face as Sir Geoffrey Howe continued his speech. It was a repudiation of her as a person, and her style of government, but above all, her attitude to her colleagues in government at home, and her fellow leaders in the EEC. The speech ended with what many regarded as a coded call for someone to challenge her: 'The time has come for others to consider their own response to the tragic conflict of loyalties with which I have myself wrestled for perhaps too long.'

I was not in the House to hear it. I was in my office in the department with about a dozen members of the 'No Turning Back' Group who had at their request come to talk about transport policy. In the group were Nicholas Bennett, Michael Brown, John Butcher, John Butterfill, Tony Favell, Gerald Howarth, Robert Jones and Allan Stewart. We were told by one of my staff that Sir Geoffrey was speaking and we moved over to watch it on the television. We realized at once that the speech was extremely damaging to the Prime Minister and interest amongst the group quickly gave way to anger. Many of us felt that it was totally out of character for Geoffrey to be so bitter and personal and there was a feeling that Elspeth had contributed much of the sentiment if not the wording of the speech. When it came to an end we all knew that a leadership contest was inevitable and that Michael Heseltine would be a candidate. The NTBG members left, anxious to get back to the House and to discuss the afternoon's events with their friends.

I had been trying to see Michael Heseltine for two or three days, but he had been on a visit to Germany, where he made a number of speeches before rushing back to London to be in the House of Commons to hear Geoffrey's speech. I had arranged to meet him later that evening in my room in the House of Commons. My aim was to try to persuade him not to stand as a candidate if there was an election. In fact, I am sure there would not have been an election if he had not stood against her. No one else would have done so.

I got to know Michael in 1972 when I became his first Parliamentary Private Secretary on his appointment as Minister for Aviation. During the nineteen very happy months I spent working for him, I developed a great liking and respect for him and we had remained friends.

We met at 7.0 p.m. – about an hour after Geoffrey's speech. I explained briefly to him why I thought he should not be a candidate. I felt that he would lose, would split the party and destroy his chance of ever being leader. I urged him to put out a statement, explaining that although he was under pressure to stand against her, he had decided not to do so, in the interests both of the country, which was not only in severe economic difficulty, but also faced the prospect of war in the Gulf, and of the party, which in the run-up to an election could not afford to divide itself. I argued that a leadership election would be a huge bonus for our opponents. He listened politely but when I finished speaking, he said quite simply, 'Cecil, she is finished. After Geoffrey's speech, she's finished.' We talked for a few more minutes, and I explained that I would be campaigning for Mrs Thatcher. As he left, he stopped in the doorway and said with a grin, 'Say what you like, but vote for me.'

Geoffrey Howe's speech made the leadership election inevitable. Until that speech, I am sure that Michael Heseltine had not made up his mind to stand. That speech tipped the balance. By creating a position for Geoffrey after the reshuffle in July 1989 instead of sacking him, she had provided him with a platform from which to launch his attack on her. Had she sacked him in 1989 and had he made that speech, it would have been treated as the speech of a disappointed man who had lost his job. As it was, he made it as the Deputy Prime Minister who had given up his job because he could no longer stand working for the Prime Minister.

The next morning Michael announced that he would be a candidate. The army of the disaffected on the back benches had acquired a general to lead and organize them, and a very formidable general at that.

The contrast between the campaigns of the two candidates was stark. The Heseltine campaign was directed by him and controlled by Michael Mates and Keith Hampson, both highly competent operators. For many of those working for him this represented probably their only chance of ministerial office, if their man won. There was a drive and urgency about the campaign which reflected the passion and commitment of the candidate. Knowing that whatever was said by the newspapers and on the television the only people who really mattered were the 372 MPs who would be the only people with a vote, they put a massive effort into courting individual Members. Michael was available in the House at every possible moment. It was virtually impossible not to meet him at least two or three times a day.

By contrast, the Thatcher campaign led by George Younger, who was by then Chairman-designate of the Royal Bank of Scotland and naturally reluctant to be involved in controversy, was discreet to the point of being invisible. The Prime Minister could not be as available in the House and would be abroad for the last two days at the European Defence and Security Conference in Paris. The conference was the official recognition that the cold war, which had divided the west from the east since the end of the Second World War, was at an end. It should have been a particular moment of triumph for Margaret Thatcher who, together with President Reagan, had ensured that the west had kept up its defences and had seen the collapse of the Soviet empire. The leadership election put a cloud over the occasion for Margaret Thatcher, but she was determined to play her part in the conference, even if it meant being away from London for the last few hours of the campaign.

The Prime Minister's unavailability should not have affected the ability of those around her to organize an effective campaign. Yet it was a shambles. Various people such as Michael Jopling and John Moore (who was in America at the time) heard through the press that they had been appointed to her team. On his return John Moore did all he could to help, but Michael Jopling refused to play an active role and apart from voting for her he took little part.

I was asked to concentrate on the media, and I did many radio and television broadcasts, but most of them were arranged directly between me and the various producers, and it was left to me to liaise over my activities with the campaign office with which I otherwise had little contact. There was no attempt to make my efforts part of a coordinated campaign.

The difference between the two campaigns was perhaps best summed up for me by a backbencher who was a little uncertain about supporting Mrs Thatcher but was persuasible. He told me that he had received three approaches from Heseltine personally, but none from Mrs Thatcher's team. I asked one of her team about this. 'Oh, he has been approached but he didn't realize it,' was the answer. I felt this was carrying the soft sell a shade too far.

On the Sunday, I was due to appear on the Brian Walden programme to discuss Mrs Thatcher's prospects. I thought I had better speak to her before the interview so that I could, if asked, give an up-to-the-minute report on her feelings. Mrs Thatcher never takes elections for granted. She has always regarded Finchley as a marginal seat and fought it as such. Even as Prime Minister she held regular surgeries in the constituency and carried out well over a hundred constituency engagements a year. She herself told me that on election night 1979, just before leaving for the count at Finchley, she had called her family together and told them, 'I must warn you, that although our party is going to win the election overall, I could lose Finchley.' She was not taking this election for granted either, but she told me that Peter Morrison, her PPS and a key member of her team, had assured her that even after 'aiming off' for those who might be promising support but planning to vote for Heseltine or not vote at all, she had 250 votes in the bag. This would have given her a comfortable victory, and although she was predictably cautious, she obviously felt she had reasonable grounds for optimism.

The interview with Brian Walden seemed to go quite well. His basic argument was that the Prime Minister was irredeemably unpopular, the government had lost its way and a change of leader was necessary if we were to have a hope of winning the election. I argued very strongly that Mrs Thatcher was easily the best qualified person to be Prime Minister, that the government was unpopular because of the recession, and that, as the economy improved, the standing of the government and Mrs Thatcher would recover. I argued that it was a cruel form of escapism to personalize our problems, lay the blame for them on the Prime Minister and to pretend that, by changing the leader, we would in any way change the underlying problems, which had already been tackled and were on the way to being solved.

Much of the interview was taken up by the poll tax, as the community charge had become known. The reform of local finance had been a major part of our election manifesto in 1987, but the legislation and the introduction of the tax had proved highly controversial. Polls showed that it had been the leading issue in British politics for some time, but that this interest had peaked in April 1990 with the sending-out of the first bills. After that public concern had declined steadily, and in the Eastbourne by-election research showed that the poll tax ranked only ninth in importance on the list of issues of concern to the electors; the economy, health and the Gulf were of far more concern to them. National polls confirmed a similar pattern over the country as a whole. Following its introduction, Chris Patten and his new Minister for Local Government, Michael Portillo, had carried out a thorough review, and with the help of the Treasury had come up with a number of proposals to make the tax more acceptable. Indeed Michael Portillo had received a standing ovation at the party Conference for his explanation of the tax. He told the Conference that, 'Far from being a vote loser, with your help it will be a vote winner and launch us on our fourth term.' It looked as if the great poll tax argument was beginning to simmer down, and that the worst was over for the government on that particular subject.

Michael Heseltine had always been opposed to the poll tax. During his stint as Environment Secretary from 1979 to 1983 he had examined the whole question of the financing of local government. In 1981 he had published a Green Paper, 'Alternatives to Domestic Rates', which considered the arguments for replacing domestic rates with a poll tax. The conclusion had then been that a poll tax would be too expensive and 'would almost certainly not be a practical proposition'. However, after the 1983 general election, his successor, Kenneth Baker, supported by the Minister for Local Government, William Waldegrave, had reviewed the idea and had convinced the Prime Minister and the Cabinet that the poll tax was the answer. There were a number of critics in Cabinet of this decision, of which the most notable was Nigel Lawson, the Chancellor of the Exchequer. This was one of the rare arguments that Nigel lost in Cabinet. He accepted the collective decision of Cabinet with barely concealed distaste. Later, when Michael Heseltine announced details of his plans to replace the community charge with the property-based council tax and Nigel was free to speak his mind, he told the House of Commons that there would be 'widespread relief' that the 'government had had the courage and common sense to consign the poll tax to oblivion'. But despite his reservations the government pressed ahead with its plans. Michael Heseltine opposed the legislation in the House and remained a persistent critic of the tax.

He made the poll tax a central issue in his campaign. He promised, if elected, to scrap it. The poll tax thus became not only the main focus of the leadership election, it dominated domestic politics for months afterwards. Even the events in the Gulf did not succeed in stifling the argument. The tax was finally killed off by a double blow. Firstly, from the Chancellor, Norman Lamont, who arranged in his first Budget that a substantial tranche of local government expenditure would be funded by a 2.5 per cent increase in VAT. Secondly, by Michael Heseltine himself. Back in his old job as Environment Secretary he announced in March the return to a property-based tax.

Michael Heseltine's clear commitment to scrap the poll tax and his approach to Europe undoubtedly attracted supporters into his camp, including two leading women MPs, Emma Nicholson and

Edwina Currie. Emma had been appointed by Mrs Thatcher as a Vice-Chairman of the party, in charge of women, at my suggestion, in 1983. She had subsequently been selected as candidate for the safe seat of Devon West and Torridge which she won in 1987. She owed a great deal to Mrs Thatcher, but was disappointed that she had not become a minister. Edwina had been a high profile and controversial minister and had resigned following a careless remark about eggs and salmonella which had threatened to destroy the British poultry industry. The common view about Edwina was that it was only a matter of time before she would be recalled to the government. Mrs Thatcher was known to have a high regard for her abilities. Both women appeared to have good prospects if Mrs Thatcher won, and it was a shock to the Thatcher camp when they announced that they would be supporting Heseltine. To me, it was worrying evidence that disaffection with Mrs Thatcher was more widespread than her campaign team appeared to believe.

Whilst the Heseltine camp continued to issue bulletins about the growth of support for Michael, the Thatcher team remained quietly confident. I found it both disturbing and amusing that the total votes pledged to the two candidates exceeded the number of voters. A number of colleagues were obviously taking no chances and promising support to both sides in the happy assurance that whoever won would be grateful to them.

Each member made his decision in his own way. Some took elaborate soundings in their constituencies before announcing their choice of candidate. Others consulted very widely with constituents but kept their decision to themselves, and still others felt it was their decision and did not consult at all. I made my position clear from the beginning. I was totally committed to the Prime Minister and to campaigning for her, although I did have an opportunity of discussing the election with a very large number of constituents and friends.

On Saturday 18 November we were due to hold our annual constituency ball. This was normally attended by about 200 people and held in a local hotel. On this occasion the venue was a large house in the constituency. Shenley Lodge had been converted into offices some years earlier by a group of companies, the Midas Group, whose Chairman, David Robertson, was a keen Conservative supporter, and who allowed us to use the house for social events from time to time. When we arrived I received a great surprise. It was twenty years to the day since I had first been elected to parliament, and to mark the occasion it had been decided to hold a special ball. Over 500 people had come and a huge marquee had been erected in the grounds. It was a brilliantly kept secret and a splendid dinner. The President of my constituency Association, Keith Carmichael, made a short speech, before presenting me with a handsome antique writing case. An old friend, Sir Geoffrey Leigh, gave me a battery-operated golf trolley and there were toasts to Ann and myself. There was also a certain amount of talk about the next twenty years and this put me in an awkward situation. I had decided some time before to leave the Cabinet the following July and not to be a candidate at the next general election. I was sure, even then, that we would not have an election before the autumn of 1991, but I accepted that if we did have an early election I would have to fight it. In my reply, I reminisced about the previous twenty years in parliament and thanked those with whom I had worked during that time. I did not mention the future, but it was a happy social occasion and only one person, a local councillor, noticed.

In the only serious part of my speech, I talked about the leadership election and of my support for Mrs Thatcher. This was received with loud applause and it was clear that she had the overwhelming support of those present. In the course of the evening I spoke to dozens of people individually and the message from virtually all of them was the same. There was also a great deal of criticism of Michael Heseltine for challenging her, and of Geoffrey Howe's 'treachery'.

After dinner Nick Gibb, who had worked for me during the 1987 election and who had recently been selected to fight his first parliamentary seat, showed me a copy of a statement that he and others had written. It was being supported by eighty-three per cent of Conservative candidates at the next election and stated that they were firmly behind Mrs Thatcher.

From the various polls and other soundings by newspapers and television it seemed that party workers all over the country were taking a similar view. I hoped that this support in the constituencies might consolidate Mrs Thatcher's vote and that a number of wavering MPs would return to her camp.

Sunday's newspapers did not contain encouraging news. Many had polls which indicated that, if Michael Heseltine were leader, the Conservatives would have a lead over Labour of between five and ten per cent and *The Sunday Times* in a critical leading article described Mrs Thatcher as a 'handicap' to her party's chances of re-election and concluded: 'The issue before Tory MPs this weekend is not the re-election of Margaret Thatcher; it is the defeat of Neil Kinnock. That requires saying a reluctant goodbye to Mrs Thatcher and the endorsement of Michael Heseltine.' Of the other nine national Sunday newspapers only the *Sunday Telegraph*, the *Sunday Express* and *The News of the World* declared themselves unequivocally for Mrs Thatcher. *The Independent on Sunday* and *The Mail on Sunday* strongly backed Heseltine whilst *The Observer* gave him lukewarm support. The others – the *Sunday Mirror*, *The Sunday Correspondent* and *The People* – supported neither candidate.

On the Monday I had a very full day in the department before leaving for Birmingham where I was due to speak at a dinner and to present an award to the Midland Businessman of the Year. I was glad to leave electioneering behind for a few hours.

I found great difficulty in concentrating on government business the next day. Although my main concern was for the Prime Minister, I was obviously aware that if she lost then this could be my last day in government. Having decided to leave the government there would have been little point in starting with a new leader and causing a reshuffle a few months later.

I had a series of meetings, the first with my ministerial colleagues other than Chris Chope who was away from London attending a family funeral. He had given me a letter authorizing me to vote on his behalf. A deputation of northern Labour Members came and went, followed by Conservative London Members and after seeing them I went over to the House to vote. Voting took place in committee room 12 and the corridor outside was packed with journalists. Inside, it all seemed remarkably peaceful with Cranley Onslow, Chairman of the 1922 Committee, sitting in the chair normally occupied by the committee Chairman, and Janet Fookes and Michael Shaw, sitting on either side of him. I handed over Chris's letter, took two ballot papers and moved to the other end of the room, put the crosses by Margaret Thatcher's name, put them in the ballot box and left by the other door. It was all over in about a minute.

The voting rules for the Conservative leadership were extremely complicated. They had been devised by Humphry Berkeley following the controversy of 1963 when Alec Douglas-Home had been selected after what was described as the usual process of consultation. The decision was then taken that in future we would elect not select our leader. Humphry Berkeley had subsequently left the Conservative

Party to join Labour and many of us wish that he had taken his rules with him. To win on the first ballot a candidate must achieve an overall majority of Conservative MPs and have a margin of fifteen per cent over the next candidate. So, if all 372 Conservative MPs voted, Mrs Thatcher would have needed to win 187 votes to achieve an overall majority and be fifty-six votes (15% of 372) ahead of Michael Heseltine. In the second round the rules become much simpler. New candidates are allowed to enter and the winning candidate must achieve an overall majority of those entitled to vote.

I had been asked to appear on a live television programme during which the result would be announced. When I got back to the office after voting, Elizabeth Buchanan came to see me. She had been in touch with John Whittingdale, the Prime Minister's Political Secretary, and he had given her the line which Mrs Thatcher and those supporting her would take depending on the result. There were three draft statements which had been agreed before she left for Paris. They covered the range of possible results: the first if she had won well, the second if there was to be a second ballot, and thirdly there was a short statement if she had lost. In the event the second statement was used.

The result was announced just after 6.30 p.m. Mrs Thatcher polled 204 votes to Heseltine's 152 with sixteen abstentions. She failed by four votes to win an outright victory: if just two MPs had switched from Heseltine to Thatcher, the second ballot to be held the following Tuesday would have been unnecessary.

By the time this was announced publicly Mrs Thatcher had already had the result for ten minutes, and she decided to come out of the British Embassy in Paris and make the agreed statement. In it Mrs Thatcher was to say that it was her 'intention' to contest the second round. The theory was that 'intention' would sound less dogmatic than saying she would definitely stand again. The actual remarks she made were a paraphrase of the original statement but included the word 'intention' and in my opinion conveyed the spirit of that draft. What was totally misleading was the impression given by some critics that Mrs Thatcher, having heard the result, charged out within seconds and made a totally impromptu statement. She had consulted, she had considered what she should do, and she went ahead and did it. Everything had been settled before she left for Paris.

I had a long-standing dinner engagement with Lord Tombs, the Chairman of Rolls-Royce, and some of his colleagues and was excused from voting in the House of Commons for the rest of the evening. After doing a couple of radio and television interviews I went off to dinner. I did not go back to the House that night. I was happy to be away from the place and to have the opportunity to get the day's events into perspective. The pity was that very few other colleagues did the same.

The next morning, a Wednesday, my home telephone rang early and frequently. The first caller was Norman Lamont, an old friend and then Chief Secretary to the Treasury. He was keen that we should meet as early as possible. I said I would be in my office until about 10.15 after which I had an engagement to open the newly modernized Marylebone Station and would be back at about noon. He asked me if I would mind going to his office since he was expecting 'a lot of telephone calls'. We agreed that my office would contact his and make the necessary arrangements. I then went off to do a number of media interviews, and from conversations before and after these was able to piece together a picture of events at Westminster following the announcement of the result. In Mrs Thatcher's absence, and in the absence of anyone to act for her, the party had kicked over the traces. Heseltine supporters had been very active in the House. Their message was simple. Support for Mrs Thatcher was haemorrhaging away, Heseltine's was growing and she would lose in the second ballot. Much was being made of her precipitate action in announcing that she would be a candidate in the second ballot without consultation. This was, of course, incorrect.

After the ten o'clock division a group of younger ministers including five members of the Cabinet, Norman Lamont, Tony Newton, Chris Patten, Malcolm Rifkind and William Waldegrave, had met at Tristan Garel-Jones' home in Catherine Place. Those who believe that there was a conspiracy to replace Mrs Thatcher with John Major or Douglas Hurd, having first used Michael Heseltine to bring her down, see this meeting as sinister evidence of a well-laid plot. They see Tristan's central role in arranging the meeting and holding it at his home as proof positive of such a plot. Over a period of years in the whips' office, latterly as Deputy Chief Whip, Tristan had acquired a well-earned reputation as a schemer and was deeply distrusted by Thatcherites. His move to the Foreign Office in the reshuffle in 1989 was welcomed as evidence that the Prime Minister was reasserting her control over the whips' office. It is interesting that only three of those present would have been regarded as Thatcher supporters:

Norman Lamont, Richard Ryder and Alan Clark. At this meeting a consensus emerged that Mrs Thatcher should resign and that Michael Heseltine should not be allowed to win. I have no doubt that this meeting was decisive in confirming people to whom the Prime Minister would naturally have looked for support in their view that her time was up. Their acquiescence was widely used as evidence of her crumbling support, and many of those present left the meeting determined to persuade other Thatcher supporters to abandon her.

My criticism of those present is not that they were part of a conspiracy, but that without consulting anybody they claimed to be able to interpret the mood of the party. They were not a representative group. With one or two exceptions they spent no more time in the House than they had to and were somewhat divorced from the back benches. Nevertheless the conclusions of this meeting were widely discussed around the House the next day and were repeatedly cited in support by those seeking to prove that Mrs Thatcher should resign.

I knew little of this when I left home just after 7.30 a.m. on the Wednesday to do a number of interviews for radio and television programmes. So far as I was concerned, the Prime Minister had declared that she would be a candidate and would be fighting to win, and I felt confident that, with better organization and a lot of hard work from those who supported her, she would win. I had only been in my office a short time when John MacGregor rang. He wanted me to tell him whether I would be supporting the Prime Minister in the second ballot and whether I thought she should carry on. I answered both questions with an emphatic 'Yes'. He then asked if I would find out how my ministerial colleagues felt. I replied that I was sure from many discussions with them that they all held the same view as mine, but that I would check with them, and if I was wrong, I would let him know. I also told him that I thought that the whole exercise was a mistake, and that if the fact that he was telephoning around got out, which was bound to happen, it would be immensely damaging to the Prime Minister. She had made her decision and we should be preparing to support it and to win. I then heard that the Chief Whip had been to Willie Whitelaw's for breakfast, which could only mean that the Chief Whip was wobbling. What I still find fascinating is that a party that had decided to abandon behind-closed-doors consultation as a way of changing its leader, ignored the result of the ballot box and embarked on a series of consultations behind closed doors which resulted in the resignation of the elected leader.

Just before I left to reopen Marylebone Station, my Private Secretary told me that my meeting with Norman Lamont was fixed for 12.15, and after a hectic morning I arrived at the Treasury building, going in through the entrance in Whitehall. It is a rather grand building, but a bad advertisement for a department that prides itself on keeping a tight rein on expenditure and getting value for money. Ceilings are high, corridors wide, ministerial offices are huge and even more than in other departments officials seem to hunt in packs. Ministers are always accompanied or policed (I was never sure which) by a number of civil servants. Since I was there on party business, I was shown straight into Norman Lamont's office and on this occasion he was alone. Whilst I sat in an armchair he paced around the room, seeming ill at ease, and after a few desultory remarks he came straight to the point. He wanted to know whom I would support if Margaret Thatcher resigned. I said she was not going to resign and therefore his question needed no answer. He persisted, but I said that I was not prepared to say anything which could be represented as an acceptance by me that she might withdraw from the contest. Westminster was awash with rumours and I did not want to add to them. We talked for about half an hour and just before I left he summed up his position by saying that although he would support Margaret Thatcher if she stood, he was convinced that she would lose. He felt sure that she would realize this, and withdraw. I told him that I disagreed, but that we should keep in touch. Norman ended by expressing the hope that John Major would have my support. With that I left for lunch at the Garrick with Simon Jenkins, the recently appointed editor of *The Times* newspaper.

The Times had been a strong supporter of Mrs Thatcher. That morning's leading article had argued that the best interests of the Conservative Party would lie in 'Mr Heseltine honourably standing down', but recognized that this was unlikely. Simon Jenkins took the view that Mrs Thatcher should stand, that she could win, but that it would require a huge effort from all her supporters, not least her proposer and seconder, Douglas Hurd and John Major. They would need to spell out to their supporters that their way of demonstrating their support was to vote for Mrs Thatcher. For her part Mrs Thatcher should emphasize the fact the government was a team and not a one-woman show. We both agreed that it would have been far easier for her to win on the first ballot than it was going to be on the second.

Mrs Thatcher had returned from Paris that morning and was

having lunch at Downing Street with a number of colleagues. Amongst those present were Kenneth Baker the Party Chairman, John MacGregor, John Moore, Peter Morrison her PPS, Cranley Onslow the Chairman of the 1922 Committee, Tim Renton the Chief Whip, Norman Tebbit and John Wakeham.

Tim Renton told her that her support was dwindling. Others, including Kenneth Baker and Cranley Onslow, were more optimistic, but it was a subdued meeting. Mrs Thatcher was due to go to the House to make a statement on the Paris Summit and as she left she told the assembled media representatives, 'I fight on, I fight to win.' What she had heard over lunch had shaken her, but she still believed at that point that she could and would win. She had however been persuaded to consult her Cabinet colleagues one by one.

I went straight from the Garrick to the Commons and found the place in a turmoil. Small groups of anxious-looking Tories were standing in the division lobbies and in the small lobby behind the Speaker's chair, and the only questions being discussed were whether Mrs Thatcher could win or whether she should go. The House of Commons can manufacture rumours more quickly than Rowntree can make Smarties and that afternoon the rumour machine was in overdrive. Mrs Thatcher's support was alleged to be melting away, and when I asked for evidence I was shown a list with three names on it, two of which I knew from direct contact with the individuals concerned to be wrong. The common line was that the person speaking would support her but others wouldn't. I argued with various Cabinet colleagues that if they would stop their remarks at 'I will support her', without adding the rider that others wouldn't, they would be astonished how much more staunch 'the others' would become.

Douglas Hurd and John Major had already made it clear that they would not oppose Mrs Thatcher if she was a candidate. This meant that the second round would be a replay of the first. My own theory was that, in the first round, a number of people had voted for Heseltine in the hope that they would prevent Mrs Thatcher winning and open the way for new candidates in the second ballot. John and Douglas were the preferred new candidates but they couldn't stand as long as she was in the field. Given the choice between Mrs Thatcher and Michael Heseltine the tactical voters would have gone back to Mrs Thatcher. I was convinced that there was a solid anti-Heseltine majority and it was notable that at Catherine Place the night before all those present were bent on stopping Heseltine. It was also notable at Cabinet the next morning. We were unanimous in thinking that the new leader must be someone other than Heseltine. If Mrs Thatcher had not allowed her Cabinet to talk her into resignation, if she had kept her nerve for a few more hours, thus ensuring a head-on contest with Heseltine, combined with a determined campaign, I believe she would have won well.

As usual she handled the statement to the House superbly. She told MPs: 'The word "historic" tends to be used extravagantly these days, but I believe that this Summit was an historic gathering. It marked the end of the cold war in Europe and the triumph of democracy, freedom and the rule of law.' Although she did not claim it, few could doubt the important role that she had played in bringing about this triumph. Afterwards she was taken by Norman Tebbit and others into the tea room and around the corridors of the Commons where she received a warm reception. Then the next consultative exercise started. This had been suggested to Mrs Thatcher by John Wakeham, who had replaced George Younger as her campaign manager. He persuaded her to see all her Cabinet ministers one by one. Once again, the exercise had been hijacked by the Catherine Place gang and their newly recruited colleagues. Instead of receiving their individual views she was given a prearranged message from a procession of colleagues. It had a demoralizing effect. The person who prided herself on giving leadership and looked down on 'those who led by following' effectively allowed one of the most crucial decisions of her life to be dictated by a handful of her subordinates.

I had been asked to meet her in her room at 5.10 in the afternoon for the so-called consultation. Because of the statement and the walkabout in the House she was running late. I was waiting in the small secretary's office next to the Prime Minister's office when she came back from her tour. She obviously felt she had had a good afternoon and was in ebullient mood. One rather startled junior minister who happened to be in the office, suddenly found himself being tapped on the chest by the Prime Minister who said, 'I know, you worked hard last time, Robert, but you are going to have to do even more over the next few days.'

I told her that she must carry on, that with better organization and hard work she would win, and I then left to meet some constituents who had been waiting to see me. It was about six o'clock when I went back to my office in the Cabinet corridor. At that point I felt her campaign was firmly on the rails. She had made up her mind to fight. But between then and 8.30 she began to change her mind. At 7.30 Andrew Turnbull, her Principal Private Secretary, sensing that her mind was turning towards resignation, telephoned Downing Street to suggest that thought should be given to a resignation statement. Only Kenneth Baker and Peter Brooke had joined me in telling her she could win. What devastated her was the succession of younger ministers who made it clear that she should go, subject to the customary rider that of course, 'I would support you.' One or two were quite blunt, telling her that not only would they not support her, but that they would resign if she didn't. Her lack of friends and supporters in the Cabinet, which had been obvious to me for some time, was brought home to her most cruelly.

She returned to Downing Street at 8.30, where her most trusted friend, Alistair McAlpine, had been waiting to see her. He had been with Charles Powell when the instruction to begin drafting her resignation statement came through from the House of Commons and he expected their meeting to be postponed. Mrs Thatcher insisted that he stay and they went up in the lift to the private flat. There they found Denis Thatcher pacing up and down, waiting for them to arrive. She told him that she would probably go, to which he replied that nothing would please him more. She asked Alistair for his views. He felt she could win but that she would be in for an unpleasant few days, and that even if she did win she would be damaged. She was not angry, but deeply hurt. What troubled her most was that a number of the Cabinet, each one of whom she had appointed, were not prepared to work for her in her hour of need. Alistair told me later that during this conversation he found himself thinking of the old Chinese saying, 'Dragons in shallow waters are the sport of shrimps.' This phrase seems to me to sum up Mrs Thatcher's predicament perfectly.

Many factors contributed to her resignation. The unpopularity of the government and the recession which was the main cause of that unpopularity were blamed on her. Having been Prime Minister for nearly twelve years she had a large number of disaffected colleagues on the government benches – including people who had been dropped from the government, people who had never been asked to join the government and people in government who felt that their abilities had not been recognized sufficiently. There were also people in none of these categories, who just did not like her, and others who felt that a change of leader would improve their chance of being re-elected.

The Euro-enthusiasts in the party were increasingly angry at her attitude to the Community and some of its leaders. Many with marginal seats especially in the North and Midlands still had strong reservations about the community charge and found the idea of getting rid of it, which Michael Heseltine supported, attractive. The damaging speeches of Geoffrey Howe and Nigel Lawson enhanced the doubts of still more colleagues. Another factor was the death of Ian Gow, who would, without doubt, have corralled a number of waverers and doubters, and whose friendship with both Margaret Thatcher and Geoffrey Howe might well have averted the crisis over Geoffrey's resignation.

Critical mistakes were also made: the decision to have an early election for the leadership and to pick a time when Mrs Thatcher would be abroad for the critical last two days; the appointment of a campaign manager who did not want the job and could not do it properly because other commitments prevented him. All these factors and others played their part, but it was the erosion of her support in Cabinet which finally tipped the scales and made her feel she could not carry on.

The announcement of Mrs Thatcher's resignation was made publicly at 9.42 on the Thursday morning. As I left Number 10 about half an hour later, my driver gave me a message that Michael Heseltine wanted to speak to me: he had left three alternative numbers. They were all engaged, but I did eventually get through. He reminded me that our friendship went back a long way and said that, since Mrs Thatcher was no longer a candidate, he hoped I would come out in support of him in television and radio interviews which his team would arrange. I pointed out to him that I had spent a considerable amount of time arguing that his economic views made it impossible for me to support him in the first round, and so far as I knew they had not changed. He replied that he believed himself to be just as sound or unsound as the other two candidates, and asked me to think it over and not to campaign for anyone else until I had spoken to him again. This I agreed to do.

On my return to the Department of Transport I called the ministers and PPSs and my Special Adviser together to tell them what had happened in Cabinet. I also informed them of my decision to leave the government at the same time as Mrs Thatcher, which would be the following Wednesday, or if there were a third ballot, the following Friday. I was very touched that after the meeting, each of those present came to see me individually and urged me to stay. I had made up my mind and had told Mrs Thatcher the previous July that if there were to be a change of leader I would not wish to start with a new one. It seemed a strange thing to say at the time, we were having tea in Number 10 the day before she went away for a summer break. She told me she had no intention of leaving and so the situation would not arise.

A number of people have expressed surprise at my decision to leave parliament, but I wanted to go while still young enough to pursue other interests. My wife and I agreed in 1987 that that would be the last general election we would fight. We both felt that it would have been wrong not to fight it. I still believed I had a contribution to make to the government and I was as committed to the policies and to the Prime Minister as I had ever been. Besides, I was determined to demonstrate that the line run by sections of the press that the public had rejected me after the events of 1983 and that I was unacceptable to the Conservative Party at large was untrue. When I resigned over the Keays affair I received over 16,000 letters of support and less than fifty hostile letters. I was swamped by invitations from Conservative Associations from all over the country to speak to their members, and wherever I went, we had large and enthusiastic audiences. Colleagues in parliament on all sides were tremendously supportive, and yet sections of the press persisted with the notion that I was some sort of outcast. The election result proved them wrong. I was returned with a record majority. I was pleased to be back in government, but that did nothing to change my determination to leave parliament at the next election. I had however become alarmed as a succession of colleagues left the Cabinet between July 1989 and December 1990. It seemed to me that there was a danger of Mrs Thatcher becoming so isolated in her Cabinet that I would have found it very difficult to leave in July 1991 as I had planned. It would have been hard to have escaped the feeling that I was letting her down, but I still hoped that if at all possible I would leave government in July 1991. By that time I would have seen through the biggest legislative programme the Department of Transport had had for many years, and the record investment programmes on road, rail, underground and air traffic control would be well under way.

The events of the previous few days and the shabby treatment of

Mrs Thatcher underlined my wish to leave. The performance of some of my Cabinet colleagues between the announcement of the result of the first ballot and the time of Mrs Thatcher's resignation killed any desire to continue working with them.

On that Thursday I was the guest speaker at a lunch at Grosvenor House and I spoke about London, its transport problems and the policies we were pursuing to improve the situation. I talked about the modernization of the existing underground system, the new lines, the huge investment programme on Network South East, the red routes scheme to clear 320 miles of the main arterial roads into London, all of which I had talked about dozens of times before and all of which seemed to come as a complete surprise to the audience.

It is one of the frustrations of politics that even after the politician has become sick of repeating certain facts, the public has still not heard them. This was brought home to me when I was Party Chairman and unemployment was the overriding issue. I discovered that every Labour government in history had been elected on a promise to reduce unemployment and that no Labour government had ever kept the promise. There were always more people out of work when a Labour government left office than when that same government took power. I had repeated this in virtually every speech, broadcast, interview, and press release for about eighteen months. One night on a by-election programme I repeated it again. Neil Kinnock who was also on the programme was asked by Robin Day whether this was true. He gave a typical Kinnock answer, 'statistically speaking, it is true', which I thought was a long-winded way of saying 'yes'. The next day Michael Heseltine came up to me just before Cabinet, and asked me if it really was true that no Labour government had ever reduced unemployment. I thought I had planted this idea firmly in the minds of the nation, and I hadn't even got it over to my Cabinet colleagues.

The chairman of the lunch paid a very warm tribute to Mrs Thatcher, and the audience reacted enthusiastically. I realized that at that time she would be preparing for what would almost certainly be her last Prime Minister's question time and that she then had to speak in the censure debate which the opposition had called. I wondered how she would cope, and I wanted to be there to show my support.

I arrived back at the Commons shortly before 3.0 p.m. and went immediately into the crowded chamber. I found a place on the front bench. Shortly afterwards John Major came in and sat beside me. He looked pale following his tooth operation and I asked him if he would like a glass of water. The Speaker's Clerk heard me, poured a glass of water and passed it over. Then the Prime Minister arrived to take her place to tremendous cheers. It was the first opportunity most colleagues had had of demonstrating their feelings, and they took full advantage of it. It was hard to believe that a leader who could provoke such cheers, could not command the same support in the ballot box. I suppose the cheers were fuelled by a mixture of loyalty, sadness, relief and bad conscience.

Whatever her private feelings, and she was deeply upset at her treatment by her colleagues, she reacted in typical Thatcher fashion. Question time was handled in a very businesslike way with no suggestion that she felt sorry for herself or was inviting sympathy, but her speech took the House by storm.

To read it now in Hansard the speech does not appear extraordinary. Yet at the time it was. Here was a Prime Minister at the height of her powers, undefeated in three general elections, who was being forced to resign by her own supporters. One could have understood had she made a bitter speech, but instead she delivered an eloquent, fiery and witty exposition of the policies and beliefs that had been the hallmark of her governments. It was, as Paddy Ashdown was generous and honest enough to admit, a bravura performance, unforgettable not only by those of us fortunate enough to be in the chamber, but also by all of those who saw it on television. The House hung on her every word and dissolved into noisy laughter at her reaction to a suggestion by Dennis Skinner that she should become the Governor of a Central European Bank. 'What a good idea. I had not thought of that,' she retorted, breaking the tension. A few moments later, in full flow, she paused and said, 'Now where were we? I am enjoying this.' So was the House.

She sat down to a rousing ovation marred only by the sight of a number of colleagues who had worked against her re-election standing, cheering and waving their Order Papers. It seemed incongruous and hypocritical that they could put on a display of support for the person whom they had just brought down.

For some time Neil Kinnock had been pretending that Mrs Thatcher was a great electoral asset for the Labour Party and that he wanted her to stay as Prime Minister. That afternoon she reminded us and him that she and he played in different political leagues. She recalled him, without actually being specific, those innumerable Tuesdays and Thursdays when she had made him look lightweight and foolish at Prime Minister's questions. It was no coincidence that he looked more composed and sounded more authoritative after her resignation. She simply outgunned him week after week in parliament, and he took his refuge in bluster and bravado away from parliament and usually to selected party audiences.

I found great difficulty in arousing any interest in the second ballot for the leadership. I had made my views known, I regarded Mrs Thatcher as far and away the person best qualified to lead us, and, in my anger at the way her resignation had been engineered, I felt tempted to say, 'A curse on all their houses', and not get involved. This mood prompted me to say to a friend, 'The Labour Party is led by a pigmy and we are led by a giant. We have decided that the answer to our problems is to find a pigmy of our own.' This was grossly unfair to the three candidates, but if fairness had been the criterion for choosing our leader, we would not have been having an election.

I knew Michael Heseltine better than I knew John Major or Douglas Hurd, and some months earlier I had caused a bit of a stir by saying in a television interview with David Frost that he could handle big issues and had many of the qualities of a leader. I then went on to say that his economic views and ideas ruled him out as a potential Prime Minister so far as I was concerned. Nevertheless, the next day *The Sun* newspaper headlined its report of the interview 'Parkinson in swing to Tarzan'.

The fact that as a supporter of Mrs Thatcher I could say anything good about a rival of hers who was a friend of mine was regarded as amazing. My respect for Michael was based on watching him in action when I had been his PPS. He is ruthless, sure of himself to the point of arrogance, and utterly convinced of his qualifications to be Prime Minister. He has little time for ideology, regards government as a management problem, and believes that he is the man to be the manager. For all his good qualities, I felt that under his leadership we would be taking a step backwards, towards the corporatist policies of the sixties and seventies, and for that reason I did not support him. Having told Brian Walden less than a fortnight before that Michael's economic views were a 'fundamental disqualification' for the position of Prime Minister, I was not prepared to swallow those words.

I had known Douglas Hurd for almost as long as I had known Michael, but had never worked closely with him except when we had been jointly in charge of a bill imposing economic sanctions on Iran at the time of the American hostage crisis in 1980. I had seen him in action at various Cabinet committees and between 1981 and 1983 in Cabinet when he attended in Peter Carrington's or Francis Pym's absence. He was always impressive and his contributions in discussion were well thought out and informed. He was somewhat distant and did not seem to have or to want many close friends. Perhaps, even more important in politics, he had no enemies and was widely regarded in all parts of the House as a civilized, capable minister who had been promoted to the Cabinet on merit and in spite of his previous strong connection with Ted Heath. Having been successively Northern Ireland Secretary, Home Secretary and Foreign Secretary, he had served in government for longer and at a higher level than either of his rivals. Whether from a natural diffidence or lack of compelling ambition, he did not seem to want to win quite as much as either of the other two.

John Major was the most surprising candidate. Only seventeen months before he had been the most junior member of the Cabinet as Chief Secretary to the Treasury. In the meantime he had become successively Foreign Secretary, Chancellor of the Exchequer, and candidate for leader. It was an amazing rise by any standards, but by the perceived standards of the Conservative Party, it bordered on the miraculous.

Major was appointed Chief Secretary in 1987 following the general election victory. The job is not a glamorous one, being hugely demanding and requiring enormous attention to detail, in addition to an intimate knowledge of the financial workings of each department. It also involves the holder in an annual confrontation with each of his Cabinet colleagues as they negotiate in the annual public spending round, and in a daily war of attrition throughout the year as circumstances change and agreed figures need revision. The Chief Secretary therefore has a pivotal role. John did the job brilliantly. He was always supremely well briefed, determined that the Treasury should win the argument, but, unlike most of his officials, not wholly unreasonable. It was possible after very hard bargaining to reach a sensible agreement and the process was surprisingly enjoyable because he was very pleasant to deal with. In Cabinet he defended the indefensible with skill and conviction, and he deserved his reputation as a very good minister. He was also popular, which is rarely the case for Chief Secretaries. Major had clearly made a great impression on Mrs Thatcher and his promotion was inevitable. When it came in the reshuffle of July 1989 with his appointment as Foreign Secretary it took everybody by surprise, including him. The switch from the obscurity of Chief Secretary to one of the most high-profile jobs in government seemed to many to be a mistake.

Within weeks Nigel Lawson had resigned and John was moved to what had always seemed a more likely post, Chancellor of the Exchequer. He took over in the middle of a recession and handled a very difficult situation well. In October 1990 he had also persuaded Mrs Thatcher to allow him to take sterling into the ERM. He was clearly identified by her as her preferred successor.

The three candidates represented a strange and total contrast. In appearance, background and achievement they could not have been more different: Heseltine openly ambitious, flamboyant, able, rich; Hurd diffident, reassuring, established and supremely competent; Major quietly determined, relatively inexperienced, popular and capable. It is very common at party Conferences for speakers to refer to the Conservative Party as a 'broad church'. Few people outside the party who hear that rather hackneyed assertion believe it, but the range of choice provided by these three candidates illustrates that it is true.

After my initial anger and disillusionment I accepted that I would have to make a choice. It seemed to me important to choose a leader who would pursue the central economic policy, and I came to the conclusion that John Major was the one most likely to do so. I spoke to Norman Lamont, who was managing the Major campaign, and we agreed that I would declare my support on the Monday. He was anxious for the campaign to maintain momentum and was arranging for different Cabinet ministers to declare their support on successive days, so he asked me not to announce my decision until then.

Immediately after Mrs Thatcher's resignation my Cabinet colleagues had started to line up behind one or other of the candidates in the second ballot. Only David Hunt announced his support for Michael Heseltine, the remainder divided between John and Douglas. Norman Lamont, Peter Lilley, Michael Howard and John Gummer declared their support for John Major, whilst Ken Clarke, Tom King, Chris Patten, Malcolm Rifkind and William Waldegrave backed Douglas Hurd. Over the next few days the rest of the Cabinet (with the exception of John Wakeham, Mrs Thatcher and Kenneth Baker, whose position as Party Chairman made it impossible for him to support any candidate publicly) declared their intentions to an expectant media. On Friday John MacGregor threw his weight behind the Major campaign to be joined over the weekend by Tony Newton and David Waddington. Peter Brooke announced that he would vote for Douglas Hurd.

Over the weekend a number of Thatcher supporters, deeply angered by her treatment, telephoned me to discuss what we should do and I told them in confidence of my decision, but to the media, as requested, I said nothing.

On Sunday I spoke to Keith Carmichael, the President of my constituency Conservative Party, and told him that I would be leaving the government at the same time as Mrs Thatcher and would not be standing at the next election. He tried to persuade me to reconsider, but I made it clear that my decision was final, and that I would be announcing it after seeing Margaret Thatcher the next day.

Monday was a hectic, surreal day. Early in the morning I rang Michael Heseltine to inform him that I would be announcing my support for John Major later in the day. We were due to answer transport questions in the House that afternoon. This was to be my final appearance at the dispatch box. We normally prepared meticulously for questions, but it scarcely seemed worthwhile that day. Nevertheless we had a brief meeting of the full ministerial team after which I left to attend a lunch at Number 10, which Mrs Thatcher gave for twenty-four of her friends and supporters. It was a sombre occasion and she was very subdued and pensive. She spoke at the end of the lunch, but by that time I had left to get to the House for question time. The leadership election was dominating parliament and our monthly question session was low-key and mundane. The only moment of any note came when John Prescott, the Labour transport spokesman, suggested that I was to be sacked. It was a typical Prescott question – ill-tempered and inarticulate: 'Is the Secretary of State aware of the statement made recently by the right honourable Member for Henley [Mr Heseltine] that he intends to devote far greater resources to railway investment, even at the expansion [sic] of a reduction in tax? As that is clearly at odds with what the Secretary of State has told the House, is not it time that the right honourable gentleman accepted my suggestion that he should resign, before he is sacked in three days time?' To which I replied that the honourable gentleman's English was 'matched only by his powers of logic'. Prescott was right that this would be my last appearance; what he didn't know was that I had arranged to see Mrs Thatcher at 5.15 that afternoon to tell her of my intention to resign.

Immediately after questions I left the chamber and went across to College Green, where the television and radio teams were camping out. They had turned what was normally a stretch of lawn into a media village, and there in the course of the next half hour I announced my support for John Major in a number of radio and television interviews which, to my surprise, became the lead items on the early evening news programmes.

Later that afternoon I went round to Number 10 to see Mrs Thatcher. There was a funereal air about the place. The policeman outside and the doorman inside looked grim and sad. I was told that the Prime Minister was waiting for me in her study on the first floor and I went straight up the staircase lined with pictures of former Prime Ministers. There seemed to be no room for another, and I wondered where Margaret's would go. The attendant opened the door for me and I found the Prime Minister sitting behind a strangely empty desk signing a small pile of letters. We sat down in the armchairs at the other end of the room and talked for about an hour. I told her that I wished to make my resignation to her because she had appointed me, but I realized very quickly that it was not fair to add to her problems and said that I would sort it out with whoever won, hopefully John. She thanked me for my support, and revealed that what mattered most to her now was that John Major should win. She told me of the efforts she had been making to convince waverers that they should support him. I could not help thinking that she had done far more for him in the second ballot than she had been able to do for herself in the first. She was distracted and unhappy but in total control of herself. We discussed her resignation and the events leading up to it the previous Wednesday evening, and she repeated her deep disappointment at the behaviour of some of the younger members of the Cabinet, in whom she had, in my opinion, wrongly placed such high hopes.

My abiding memory of that last conversation with Mrs Thatcher as Prime Minister is of feeling that she had already effectively ceased to be Prime Minister and seemed to have lost her authority. The sense of power which one had previously felt in her presence had disappeared. I had once before been near a Prime Minister who had just lost office, in 1974. I was then the most junior member of the Heath government, the Junior Whip. On the night of 7 February 1974, Ted Heath as Prime Minister spoke to the 1922 Committee and announced to tremendous cheers that he had decided to call a general election. Afterwards he came into the government whips' office to have a drink with us. He was hugely impressive and had about him an air of greatness. Four weeks later, he spoke to the 1922 Committee again, having resigned the previous night after failing to reach an accommodation with Jeremy Thorpe and the Liberals. He again came to the whips' office after that meeting but this time it was to the opposition whips' office on the other side of the Members lobby. He seemed almost physically diminished and, instead of being impressed by him, one just felt very sorry for this desolate and lonely figure. The contrast between the Mrs Thatcher who had returned from Paris only five days earlier and the sad person sitting in her study was equally stark. She was clearly finding great difficulty in coming to terms with what had happened to her. To add to her confusion letters of support and sympathy were pouring in at a rate of more than 10,000 a day and flowers sent by hundreds of well-wishers and friends were avalanching into Downing Street.

I went back to Marsham Street to clear my desk and prepare for my own departure from government. I had been asked by the Major team to do a number of media appearances on his behalf on the Tuesday, to appear on the programmes to be broadcast live during and after the count, and to attend a meeting at 4.15 in the afternoon at Number 11. When I arrived I was surprised to find about a hundred people there. The size of the team, the very thorough report and briefing given by Francis Maude and Norman Lamont, and the confidence and enthusiasm of all present made me feel that John was well on the way to victory. The Treasury team of Norman Lamont, Francis Maude and Richard Ryder were clearly the mainspring of the campaign and they put up an impressive performance. In five days they had planned and carried through a superb campaign. The result was announced at just after six o'clock. It was:

Major	185
Heseltine	131
Hurd	56

Hurd and Heseltine immediately conceded defeat and announced their support for John Major. In theory there should have been a third ballot, but to the delight of the party Cranley Onslow, Chairman of the 1922 Committee, made it known that he had decided to dispense with that particular part of the rules and that John Major was the winner. After a five-day campaign and with 185 votes John Major replaced a leader who had won an historic three general elections and who had moreover polled 204 votes in the earlier ballot. Mrs Thatcher's much-quoted remark that 'It's a funny old world' seemed an appropriate way of summing up the events of the previous week.

I was due to make three speeches that day, the last one to a business group over dinner at the Ritz. It seemed as good a thing to do as any, so I went. They told me that their first guest had been the Chairman of British Satellite Broadcasting and that he had resigned the next day. I was their second guest speaker, and I told them that I would be doing the same. We joked that if news of this got out they would have great difficulty in getting speakers for their future meetings.

I had to get back to the House to vote at 10.0 p.m. and I went into the division lobby just as John Major came in through another door. There was a loud spontaneous cheer, and he said a few words which were followed by even louder cheers. Everyone looked relieved that we now had a new leader and that the election process which seemed to have been going on forever had come to an end.

As I walked into the chamber I met Michael Heseltine. It seemed obvious that John would feel that he had to offer Michael one of the top three cabinet jobs – Home Secretary, Foreign Secretary or Chancellor. Douglas could clearly not be moved from the Foreign Office. The right would never accept Michael as Chancellor. This left the Home Office. I said to him 'Well, it's the Home Office for you.' 'I know what they're up to,' he replied. 'It's a political graveyard. I don't want it.' The Home Secretary is Her Majesty's Principal Secretary of State. It is one of the highest offices in the land. Michael, quite clearly, still had his sights set on an even higher office, the leadership of the party to which John Major had just been elected, and the premiership to which he would be appointed by the Queen the next day.

I arrived in the Department of Transport early the next morning, and placed a call to John Major. I also asked my Special Adviser and Press Officer to draft a resignation statement. We discussed what it should contain and then worked on it together.

John Major telephoned me a few minutes later. Neither he nor Mrs Thatcher had yet been to the palace, so he was still not technically Prime Minister. After congratulating him on his election as leader I told him that I did not wish to continue in government, and that I had told my Association that I would not be standing at the next general election. He said that Margaret had reported our Monday conversation to him and that he accepted my decision. I assured him of my total support and wished him every success in the years ahead. I put down the telephone a few minutes later as the ex-Secretary of State for Transport, just in time to see Mrs Thatcher on the television leave Number 10, on her way to Buckingham Palace to become the ex-Premier. Her resignation marked the end of an era in British politics. Mine brought to an end a personal political journey begun in Lancaster more than fifty years before.

2 Diffidence and Deference

I was born in the Royal Infirmary in Lancaster on 1 September 1931, but my parent's home was in the small town of Carnforth, seven miles north of Lancaster.

It was a plain town in the 1930s and 1940s. Daily life was dominated by the railways. The main west coast line from London to Scotland ran through its heart and the station was also the starting point for the Furness line which weaved its way around Morecambe Bay through to Barrow-in-Furness. The town was also split by the A6, then the main road to Scotland and the Lake District. As in many small towns, no time or imagination had been wasted in naming the streets and roads – Scotland Road, North Road, New Street, Market Street were typical and they reflected the simple utilitarian nature of Carnforth. But they gave no clue to the pleasantness of the town as a place in which to live and grow up.

Carnforth, pronounced Carnfuth, lies by the shores of Morecambe Bay surrounded by beautiful countryside. Lovely little towns and villages such as Silverdale, Arnside and Grange-over-Sands which nestled by the shores of the bay were all within range of a short train or bus journey and were all beautiful places for walking, picnicking and swimming. The Lake District was just up the road, and inland, if one could summon the courage to cross the Yorkshire border, were the dales, hills, and waterfalls of Ingleton and the Lune valley.

In many ways those who are today seeking a classless society need look no further than Carnforth in the 1930s and 1940s. It was a very poor town, with a settled population. As a result it was almost totally devoid of pretentiousness and jealousy. People enjoyed other people's success. When Carnforth children won scholarships to one of the excellent local grammar schools their success was a matter of local pride. Without being unduly nosey or prying, people knew a lot about each other, and assumed airs and graces did not impress. I have vivid memories of a local man who set up a mobile greengrocery shop. He seemed to prosper mightily and one day he appeared driving a Rolls-Royce. Nobody envied him his new-found prosperity but nobody was convinced by it. A year or so later his wife, an accountant, was charged with defrauding her employer and robbing him of thousands of pounds. Nobody enjoyed their downfall, although it confirmed a collective view that something not quite right had been going on.

My father was also born in Carnforth and his three brothers and a sister all lived there. His parents were a respected couple in the town and my grandmother was formidable to the point of being fearsome. She was the local midwife and combined this with being the head of the Mothers' Union and the Women Unionists in her spare time. Her profession ensured a steady stream of recruits for both her organizations. She was a die-hard Conservative, and one of my earliest political memories is of her talking to a friend about Neville Chamberlain and saying that unless the Conservatives got rid of him as their leader, Hitler would win. She died when I was 10, and for several years after her death my grandfather and I would walk on Sundays through the fields to matins in the village of Warton about three miles away, and from time to time we would lay flowers on her grave. Apart from socialists and Germans her other pet hate was the people of Yorkshire. Her favourite expression about them was that 'a Yorkshireman would skin a louse for its hide'. She had strong views and was very good at expressing them.

My grandfather was the opposite. Like eighty per cent of Carnforth men he had worked on the railways, but by the time I knew him he had retired. He was handsome, placid and kindly, with snow-white hair. His greatest delights were to smoke his pipe, drink a pint of beer and chat with his friends about sport, and he was happiest when he could spend an evening doing all three.

My father was the youngest of his three sons, and inherited from him his love of sport and his ability to make friends. My mother was 'an outsider' which was the description attached to anyone not born in Carnforth. The youngest member of an Irish Catholic family of seven children, she was born in Ireland. Her mother and father left Belfast during the Twenties and moved to Barrow-in-Furness where the boys went to work in the shipyards and the girls went into service with well-to-do families. My mother was sent to work for a family which lived near Carnforth and it was while she was in their employment that she met my father.

I was born two years after their marriage and my sister Norma was born eighteen months later. It was always a puzzle to me why we were not brought up as Roman Catholics since my mother's family were strict adherents to the church. The mystery was only solved on the death of my mother in 1991 when I asked my father about it. He told me that to the fury of both families he and my mother had eloped and had been married in a registry office in Manchester precisely because neither family could agree how any children should be brought up.

My earliest childhood memories are dominated by three events – King George V's Silver Jubilee, the first run of the Coronation Scot and preparations for war. The Jubilee was a great event. The whole town took part with sports, street parties, church services and a carnival parade culminating in the crowning of a carnival queen. The dull streets were bedecked with coloured ribbons and decorations and I remember there being commemoration mugs for all the children. Although the whole concept of kings and queens and even parliament seemed remote from the lives of the people of Carnforth, our commitment to the monarchy was absolute.

The death of King George V, swiftly followed by the abdication of Edward VIII and the crowning of George VI, registered with me only as a series of school holidays. These events had little significance for us in Carnforth. Nobody felt that the future of the monarchy was in doubt. Events were taking place a long way away, but nobody doubted that the problems would be sorted out and that there would be a king and a queen at the end of it. A lot of grand people who had the minimum of contact with the millions whose views they claimed to articulate told the newspapers what the people thought, and the people read these views without in any way believing them. The same tactics were used at the time that Princess Margaret was pressured not to marry Group Captain Townsend. Great personages claimed to articulate the views of the people while these same people, unconsulted and amazed, watched two lives being blighted in their name.

I don't remember the celebrations for King George VI's coronation, but the day I joined what seemed like the whole of Carnforth in lining the bridges and streets of the town to catch a glimpse of the Coronation Scot lives on in my memory. It was a stunning locomotive and the streamlined design gave the impression of power and speed. As it roared through Carnforth station on to a long stretch of straight flat line it neared its maximum speed of over a hundred miles an hour. Travelling between Euston and Glasgow in six and a half hours it cut fifty-five minutes off the previous best time, and between Euston and Carlisle it was the fastest train in the world over such a distance non-stop. Watching the Coronation Scot thunder through Carnforth was an awe-inspiring sight and made me a railway enthusiast at a stroke. It made all the more ironic the accusation levelled against me years later when I was Transport Secretary that I was anti-railways.

But for all the excitement of the Coronation Scot it was Neville Chamberlain's broadcast to the nation on 3 September 1939 that stands out above all other events in my memory of the Thirties. I had been to church and arrived home in time to hear him. I had reached my eighth birthday two days earlier but even at that age it was clear that something hugely important was being said. I still remember that rather sad, defeated tone of Chamberlain's voice. For months before, the newspapers of which I had become an avid reader had been filled with stories of wars, in Abyssinia, in Finland, and of preparations for war. I found it all very confusing. At different times Hitler and Stalin vied for first place as prime villain, and Mussolini was dragged in for deadly comic relief. The British seemed to want peace at almost any price. This was a puzzle to the people of Carnforth who were convinced that we only needed to make up our minds to sort it out and it would be sorted out – such was our ignorance and our self-confidence.

The actual declaration of war came almost as a relief, but once again there was this familiar Carnforth feeling that life was either preordained or beyond our control and our role was to put up with it. Many young men from Carnforth went off to play their part, joining the forces or serving the country in other ways. My father was too old to fight and was sent off to Durham as a 'Bevin boy' to work down the mines. It nearly killed him and I remembered his vivid description of life underground when I became Secretary of State for Energy.

After a time he became too unwell to continue. To make matters worse, my mother was also very ill at this time and so he came home where he was directed to work on the railways. He remained there for the rest of his working life.

The feeling of being unable to influence events, the almost total acceptance of the authority of others was a hallmark of Carnforth and hundreds of other small towns and villages in the Thirties.

The gradual erosion of this diffidence and deference has made our democracy so much more broadly based and secure in the years since the Second World War. A growing resentment of this fatalistic view of the world led me to join the Labour Party. At the time it seemed to me to be the only party which wanted to give the people a say in the decisions which affected their lives.

There were two schools in Carnforth, both primary schools, the Council School and the Church School. They were great rivals but since neither had any playing fields, that rivalry was confined to the classroom and to exam results, especially the numbers of 11-plus examinations passed.

I went to the Church School. The headmaster, Mr Fred Gander, was a fierce disciplinarian with an appropriately fearsome appearance. He and his team of Miss Johnson, Miss Moore and Miss Mason made us work. Mr Gander taught the top class and he set high standards. He believed in corporal punishment but used it sparingly. It was here that I saw at first hand the power of deterrence. The other notable feature of the school was the visit at assembly time on Monday of the vicar, Canon Mercer. He came, amongst other things, to ask those who had not been to church the previous day for an explanation, and very few were regarded as acceptable. In Canon Mercer's presence it was much easier to believe in a vengeful rather than a loving God. Nevertheless, as a result of this Monday inquisition church and sunday school were well attended if not enthusiastically.

By 1941 I was totally obsessed by the war and was reading everything I could find. I developed a particular enthusiasm, bordering on fanaticism, about a Russian general, Marshal Timoshenko, who in my eyes was Robin Hood, Sir Lancelot, the Duke of Wellington and Dixie Dean rolled into one. The Russians were emerging as the great heroes. It was socialism that was defeating fascism, or so I thought at the time. Our enemy's enemy was clearly marked out as our friend, and I developed a great admiration for Russia and all things Russian. This feeling persisted for some time after the war and in 1949 I attended one or two Communist rallies. One in particular, addressed by Arthur Horner, the General Secretary of the National Union of Mineworkers, lives in my memory. His vicious attack on the system which had allowed the war to develop and seen millions of people slaughtered struck a strong chord with me. One of my companions that day never recovered. He went on to Oxford University, married, gave his first son the Christian names Joseph Stalin, and when I last heard of him in the early Sixties he was a left-wing Trade Union organizer in the motor industry.

In 1942 I learnt that I had been selected to take the 11-plus exam. I passed and along with two or three others was admitted to Lancaster Royal Grammar School. The school, founded in 1469, was for boys only and had a very strong academic and sporting tradition. It was made up of two boarding houses and seven day-boy houses and played an important part in the life of Lancaster. On the basis of their brains and regardless of their parents' income, thousands of local boys had gone on to universities and achieved success across the whole spectrum of professions, equipped with an education that enabled them to compete against people from more privileged backgrounds. The school had received a Royal Charter from Queen Victoria and had the right to sing a unique second line of the National Anthem:

God save our gracious Queen
Long live our noble Duke
God save the Queen

After a controversial and difficult time in the 1930s the school had revived under the guidance of a new headmaster, R. R. Timberlake, who had arrived in 1939 via Berkhamsted, Emmanuel College, Cambridge, and Rugby. He was a superb administrator and fine classical scholar. Under him and a string of well-chosen successors, the school flourished. Academic standards rose sharply and new sporting standards were set. There was a tremendous enthusiasm throughout the whole school which continues to this day. Now it has over 800 pupils, almost every single one of whom would expect to go on to university, polytechnic or other higher education.

Yet the school is lucky to have survived. It was only saved by the division of responsibility for education between central and local government. When we had a Labour government intent on destroying it, we had a Conservative County Council helping to protect it and vice versa. But in 1979 the school had reached the end of the road. By then I was a governor and with great reluctance the governors applied to leave the state system and to go private. The alternative would have spelt the destruction of the school. Its only offence was its enduring success. Fortunately, following the Conservative victory at the general election, we were able to withdraw our application and remain part of the state system. It was particularly irksome to many of us that Shirley Williams, herself the product of a privileged background and a private education, should be the Labour Party's chosen instrument for the destruction of the grammar schools. Years later, when she was the candidate for Crosby in a by-election and I was the Chairman of the Conservative Party, I spoke in the town. I pointed out that Merchant Taylors' School in Crosby, which had once been available solely on ability to anyone in the town, was by that time only available on the basis of parental income to a limited number. By then at least two generations of local boys had been denied their opportunity as a result of her efforts, but this still did not stop her holding herself up as the supporter of the party of opportunity, or portraying us as the party of privilege.

Lancaster Royal Grammar School seemed massive to me after the small school at Carnforth. Suddenly I was meeting boys from a far wider range of backgrounds and affluence. The great levellers were work and sport. Thanks to the excellent education I had received in Carnforth I was placed in the alpha stream which took the School Certificate in four years as opposed to the more usual five.

Fairly soon after arriving at LRGS I was elected captain of my form, a position I was re-elected to each term for the next four years. That was the good news; the bad news was that as a result of my success in my first year, I was placed in the classical stream, and gave up science, geography and other subjects so that I could concentrate on Latin, Greek and Ancient History. It was bad news because I never mastered the languages well enough to enjoy the literature, but above all because I soon had to give up English History which I have always regretted.

The other piece of bad luck was to have been earmarked as a cross-country runner. Shortly after starting at the school I had taken part in the school cross-country run and come third in the Under-14 race out of more than 300 boys, many of them older than me. I was immediately drafted into the school team, but I never enjoyed it and it was a relief when at age 15 I broke the school 440-yards record, and it was discovered that I was in fact a sprinter. The following year I became Victor Ludorum at the school sports and developed a love of athletics which persists to this day. Since I had proved I could run, I was placed on the wing in the school rugby second team and after only one game, because of injury to one of the first team, I played in the first fifteen and, as luck would have it, scored the only try of the match, depriving our opponents, Rossall, of an unbeaten record in their last match of the season.

Five years later on my first day as a management trainee with the Metal Box Company I met a blond-haired Oxford graduate. We started talking about rugby and I soon established that he had been the captain of Rossall on that fateful day. We became firm friends and a few years later Douglas Peters joined my wife's family business as Chief Executive and is now Chairman. That defeat still rankles with him after all these years.

I loved my time at Lancaster. Besides work and sport my other great love was the debating society. It was named after one of the school's most distinguished old boys, William Whewell. The son of a Lancaster master carpenter, Whewell had gone on to become Master of Trinity College, Cambridge. There is a story told of a visit paid to Cambridge by Queen Victoria during Whewell's time at Trinity. He was escorting the monarch along the banks of the River Cam, which at that time was also the city's main sewer. Suddenly, Queen Victoria stopped and, pointing to the river, asked him what the small pieces of paper floating down the river were. Whewell, who was understandably reluctant to tell the Queen that these were in fact pieces of lavatory paper, immediately responded that they were little messages warning the students not to bathe. Whether this story is true or not I do not know, but the society which bore his name at Lancaster was an important influence in developing my interest in politics.

The Whewell Society met on Wednesday evenings and was surprisingly well attended especially by the boarders to whom any break in a highly regimented routine was welcome. By the time I joined I had become a firm supporter of the Labour party and invariably spoke from an extremely left-wing point of view.

My form master for the first four years at Lancaster was a clergyman, the Reverend J. W. Packer. I admired him tremendously and he for his part encouraged my already strong involvement in the church. Christ Church in Carnforth was a high Anglican church. The Reverend Anderson, who had succeeded Canon Mercer, was different in virtually every way from his predecessor. He was large, friendly, approachable and a football fanatic who involved himself in all aspects of the life of the town and was hugely popular. He prepared us for confirmation. I became an altar server and a very active member of the church. Over the years I developed a strong feeling that I wished to become a clergyman and in 1946 when Edward Welbourne, the Master of Emmanuel College, Cambridge, presented the prizes at Speech Day it was arranged that I should meet him. To my astonishment a few weeks later a letter from him arrived at my home offering me a place at Emmanuel to read Divinity, subject to my passing the necessary matriculation examinations. The letter went on to suggest that I should sit the scholarship exams in due course, but a place was assured.

I never did sit the scholarship exams because National Service was extended to two years in the late summer of 1950, and if I was to take up my place in October 1952, I had to get into the forces quickly. I already had a state scholarship on the basis of my Higher School Certificate which covered all tuition fees and I also qualified for the optimum grant. It was not enough to live on, but by working in the summer holidays, and with the help of an obliging bank manager I was able to enjoy three happy years at Cambridge from 1952–55.

Many years later I sat in the white sitting room at Chequers with Margaret Thatcher, Keith Joseph and William Waldegrave, discussing the subject of student loans and whether we should commit ourselves to them in our 1983 election manifesto. I was opposed to the idea. I was quite convinced that working-class parents, like my own, who had an almost pathological fear of debt, would find a loan scheme totally unacceptable, with the result that many bright children from poor families might be denied a university education.

I won the argument that day but with the benefit of hindsight I think I was wrong in principle for two main reasons. A combination of free tuition, means-tested grants and favourable loans which we now have makes students in Britain better supported than in virtually any other western country. Financial barriers against going to university in Britain are very low. Yet we attract a smaller proportion of those eligible than countries where the financial barriers are much higher.

In practice I still think I was right at the time. We were in a huge recession, more than three million people were out of work and the figure was rising. It would have looked vindictive to appear to be discriminating against the children of the poor, and it would have looked as if the government had got its priorities wrong in pursuing such a marginal issue as student loans at a time of national economic problems.

I joined the Labour Party in 1947 when I became treasurer of the local Labour League of Youth – one of the succession of Labour youth organizations that eventually got out of hand and were disbanded. In 1972 I was travelling up to Norwich with the Labour Member for Tottenham, Norman Atkinson, who was then challenging Jim Callaghan for the treasurership of the Labour Party. Atkinson always belonged to the left wing, though in 1986 he was deselected by his local party on the grounds that he was not left-wing enough. On the train to Norwich he told me the story of his political career. He had started as a shop steward at Metro-Vickers in Manchester and was making his reputation in the local party when he was approached by a wealthy Labour supporter who wanted to start a youth wing of the Labour Party in the North West and offered to fund a full-time organizer. He offered Norman the job. He accepted and made a great success of it, founding many branches all over the area. Looking back he regarded this as one of the most enjoyable periods of his political career. I asked him if he remembered the Carnforth branch. He remembered it vividly as one of his best branches. I then told him that I had been the first treasurer of that branch. He was silent for a moment and then he said with a rueful smile, 'Bloody hell, I give five years of my life to promoting the Labour Party amongst young people, and all I produced was a bloody Conservative MP.'

The first general election in which I campaigned was in 1950. Lancaster's MP was Fitzroy Maclean, 6 foot 6 inches tall, and a man whose war-time exploits were legendary. Parachuting behind the enemy lines, working with Tito in Yugoslavia, he was an authentic hero and hugely popular.

Labour's candidate was Bert Farrer, a manager at a local engineering works. Although he did not share Maclean's legendary status we were optimistic about his chances. As a result of boundary changes the Lancaster constituency had lost Conservative Morecambe and gained my home town of Carnforth. We were confident that this would tilt the balance in favour of Labour. I don't remember much about the campaign except that Fitzroy Maclean won and that I saw a Prime Minister in person for the first time when Clement Attlee came to Lancaster. He was due to speak from the Town Hall steps at 10.30 a.m. This coincided with the morning break at school, and I decided to run the half mile down the hill to hear him. He was late, and it wasn't until about 10.50 that a small unaccompanied Morris 1000 came round the corner and pulled up in front of the Town Hall.

Attlee was in the passenger seat and he looked pale and tense. When I mentioned this to the person standing next to me, he told me that Mrs Attlee was a famously appalling driver and that if I had been riding alongside her, I too would be looking pale and tense. The Prime Minister spoke for about ten minutes quietly and in a very matter of fact way about the need for a new mandate so that he could continue with his work of creating a fairer, more prosperous socialist Britain. He did not, in any way, seek to dominate the crowd, but he did impress them. There was no heckling. Attlee was guarded by a solitary unarmed policeman, who stood near him on the steps, and he left in his car without an escort.

By the time I got back to school it was 11.30 and it was my misfortune to meet the headmaster as I walked up the road. He asked me where I had been and when I told him he invited me to go to his study where he thanked me for my honesty and said that in view of this he would ask me to write out only 500 lines of Virgil. It seemed a reasonable price to pay, but I've often wondered what the punishment would have been if the speaker had been Churchill.

In the 1951 general election Labour selected a new candidate whose war-time experiences matched those of Fitzroy Maclean. Her name was Dodo Lees. Miss Lees was almost as tall as Fitzroy Maclean, she was as beautiful as he was handsome and she too had parachuted behind enemy lines. She had worked with the Resistance in France and been decorated by the allied governments for her bravery. Although we worked hard, we failed to oust Fitzroy Maclean but we did manage to reduce his majority.

The other great event of that period was attending the Labour Conference in Morecambe in 1952. It was the first party Conference since Labour had lost power and, perhaps inevitably, it was a bad-tempered affair with each side blaming the other for the failure at the polls. There was little doubt where the sympathies of the grassroots at the Conference lay. The left was in the ascendancy and the brightest star was the charismatic Aneurin Bevan. Bevan and his supporters – Barbara Castle, Richard Crossman, Tom Driberg, Ian Mikardo and Harold Wilson – almost swept the board in the constituency section of the national executive election.

The event that week which sticks most in my mind is a meeting organized by Tribune at which Bevan and his leading supporters spoke. The meeting, held in the Winter Gardens, was packed. Even before the meeting began a queue many yards long had formed.

Hundreds of people were turned away at the door. The atmosphere inside the hall was unlike anything I had experienced before and when Bevan rose to speak the expectation was immense. The audience was not disappointed. We witnessed a magnificent display of political oratory.

One of my best friends at school was Robert Woof, the son of a local farmer. We met through the debating society and discovered a mutual interest in politics, reading and music. At the time we felt that Lancaster was a bit of a cultural desert, but in fact, there were quite a number of events. I recall concerts by the Hallé Orchestra, a piano recital by Louis Kentner, regular visits by the D'Oyly Carte company and the Carl Rosa touring company. Madame Butterfly and Pinkerton struggling with the acoustics of the Morecambe Winter Gardens still contrived to make an impression. In 1947 we decided to go to the first Edinburgh Festival. Robert and I spent days packed with concerts, plays, exhibitions and operas, and I had my first encounter with Richard Strauss and *Ariadne auf Naxos*. The experience was bewildering and only in 1990 at Covent Garden did I fully begin to appreciate this opera. It was a thrilling week which was followed by a week of walking in and around Pitlochry and my first experience of a Highland games. The people in Edinburgh thought we were mad to go walking. The people in Pitlochry thought we had been wasting our time in Edinburgh. Throughout my life I have found that people love to pigeonhole others. The chattering classes in London seem to feel that to say one enjoys sport and music, loves running and singing means one cannot be serious about either. I find intolerant aesthetes the most unattractive of people.

Lancaster had one continuing source of musical delight for me. The Priory Church set by John of Gaunt's Castle and overlooking the Lune has always had a fine choral tradition and the Forties and Fifties were no exception. Matins and evensong were beautifully and ambitiously sung, and from those days I have maintained a love of church music.

I left Lancaster Royal Grammar School as a Labour supporter, with a place at Cambridge, a love of running and rugby, an interest in music and literature and sadly, a dislike of Latin, Greek and Ancient History. But above all I left feeling that life was not as good as it should be for the majority of the British people. I was burning with desire to do something about it and this zeal made me intolerant, angry and articulate.

I did not enjoy my National Service which I served in the RAF. At this time I was virtually a pacifist and I agonized about whether to be a conscientious objector. It mistakenly seemed to me that I was being ordered to join up to oppose the one allied country which had paid a huge price for the freedom of the west with the lives of millions of its people – Russia. In the end I was persuaded to join, but I resolved to involve myself to the minimum possible degree. I became an NCO in charge of a signals unit in the Midlands. I played sport, learned how to drink beer and passed nearly two years pleasantly enough. I was described in my discharge papers as 'competent and intelligent with no interest in the Service'. Now I feel that I missed an opportunity in the RAF, but my frame of mind and my political views at the time made that inevitable.

I have a vivid memory of the address given to us by our drill sergeant when after four weeks of recruit training we were to be allowed out of camp in uniform for the first time. He advised us about the temptation of the outside world and, in particular, of the wiles of women. 'Just remember,' he said, 'if you want it, you'll find it; if you find it, you'll get it. If you get it, you've had it.'

The most important, in fact the only, decision I took during this period was that I did not wish to read Divinity at Cambridge. I had given up my ambition to be a clergyman and wrote to Dr Welbourne, Master of Emmanuel, telling him that I wanted to read for the English tripos instead. His reply was brief but cutting. It would be possible for me to read English, but the next time I changed my mind would I please write an enquiring letter, because 'it is difficult to deploy our staff to meet the changes of intention'. I later discovered that he had an almost pathological dislike of those who taught and those who studied English. This stemmed from a battle that raged over many years between Welbourne and F. R. Leavis. They were the two most brilliant young men of their generation at Emmanuel just before the 1914–18 war. When war was declared Welbourne joined up, was commissioned, and was awarded the Military Cross for bravery in battle. Leavis was a conscientious objector and served as an unarmed stretcher bearer, which many would consider also showed great courage. For Welbourne, however, this was tantamount to treachery and after the war these two fought a bitter battle. Leavis eventually left Emmanuel and moved to Downing. From that time Welbourne – a man of infinite prejudice – became convinced that anybody connected with the English faculty was a potential conscientious objector and his aim was to keep the numbers studying English down to a minimum. His lack of enthusiasm for students of English was matched only by his conviction that the college owed it to the Church of England to provide a steady stream of would-be clergymen. My letter annoyed him, therefore, on two counts, and meant that for my first two years in Cambridge he refused to speak to me.

In 1951, Labour lost the general election and along with millions of others I began to have doubts about socialism. I did not actually join the Conservative Party until 1959, but I had stopped supporting the Labour Party several years before that. When I went up to Cambridge in 1952 I still viewed events from a left-of-centre point of view and I found the university Conservative Association a puzzling group of people. Most of them had already decided to be Cabinet ministers and they all dressed like mini Cabinet ministers. The chief aim of the committee members seemed to be to invite as many Cabinet ministers as possible to come and speak to them. The speech of the visiting politician was quite important. The meal with him afterwards was all-important.

Many of the leaders of the Cambridge University Conservative Association and the Union of the Fifties and Sixties did indeed emerge in the so-called 'Cambridge Mafia' as members of the Heath, Thatcher and now the Major Cabinets. I marvelled at how these students in their early twenties could be so sure of themselves, of their views and of their ambitions. I was impressed by their competence and above all their ability to speak and the confidence with which they put forward their views.

3 The Imaginative and the Contrived

When I went up to Cambridge in October 1952 the university was still trying to decide whether the 1939–45 war had been an aberration, an interruption to a way of life that would shortly be resumed, or whether it would have to adapt itself to a fundamentally changed world. The war and its aftermath had left its mark, and the Labour government which had been in power for all but a few months since the war, had, by the enormous increase in state scholarships, opened Cambridge to a host of people like myself who would not previously have had the chance. Because of rationing and the need to pool resources, communal living with most people eating most meals together had become the norm. A different mix of people living in a different style at least offered the possibility of change, but seven centuries of tradition would not easily be overturned even by Hitler. Moreover, Mr Churchill was recently back in power, rationing was shortly to be abolished and there was a growing feeling that normality would soon resume.

Emmanuel College was, in the words of its Master, 'perhaps still in the Seventeenth Century, and goes its way a little outside the full stream of University life'. It provided 'few of the men in fancy dress who lounge in King's Parade'. This was, to many of us, an expression of hope rather than a statement of fact. Edward Welbourne was describing his beloved Emmanuel as he was determined to keep it. He was a most unusual man, quite tall and powerfully built, but his head and particularly his forehead were huge and massively out of proportion to the rest of him. Piercing eyes and a rather loose grinning mouth added to the intimidating impression which he invariably made and, I sometimes felt, intended to make. He had spent his whole life, with the exception of the years 1914–18, in the services of Emmanuel as Fellow, Tutor, Senior Tutor and finally Master. It was as Senior Tutor that he made his greatest mark on the college. He personally selected every man during thirteen years in that office and he made sure that he produced the college he wanted, reaping success in the whole gamut of undergraduate activities. The college thrived under his direction. Welbourne recognized that the massive increase in state-supported students needing to prepare themselves to earn a living could make Cambridge an earnest, dull source of vocational training and he set out to guard against that particular danger in his own way. In the Emmanuel College Magazine he wrote : 'Men do not see themselves as adventurers into the world, but as neatly formed pegs for the square and round holes, but we are not without men who cultivate their personalities rather than train for the foreseen demands of the Appointments Board'. We were not without such men because Welbourne made sure that we had more than our share. That is how a leading member of the university draghounds came to be sitting under a tree in the college grounds on the day before his first examination reading *Teach Yourself Economics* and saying to a friend, 'This economics can be bloody difficult, can't it?' That is how the university came to acquire its best soccer player in decades. That is why we had students from all parts of the Commonwealth. That is why we had undergraduates with such a wide variety of backgrounds and interests.

I had decided to read English because for the first time in my life I wanted to study literature without the barrier of language. My supervisor to whom I was invited to introduce myself was Peter Furbank who subsequently became well known as the biographer of E. M. Forster. He was extremely kind and likeable, but painfully shy with a stammer which I found catching and which became more pronounced the longer the supervision period went on. It was a relief to him and all who worked with him when the weekly supervision came to an end. Nevertheless, after discussing the reasons behind my decision not to read Divinity and my almost total ignorance of the subject I had chosen to study, he drew up a crash course of reading and lectures which would create a framework of knowledge on which I could build. I spent two very happy years doing as work what I had previously done for pleasure – reading voraciously. The highlights of this period were the lectures of F. R. Leavis and in a totally different vein those of Sir John Sheppard, the legendary head of King's College. Leavis, small and slight, arrived at the Mill Lane lecture rooms on a butcher's boy's bicycle with his papers in the front holder. I found him most unattractive as a person. He always seemed to be at war with somebody, and enjoyed nothing more than tearing the reputation of his current hate to shreds. What made him fascinating was his total intolerance of the shoddy and the second-rate, and his wonderful ability to demonstrate why the chosen writer, poet, or critic deserved his contempt. His fundamental distinction between 'the imaginative' and 'the contrived' has stayed with me all my life, and extends itself, as he intended that it should, far beyond literature as an infallible touchstone. Brian Walden's speech in the debate on the Industrial Relations Bill twenty years after I last heard Leavis, when I was a new Member of Parliament sitting on the opposite side of the Commons, summed up for me all that is imaginative. In a passionate defence of the right to join trade unions and of the continuation of the closed shop, Brian Walden argued: 'It is very difficult for people with a certain background, with a certain temperamental inclination, with a certain view, for instance, of patriotism and of the courts, who have a certain view of responsibility and of duty, people with a background that has been not only in their own lives but in their training basically individualistic, to grasp how much so many of us on this side are shaped by a different set of values: no better, no worse – just different. They are collective values. They are values very well understood. Indeed, the whole reason why the Labour Party exists is that we were able to stand together as a group when we were anonymous.' In contrast, virtually any speech by Bryan Gould or Roy Hattersley is contrived in the full Leavis meaning of the adjective.

Sir John Sheppard who was alleged to have decided to become old and doddery at the age of about 30 was altogether different. I had never before come across a person who could genuinely be described as exotic. His performance in preparing to deliver his lecture consisted of climbing on to the high dais, crawling across it and then sitting, legs dangling over the edge, facing a drop of about eight feet which would almost certainly have killed him. One felt one was in the presence of a great scholar and a great eccentric, and although I do not now recall a single word he said, I and the hundreds of others who went to Mill Lane on Wednesday afternoons felt we had spent our time well.

After two years of reading English, I began to feel that it was time I stopped indulging myself and started doing something that might be useful and make me employable. I switched to the Law tripos for my final year and applied myself to getting to grips with contract tort and real property. The Tutor in Law at Emmanuel was Freddie

Odgers. He was hugely popular both as tutor and university lecturer and was proud of the consistently high attendance rate at his lectures. This was unusual. Most courses started term with a large audience but by the end of term only a devoted few would usually be attending. Amongst the group attending Freddie's lectures were two very pretty, auburn-haired girls. To his disappointment they both stopped coming. He asked if any of us knew why. A very earnest member of our group volunteered the information that although Julia was no longer coming to the lectures, she was receiving the lecture notes from him. Freddie asked which one of the two was Julia. Jonathan replied that she was the one who had been presented. Another member of the group, irritated by Jonathan's pomposity, said rather innocently, 'Isn't that what they do to heifers?' 'No,' replied Jonathan, 'heifers are served, young ladies are presented at court.' 'How can you tell which has done what?' was the answer. Supervisions with Freddie were a mixture of laughter and hard work and it was to his great credit that all his students graduated, regardless of the depth of their commitment to the law, and that a substantial number followed successful careers as barristers and solicitors. I had no interest in becoming a lawyer and had decided to join an industrial group as a management trainee. This was regarded as an unusual choice in Cambridge in 1955. Even in that year as many people joined the colonial service and went abroad to take up 'the white man's burden' as went into business.

One of the joys of Cambridge, especially for an 'Arts student', is the amount of time available for other pursuits even when one has set aside, or attempted to set aside, a reasonable amount of time for work. The scientists, engineers and medical students have a much more controlled life, but for the arts student, the weekly essay, the weekly hour spent with a tutor, and the end of year examinations represent the only fixed points in an otherwise flexible diary, and the variety of ways of filling the rest of the time was truly infinite.

Emmanuel Athletic Club was founded in 1855 and is the second oldest in the world. St John's Athletic Club was founded one week earlier. Although I had won the Victor Ludorum twice at school, I knew that the standard at Cambridge at that time was extremely high. My chances of running for the university were not helped when Harry Whittle, the captain of our Olympic team, came up to Cambridge for a year's postgraduate work. Nor was my confidence improved when the secretary of the university club, P. J. Robinson, an outstanding miler who had rooms in the same house as I did, told me as we walked to dinner one night that it was a great pity that Emmanuel did not seem to attract good athletes like John Macve. John, a charming Old Marlburian, happened to be my rival for a place in the freshman's team to run against Oxford two weeks later. In the event John was selected ahead of me and I resigned myself to sitting out the meeting as reserve. However, following a late withdrawal, I was included in the team and won both the 100 and 220 yards, finishing just ahead of John Macve. The following week I was pleasantly surprised to read in *Varsity*, the Cambridge student newspaper, of my 'unexpected double victory in the sprints. Selected at the last minute, he won both in times that promise much for the future.' My athletics career at Cambridge had got off to a good start.

After the match I had a long talk with one of the judges, an old man who had won an Olympic gold medal way back in the dark ages, and who wrote about athletics for *The Sunday Times*. His name was Harold Abrahams and years later, when I saw *Chariots of Fire*, I realized that Abrahams was only in his early fifties, as must have been the other judges, Lord Burghley, Henry Stollard and Euan Montague, all of whom also featured in that superb film. Such was the pre-eminence of Oxbridge athletics at that time that even the freshman's match was reported in the national press. It was hardly surprising, since this was the era of Roger Bannister, Christopher Chataway, Derek Johnson, Chris Brasher, Herb Elliot, all world record holders or Olympic medallists, and some of them both. For me the outstanding home-produced athlete of this period was Derek Johnson. He failed by a fraction of an inch to win the Olympic 800-yards final in Melbourne in 1956, but during his career at Oxford he ranked among the top ten in the all-time British list in, I think, eight events and for good measure he won the inter-university cross-country event. He also seemed to manage it with rather less training and a more active social life than most of his rivals. Even in the early 1950s, training for athletics was becoming more scientific and demanding, and it was the good fortune of those at Oxford and Cambridge to have both the time and the facilities available, not to mention first-class coaches. This undoubtedly gave us an advantage over many other fine athletes who had to earn a living and could only train in their spare time, often after travelling long distances to the nearest track. The wheel has turned full circle and now it is Oxbridge athletes who are at a disadvantage. In the absence of National Service they leave university in the main at the age of 21 having spent their three years pressured by exams, so they find it hard to compete with the older, stronger, full-time top-class athletes of today.

In addition to inter-university athletics there was ferocious competition between college teams for the university championship, the Rouse Ball Cup, and it was a matter of great satisfaction to me that after a number of years of being runners-up and sharing the championship we won the cup in our centenary year, 1955, by which time I had become President of the club.

I was not chosen to run against Oxford in 1953, but in 1954 and 1955 I was. I also ran against Cornell, Pennsylvania, Yale and West Point for the combined Oxford and Cambridge team. Athletics can be a lonely and rather grim sport involving hours of training often to the point of exhaustion and sickness. What made Cambridge athletics so enjoyable was the camaraderie and the traditions which were such a feature of the club. Athletics was a winter sport in Cambridge. The match against Oxford took place in March. We ran at Fenners on an irregularly shaped cinder track round the perimeter of the cricket ground. The track was over 500 yards round and we ran in a clockwise direction. Every other track was 440 yards in circumference and one ran in an anti-clockwise direction. In the pavilion at Fenners there was a room called the Alverstone Room where the university athletes changed and where our masseur, Freddy, dispensed massages and advice. 'Always take a good look at the young lady's mother before you propose, because that's the way she'll be when she grows older' was a typical piece of Freddy counsel. We were all treated as young gentlemen and after training would sit around the fire drinking Horlicks which was provided for us as a form of primitive sports sponsorship. We would while away the time waiting for our massage inventing slogans for our sponsor.

The team for the match against Oxford was chosen after trials at Fenners, which took place about three weeks before the match. Once selected the team went off for a long weekend at a fine hotel, the Cavendish at Eastbourne. We would run as a group to Beachy Head once or twice a day, eat marvellous meals and change into dinner jackets for dinner. It was a very civilized but rather unusual way to prepare for an athletics meeting.

The match took place at the White City track in London and was attended by a few thousand people. It was followed by a splendid dinner for both teams and old blues at which we set out to undo some of the good that months of training and abstemious living had done. The day concluded with the Achilles Ball at Gunters in Park Lane. After the dance we usually went on to a rather less formal party in somebody's house and got back to our hotel as the dawn broke. It all added up to an unforgettable day, and the effort one had to put into becoming a part of it seemed then, as it does now, more than worthwhile.

After the university match the two teams combined to run against the American universities and later as the Achilles Club to tour at home and overseas. Through these tours, in particular, Oxford rivals became friends. Those friendships still continue, and even after a break of years, they are revived effortlessly when we meet now.

In 1990 one of my contemporaries at Emmanuel became Lord Mayor of London, and to mark the occasion, a dinner was held at the Mansion House to launch a society for former members of the college. I was asked to speak at the dinner, and in the course of my remarks said that it was no surprise to any of us that Christopher had become Lord Mayor. His family had a long tradition of public service in the City and even as an undergraduate he had shown a deep commitment to the common good. I added that, in view of my interest in politics, I hoped it was no surprise that I had become a member of the Cabinet, but I was sure that it was a surprise that it was a Conservative Cabinet.

When I arrived at Emmanuel I had become disillusioned with the Labour Party. I did not doubt their motives, but it seemed to me that the people they cared about most appeared to do worst under them. In particular, nationalization which, in theory, should have produced greatly improved industrial performance had produced exactly the opposite. Where there should have been industrial harmony with management and labour working together for the good of the new owner, the British public, we had industrial strife and appallingly low productivity. All the signs were already there that nationalized industries would be trade-union dominated and producer-driven, with the public getting a poor and expensive service as customer and a large bill as taxpayer. I still saw events from a left-of-centre point of view and, in spite of feeling a great admiration for Churchill, I regarded the Conservative Party as the defenders of privilege and the protectors of the well-to-do. The first debate I attended at the Union was on the motion 'That this house has no confidence in Her Majesty's government'. The leading speaker in favour of the motion was

Herbert Morrison, who had lately been Foreign Secretary and was a leading figure in the post-war Labour government. Against him was Iain Macleod, then newly appointed to the Cabinet as Minister for Health after only a few months in the House of Commons. It was no contest. Morrison totally misjudged the audience and played the wise old uncle, there to give the students the benefit of his experience. Macleod took him apart, with a vicious analysis of the failings of the Labour government and of Herbert Morrison in particular. He cuttingly dismissed Morrison's arguments by saying, 'he is old enough to be my father, wise enough to be my son'. Macleod delivered his attack without notes, in a rather piping, icy voice without any change of expression. It was a devastating speech, rapturously received by what seemed to be a totally Conservative audience. An equally brilliant speech in support of Macleod came from an undergraduate, John Biffen. That evening summed up for me my political dilemma at the time. My sympathy was wholly with Morrison, but I was forced to face the fact that Macleod and Biffen had won the argument hands down. Moreover, neither Biffen nor Macleod conformed to the traditional picture I had of a Conservative politician. Both had clearly achieved their positions on merit. Nevertheless my side had lost and fuelled by anger rather than reason I resented the Macleod/Biffen victory. It was the first of many times I heard Iain Macleod speak. To this day I do not know where the picture of him as a consensus politician comes from. He was far and away the best partisan orator the Conservative Party has produced since the war. The highlight of the party Conference year after year was Macleod's demolition of the Labour government or Shadow Cabinet. I particularly remember his speech in 1967. He was working his way through the Labour Cabinet, person by person, and he finally came to Jim Callaghan, the Chancellor. 'He is by a long chalk the best of them,' he said, 'although, as Shakespeare said, "There is small choice in rotten apples".' Eighteen years after the Union debate, following Macleod's tragic death after only thirty-two days as Chancellor of the Exchequer, I was selected to succeed him as the Conservative candidate for his parliamentary seat of Enfield West. Shortly after that I was introduced to a parliamentary colleague whom I felt I had met before. We soon established that it was the person who had supported Iain Macleod in the Union in 1952, John Biffen.

Emmanuel College was founded in 1584 by Sir Walter Mildmay, for many years Chancellor of the Exchequer to Queen Elizabeth I.

His aim was to create a college 'to train learned and devoted ministers of the Church of England'. His secondary purpose was to create a Puritan stronghold in the university, and this he succeeded in doing to such effect that, following the accession of Charles I when many clergymen felt that emigration was the only alternative to betrayal of conscience, many Emmanuel men left the country. Of the first one hundred university graduates to settle in New England, no less than one third were Emmanuel men. The best known of them was John Harvard who, by the bequest of his books and half his estate, gave his name to a college founded at Newtown. Newtown was subsequently renamed Cambridge by way of compliment to the first minister there, Thomas Shepherd, who was also an Emmanuel graduate.

Each year, as living evidence of the link between Emmanuel and Harvard, a newly graduated Harvard man came to spend a year at Emmanuel. The person had normally had an outstanding career at Harvard, had graduated well and usually had a fine sporting record. The three Harvard scholars who came to Emmanuel during my years there were Louis McCagg, an Olympic oarsman, Charlie Ufford, a fine squash and tennis player, and John Culver, an outstanding American football player. Each of them subsequently had successful careers, the most notable being John Culver who became a well-known Democratic congressman and subsequently Senator of Iowa.

The Harvard scholar lived in a set of rooms in one of the oldest buildings in the college, called Old Court and completed in 1634. Old Court had no central heating and the bathrooms and lavatories were fifty yards away behind the library. Being exposed to an English winter in this elegant but spartan setting was a considerable shock to the system of these young Americans. The Master for his part recognized the special needs of our transatlantic visitors and had installed in the Harvard rooms an ugly anthracite-burning stove which he was convinced transformed the rooms from an ice-box to an oven. Nobody had the nerve to tell him that the stove produced dust and smoke, but very little heat. Nevertheless the Harvard men quickly adjusted, and became popular and active members of the college. In my second year I shared a set of rooms, a sitting room and two bedrooms, just opposite the Harvard rooms with a friend, Bob Mackley. As a result we got to know Charlie Ufford well. He was a very tall, rather shy, delightful New England Quaker. After he had been in Cambridge for a couple of months I asked him how he felt he was getting on. He said that with two exceptions he was getting on well. The first was the Master, who made him feel inadequate. I assured him that that put him on a par with all the rest of us. The second was the man who cleaned our bathrooms and lavatories, whose name was Billy but whose nickname was Billy Boggs. Charlie explained that every morning when he went into the bath-house to shave and clean his teeth, he would say to Billy, 'Good morning, Mr Boggs,' and, for some reason he couldn't understand, the more politely he said it the more hostile Billy became.

In 1953 when Charlie came to Emmanuel, a black American called Jim Gibbs came from Cornell to do some postgraduate work. He was a charming fellow, and Bob and I invited the two visiting Americans to tea to introduce them to each other. The first half hour was surprisingly difficult for some reason which we didn't understand. After that we all got on well together, and Bob and I thought no more of it. It was a little later that Charlie explained to us that he had not previously socialized with a coloured person, not because he had avoided it but because the opportunity had never arisen. By the end of the year they were firm friends. I had never been to America at the time and knew few Americans. The fact that two civilized, devout Americans had to come to England to learn how to talk to each other demonstrated to me the divisions and segregation in American society far more than the obscene rantings of Senator McCarthy did.

John Culver, who followed Charlie, was quite different from the normal run of Harvard scholars. They were usually privately educated from New England and very much established. John was from Iowa in the Mid-West; he was huge, outgoing, athletic and a man of very strong views. He had been friendly at Harvard with Teddy Kennedy, who had been in the football team with him. Kennedy's brother had been elected to the senate two years earlier, and during his time at Cambridge John Culver was seeking the senator's help to get into the marine corps after Cambridge. Such Americans as I did know assured me that it was the norm for people in John's position to use whatever influence they had to keep them out of the marine corps.

Teddy Kennedy came to stay with John once or twice and I remember one uproarious dinner in the Harvard rooms. He was clearly set for a career in politics and, although already rich and destined to become richer, he was at that time very pleasant, easygoing and quite unaffected. It surprised me that John, who also had political ambitions, seemed to accept that his own career could never match that of Teddy's. John Culver was the more able of the two, more intelligent, a better athlete, and had been more successful in every area in which they had competed. It was quite an eye-opener to me that in the land of the free and the home of the brave, money and influence should count far more than ability. After serving for three years in the marines and then graduating from Harvard Law School, John became a senior member of Teddy Kennedy's staff. He was a liberal Democrat who lost his seat in the Senate in 1978 and is now a successful Washington lawyer.

Emmanuel, like every other Cambridge college, was riddled with clubs and societies of varying degrees of exclusiveness. Many of them, like the sporting clubs, the debating society, the law society, were open to any member of the college who wished to attend, but some were restricted in numbers and one only joined if elected and invited. The Lions, for instance, was a club for sportsmen in the college. Membership was limited to twelve and any one member could veto the election of a new member. This could be irksome, and proved to be in one particular case, where ten members were keen to elect a new member and the other member, on very slender grounds, was opposed. Eventually a meeting of the club was called to discuss a change in the rules, and it was agreed that, in future, not one but two blackballs would be needed to exclude a person from membership. Everyone present was satisfied that a sensible compromise had been reached, and were all surprised when a Jamaican member got up and left the room, looking very angry. We were all sitting wondering what we had done to upset him when the door opened, and a grinning face appeared round the side of the door. He explained that under the newly agreed blackball rules he might be excluded from membership.

Most of the clubs and societies, whatever they started out to be, ended up as dining clubs, but the two most senior clubs in the college, the Mildmay Essay Club formed in 1883 and the Twelve Club formed in 1889, were the exceptions to that rule. The Mildmay which numbers amongst its past members bishops, authors, judges, academics and politicians, including Hugh Walpole, Lord Birkett, F. R. Leavis and Sir George Porter, was limited to twelve under-graduate members, and met about ten times a year. Each member had to produce two essays during his time as a member and on the evening on which he read his essay to the club he also entertained the club to food and drink. It was a nerve-wracking experience to be the host and essayist. After the formal opening by the President, the victim was invited to read his essay. At the end of the reading, the President used a traditional form of words to launch the supper. He simply said, 'In accordance with the ancient and honourable traditions of the club, I call upon members to help themselves.' Then followed several hours of conversation and argument. The choice of essay was entirely a matter for the member and the subjects ranged widely from 'When pigs can fly' and 'Chocolate-box art' to 'Where there's muck, there isn't always brass' and 'That Aarlot Reason'. My own essays were entitled 'Pantisocrats' and 'Random harvest', the first about idealism and the second about the evolution of the English theatre. The fact that being a member involved making an effort made the social aspects of the club all the more enjoyable. One really felt one had earned one's enjoyment. The rival club, the Twelve, also started as an essay club, but from 1899 they met and continue to meet to read plays. Every year the two clubs competed in one form of sporting contest, usually on the river. A leading member of the Twelve during my years in the Mildmay was Tom King, who later became a Cabinet colleague.

In my final year I was elected to the Emmanuel Singers who met each Monday evening in the Dean's rooms to drink his port and sing Gilbert and Sullivan. An evening a week at the theatre, regular visits to the cinema, evensong at King's on Sunday, and occasional visits to London filled what was left of the time available and it was almost with relief that one returned to Carnforth in the vacations to catch up on sleep and, in the summer, to earn some money.

In my final year I started to think about how I was going to earn my living, and after a visit to the Appointments Board, I decided on a career in industry. After a number of interviews I accepted an offer to become a management trainee with the Metal Box Company, a large packaging concern. They were one of the relatively few companies to have an established training scheme, and most of their directors were former trainees. Other than that I knew very little about them or about industry for that matter.

In the summer of 1955 after the May-week round of parties and balls, Emmanuel and St John's athletic clubs combined to tour schools and universities in the West Country. We ran against Bristol and Exeter Universities, and the Royal Navy, and gave coaching at schools such as Bryanston, Allhallows and Marlborough. At the end of the tour we went back to Cambridge where I took my degree in person in the Senate House. I stayed on for a few days in Emmanuel, reluctant to make the final break with Cambridge, but in mid-June on a lovely morning, I very sadly said goodbye to the Head Porter, Mr Freeman, and caught the train back to Carnforth.

4 *Laying Foundations*

I was not due to join the Metal Box Company until mid-September 1955 so I accepted an invitation to tour Norway and Sweden with an Achilles team. We ran at international meetings in Gothenburg, Oslo and Stockholm, and at smaller meetings in various other towns and cities in the two countries. At that time the antipathy between the Swedes and the Norwegians was particularly strong, following Sweden's neutrality in the recent war, and the invasion of Norway by the Germans. As British athletes we were made very welcome in Norway, and treated in a much cooler fashion in Sweden. We were due to arrive back in England early on a Sunday morning and I had to report to the company headquarters at the Langham, Portland Place at 9.0 a.m. the next day. We travelled by boat from Gothenburg to Tilbury, but heavy storms delayed our crossing and we docked at Tilbury twenty-four hours late. As a result I arrived three hours late for work on my first day with the company. My boss appeared to be very understanding, introduced me to my twelve new colleagues and promptly invited us all out for what he called a typical Metal Box four-course lunch, consisting of three pints of beer and a sandwich in a local pub.

The name, Metal Box Company, was in fact a misnomer. Although the company had a virtual monopoly of food cans and most other metal containers from biscuit tins to judge's-wig boxes, it also had substantial paper-printing, board-printing and polythene-extruding subsidiaries. In my first few months with the company I was seconded to different factories throughout the group and in different parts of the UK to gain experience of the range of products and processes, and to meet as broad a spectrum as possible of the personalities and personnel in what in the Fifties was regarded as a very large British concern. Because most of the senior management of the company had started as trainees, the departments to which new recruits were attached handled them with a certain amount of care. As one foreman explained to me, 'You might be back here in a few years time as my boss, so I'd better be careful.' Nevertheless, spending eight hours a day watching a can-making machine produce thousands of cans an hour could be mind-numbing. I had some sympathy with the trainee who, after spending two hours on his first day in a noisy plant with machines thumping away producing cans and watching thousands of tin cans whizzing around overhead on high-speed conveyor belts, said to his supervisor, 'This can be bloody boring, can't it.' He had caused a certain amount of interest by driving into the car park in a shooting brake with a collapsible canoe attached to the top. 'For duck shooting,' he explained when asked what it was for. He had just been sent to a large factory in Worcester and after a few days he put an advertisement in the local paper: 'Gentleman seeks accommodation in country house, garage for two cars, dog later in the year.' He got a reply within twenty-four hours from the owner of a beautiful house, who asked only two questions. 'Are you the gentleman who owns the famous vintage Bentley and is that your second car?' The answer to both questions was 'Yes' and Hamish found a home, a garage for his two cars and did acquire a gun dog later in the year. He also decided that he and can-making were not meant for each other and after a year he left to become a stockbroker.

Each trainee had to write a weekly report to the factory manager and they in turn wrote an assessment of each of us at the end of every secondment. On the basis of these reports it would be decided in which part of the group we would eventually work. After two months we were reunited as a group at Ashridge College in Hertfordshire, one of the first British management colleges, and there we spent an intensive three weeks along with trainees from other companies, being introduced to a range of management techniques and theories. Ashridge is now well established and sought after, but in the Fifties there was little demand for business schools, and the management college shared the premises with the House of Citizenship. The latter offered secretarial and business training plus a wider citizenship course, and was attended by about 120 girls aged 18 and over from all over the world. They shared a dining room with the management trainees and were encouraged to mix with us, subject to strict supervision. On my third night there I was introduced after dinner to a very pretty young woman who, with a group of friends, was drinking coffee with my group. Her name was Ann Jarvis and for the next two weeks we saw each other regularly. I even joined the choir of which she was the leader so that we could see each other more often. Her college was residential, but her home was only about twenty miles away and one weekend just before Christmas I was invited to have lunch and to meet some of her friends. A few days later I left Ashridge for home and after Christmas for Carlisle where I was to spend three months at one of the original Metal Box factories, the Hudson Scott branch. Ann and I kept in touch by telephone and letter, but there seemed little prospect of meeting until she invited me to her twenty-first birthday party in March 1956. By this time I had started playing rugby for Carlisle, as a way of meeting people and of doing something which I enjoyed. Unfortunately a few days before Ann's birthday I was badly concussed and was forbidden to travel. I was surprised at how disappointed I felt, and delighted to learn from Ann that she too had been looking forward to seeing me. A few days later I was summoned by the company to London to be told that I was to join the food-canning division and that I would be based at Neath in South Wales for the next year. I had only been to South Wales once before to visit the steel works at Port Talbot, the tin-plate works at Llanelli and the factory at Neath. It had poured with rain during the whole visit and my overwhelming impression of South Wales was of grimness, greyness and grime.

The only consolations were that I would be going with a fellow trainee and friend, John Hoblyn, who had a car, and that Neath was nearer to Hertfordshire and Ann than Carlisle had been. I arrived in Neath full of apprehensions and fearing the worst. I could not have been more wrong. The company owned a beautiful house just up the valley from the town. It was normally used by senior management, but we were given permission to stay there for a few weeks until we found somewhere to live. In the factory we were attached to a delightful Metal Box character, Bob Mackie, who had the rather grand title of Methods and Mechanical Handling Manager. His remit was to roam the factory seeking ways of taking the drudgery out of the work as well as improving the conditions of the work force and the productivity of the factory, two objectives which I quickly learnt are very often mutually compatible and not, as industrial cold war warriors would have us believe, mutually exclusive. Bob was also a great company politician and gave careful instruction to his trainees on the politics of the Neath factory in particular and the company in general. His wife ran a shop in Porthcawl which he referred to as 'The Emporium', and as a secondary subject, he taught us the economics of the family-owned grocer's shop. His favourite way of ending an argument, as his wife reminded me only recently on his eightieth birthday, was to say, 'Cecil, I'm not always right, but I'm never wrong.'

After a few weeks John and I and a more senior trainee, Alan Marsh, found a flat in Swansea and we began to enjoy our life. The work was interesting, the people were very friendly, the Gower peninsula with its lovely beaches was only a few miles away, and Ann and I were meeting regularly, either in London where she now worked, in Neath or in Swansea. One Friday as she was travelling on the underground with her suitcase, she met a mutual friend from her home town who asked her where she was going. She told him she was coming to see me in Neath. He replied, 'Blue train?' She said, 'No, Red Dragon,' – the name given to the London to South Wales express. When she returned home after the weekend she found her home town buzzing with the news that she and I had spent a weekend together in Nice.

During one of her weekend visits, which our landlady insisted were fully chaperoned, I asked Ann to marry me. She agreed and the following weekend I travelled to Harpenden to meet her father, Tony Jarvis, and to ask his permission. He was only 42 and, having trained at Cambridge as an architect, was running his family building firm. He was a first-class golfer and skier, and had followed his father and a number of his cousins in playing in the Wimbledon tennis championships and captaining his county tennis team. He also had a very fine war record. Tony made what might have been a difficult meeting very easy. He said, 'I suppose I ought to ask you about the state of your bank account, but on the other hand, you might ask about mine, so we'd better leave the subject alone.' Ann's parents were divorced and her mother had married again. Arthur and Barbara Slater lived in London and later that day we travelled up to see them. They were also very welcoming.

A few weeks earlier I had been invited to spend a weekend with them. When I arrived I found that a number of relatives had turned up unexpectedly and that I was to be boarded out with their next-door neighbours. I was taken over to be introduced to them, but I missed their surname. I was wearing a Hawks Club tie, which my host recognized and asked me if I was still at Cambridge. I explained that I now worked for the Metal Box Company and asked him if he'd ever heard of it. He asked me how they were treating me and explained that he was the Managing Director of the company. The story of the trainee who asked the MD if he had ever heard of the Metal Box Company whizzed around the company.

The Metal Box factory at Neath employed about 3,000 people and was a trade union closed shop. Just before I arrived there had been a strike, the first in the history of the company. Relations between management and the work force were improving but were still not good. The other trainees and myself were seen as part of management and treated correctly, but kept at arm's-length. A new sports field had been created by the company as a gesture of good will and I used it to prepare for the athletics season. The Chairman of the company was Sir Robert Barlow, and each year all the factories in the group, and there were nearly forty of them, sent teams to London to compete in the company athletic sports for the Barlow Trophy. I approached the secretary of the Sports and Social Club and said that I would like to join the team, would be training three times a week and would be happy if others would care to join me. He put up a notice, and to his surprise and mine about thirty people turned up for training. The standard of the athletics competition was low, and even the limited training we had done gave us an advantage. We won the Barlow Trophy easily and Sir Robert congratulated Charlie Gaiger, our General Manager, on a fine result which was evidence that the strike problems were behind us and morale had been restored.

Although I enjoyed factory life and was happy in the Metal Box Company I had become more and more convinced that I wished to emigrate to Canada. One of my best friends at Cambridge, a man called Drew Chambers who was an engineer, had gone to Canada and wrote to me regularly, singing the praises of his adopted country as a place to live and work, and urging me to join him. I remember that in one of his letters telling me of his life in Canada he announced that he had four suits in his wardrobe, a new car in the drive and was buying his own house. On top of this he was taking flying lessons. He wrote that at 25 he was living the kind of life that a man of 45 would hope to live in Britain. It was a tempting prospect. He made one proviso which was that Canada at that time desperately needed people with a professional qualification. One day, looking through *The Times*, I saw an advertisement for trainee accountants in Toronto. A large international firm was offering to pay the fare out and a living salary during training. At that time in the UK one had to pay to be trained as a lawyer or an accountant, but in Canada that system had already been abandoned. I applied and was asked to come for an interview on the Monday after the company sports. I spent the weekend at Ann's mother's home. Just before I left for the interview the telephone rang. It was the Metal Box Chairman's office. The Chairman had noticed me at the sports and had asked to see my CV and my company dossier. I was asked to confirm the details which I did and then left for the interview for the Canadian job. It was my first contact with a senior partner in the City and it was an eye-opener. He had clearly had a very good lunch, was obviously uninterested, knew nothing about me, had not read the file, and offered me a job, subject to a further interview with the representative of their Toronto office, which took place that afternoon. It went well and we agreed that I would start in Toronto in the middle of September.

I travelled back to Wales that night and the next morning was called into the General Manager's office. He told me that the Chairman and he were pleased with my progress and that he wanted to promote me to become his Personal Assistant. It was with some regret that I told him that I was planning to leave the company and emigrate to Canada. We agreed that I would leave six weeks later.

Two weeks later my father had a series of heart attacks and the doctors told me that he would not live for more than three months. My sister and mother were not well either and it was clearly impossible to emigrate at such a time. I was in a dilemma. I had given up my job at Metal Box and could not take up my new position in Canada. I was also engaged to be married. Two days later a letter arrived from Ann's stepfather, Arthur Slater, saying that he had heard from Ann of my problems and offering me articles with the firm of chartered accountants of which he was senior partner. It was a very old firm called West Wake Price & Company in the heart of the City. He offered to pay me £3 per week for the first year of my articles, £4 for the second and £5 for the third, pointing out that this would make me the highest-paid articled clerk in the history of the firm. He made it clear that he expected me to move on as soon as I had qualified and that there was no vacancy for a new partner. None of this mattered to me. My aim was to qualify and then emigrate to Canada, by which time my family problems would be resolved. By the time I qualified three years later, I was married, had a child, a dog, a tiny Elizabethan cottage and had been offered a partnership. I never did get to Canada. My father for his part is now 86 and has just given up golf in favour of bowls. Drew Chambers, on the other hand, was not so lucky. About a year after my decision to postpone my move to Canada his letters stopped coming. I subsequently discovered that he had been killed in a flying accident.

With the benefit of hindsight, I now see that Metal Box was a very well-run company. They were pioneers in market research and financial forecasting and controls. They were very aware of their monopoly position and made great efforts to avoid abusing it. In fact I sometimes felt that they allowed themselves to be pushed around by their customers in their efforts not to be open to the accusation of exploiting their monopoly. Management recognized that much of the work was arduous, noisy and dangerous, and was constantly seeking ways of eliminating or reducing risk, and of automating wherever possible. The group had originally arisen from an amalgamation of a number of family-owned businesses, and every effort was made to delegate real authority to individual factory managers. As a result individual trade union organizers were happy to deal with local management, and disputes and difficulties were quickly sorted out, so labour relations were good. Management knew their workforce and vice versa. All this showed me that you can run a huge organization efficiently and well, and still identify those who work in it as individuals. Although in-house pundits spent a great deal of time studying the genealogy of newly promoted management and tracing their (usually imaginary) relationships to the Chairman, promotion was in my opinion on merit, although, as my experience at the company sports had taught me, in any large organization you do need a certain amount of luck.

I left Neath on a Friday afternoon and reported to the City office of my new employer the following Monday morning. I was told that I would be leaving that evening for Cardiff to work on the audit of a large engineering company for the next six weeks. Having just said goodbye to my friends in Wales, we found ourselves having our first reunion only five days later.

The aim of the audit was to check the books and accounts of the business in question so that my firm could report to the shareholders that the management was running the business properly, that the profits were accurately stated, and the balance sheet showing the assets and the liabilities at the chosen accounting date gave a true and fair view. We had various methods of checking the accuracy of the figures, and of trying to detect fraud and attempts to mislead. This was in pre-computer days and, although data-processing equipment was being introduced by bigger companies, many of the records of smaller and medium-sized businesses in which West Wake Price specialized were handwritten. The work of checking all these detailed records was monotonous and to a very considerable degree unproductive. On only two or three occasions did we detect dishonesty and then almost invariably by accident not design. On one occasion a bored audit clerk flipping through a pile of copy invoices spotted that the numbers did not run consecutively. A check was made against the despatch notes issued when the goods were sent to the customer. It was discovered that goods were being sent but not being invoiced, and that the accounts clerk and not the company was being paid for them. Such incidents were extremely rare and the end result of our efforts was to establish that the books were properly kept and that the various assets which the company owned did in fact exist. At that point we disappeared from the scene and the managers and the partners took over. It was for them to decide the issues of principle: whether the stock was properly valued, whether the provision for bad debts was adequate, whether the assets were worth what had been paid for them, whether they were being adequately depreciated. It was issues such as this which decided the profits and affected the balance sheet – issues of accounting principle and not of book-keeping.

All of this represented a totally new world to me and the methods of training ensured that it remained a mystery for far longer than it need have done. As an apprentice accountant, or articled clerk, I was in theory articled to a partner in the firm who was a chartered accountant, and the theory was that the articled clerk would learn, in part, by working with that partner. Each partner was entitled to have four articled clerks at any given time, and most of them did. The articled clerks were, in the main, unpaid, and many of them had in fact paid a premium for the privilege of becoming articled. Although unpaid, they worked quite hard and the clients were charged substantial sums for their services. The articled clerks felt exploited and were under the impression that the partners did not really care about them. This was not just true of West Wake Price but of virtually all firms of accountants. Eventually the partners got wind of this dissatisfaction and a meeting was called of all the articled clerks and partners. The senior partner opened the meeting by explaining that, contrary to rumour, the partners did take a tremendous interest in the welfare of the articled clerks in general and their own articled clerks in particular. He then pointed to one of the articled clerks called Mike West. 'Take you, West,' he said, 'who are you articled to?' 'You, sir,' was the answer. The meeting was brought to a speedy conclusion.

In addition to practical on-the-job training, all articled clerks had to sign up for a correspondence course, to be done in our spare time in the evenings and at weekends. Before each of the intermediate and the final examinations, we were allowed six weeks' 'study leave'. Most articled clerks went into articles straight from school, and then did five years of articles; the minority who had degrees did three years. After the very leisurely life at Cambridge, it required a major effort to work during the day and then study at night. I decided in addition to go to a course at a firm in the City called Hargreaves & Mason. Most of the people on the course had failed their exams on a number of occasions, but a few of us were taking them for the first time. One of these was a tall blond Oxford graduate called Heseltine. Although, in theory, training as an accountant, he was already running his own business. He attended the course very irregularly, failed the exams, gave up accountancy and became a politician. I passed my exams, and became an accountant before going into politics. Fifteen years later I was his PPS. Ten years after that we were to serve in the Cabinet together.

Once I had passed the first exams I found that I was given more responsibility. West Wake Price was the ideal size of firm with which to train. Its clients ranged from large public companies to a wide variety of medium-sized and small businesses in all branches of industry, commerce and the professions. One month we might work on the finances of a large engineering group, the next on the accounts of a Harley Street surgeon, a small building company, a wholesale jeweller, a specialist toolmaker, a stockbroker or a large retail group. The range was almost infinite. In addition to looking after the firm's finances we would also act as financial and tax advisers to the families who owned them.

As a relatively junior trainee one had access to the innermost financial workings of the client's firm. One could analyse what made one firm or one person more or less successful than a rival. I found this work interesting, constructive and instructive mainly because I felt that we were able to help our clients to develop and expand their businesses, and it was that aspect of the profession that I enjoyed most, and on which I subsequently concentrated.

The City at that time was proprietor- and family-dominated. Firms were still run by the founder or the founder's family. Even the joint stock banks such as Barclays were dominated by members of the families who had owned the individual local banks and which had merged to become Barclays. This remained true until Sir John Quinton became Chairman in 1985, but in the Fifties and Sixties it was particularly noticeable and Barclays were the rule not the exception.

Lloyd's, the Stock Exchange, the Baltic, the merchant banks, and all the other markets which together make up the City were family-controlled and family-run. The gap between owner and employee was vast and the prospect of moving from one category to the other was limited. The owners dressed differently, arrived later and left earlier. Anyone arriving at Liverpool Street at 8.0 a.m. would find the place relatively quiet. The busiest time was about 9.30, but the senior partners almost as a matter of principle did not arrive before 10.0. There was a City version of Parkinson's law which was that the more senior the person, the shorter the day, the longer the lunch hour. The City was dedicated to the cult of the amateur. It really was the case that it wasn't what you knew, but who you knew that mattered.

A friend of mine who was at Oxford applied to work for a leading merchant bank and was told quite bluntly by the director who interviewed him, 'We only take family or firsts.' He was left in no doubt that even then the prospects for the family were better than for those with first-class degrees. Insider trading could not have been made illegal in the Fifties, it was almost a way of life. The best stockbrokers were the best connected. Through their connections they found out what was going on, and passed on to their clients as 'tips' the information gained quite often over that famous institution, the two-hour City lunch. Years later I asked a fellow MP, who was a partner in a leading firm of brokers, what he thought of Phillips & Drew as a firm. 'They're awful, they're all qualified,' was his answer. The partners in Phillips & Drew were almost all chartered accountants or actuaries by profession and had subsequently trained as stockbrokers. Their emphasis was on skill and knowhow and they were regarded with great suspicion and a certain amount of distaste by their competitors. In later years they were totally vindicated, and others found to their cost that without matching expertise they could not survive.

I now find it difficult to believe that for fifteen years I wore the City uniform of dark suit with waistcoat, dark tie, white shirt with detached starched cutaway collar, black shoes and a bowler hat. Anyone wearing such an outfit now would provoke incredulous stares, but in those days it was standard dress for thousands who travelled into the City daily.

I found the autocratic City attitude quite hard to take after the relatively egalitarian life in the Metal Box Company but I enjoyed the less regimented, more individual way of life and I soon became convinced that, once qualified, I wanted to work for myself.

Three months before I was due to take my final examinations in the autumn of 1959 the senior partner sent for me. He told me that the senior partner of another firm had told him that they wanted to offer me a job, leading to a partnership, in due course. I was surprised by this, but even more surprised when he said that he had talked it over with his other partners and they had decided to invite me to join them. There was one proviso, that I pass my finals first time. I was delighted. I knew and liked my future partners. The firm was over seventy years old, had a good reputation and an excellent list of clients. Having been well placed in the intermediate exams the previous spring I felt reasonably confident about the finals, but now they suddenly took on a new significance. The results came out in December 1959. That morning, after a sleepless night, I pursued the village postwoman all round Flamstead. I eventually found her in Trowley Bottom, the far corner of the village. To my great relief I discovered that I had passed. After seventeen years of almost continuous examinations, I had taken my final one.

My first job after qualifying was an unusual one. John Stone was a long-standing client of our firm. He and his brother had arrived from Hungary in the 1890s as penniless refugees before they had reached their teens. Somehow they had managed to open a small shop selling gas mantles. They had prospered and, by the time they retired in the late Fifties, they had each built up a chain of more than 200 shops selling radios, televisions and all sorts of electrical goods, and they were chairmen of substantial public companies and millionaires. John Stone was bored in his retirement and without consulting anyone invested £150,000 in a greetings card company in Bedford. He was becoming concerned about his investment and asked us to investigate the company. The job was assigned to me and I arranged to go to Bedford with him the next day. We quickly came to the conclusion that he was right to be concerned. The directors had taken a lease on a large modern factory which seemed to be packed full of boxes of unsold greetings cards. I said, jokingly, to the man in charge, 'What you need is a good fire.' To my astonishment he replied, 'Syd would do it for £200.' For the next four months I struggled to save the business and in the end I sold it as a going concern to a person who became a client and friend.

I was made a partner on 1 June 1961, and as well as inheriting a number of existing clients I acquired new clients over the next few years in a variety of ways. Many of them were contemporaries who wanted to set up their own businesses. In the Sixties there were very few sources of capital for the would-be entrepreneur. Merchant banks were prepared to back projects but they normally wanted a controlling interest. The joint stock banks would lend limited amounts but were not in the business of supplying fixed capital. There was an organization, ICFC, which would invest and leave control in the hands of the founder, but they had fairly limited resources. I found that I spent an ever-growing proportion of my time working with entrepreneurs who had ideas but little or no capital, getting their businesses started, and making sure that they retained control and were the principal beneficiaries of their own efforts. A number of these ventures became substantial businesses over the years and many of their owners grew very rich. I am still pleased to have played a small part in their success. By 1966, I had decided that if my advice was worthwhile I should be taking it myself and I started to look for a business of my own.

My first attempt was not successful. One of my clients, who must have been well into his seventies, was keen to sell his business. It occurred to me that this might be the perfect opportunity for me and so I asked how much he would be prepared to accept. Although the price of between £25 and £30 million was high, it seemed fair and so I approached a friend who agreed that the price was realistic. He was confident that we could raise the money. I then approached the owner with a firm bid. However, it soon became clear that he was not prepared to sell his life's work to two such relatively young people. This rebuff taught me two things. Firstly, that it would have been better if negotiations for the sale had been conducted on our behalf by a more established businessman, who could have acted as a front for us, and secondly, that we should try to start our business careers in a more modest way.

Early in 1960, I had started to work with Ann's father, Tony Jarvis, as a part-time unpaid adviser on Saturday mornings. The building company had been started by Ann's grandfather and his brother, just after the turn of the century. It had a reputation for outstanding workmanship but its profits did not reflect its reputation. My first task was to analyse every job done by the firm in the previous five years and to divide them into a number of categories : small works, housing, heating, contracts. We discovered that the business was very profitable in three of the categories, but losing in the fourth. By eliminating the losses we became overall very profitable. Together Tony and I devised new financial controls, budgets and targets, and improved middle management, and the business started to prosper.

One Sunday morning in 1967 I was playing golf with a friend. He told me that his father had just given him and his two brothers and sister a quarter each in the shares of a small but successful building business in Stockport, Cheshire, where his father lived. With taxes at over ninety per cent on investment income they had decided they must sell, and he wondered if Tony and I would be interested. They wanted £95,000 for the business. Tony said that he was not interested. Nonetheless I went up to Stockport to meet the people running the business and especially the Managing Director, Reg Bradbury. It was clearly an extremely well-run, successful company employing about seventy people. I decided to buy it, but I felt I needed a partner to share the risk, and also to take a more active part in maintaining day-to-day contact with Stockport than I was able to. On my return to London I asked a friend, Billy Hart, who was a barrister by profession but who had decided not to practise at the Bar, if he would like to join me in buying the business. We agreed to meet the next day, and after some discussion, a further visit to Stockport, and a visit to the National Westminster Bank in Finsbury Circus, we made an offer of £95,000 which was accepted. Billy and I invested £7,500 each in a new company formed for the purpose called Parkinson Hart Securities Ltd and the bank loaned us the remaining £80,000. We subsequently took over a number of other businesses in engineering and specialist civil engineering, and between 1967 and 1979 our group grew from an initial turnover of £120,000 to several millions. We financed all our growth from retained profits and never had to increase our initial investment of £7,500 each. We believed very strongly in profit-sharing for executives and bonuses related to results for those who worked for us. We wanted all who contributed to the success of the group to share in that success, and the results proved that we were right. Although the trade unions tried to become active in some of the companies, the workforce preferred, as we did, to remain non-union businesses. We all had a common purpose, and Billy and I were pleased that our workforce felt they did not need a union to protect their interests.

The logical next step would have been to find a small publicly quoted company and to bring about a reverse takeover – to allow the business to be taken over in exchange for shares which would give us control of the company which took us over. We would then have had quoted shares which we could use to buy other businesses. It was a technique widely used in the Sixties and early Seventies and we were tempted. We had always paid cash for the businesses we took over and had retained one hundred per cent control of our group. We decided that we would rather stay that way even if it meant slower growth. A few years later we had cause to be relieved at that decision as one after another of the takeover kings came a cropper.

We found the businesses we bought in a number of ways, but one of our best buys was from a large contracting group which had a small subsidiary in a very specialized area, foundation engineering. Little interest had been taken in the subsidiary and in due course it was decided to close it down. We had worked with the company and liked its people and its product. We paid £30,000 for its machinery and agreed to take over the seller's obligations to the thirty staff who joined us. Within two years the company was making more than £80,000 profit and remained a consistent profit-maker. I am sure that in most large groups there are similar lost opportunities tucked away, and that if they can be prised from the grip of the partially interested owner and become the prime concern of their new owners they can be developed. In 1981 I was putting this theory forward to a group of businessmen on my way back from the Leipzig Fair which I had visited as Minister for Trade. I gave the example given above, and was asked by the Chairman of a large company who was in the group, 'Which company did you buy that business from?' 'Yours,' was the answer.

5 Just Another Useful Vote

Ann and I were married in February 1957 and, after living in a flat in her home town of Harpenden for a few months, we moved into our first house, a small Elizabethan cottage called Blacksmith Cottage, in the nearby village of Flamstead. It had a living room, kitchen and bathroom downstairs and two bedrooms upstairs. It had been built in 1450 and we paid £2,500 for it. Six months later we bought the next-door cottage, which was semi-derelict, for £400 and Ann's grandfather, Frank Jarvis, who loved old buildings and specialized in restoring them, set about drawing the plans to convert the cottages into a single home. The original timbers were as hard as iron and needed no restoration, but the brickwork was in a terrible state, and a great deal of it had to be replaced. Frank found a stock of two-inch Elizabethan bricks from a house which had been demolished some years earlier. These were used in the restoration, and as the result of Frank's efforts we had a beautiful and comfortable home with magnificent beamed ceilings and a lovely original inglenook.

These were busy times for us. Ann was running a travel agency in Luton as well as being the business manager of the first commercial airline to fly out of Luton. Luton Airways was started by her father and his friend, Moorton Fisher, and owned three De Havilland Rapides. The business was subsequently sold to a much bigger outfit, Derby Aviation. In those days Luton Airport had only a grass runway and the control tower was the terminal. I was qualifying as an accountant, commuting into London daily, working on my correspondence course in the evenings and helping Ann with her bookkeeping. We took little part in the life of the village, but after a few months, in 1959, our next-door neighbour, a barrister, Spencer Maurice, called and asked us to join the Conservative Association. That was the first time I had been a paid-up member of the party. In December I learnt that I had passed my finals and two weeks later,

Ann, who had given up work in October, gave birth to our first daughter Mary.

We loved living in Flamstead. I enjoyed my work and we began to make friends in the area. In 1961, neighbour Spencer approached me again. He explained that Flamstead always entered a team in the Conservative national speaking competition and he wondered if I would like to join another neighbour, Mike West, to form the team. A team consisted of a chairman and a speaker, who were allegedly addressing a public meeting on a chosen subject. The chairman had to introduce the speaker, control the meeting and thank him. The speaker had to make the speech and answer questions. The whole operation was carefully timed and had to last fifteen minutes. Mike was the speaker, I was the chairman. We won the first round, the constituency round. The second round, the area final, took place in Cambridge, and about a dozen teams from all over the Eastern Area took part. We won that and so qualified for the national final in London where we came third.

In September 1961 our second daughter Emma was born and we realized that if we were going to have any more children, we would have to move. Spencer solved our problem. In 1963 he told me that the Chairman of our branch, Leslie Hyatt, was moving to Chepstow, to take charge of the building of the Severn Bridge. Spencer would become Chairman, thus creating a vacancy for Treasurer, and he wondered, since I was a chartered accountant, if I would take it on. Living in a village I had already discovered that one of the occupational hazards of being an accountant is that it is only a matter of time before one becomes Honorary Treasurer of all the organizations of which one is not the honorary auditor. The Conservative branch was therefore added to a fast-growing list. I told Ann that the Hyatts were moving and we decided to buy their house, a very pleasant Regency house with two cottages and a large garden about fifty yards from Blacksmith Cottage. We lived in Westfield House for the next ten years. They proved to be very eventful years indeed.

We moved in the autumn of 1964 not long after the general election. Flamstead was part of the Hemel Hempstead constituency, whose Member of Parliament was James Allason. It was a huge constituency. The biggest town was Hemel Hempstead, a fast-growing new town dominated by the Labour Party. The rest of the constituency consisted of a number of towns and villages which were predominantly Conservative. James Allason held meetings in virtually every town and village during the campaign, speaking at four or five different meetings every night. He needed a team of supporting speakers of which I became one and I spoke on about half a dozen occasions to meetings of various sizes. I spoke without notes, or from a piece of paper with just a few headings, mainly about the economy, and the speeches seemed to go down well with the audience.

I always tried to speak from my own experience. The very first public speech I made came whilst I was in the process of buying Westfield House. The day before, a surveyor had inspected the house and he rang me the following morning to tell me that the house had about thirty-nine faults. Some, such as the fact that one of the main beams did not meet the roof, were quite serious, but most were trivial. I thought that he was telling me that I should withdraw my offer. 'Good Lord, no, it's a fine house,' he replied, 'it just needs putting right.' On my way to deliver my speech that evening it occurred to me that this advice could just as easily be applied to the nation's economic problems. So I used the incident as the theme of the speech. There were, I said, many problems with our economy – inflation, strikes and low productivity – but Britain was fundamentally sound. There might be thirty-nine problems, but there were a thousand good points. Together, we just needed to put the problems right.

Although we lost the election nationally, James Allason held Hemel Hempstead and one of the highlights of the campaign was a visit from the Prime Minister, Sir Alec Douglas-Home. I met him briefly and was stunned by the contrast between the warm and approachable person I met, and the appalling caricature of him which the media had projected.

Shortly after the election the Conservative agent for Hemel Hempstead, David Smith, asked me if I could spare an evening a month to become Chairman of the constituency Conservative Political Centre Committee. I asked him how many members it had, and he replied, 'One, if you say yes.' He said I had carte blanche to form a committee and to invite whoever I chose to join it. I telephoned a friend who was Chairman of another village branch. He was an airline pilot and as an active member of the British Airline Pilots' Association he was on strike at the time. I invited him to become Vice-Chairman of the CPC. He asked me, 'How many members are there?' I replied, 'Two, if you say yes.' That was how Norman Tebbit and I formed the CPC in Hemel Hempstead. It marked the beginning of two political careers that have remained interwoven ever since. I had no interest in a political career at that time and had not even considered it as a possibility. Norman subsequently told me that he had considered it, but only remotely. We drew up a list of people we would like to join our committee and were delighted that we had no refusals. We found that there was tremendous interest in making the Association a political as well as a fund-raising, election-organizing body. Two of our first members were Michael Angus, who lived in Tring and worked for Unilever, and Chris Lawson, who lived in Berkhamsted and was a senior manager with the Mars Corporation. Michael was a superb speaker. Though tempted by politics he decided to concentrate on his business career. He became the Chairman of Unilever in 1986. Chris had an outstanding career in his company and, having retired early, played a key role as Director of Marketing at Conservative Central Office in the 1983 general election.

Our first venture was to form a political supper club and invite young MPs or candidates to come and speak to us. Douglas Hurd, Michael Heseltine and Nigel Lawson were amongst our early speakers and all our suppers were over-subscribed. We also organized public meetings with audiences of several hundreds for such speakers as Enoch Powell and Reggie Maudling. We decided to follow the example of a group who called themselves the Hyde Park Tories and who spoke at Hyde Park Corner on Sundays. A team of speakers would harangue the crowd, each speaking for about a quarter of an hour. We invited their Chairman Ben Paterson, now a Euro MP, to come to Hemel and show us how it was done. A team of about six of us including Norman and myself met him one Saturday morning in Hemel and, having selected our pitch, put up our soapbox and started to speak. We quickly had a small crowd and the exchanges were lively with plenty of heckling. When my turn came, one particularly persistent large lady interrupted me every few seconds. She was becoming a little obstreperous, and finally, in desperation, I interrupted her. 'May I ask you a question, madam?' 'Yes,' she said, 'what is it?' 'Have you ever considered trying to slim?' She was furious and, to my relief, went away. I was followed on the soapbox by another member of the team, David Sawter. The lady returned with two large red tomatoes which she threw at him. Fortunately she missed, but as I pointed out to him, she taught us a valuable lesson – never to speak second in politics.

The 1966 general election, which saw the re-election of Harold Wilson's Labour government with a much increased majority, was a very difficult one for the Conservatives in Hemel. The new town had grown dramatically and the old tactic of leaving the new town untouched and concentrating on the Conservative areas was no longer sensible. Our agent, David Smith, set out to create an organization in the town drawing on help from all the surrounding areas. We found that there was a substantial Conservative minority vote and, by the time of the election, we had ten active Conservative branches in the town. It was enjoyable and rewarding but, above all, effective, and James Allason was comfortably re-elected. These early days in politics confirmed my view that the successful political party needs ideals and organization. The one without the other is a recipe for failure. Shortly after the general election, the Association was due to choose a new Chairman. The year before, Ted Heath had become the first elected leader of the Conservative Party, and it was decided that what was good enough for the parliamentary party was good enough for Hemel Hempstead. We held our first-ever election for Chairman. There were three candidates, of which I was one. Mike West, my old speaking competition partner, was another and the third was Ken Dunkley, who was older and had fought Lichfield and Tamworth in the 1964 election. We were all chartered accountants, all married and, following the birth of our third daughter Joanna in December 1963, each of us had three children. At a crowded AGM attended by over 500 people as opposed to the usual eighty, I was elected. I was 34 and younger than any of my predecessors by more than twenty years. In my short speech after the result was declared, I set out three objectives for what I hoped would be a three-year term. The first was to buy and pay for a new headquarters building for the Association which was then housed in small rented offices, but had been given notice to quit. The second was to win control of Hemel Hempstead Council and elect a Conservative Mayor. At the time we had three councillors out of twenty-seven. The third was to bring our rules and constitution up to date.

I retired as Chairman in June 1969, and one of my happiest moments in politics occurred the night before, when for the first time for nearly twenty years we elected a Conservative, John Doyle, as Mayor of Hemel Hempstead. After three exciting years, we had twenty-six of the twenty-seven councillors, but above all we had proved that by hard work and organization we could oust Labour from areas which they regarded as theirs. We had also recruited into our party organization people who had previously almost instinctively accepted that there would be no place in it for them. Ted Heath's election as leader gave us a tremendous boost. He had clearly made his way in the world by his own efforts, and his very presence at the head of our party was proof to many that you did not need to be rich, privileged or well-connected to succeed in the modern Conservative Party.

We held the AGM in 1969 in our new headquarters. The Association had bought an old church hall, and virtually rebuilt it. It provided excellent offices and a large meeting hall, but above all, we now had a permanent freehold home. We also adopted our new rule book at the same meeting, so all three of my rather optimistic objectives had been achieved.

In late 1966 Norman Tebbit had decided to go on the candidates list and asked me as Chairman to be one of his sponsors. I felt he would make an excellent MP and said so. A few months later he was adopted as candidate for South West Islington, a Labour seat which, as he put it, he could win with a swing to Conservative of 'only' twenty-eight per cent. He moved into his new constituency and gave up his vice-chairmanship of Hemel. I was particularly sad to see him go. He and Margaret and Ann and I had become good friends and have remained so ever since. Norman has changed very little over the years. He was always spoiling for a fight with his employer BOAC, socialists of any colour, and from time to time with the Tory establishment. He was never a cosy person, and could lose his temper easily, but he has a sardonic sense of humour which habitually surfaces at the critical moment. Our views coincided in many areas. We had not acquired them by instinct or by inheritance, but each of us had arrived at them by ourselves. We both regarded socialism as a scourge and the failure of the Conservative governments of 1951–64 to reverse the Attlee experiment as deplorable. From his career in BOAC he had developed a healthy disrespect for nationalized industries and their management. He had very strong views about industrial relations and the role of the trade unions. I for my part was sceptical about the City with its rigid, autocratic, class-conscious, closed-shop attitude. Resistance to change and entrenched attitudes were the common factors we encountered daily in our respective places of work. Less than twenty years after our first meeting, he was Secretary of State for Employment promoting the changes in trade union law, and I was at the Department of Trade and Industry launching changes which played a major part in transforming the City. In the Sixties we were both acquiring the practical experience leading to conviction which made us promote those changes years later with enthusiasm in the face of opposition within our own party.

Early in 1968 I had lunch with the Hemel Hempstead agent, David Smith. We talked about Norman and he asked me whether I would be applying to go on the candidates list. I told him that I had been thinking about it, but was not sure that I would measure up. I had never been to Westminster, knew few MPs and had little idea of what would be involved. David is a very down to earth Derbyshireman. 'You ought to do it,' he said. 'I know quite a lot of them, and they're no better than you.' In the summer of that year I applied to go on the list and a few weeks later was summoned for interview. There were two interviews, the first with an MP and the second with Richard Sharples (later murdered in Bermuda), then Vice-Chairman of the party in charge of candidates. The meeting with Sir Walter Elliot, MP for Carshalton, could hardly have been more chaotic. He asked what I had done since leaving Oxford. I told him I was at Cambridge. He asked me about my membership of the Bow Group. I told him I had never been a member. After two or three more questions, he began to realize he had the wrong file. 'What did you say your name was?' 'Parkinson.' 'Oh dear,' he said, 'let's start again.' A few days later I received a letter telling me that I was now an approved candidate.

In September I was invited to go to Truro who were looking for a successor to the retiring Conservative Member, Geoffrey Wilson. I telephoned a friend, Joan Crofts, the deputy Central Office agent for the Western Area, to ask about the seat and to point out the difficulty of combining a partnership in a busy City firm, living in Hertfordshire with a family of three small daughters all under 9, with trying to nurse a parliamentary seat 300 miles away. 'Oh don't worry,' she said, 'you won't get selected, but the experience of being interviewed will be valuable and you'll make your mistakes a long way from home.' Thus encouraged, I travelled to Truro for the first interview. Knowing that I was not in the running and feeling under no pressure, I apparently did well, and was asked back for a second interview a week later. The thirty who had originally been interviewed had been reduced to six and we were asked to make a ten-minute speech on a subject of our choice before answering questions. Still confident that

I could not win, I was very relaxed and again did well. The next day, Joan Crofts telephoned me to tell me that I was in the last three and could win if I did as well as I had in the previous rounds. This news had the opposite to the desired effect. Having got so far, I wanted to win, but equally I realized that if I won I would have to change my way of life in a way for which I was not prepared. In the event, all was well, I finished a respectable second to Piers Dixon who had fought a tough seat before and deserved his win. He was married to Edwina Sandys, Sir Winston Churchill's granddaughter, and one of my abiding memories is of a large picture of Sir Winston glowering at me from the wall opposite as I stood up to speak.

In November, I was invited to go for interview to Northampton who were looking for a candidate to unseat the redoubtable Labour Member, Reginald Paget. He was a popular Old Etonian millionaire, a master of foxhounds, and had held the seat since 1945. His majority was about 8,000 and Northampton was not on Central Office's list of winnable seats. It was about forty miles from my home and I felt that we could win it. I went up to Northampton twice before the interview, met a group of local businessmen, and arranged to have the daily local newspaper, *The Chronicle & Echo*, sent to me for the week before the interview, so that I would have some knowledge of current local issues. The selection procedure was much simpler than at Truro. Fifteen people were interviewed, and a shortlist of three was chosen. I spoke about why I had left the Labour Party and become a Conservative, about the need for each of us to play our part in arresting the decline in Britain's standing and Britain's prospects. Earlier that year I had been to a conference at the Hudson Institute just outside New York, on the subject of 'The World in the 1980s'. Herman Kahn, who had founded the institute, made the keynote speech and led two days of intense discussion. His two main predictions were that Japan in the Eighties would be an economic superpower and that Britain's economic decline was irreversible. By 1980 we would be the poorest major country in the west with a standard of prosperity of at best seventy to eighty per cent of that of our neighbours, at worst fifty to sixty per cent. We were simply being outdistanced and we didn't seem to care. His forecasts were in fact too optimistic; we arrived at the lower end of his predictions by the mid-Seventies not the Eighties. His forecasts were based on extrapolations of established patterns of growth and have proved broadly correct. From that time I made the dangers of economic decline and the need to arrest that decline a main theme of my speeches. I found that there was a great reluctance to accept the extent of our national problem. It was not only amongst the public that this ignorance persisted; politicians were equally ill-informed.

In 1971 Ted Heath called the junior ministers to Chequers for a presentation by Lord Rothschild, the head of the Think-Tank, at which he spelt out the same message. At the end of the presentation Ted asked those present how many of them had realized the full implications of just carrying on as we were. Only three of those present claimed that they had known beforehand what Lord Rothschild had told them.

The final selection for Northampton was made at a meeting of about 300 people in the Town Hall. The other two candidates were Tony Newton, leader of the House of Commons following the 1992 election, and a local county councillor. I was the last speaker, and elaborated for ten minutes on why I wanted to fight Northampton and why the country needed a Conservative government. Ann had to appear on the platform with me and say a few words. We were then shown into an antechamber where we met the other two couples, and after a few minutes Philip Branch, the Chairman, came into the room, thanked the other two and announced that I had been selected. We then went back into the hall where we were greeted with an enormous cheer and over the course of the next hour we met dozens of people, all of whom claimed to have voted for me. Half of them told me that Paget was really a Conservative.

We drove back down the motorway to our home in a jubilant frame of mind, and were so preoccupied with discussing what we would do that we failed to notice the speed at which we were travelling. Unfortunately, the police did notice and just outside Luton we were waved down by a policeman who told me I had been travelling at ninety miles per hour. I was prosecuted and fined £40, so the night of my selection as a prospective parliamentary candidate was doubly memorable.

The Northampton Conservative Association employed a full-time agent, Tommy Hood, had its own headquarters in the centre of the town with a small but active membership, and controlled the town council by a substantial majority. From the first day we were made welcome and a series of social events was arranged so that we could meet the party workers in the eight branches which covered the town. We quickly realized that we had to find a way of making contact with a wider group of people and with the help of one of the members, Gyde Harrocks, Ann and I decided to spend two nights each week canvassing in different parts of Northampton. Gyde became one of our closest friends and by the time the election was called eighteen months later we calculated that we had called on almost 10,000 electors. It was a laborious way of getting to know the town and its people. When the local elections took place the following May we canvassed with each of our nine candidates. The local paper was intrigued by all this activity and telephoned Reggie Paget's agent to ask if he would be following my example. The reply was short and to the point. 'The people of Northampton do not expect to meet Mr Paget on their doorsteps. As long as they see him on the back of his horse at the annual British Timken horse show accompanied by the huntsman and the pack of hounds, that is the way they prefer to think of him.' I realized that my Labour opponent's reputation as a most unusual socialist, was very well deserved.

In addition to canvassing and the normal run of political activities, I visited factories, schools, hospitals and sports clubs, so by the time the election was called in May 1970 I felt I was beginning to know the town and to be known by the people. I liked the town and the people and felt that we could, with luck, win.

Although I played rugby at school and subsequently for a number of clubs such as the Vale of Lune, Carlisle, Rosslyn Park, and finally Harpenden, I have always preferred to watch soccer and from boyhood have been a supporter of Preston North End. One of the Conservative councillors, Fred Tompkins, was a director of Northampton Town and invited me to join him in the directors box to watch a match. Northampton were in the process of making football history. They moved from the fourth division to the first in four years and then back to the fourth without playing in the same division for two consecutive seasons. When I went to see them they were in the third division and were moving down. They lost the match and as I left the directors box I was grabbed by an irate fan who threatened to have me sacked from the board if the team went down.

Having spent a few hectic days getting up to date with my accountancy work, I left the office at 2.0 p.m. to travel to Northampton for the adoption meeting. I was wondering what to say, when the train stopped at Radlett and gazing out of the window I saw a large poster which said, 'It's not your fault that Britain is going down the drain. It's the fault of the chap standing next to you.' It seemed to me to be a very apt comment on Britain at the end of the Wilson years and I decided to make it the theme of my speech, so I spoke of the need to stop Britain's drift to mediocrity, and of the need for government to remove the disincentives which had been piled on the individual by socialism, arguing that a massive effort by each and every one of us must be made.

Northampton was not regarded as winnable by Central Office and the only visiting 'firemen' to pass through on their way to more critical seats were Michael Heseltine and John Eden. James Allason, the MP for Hemel Hempstead, came and spoke at two meetings. Otherwise we were on our own, and in addition to some excellent local councillors, such as John Poole, John Barnes and Jack Corrin, I invited a number of friends such as Richard Morris-Adams and John Bradshaw who had never made a political speech in their lives to join me. About thirty other friends also came to Northampton to help and the whole campaign proved immensely enjoyable. We were finding great enthusiasm everywhere we went and yet, each morning as the national opinion polls were produced, they were bad news for the Conservative Party. Ann and I stayed in a local hotel from Monday morning to Saturday afternoon. The girls, Mary, Emma and Jo, were brought up to join us on the Saturday morning and helped us hand out election leaflets. Emma, then aged 9, showed early and strong commercial instincts by selling hers for sixpence each, until stopped. We all travelled home together and our Sundays together as a family were the highlight of our week.

It was an exciting campaign. In my election address, I concentrated on the economy and on Labour's record over its five and a half years in office. 'We have seen the pound devalued, the cost of living rise at a record rate. We have seen higher unemployment for a longer period than at any time since the war. We have seen taxation increase by £3,000 million.' I argued that 'Britain must make a fresh start' and pledged my support for the radical Conservative manifesto which Ted Heath was presenting to the electorate.

Aside from the economy, it was housing, education and Europe which dominated the campaign in Northampton. I attacked Labour's dismal record over house building and promised that the next Conservative government would get the house-building programme back on course and that we would remove the restrictions on councils who wished to sell their houses. On education I argued that local authorities should be able to decide whether to move to a system of comprehensive education. I was a strong supporter of direct grant grammar schools and the right of parents to choose whether to send their children to state or private schools. My Old Etonian Labour opponent argued passionately 'that it was socially objectionable' that some people could 'buy advantages in education'. He didn't, of course, reveal that he had sent his own children to private schools. This was not the last time that I came across socialists who preached one thing but quietly practised another.

On Europe, both Reggie Paget and myself were what today would be called Euro-sceptics. At one public meeting I argued that the question of Britain's entry into the EEC was a great national issue. It would be, I pointed out, 'probably one of the three biggest decisions taken this century' and I believed that there ought to be a referendum on the issue. Reggie Paget strongly disagreed. At this time few people supported a referendum on our membership of the EEC – it was certainly not Conservative Party policy – and I admitted that I doubted that there would be one. I was not to know that the next Labour government, under pressure from Tony Benn and Labour's left-wing anti-marketeers, would hold a referendum and that I was to play an active part in supporting Britain's membership.

Reginald Paget had no doubt that he would win and his election address reflected this complacency. His personal message to the voters was almost word for word the same as he had used at the 1966 election. He clearly did not think that he had to make any real effort to retain his seat. But, in spite of the occasional harsh press release and angry word at public meetings, I thoroughly enjoyed all my meetings with Reggie. On the first Monday of the campaign, he and I spoke to a joint meeting of all the sixth forms from Northampton's schools. He, as the sitting Member, spoke first. He said, 'You will find that Mr Parkinson and I disagree about very little but we do disagree about one thing – Mr Parkinson dislikes Mr Wilson, the Prime Minister. I hate him.'

Three weeks later after a series of joint meetings and lively exchanges through the columns of the local daily paper, we walked out of the Town Hall with the Returning Officer to announce the result. Paget had won, but his majority had been cut from 7,489 to 1,242, his lowest ever, and our vote at 26,182 was one of the biggest ever. As we came out I congratulated my opponent, and added, 'but it doesn't look as if Mr Wilson will be back in Number 10 tomorrow night.' 'No,' he said, 'and I for one will shed no tears about that.'

The next day we travelled home exhausted and deeply disappointed that we had come so close, but had lost. Norman Tebbit had won at Epping and I telephoned him to congratulate him. Northampton was due to be redistributed and divided into two difficult but winnable seats, Northampton North and Northampton South. The local party offered me the choice of the seats and I decided I would like to stay at Northampton and take one of them. After a few days we went off to Portugal for a golfing holiday during which I wrote more than 1,100 letters of thanks to the people who had helped with my campaign. On my return I went back to work in my accountancy firm and accepted that it would be at least four years before I entered parliament. In August we went off to Cornwall with the girls for a holiday in the new house we had built at Trevose, near Padstow.

One morning we were sitting having breakfast when the telephone rang. It was Jeffrey Speed, the Conservative agent for Enfield West. He told me that fifteen people had been selected for interview out of 464 who had applied for Iain Macleod's seat, following his death, and that I was the only one who had not replied to the invitation. I explained that I had not seen the letter, but that I understood that Iain's widow, Eve, had wanted the seat and that I would not wish to oppose her. He replied that I could always pull out at a later stage, and that Eve might herself withdraw. In the event she did withdraw, and so after two interviews, I found myself on a shortlist of three, the other two being Kenneth Baker and John Cope. Before the final meeting, Kenneth was selected to follow Quintin Hailsham at Marylebone, and John and I were left to fight it out. I won, and six weeks later was elected in the by-election as the Member of Parliament for Enfield West. My delight was rather muted by the fact that the Home Secretary, Reggie Maudling, in the middle of the by-election adopted the report of the Boundary Commission which meant that at the next general election Enfield West would cease to exist and I would have to go through the whole selection procedure again.

Three incidents in particular stand out in my memory of this period. The first was the adoption meeting which launched the campaign. I was very conscious that for twenty years the members of the local Conservative Association had listened to one of the greatest post-war Conservative orators whenever their MP addressed them. I therefore put a great deal of effort into my speech. The meeting was held in a large school hall in Potters Bar and about 500 people were present. The speech was going well and the audience was listening attentively. I was approaching the last two minutes of my remarks and building up to a rousing peroration when the school caretaker entered the back of the hall and stood there waving his arms. The Chairman, Tony Simons, asked him what he was up to. The caretaker shouted, 'Would the owner of the grey Daimler please remove it. It is blocking the drive.' It was, inevitably, my car and I had to fish my car keys out of my pocket and hand them to Jeffrey Speed, who had to walk the length of the hall in full view of the audience, who saved the day by hooting with laughter.

The second was that in the booklet which had been prepared for the by-election for the benefit of the media, I was described at the end of my CV as the 'unsuccessful Conservative candidate for Northampton'. Every journalist who came to the by-election included that phrase in his description of me. The Liberals described their candidate as 'a proven vote-winner'. Labour called theirs 'a doughty fighter'. Those descriptions were also used by the press. In the end, I pointed out that in the general election, I had polled 26,182 votes – nearly twice as many as the proven vote-winner and the doughty fighter put together. Years later, as Party Chairman, I issued an instruction that the adjective 'unsuccessful' should never qualify the noun candidate if the intervening adjective was Conservative. By a coincidence the person to whom I gave the instruction was the person who had written the booklet at the by-election.

The third notable feature of the campaign was the presence of a National Front candidate. Iain Macleod as Colonial Secretary had been responsible for bringing many of our former African colonies to independence and this made him a target for the National Front. They always opposed him and they decided to oppose me. They organized no meetings of their own. Their aim was to disrupt other people's and this they did by constant harassing and yelling racist abuse. I found that their presence united the audience behind me. After coming to a couple of meetings they disappeared only to reappear at the count where they staged a mini-riot after the result was declared. They were a tiny group who struck no chord with the electorate, but they certainly received a totally disproportionate amount of media attention.

The by-election took place only five months after the general election. There was little interest outside the constituency and, apart from a devoted group of party workers, very little inside. I felt that the whole electorate was numbed by the loss of Iain and had little interest in who succeeded him. Eve Macleod was magnificent and, in every way open to her, helped and encouraged Ann and myself. Peter Thomas, the Party Chairman, spoke at the final meeting and from that time on took a great interest in my career. Jeffrey Speed showed himself to be a superb organizer, and it was a delight to me that twelve years later, when I was Party Chairman, he became one of our youngest and most successful area agents in the East Midlands. One of the other professional agents who came to work in the by-election was Roy Longstone, the agent for Finchley. Three months after my election, he invited me to be the guest of honour at the Finchley annual dinner and there for the first time Ann and I met Denis and Margaret Thatcher. It was to be the beginning of a long and valued friendship.

When the result was announced it became clear just how little interest the by-election had generated. Out of a total electorate of over 53,000 only 26,590 had voted and so it came as no surprise to see that the *Enfield Weekly Herald* headlined their report of the result: 'The Mystery: where were the voters'. However, in spite of the low turnout, I had a respectable majority of 8,279.

After the result we held a party for our workers which ended at about 3.0 a.m. and we went to bed that night in a small hotel in Enfield. Only four hours later, the telephone rang. It was Francis Pym, the Chief Whip. He congratulated me on winning, and asked me if I could take my seat on the following Monday. Ann had not been well during the campaign and we had made an appointment to see a specialist on that day. I was very concerned about her and was anxious to take her myself. I explained this to Francis, who was most sympathetic and insisted that I keep the arrangement. 'Don't worry,' he said, 'it was your vote I was interested in.' I realized that whatever I was to my family, or the electors of Enfield West, to the whips I was just another useful vote.

6 Joining the Whips

I had never set foot in the chamber of the House of Commons until Tuesday 24 November 1970, the day I took my seat. I knew only half a dozen MPs and little about the workings of parliament. The Deputy Chief Whip, Jack Weatherill, invited the whole family to lunch. I had met him some years earlier when we were both on holiday in Cornwall and he had encouraged me to think of a political career. He was an extremely kind and considerate host, and coped very well with three excited and bewildered young girls, not to mention their nervous parents.

After lunch, Ann and the girls went into the public gallery, and I was taken to meet the Chief Whip, Francis Pym, who was very straightforward. He welcomed me, told me that he knew nothing about me, but that within a couple of years they (the whips) would have a pretty fair impression of where I would fit in and of my prospects. What that impression would be, would depend entirely on my own efforts. Nobody would tell me what to do, what to specialize in, but if I wanted help or advice, I only had to ask. We then went into the corridor outside his office where James Allason, my own MP and friend, was waiting and we practised the short walk interrupted by two bows which I would make when I took my seat at 3.30 p.m. after Prime Minister's question time. Francis suggested that to ensure that we moved with military precision he and James, who would be on either side of me, would lean inwards on me. Since James was much taller and much heavier, the first time we tried it I looked rather like a mobile Tower of Pisa, with a pronounced tilt in Francis's direction.

We soon got it right and after a few minutes we went into the chamber which was crowded. The Prime Minister, Ted Heath, was answering the last of his questions and then, after a series of points of order, the Speaker called out, 'New Members desiring to take their seats'. We bowed and moved slowly towards the table where the Speaker's Clerk was waiting. In the background erupted that extraordinary rumbling noise, 'Yer, yer, yer, yer, yer' which I believe is a corruption of 'Hear, hear'. Above this din I could hear Gerald Nabarro shouting, 'No consolation in this for you, Harold,' in the direction of Harold Wilson, the leader of the opposition, who shouted something back at him. I handed a certificate of return confirming that I had been elected to the Clerk who handed me a Bible and a copy of the Oath of Allegiance which I read out. I then signed the book and shook his hand. He escorted me to the Speaker who also shook my hand and welcomed me. All this time the rumbling noise continued and the moment I had shaken the Speaker's hand there was a mass stampede for the doors. I stood behind the Speaker's chair and various members of the Cabinet, including the Prime Minister, shook my hand and made welcoming noises.

Two or three minutes later I was wondering how to find my family when James Allason came along and led me back through what I later discovered was the division lobby to central lobby, where we found them and then went on to tea. After Ann and the girls left, James showed me the library, the terrace and the various dining rooms and bars. He then took me back to the chamber where he left me very self-consciously listening to my first debate which was on the second reading of the Civil Aviation Bill. By coincidence, although I had not been in the chamber to hear it, earlier that afternoon Norman Tebbit had made his maiden speech.

The House of Commons is a very easy place in which to get lost, both physically and, as some Members discover and others relish, politically. Later that evening I was standing quite lost in a corridor behind the chamber when John Eden, the MP for Bournemouth West, came up to me, reintroduced himself and asked me if I was free to join him for dinner. We went into the Members' dining room and joined six other Members on a table. I had never met any of them before, but they could not have been more welcoming and friendly. I quickly realized that they were all Conservatives and that the dining room was divided with Conservatives at one end, Labour at the other. In the middle there were two or three tables for the Liberals and other minority parties. I found this strange at first, but I soon saw that it was a sensible arrangement for, although most Members of Parliament treat each other in a perfectly civilized way on a personal basis and there is little personal animosity, they do profoundly disagree on politics. The dining rooms are amongst the few places where Members can meet and discuss politics and personalities freely and informally. It is generally felt that the presence of Members from other parties would inhibit such discussion. That night I voted in a division at 10.0 p.m. for the first time and after a day which was eventful, confusing but encouraging, I drove home to Hertfordshire.

A major part of the government's programme was the Industrial Relations Bill, which was designed to reform the legal basis of industrial relations and to bring the haphazard ragbag of laws up to date. In November it was revealed that the number of days lost in 1970 through strikes, 8,828,000 by the end of October, already exceeded those for any year since the General Strike in 1926. Barbara Castle, then Secretary of State for Employment, had produced a celebrated white paper, 'In Place of Strife' in 1969, in which she had identified the same problems and many of the same answers as were included in the Conservative bill. Nevertheless she had been ordered by the Shadow Cabinet to oppose our bill. Barbara Castle was then at the height of her powers as a parliamentarian. A fine orator, who spoke with great passion and fervour, she found the volte-face she had to make impossible to perform. It was left to Stan Orme and Eric Heffer, two leading backbenchers who had opposed 'In Place of Strife', to mount the most effective opposition.

The bill was regarded as of such importance that the committee stage, which normally takes place in a committee room upstairs and includes only a small cross section of Members, was held in the chamber with all Members able to take part. The sessions on this bill, those on Northern Ireland affairs, and those on our membership of the EEC were for me the highlights of the Heath years. I spent days in the chamber listening to genuine debate, carried out by people whose practical knowledge and debating skills ensured a most thorough, exhaustive and fascinating discussion of the issues. Not having made my maiden speech, I could not take part but I scarcely missed a speech.

The debates on Britain's entry into the EEC were truly historic and saw the House of Commons at its best. Although the House had supported the principle of entry into the EEC by a majority of 112 in October 1971, the debate had changed by the time the government brought forward its European Communities Bill in early 1972, following Mr Heath's signature to the Treaty of Accession. No longer was the House of Commons being asked in principle what its view was, it now had to decide whether to agree to give up some of its powers so that Britain could play a part in the European Community.

The issue divided the Conservative Party. The Labour Party was also deeply split. I remember being particularly impressed by the contributions of Enoch Powell and Michael Foot. Although on almost any other issue they could be expected to take contrary views, on Europe they united in defence of the sovereignty of parliament.

I did not share their fears. I believed, and still do believe, that the balance of the argument was in favour of our membership. No one who heard their speeches, no one who heard Enoch Powell's impassioned cry, 'It shall not pass!' at the end of his speech during the second reading of the bill, could have doubted the significance of the argument or the importance of the debate. At the end of the second reading in February, the bill had a majority of eight. It then went to committee which, because of its importance, was taken on the floor of the House of Commons. The government was determined to ensure that the bill was not amended in committee since it did not want to have matters of principle reopened at report stage. Finally, since the bill had not been amended and therefore there was no report stage, it moved straight to its third reading. After Mr Heath had made it clear that he would regard a vote against the bill as a vote of no confidence in his government, the bill passed through the Commons with a majority of eighteen.

Although many of the debates during the 1970 parliament were strong and passionate, there were a few lighter moments. Sally Oppenheim was the new Member for Gloucester. Glamorous, beautifully dressed and rich, she seemed on first appearance an unlikely person to be involved in a discussion of industrial relations. But coming from a family which controlled a large manufacturing business in Sheffield, she held strong and well-informed views and had the ability to put them forcefully. At first, Eric Heffer took her participation in the debates as a personal affront. He was constantly interrupting her. On one occasion he said, 'The only shop floor the honourable lady knows anything about is the floor of Fortnum and Mason.' I remember him lashing out at me once when I was sitting listening to him, and without being aware of it, shook my head to show dissent. He shouted across the floor, 'It's all very well for the honourable gentleman, but he was clearly born with a silver spoon in his mouth and has never had to struggle for anything in his life.' A few days later I met him in the corridor and we stopped to talk. I told him that I was the son of a trade unionist, that I had been a member of the Labour Party and the rest. Eric at this time had an almost pathological dislike of Conservatives and was incapable of distinguishing between people and their views. In later years he was less inclined to let his ability to disagree passionately with a person's views mar his respect for the person holding those views. He became deservedly popular throughout the Commons, and on his death in 1991 was widely mourned.

The Irish debates were a feature of the 1970 parliament for different reasons. The full spectrum of Irish political views was represented in that parliament, ranging from Willie Orr, Ian Paisley and Jim Molyneaux on one side to Bernadette Devlin, Frank McManus and Gerry Fitt on the other. One aspect of parliament which was a revelation to me was that one spends half the time listening to the views of people with whom one disagrees. This was a particularly unusual experience for Ian Paisley and Bernadette Devlin, two outstandingly gifted orators with deeply held views, but who disagreed fundamentally about everything. The debates were frequent and fierce and one learnt a great deal about the problems. It was impossible not to feel dismayed about the prospects for Ireland. The Home Secretary at this time was Reginald Maudling, an enormously capable person for whom the description 'laid-back' could originally have been invented. On one occasion, Bernadette Devlin ran across the floor of the House, grabbed him by the hair and tried to scratch his face. There was chaos in the chamber. Years later, Tony Benn, recalling the incident, said that it was such a vicious attack, it almost woke Reggie up. The conflict on the floor of the House was as real and rabid as the sectarian violence on the ground in Ulster, and one felt that, because we had a parliament which was on this occasion fully representative of the people of the province, at least some of the violence was being siphoned off and expressed in words rather than action.

I made my maiden speech on 4 February 1971, in a debate on pensions. By tradition, maiden speeches are not controversial and include passages about one's predecessor and the constituency. I started the speech by describing the constituency. In particular, I pointed to the 'beautiful rolling countryside' which formed part of the green belt in the north of London, saying that 'one of the great ambitions which I as the Member, Iain Macleod as my predecessor, and all my constituents have is to make sure, for our sake and the sake of London, that we work very hard to keep that green belt'. I went on to pay tribute to Iain Macleod: 'One of Enfield's greatest distinctions is that it was represented in this House for twenty years by Iain Macleod, one of the great parliamentarians of this or any century. He was a great man, a great patriot and a great servant of the people of his constituency.' After expressing the pride which I felt in following Iain Macleod, I pointed to his great interest in the welfare of the elderly and disabled, explaining that I felt it was therefore particularly appropriate for me to make my maiden speech in a debate on pensions.

It was a perfectly adequate speech but by no means earthshaking, and I was astonished by the fulsome praise I received from the next two speakers and from the front bench speakers who wound up the debate. I was made to sound like a cross between Einstein and Demosthenes, but I was brought down to earth with a bang by my whip who pointed out to me that these remarks would look good in my local paper, but that I mustn't believe them. He also pointed out that the next time the opposition would feel free to tell me what they really thought. Over the years I have discovered that in spite of its reputation the House is a compassionate place and that there is an unspoken consensus that only those who can take a roughing-up receive one. All new Members receive kid-glove treatment as of right for their maiden speech, but Members who for a variety of reasons, be it age, illness or just plain fear of speaking, and there are some who hate speaking, are treated with a consideration of which the House is not, to the outside world, supposed to be capable.

A week after my maiden speech I spoke in the debate on the Rolls-Royce (Purchase) Bill and from that time on I spoke regularly in debates and intervened at question time. I spoke only about subjects of which I had a working knowledge, such as the economy, industry and taxation, and about social matters such as housing and pensions, of which I was becoming knowledgeable through my work as a Member. I found that roughly the same people spoke in these debates on each occasion and one began to identify those whose views one could respect even though one might not agree with them.

I found parliament totally absorbing and it became clear to me that it was impossible to combine being a Member with being a partner in a City firm of chartered accountants. I told my partners that I would like to retire from the firm at the end of the financial year which was 31 May 1971.

The Heath government had been elected on a manifesto which

promised major and fundamental changes, an end to corporatism, a more liberal economic system, less intervention, and a major reform of our institutions. The government made a determined start and for the first twelve months seemed set to keep its promises. In the October mini-Budget, and the Budget in March, personal and corporate taxes were substantially reduced, and sweeping changes were made to the taxation system. The Prices and Incomes Board was abolished, the Industrial Reorganization Corporation was to be wound up, and the government faced up to and overcame strikes by the miners, the power workers, and the Post Office workers. The nationalization of Rolls-Royce aero engine, and marine and industrial gas-turbine engine divisions in February 1971 struck a jarring note, but the importance of the company to the nation's defences persuaded the doubters to support the government. Many people regarded the government's vacillations over the issue of Upper Clyde Shipbuilders as the real beginning of the infamous U-turn, but for me the turning point came in January, ten days after the beginning of the second miners' strike, when unemployment topped the million mark for the first time since 1947. After a demonstration of firmness, a court of enquiry chaired by Lord Wilberforce was established, and a few days later, having invented 'the adjustment factor' as an excuse, effectively recommended that the miners be bought off. The adjustment factor was based on the extraordinary argument that because the miners had been at the top of the wages league, they should be restored to that position, and the amount necessary to achieve this totally arbitrary end should be paid.

On the Sunday after the Wilberforce settlement was announced, Ann and I went to lunch with the Prime Minister at Chequers. We had been pleased but puzzled to receive the invitation. It was our first visit to Chequers and my first ever social meeting with Ted Heath. He had decided to make a prime-ministerial broadcast to the nation about the miners' strike and its settlement and left shortly after lunch to record his broadcast. It was a small party of about twelve people and the only other politician invited was Geoffrey Howe, with his wife, Elspeth. The mood was sombre and the Prime Minister was, naturally, preoccupied about what he was going to say to the nation. After he left we were shown around the house. Some months later, I asked Tim Kitson, Ted's PPS, why we had been invited. He explained that he had been trying to persuade Ted to appoint a second PPS and had recommended me. I had been invited to lunch so that Ted could get to know me, but the miners' strike wrecked the plan. I have never known whether to be grateful to the miners or not. It would have been a great honour to work for the Prime Minister, but it might have caused difficulties later.

From Wilberforce on, we reverted to prices and incomes policies, controls and interventionism, and the whole machinery of postwar collectivism was restored and more. It is now easy to see this pattern clearly, but at the time, the overwhelming consideration was that the government should survive. A few brave souls, such as Enoch Powell, John Biffen and Peter Hordern, spoke out as one election promise after another was abandoned, but the overwhelming majority, of which I was one, loyally supported the government. I spoke in a debate in favour of incomes policy in November 1973. After spending most of the speech outlining why I supported the government and attacking the Labour Party for its failure to support a policy which it had attempted whilst in government, I turned to address the critics of the policy within the Conservative Party. I quoted from a speech made by John Biffen earlier in the week and went on to reject his prognosis. In light of the policies pursued by the Conservative government after 1979, which both John and I enthusiastically supported and in which we participated, my remarks make interesting reading:

They say that it is no good pretending that there is a simple solution to our problems, and then they go on to talk about a solution which is simplistic to a degree, and use words like 'transient' and 'temporary' and 'inconvenience', and give the impression that a policy which is aimed at a strong tightening-up of the money supply will produce a short, sharp answer. The word 'temporary' and the word 'transient' are always included in the implication of unemployment which my honourable friend in his normally honourable fashion is prepared to accept as one of the outcomes of what he is seeking. I suggest that he and his honourable friends have no grounds for claiming that the hardship would be transient. A policy of the kind he and his honourable friends are suggesting could produce severe and lasting damage to our economy . . .

Some years later, I was explaining to John that I regretted having made that speech. His reply was typically honest, 'My dear Cecil, don't apologize. Go and read my maiden speech some time, you'll find it was in favour of incomes policy, but I subsequently saw the error of my ways.'

In May 1972 I received a telephone call from Michael Heseltine who had just been appointed Minister of Aviation. He told me about his new job and asked me if I would like to be Parliamentary Private Secretary to him and his newly appointed Parliamentary Under-secretary, Cranley Onslow. I told him that I knew nothing about aviation, but he explained that he wanted somebody in the team who knew less than he did, and said that since he had been there four hours that gave him the necessary start on me. I agreed to meet him in the House that afternoon and give him my answer. I wanted to make a few enquiries about being a PPS, what it would involve, what disadvantages there might be. By the time we met I had decided to say yes. Over the next nineteen months I was able to watch this formidable and impressive operator in action. I recall three incidents in particular from this period which illustrated for me the remarkable abilities of Michael Heseltine.

One of Michael's first actions as Minister for Aviation was to draw up and agree with officials a work programme for his part of the department and to set a list of priorities. Twice a week he would monitor progress. When he first arrived, he would ask for a report on some aspect of policy and when he could expect to receive it. The first offer would be 'in about six weeks'. He would say, 'No good.' The next offer: 'Four?' 'No good.' 'Two?' 'If you must take as long as that.' After a few months the officials would be apologizing that 'it could not be ready before the end of the week'. He infused a sense of urgency into the work of his officials. He set deadlines and enforced them and he got the whole place buzzing. Heseltine totally disproved the notion that ministers are at the mercy of their officials, and that Whitehall is a one-speed organization and the minister's job is to adapt himself to that speed. In his constructive and deliberate unreasonableness he reminds me in many ways of Mrs Thatcher.

The second incident showed me a different side of Heseltine. One of his responsibilities was the tracked hovercraft. This was an amazing machine which, powered by a linear motor, travelled suspended on a bed of air at huge speeds over a specially prepared track. It was a British invention much admired for its technical ingenuity and brilliance, and was alleged to be a future means of moving vast numbers of people in cities and towns and between cities and towns. There was only one problem. Nobody wanted to buy it. Michael had persuaded the Cabinet to continue to fund the project for a few more months, during which he would do everything in his power to find a customer. He did try extremely hard, but without success. There was simply no market and so, in late January 1973, the Cabinet took the decision to abandon the project. However, it was agreed not to announce the decision until negotiations to see if various parts of the technology could be saved had been completed. Unfortunately for Michael Heseltine, the tracked hovercraft had many supporters in the House of Commons, the most formidable of whom was Airey Neave, the Member for Abingdon, and the Chairman of the House of Commons Select Committee on Science and Technology. Before the Cabinet decision to scrap the project had been announced, Airey Neave and his committee decided to investigate the project and, in particular, the government's handling of it. Michael was invited to appear before them to give evidence on Wednesday 14 February. It was agreed that the decision should be announced to the committee and that a written answer explaining the decision would be published that afternoon.

On the Monday before he was to present himself to the committee, the DTI ministers were due to appear at question time in the Commons. There was a question down for Michael asking what further assistance the government intended to make available for the continued development of the tracked hovercraft. This presented him with a problem, for although the decision to scrap the project had been taken, the Cabinet was keen not to jeopardize the negotiations to save part of the technology. He therefore answered by saying that 'the question of the government's providing financial assistance for the continuation of this project is still under consideration'.

On the Wednesday, he appeared before the Select Committee and told them of the government's decision. Airey Neave and his colleagues took the news badly. They felt that their investigation had been undermined by the government's failure to make its intentions known earlier. Michael was given a very tough grilling by the committee. The next day in the House of Commons, on a point of order to the Speaker, the Labour Member, whose question on the tracked hovercraft Michael had answered the previous Monday, accused Michael of having misled the House. The chamber erupted. There can be no more serious offence in parliamentary terms for a minister or any other MP than to be guilty of misleading the House of Commons. The fact that Michael was acting under instruction was of no consequence. The fact that it was out of politeness to the committee that a government minister had decided to announce the decision directly to them, and then be available to be questioned in detail about the decision, cut no ice with Airey Neave's committee. The government had affronted the House of Commons and somebody was going to pay. Michael was the chosen victim. When the committee published its report in October, it was highly critical of Michael Heseltine. It concluded that his answer to the House of Commons on Monday 12 February was 'untrue'. As a way of expiating his crime he was forced to appear at the dispatch box in the chamber and to make a grovelling personal statement, in which he regretted that the committee had taken the view that his answer was untrue and admitted 'on reflection, that the wording of my answer on 12 February was capable of more than one interpretation and led to misunderstanding. I apologize most sincerely to the House for the misunderstanding that arose.' At the time it looked as if his ministerial career would be blighted.

I sympathized with him and told him how unfair it seemed that as a junior minister he should carry the can for the whole government. His answer was typically robust: 'My dear Cecil, that's what junior ministers are for.' I know of very few people in parliament then or now who would have ridden out such a storm with such equanimity.

The third incident demonstrated yet another side to Michael Heseltine. One of his main jobs was to find a buyer for the supersonic Concorde aircraft, and a few months after his appointment, he 'persuaded' British Airways to buy five, by lending them the money as non-interest-bearing public dividend capital, and allowing them to buy two more Boeing Jumbos. Two days before they were due to go ahead with the purchase, the entire board threatened to resign if they had to have them. Michael went to work, and two days later, I sat listening to the Chairman thanking the government profusely for giving the corporation the opportunity of a lifetime, scarcely able to believe what I was hearing. Incidentally, when British Airways was privatized fifteen years later the whole of the public dividend capital was written off and BA got its Concorde fleet for £1.

Following the first sale Michael set off on a world sales tour in Concorde accompanied by his wife, Anne, and a battery of salesmen. Their first stop was Iran where an exhibition was to be staged for the benefit of the Shah who was also to fly the plane personally. Michael inspected the exhibition just before the Shah arrived and discovered that the company had not shown Teheran on the world map. The omission was corrected just before the Shah arrived. He did take options on three planes, but was unable to exercise them before he was deposed.

The plane then went on to Singapore. Lee Kuan Yew, the Prime Minister, had a deep aversion to men with long hair. This was the era of the hippy, and before any long-haired hippy was allowed to enter his country he insisted that his hair was cut short. The plane landed, the engines were shut down, the steps were pushed against the plane, and Michael and Anne Heseltine strode on to the top step. There was a great gasp from the waiting crowd. Michael thought it was caused by the spectacular aeroplane. It was not. The thought going through the crowd's mind on seeing Michael's shoulder-length hair was, 'Will he be allowed in?'

Michael then had to come back to Westminster for parliamentary business, and George Jellicoe, leader of the Lords, took the plane on to Australia and other places. It had been arranged that the plane would end its journey at Heathrow on a Saturday morning, and Michael and Anne flew down to Toulouse to join it for this last leg. I asked Cranley Onslow, then Parliamentary Undersecretary of State to Michael, why Michael and Anne had gone. With a broad grin he said that they had gone to rub Concorde down with a J-cloth because they wanted it to look at its best when it landed in London. The anti-Concorde lobby staged a major demonstration to mark the occasion and, as the plane landed at its well-publicized time, hundreds of telephone callers jammed the Heathrow switchboard protesting at the noise. The plane was due to leave at 9.0 a.m. on the Monday. Michael decided to bring this forward to 8.30 a.m., but no notice was given to the public of the change. The plane left without incident at 8.30, but at 9.0 a.m, the advertised time, the protests poured in from people not aware that Concorde had left half an hour earlier. By his decision, Michael showed just how spurious so much of the alleged public indignation was, and dealt the anti-Concorde lobby a blow from which it never really recovered.

In November 1973, taking advantage of the Arab/Israeli war, and the ensuing uncertainty about oil suppliers, the miners decided to challenge the government for the third time in three years. The government decided it had to make a stand. Within days a compulsory speed limit of fifty miles per hour had been introduced and the use of lighting restricted in shops, offices and streets. Heating was also restricted in commercial premises and shortly afterwards the three-day working week was announced. The miners were using their economic power for political purposes, but I warned them in a speech in the House that this was extremely short-sighted. Their economic power stemmed from political decisions by governments which were capable of being changed, and must as a result of their actions inevitably be changed. The monopoly producer of electricity was forced by the government to buy all its coal from the monopoly coal producer, and coal represented eighty-four per cent of the electricity industry's prime fuels. Breaking either monopoly would curtail the power of the miners, breaking both would destroy their political and economic power. We had the prospect of North Sea oil and gas coming on stream and at that point, with the further aid of a nuclear programme, the boot would be firmly on the other foot. I argued that the miners were squandering the public's goodwill and damaging their own long-term interests. It was with real conviction that fourteen years later as Energy Secretary I presided over the break-up of both monopolies, introduced the bill to privatize electricity and committed the government to the privatization of coal.

On 7 January 1974 I went to the Bahamas for a few days. Early on the morning of the eighth I was woken from a deep sleep by the telephone. A voice at the other end, said, 'Hello Cecil, this is Humphrey.' Not knowing anyone called Humphrey in Nassau I replied in a rather guarded, sleepy way, 'Oh yes.' 'Humphrey Atkins, the Chief Whip.' 'Oh yes,' in a much more positive way from me. 'The Prime Minister is having a reshuffle and we both think it would be a good idea for you to become a whip. Would you like to join us?' 'Yes, I would.' 'Good. It will be announced in five hours time at six o'clock this evening. We are meeting in Number 12 at 10.30 tomorrow morning. See you then.' With that he put the telephone down. He clearly didn't know that I was in the Bahamas where it was 8.0 a.m. I found that there was a flight leaving at 6.0 p.m. local time which got into London at 7.0 a.m. London time. I caught the plane, went home to Hertfordshire, showered, changed and drove to Downing Street, arriving just in time for the meeting. Humphrey and the rest of the whips were friendly and welcoming. 'Where were you when I telephoned?' said Humphrey. 'The Bahamas.' 'Oh Cecil, you should have told me, there was no need for you to come back.' The Prime Minister was equally sympathetic when Adam Butler, who had joined with me, and I were taken in to see him later that day. 'I understand you were in the Bahamas when Humphrey called. How long had you been there?' 'About fourteen hours,' I replied. 'Bad luck,' he said with a smile.

In addition to the Chief Whip, the whips' office consisted of a Deputy Chief Whip and twelve other whips, one of whom was the pairing whip. The others took responsibility for keeping in touch with groups of Conservative MPs from different areas of the country, and also for working with specific government departments and the back-bench committees covering the work of those departments. I became the whip for the London Area, and for Housing and Trade and Industry.

The role of the whips is much more complex than the arm-twisting and bullying normally associated with it. If the leaders of the party are considering a contentious policy then it is the whips' job to make sure that they are aware of the likely reaction of the back benches. If a backbencher or a group of backbenchers is dissatisfied with the policies of a particular department or the performance of a minister, then those facts will be registered. As a result some measures are abandoned because the backbenchers won't accept or support them. In some cases, knowing that controversy is inevitable, and that there will be opposition within the party, the government presses on, leaving the whips to use all the means at their disposal to limit the number of rebels. The principal weapon is patronage. Members know that before there is a reshuffle the Chief Whip will be consulted by the leader and that he in turn will have consulted his fellow whips. The ambitious, and they are in the majority, know this, and realize that while a very occasional abstention or vote against the government on a point of high principle or low local interest may be accepted, regular rebellions are inconsistent with ministerial ambitions. There is, however, a substantial body known as 'the old and bold' who have no ministerial ambitions, and other ways have to be found, on occasions, of appealing to their better natures. The whips are an intelligence-gathering, talent-spotting – sometimes lack-of-talent-spotting – organization. A member of the whips' office hears every single speech in the chamber or the committee room, virtually every contribution to discussions in the back-bench committees, and the all-party groups. They are to be found having tea in the tea room, drinks in the various bars, and meals in the dining rooms, and between them have a very good idea of the mood of the House and the party. They are also a vital part of 'the usual channels', the inter-party machine which ensures that the work of parliament, and the government's programme, gets carried through in a reasonably orderly way. Enoch Powell once said, 'The whips are as essential to parliament as sewerage is to civilization.' This has always seemed to me a malodorous way of describing what is a very interesting job, in which one gets to know and becomes friendly with members from all parts of the House.

On my first day as a whip, Jack Weatherill, then the Deputy Chief Whip, subsequently the Speaker of the House of Commons, called me into his office. He explained that there were two types of whips. The first was the natural whip who would join the office and spend a significant part of his parliamentary career there. The second would spend a shorter period in the office receiving what he called 'the hothouse treatment' prior to taking up a career as a departmental minister. He left me with the distinct impression that I was in the second category. I was very flattered until I discovered that he had left everybody else in the office with the same impression having given each one the same lecture.

The whips' day was a long one. If one was the whip on a bill committee, it started at 10.0 a.m. on Tuesdays and Thursdays. On Wednesdays the whips met in 12 Downing Street, the Chief Whip's office, at 10.30 a.m. to discuss the next week's business in the House. Otherwise we met every day at 2.30 p.m. and none of us left the House until the beginning of the half-hour-long adjournment debate which ends every parliamentary day. This could be one or two o'clock in the morning and sometimes much later. It was, therefore, vital that we worked well together which is why, when there is a vacancy in the whips' office, the whips unanimously choose a candidate to recommend to the leader, who finally makes the appointment.

The early weeks of 1974 were dominated by the miners' strike and by the tremendous pressure on Ted Heath to call a general election on the theme of 'Who governs Britain?' The whips were continuously monitoring the mood of the party and Humphrey Atkins was reporting our findings to Cabinet. The Cabinet and the parliamentary party were evenly divided between those who felt we should carry on and those who felt that this represented an opportunity to discipline the miners and win a second term of office. I strongly felt we should carry on.

Three times a year the whips dine together away from the House and once a year the leader joins them. I attended my first dinner at the Carlton Club on 22 January. We had just finished a most enjoyable and boisterous dinner when the door of the Disraeli Room opened and in walked the Prime Minister and his PPS, Tim Kitson. He came straight to the point and asked each of us to express our views on whether there should be an election. We all spoke in turn and, as the Junior Whip, I spoke last. We were of no help to the Prime Minister. Seven of us were against an early election and seven in favour. I felt at the time that he did not want to call an election. But he was persuaded to have one. In my view he acted against his instincts. On 7 February Edward Heath announced that an election would be held three weeks later on 28 February.

The parliament which had started with such promise in 1970 ended with the Conservative Party in disarray. We had been elected on a radical manifesto which put the fight against inflation at the forefront of our policies. The Conservative government was determined not to be blown off course. As Mr Heath wrote in the foreword to the 1970 manifesto:

... once a decision is made, once a policy is established, the Prime Minister and his colleagues should have the courage to stick to it. Nothing has done Britain more harm in the world than the endless backing and filling which we have seen in recent years. Whether it be our defence commitments, or our financial policies, or the reform of industrial relations, the story has been the same. At the first sign of difficulty the Labour government has sounded the retreat, covering its withdrawal with a smokescreen of unlikely excuses. But courage and intellectual honesty are essential qualities in politics, and in the interest of our country it is high time that we saw them again.

By 1974 that pledge made for sorry reading. The Heath government, like its predecessors, had retreated from its central financial policies and by the October general election had abandoned its commitment to the reform of industrial relations. But in one area the government had kept a steady course. The 1970 manifesto had stated that our sole commitment on Britain's membership of the European Economic Community was to negotiate, 'no more, no less'. Yet Mr Heath's determination that we should join was unwavering throughout the parliament. What was so disappointing was that our economic and industrial policies were just as right for Britain as our membership of the EEC. On Europe the leadership was determined, elsewhere our policies were abandoned in favour of a search for 'consensus' and 'national unity'.

With the dissolution of parliament, the Enfield West constituency ceased to exist and I fought the new seat of Hertfordshire South, having been selected as the prospective candidate about a year earlier. Hertfordshire South included about a third of my old seat, the other two-thirds coming from Barnet, Watford, St Albans and South West Hertfordshire. It was a wholly artificial creation of the Boundary Commissioners, and initially the only things which the disparate parts had in common were a desire to have nothing to do with each other and a resentment at being separated from their previous constituencies. I was fortunate that the Chairman of Enfield West, Tony Simons, agreed to become Chairman of the new constituency. He quickly built up an excellent organization and was the first of a succession of fine Chairmen to whom I am deeply indebted. I had a clear understanding with him, and his successors, that they took care of the organization and I took care of the politics. Tony was, by profession, a jobber on the London Stock Exchange, a busy man, but over many years he devoted a lot of his spare time to building up, strengthening and running the organization within the constituency. As a result of his efforts and those of his fellow officers, we had more than 5,000 paid-up members in all parts of the constituency and a far better organization than our opponents.

South Hertfordshire was a much more mixed and less predictable seat than Enfield West. It included Borehamwood with its 6,000 GLC-owned houses, and no fewer than five huge mental-illness and mental-handicap hospitals with a combined, totally unionized, staff of about 8,000. Two of the areas, Borehamwood and London Colney were Labour-controlled. The Labour and Liberal parties fielded good candidates. Each of us claimed that we would win and my own party's private research showed that we should win, but that it would be very close. On polling day the local newspaper reported a 'Conservative spokesman' as saying, 'we think we will come out with a majority of 3,000'. In the end, after a grim campaign, during which the electorate became increasingly truculent about the disruption being caused to their lives by power shortages, blaming the government for their problems, our prediction proved correct and I was elected with a majority of 3,086 over my Labour opponent.

During the three weeks I spent in my own constituency canvassing, addressing public meetings, issuing press releases, meeting people in the shopping areas and outside schools and stations, I had virtually no contact with the central campaign, but one began to feel after about a week that the attempt to sustain a single-issue election was not going to work.

The miners' case had been referred to the Pay Board, who had been asked to examine relativities. The public felt that the stage was being set for a further climbdown by the government. Our position was not improved when the employer, the National Coal Board, said in evidence to the Pay Board that there was a vital need for improvement in the wages and conditions of the miners. Subsequently, on the weekend before the election, a story broke that the government had got its arithmetic wrong and that the miners' claim was justified. This was not contradicted until some time later, by which time it was established in the minds of most of the public as a fact, thus proving once again the truth of Jim Callaghan's dictum that a lie can be halfway round the world before truth can get its boots on.

Another blow to the Conservative campaign was Enoch Powell's announcement that he would not contest 'an essentially fraudulent election'. At that time Enoch still had a large following inside and outside the party. His subsequent advice to the electorate, repeated twice during the last week of the campaign, that EEC membership was the issue of overriding importance at the election and they should vote Labour, since Labour were promising a fundamental renegotiation followed by a referendum on the issue, was another significant blow to the government.

It was also a personal embarrassment to me. In 1971 I had been invited to join a small dining club, the Economic Dining Club, which was limited to twelve members, all of whom had to be members of the Commons. We dined in each other's homes and usually discussed a short paper on some aspect of the economy. We were, in the main, monetarists, and Enoch, who attended all the dinners, was our guru. At the end of the discussion which took place during and after dinner, he would sum it up. Nick Ridley was the moving spirit behind the club and only four members were members of the government, all of them junior ministers. We had agreed that come what may we would all meet for dinner at my flat in Roebuck House on the Monday after the election. Ann was particularly incensed by Enoch's behaviour during the campaign, and vowed that although she would arrange dinner she would not stay in the flat if Enoch came. In the event, he refused the invitation and the dinner took place without him. We decided at that dinner to invite Margaret Thatcher to fill the vacancy left by Enoch and she remained an enthusiastic member until she became Prime Minister, after which she came as a guest once a year, usually on Budget night. It is also worth noting that no less than eight members of the club eventually served in her Cabinet, a striking contrast with the Heath years.

For the first time in forty-five years no single party had an overall majority and, after four days of talks with Jeremy Thorpe and other Liberals in an attempt to form a coalition government, Ted Heath resigned and Harold Wilson formed a Labour administration.

It was clear to everyone that another election would have to be held within months, and Harold Wilson very astutely used the next six months to ingratiate himself and his party with the British people. Rents were frozen, food subsidies were approved, VAT was cut and a barrage of white papers on industry, sex discrimination, land, and pensions were issued before an election was called on 18 September.

They were unhappy months for the Conservative Party, which seemed totally confused about which political direction to take. Peter Walker, who was regarded as very close to Ted Heath, publicly backed the idea of a coalition government of national unity. Later that month Keith Joseph argued that the only conceivable basis for prosperity rested on 'a healthy competitive private sector – a market economy within a framework of humane laws and institutions', in other words 'the social market economy'. Far from the social market economy being a concept evolved by the wets, it was in fact at the very heart of the vision evolved by Keith Joseph and Margaret Thatcher. Ted Heath announced that he would not reintroduce the Industrial Relations Act if he were re-elected, although we had spent months in the 1970 parliament arguing that its provisions were essential in a modern Britain. In August, Robert Carr, the Shadow Chancellor, argued the case for a statutory incomes policy. In September, Keith Joseph argued the case against it and rejected consensus and any talk of a national unity government. The party was clearly split and the election result reflected this. Only 35.8 per cent of those who voted supported the Conservatives, and Labour were elected with an overall majority of three.

After the February election Margaret Thatcher had been appointed Shadow Environment Secretary. She dominated the Conservative campaign with her housing and rating proposals, which were to peg mortgages at 9.5 per cent, to give all council tenants the right to buy their houses at two-thirds of their true value, to offer help for first-time buyers with their deposits, and a commitment to abolish the rates within the lifetime of a parliament. These proposals did not convince the electorate, but they did make Margaret Thatcher much better known and more widely supported within the Conservative Party in the House of Commons and in the country. She was regarded as one of the few successes of the election campaign, but at that time Keith Joseph was seen as the leading figure on the right of the party and the natural challenger to Ted Heath for the leadership.

The situation changed as a result of a single speech in Birmingham on the moral and spiritual state of the nation. Keith argued that poorer families were least able to bring up their children without resort to the state, and yet 'proposals to extend birth control facilities to these classes of people, particularly the young unmarried girls, the potential unmarried mothers, evoke entirely understandable moral opposition'. 'But which', he asked, 'is the lesser evil?' The speech caused an uproar which upset him deeply. At that point he became convinced that he should not contest the leadership. I had for some years been the leader of the Institute of Directors parliamentary panel and attended a dinner given by the institute to mark the retirement of the Director-General. Keith was also there and we travelled back to the House afterwards to vote. He had not then announced his decision and I urged him to think again, but he was adamant. Margaret Thatcher was convinced that with Keith's withdrawal as a contestant she should stand against Ted Heath.

Following the election she had been appointed number two to Robert Carr, the Shadow Chancellor, to take charge of finance bills. Many people, including me, felt that this was a snub to her following her personal success in the campaign, and evidence even then of Ted Heath's antipathy towards her. In fact, what appeared to be a poisoned chalice proved to be a golden opportunity. Ted Heath had made his name by his brilliant handling of Britain's first application to join the EEC. What had confirmed him as a successor to Sir Alec Douglas-Home was his leadership of the Finance Bill team which opposed the Finance Act of 1965 in which Labour introduced the Capital Gains Tax. Those who were in parliament at that time talk of his superb organization of the opposition to that act.

In 1974, Labour had plans to replace estate duty with a capital transfer tax, and Margaret Thatcher set out to oppose that. By this time I had become the Finance Whip and had begun to work closely

with her. The most contentious proposals were discussed in committee on the floor of the House so that all MPs could take part. It
was in the committee stage where Mrs Thatcher really shone. I
remember one speech in particular, at the end of a debate on a
Conservative amendment to the capital transfer tax proposals. The
Chancellor, Denis Healey, had attacked her, calling her '*La pas-
sionaria* of privilege'. She responded with the most cutting put-down
of a Chancellor that anyone could remember: 'I wish I could say that
the Chancellor of the Exchequer had done himself less than justice.
Unfortunately, I can only say that I believe he has done himself
justice. Some Chancellors are macro-economic. Other Chancellors
are fiscal. This one is just plain cheap.' She continued: 'If this
Chancellor can be Chancellor, anyone in the House of Commons
can be Chancellor.' As for the allegation of privilege, she retorted
that the capital transfer tax would 'affect everyone, including people
born as I was, with no privilege at all.' It was a stunning performance
which left the Labour side sitting in glum silence whilst our own
supporters were cheering madly. She told me afterwards that the
speech would not read well because of the numerous interruptions,
but, she added, 'I sometimes think in parliament, it's not what you
say but the way you say it.'

Two days later the leadership elections were announced. Mrs
Thatcher could not have had a better beginning to her campaign,
nor could she have had a better campaign manager than Airey Neave
who offered his services. As a whip, who had accepted a job from
Ted Heath only a few months earlier, I could take no part in the
campaign. The committee on the Finance Bill had begun its sittings
and Mrs Thatcher insisted on playing a full part. We had put together
an outstanding team to fight the bill which included no fewer than
nine people – David Howell, Norman Lamont, Nigel Lawson, John
MacGregor, Tony Newton, Peter Rees, Nicholas Ridley, Margaret
Thatcher and myself – all of whom subsequently became Cabinet
ministers. We had assembled a team of expert advisers led by Keith
Carmichael, a top tax accountant, and we tabled over 400 amendments to the bill. The sittings went on into the night and occasionally
I drove Mrs Thatcher back to her home in Flood Street. It always
amazed me that after a day of high politics and detailed committee
work, her overriding concern was for her family. Her daughter,
Carol, was preparing to take her final examinations as a solicitor,
and she was worried that the publicity and media coverage might

interrupt her studies. She was also anxious about whether Denis was eating properly.

A few days before the election, Airey Neave stopped me and told me that he had a message he wished me to give to the Chief Whip. He told me that he and his colleagues accepted that Ted Heath was going to win comfortably. His concern was that after his victory Ted should treat Margaret properly and give her a job commensurate with her new standing in the party, otherwise there would be trouble. I dutifully reported this to the Chief Whip. I heard subsequently that a similar message had been given to a number of colleagues, who had shared Airey's concern and switched their votes to make sure that Ted's majority was smaller. Airey was an acknowledged master of black propaganda and I have often wondered whether this was an example of it or whether he genuinely thought she would lose. Having beaten Ted Heath on the first ballot, she won decisively on the second. She immediately went round to see her predecessor at his home in Wilton Street. But after a very brief, cool meeting with him, she had a cup of tea with his PPS, Tim Kitson, in the kitchen so that the media outside would not know how brief their encounter had been.

Margaret Thatcher had achieved what many believed was impossible. She had become the first elected woman leader of the Conservative Party. She was to go on astounding her critics and delighting her friends for the next fifteen years.

7 The Statutory Female Aggravator

In opposition a whip's job is just as onerous and time-consuming as in government but, with the exception of the Chief Whip, his deputy and one other, it is unpaid. When we went into opposition after the February election, Humphrey Atkins asked each of us whether we wished to continue in the office. Two colleagues, Ken Clarke and David Walder, felt that they had to take up their careers as barrister and author respectively, but the rest of us decided that we would carry on. I made one proviso. With my small majority I felt that the anonymity of the whips' office might be damaging and I asked for permission to make occasional speeches in the House on subjects of particular interest to my constituents or about subjects of which I had particular knowledge. There was a long-standing tradition in the Conservative Party that whips never spoke but, after considering the matter, Humphrey agreed to my request. I thus established the tradition of the talking whip. From that time on I spoke during debates on Finance Bills and played a full part in committees. It made life more interesting for me, and it meant that on major bills, when each member of our team took responsibility for a specific part of the bill, I was able to do my share. I felt that this made me a more accepted member of the team and actually helped me with my work as a whip. When I left the whips' office in November 1976, I was succeeded by Nigel Lawson, who in turn was succeeded by John MacGregor, and the practice in opposition of having a specialist whip who dealt with economic and financial subjects and spoke about them in the House was carried on.

In government, opportunities for backbenchers to speak in committee are usually limited. The government wants to get its bills through as quickly as possible, and it looks to its backbenchers for their vote, and for a helpful silence. The opposition, for its part, wants to prolong proceedings, knowing that when a vote is called it can rarely win. Oppositions use time as a weapon to force concessions out of governments. In the parliament which began in October 1974, we were in a particularly strong position to be an effective opposition. The government had a wafer-thin majority of three over all other parties and yet it was still determined to force through a very controversial legislative programme. In addition to the introduction of a capital transfer tax, the Queen's Speech following the October general election included plans for the nationalization of the aircraft, shipbuilding and North Sea oil industries, an Industry Bill which would give the government the power to take controlling shareholdings in virtually any major company, and a bill giving greater power to the trade unions. Later in the parliament came proposals to create Scottish and Welsh assemblies.

In spite of its apparent fragility, and the loss of its majority by February 1977, the Labour government carried through most of its programme and continued in office for almost its full five-year term. It was able to do this for three main reasons. Firstly, the Scottish and Welsh Nationalists were determined to sustain the government until the Devolution Bill was through. Secondly, James Callaghan, having succeeded Harold Wilson as Prime Minister in April 1976, persuaded David Steel, the Liberal leader, to join a Lib/Lab pact which gave the Liberal Party the appearance of influence, while preserving the reality of power for Labour. Finally, the Ulster Unionists had developed a deep distaste for the Conservative party and a desire to demonstrate their independence by supporting the Labour government in a number of critical votes.

The government was defeated regularly on the details of various pieces of legislation and accepted those defeats, but on the major issues it won. As opposition whips who lived to plot the government's defeat and downfall, time after time we found ourselves within a whisker of achieving our objective only to miss it because of some totally unforeseeable event. On one occasion after insisting that a member return early from the Far East, he did not turn up to vote. It transpired that, having arrived home after a long exhausting journey, he had sat in front of the fire and failed to wake up until after the vote. We lost by one.

On another occasion, a member was practising in the shooting gallery in the basement of the House of Commons. He could not hear the division bell because he was wearing earplugs to stifle the noise. Again we lost by one. Another time, one of our most reliable Members was sorting out a pile of files in her office off Westminster

Hall which had been damaged earlier that day by an IRA bomb. She waited for the division bell to ring, not realizing that the circuit had been destroyed by the bomb. She missed the vote and the government survived.

Bob Mellish was the Labour Chief Whip in the first half of the parliament. He treated his own backbenchers, and on occasions frontbenchers as well, almost brutally, but he was always pleasant to Conservative Members. Bob was dropped when James Callaghan became Prime Minister, and was replaced by Michael Cocks, the MP for Bristol South. However, throughout the parliament, it was Labour's Deputy Chief Whip, Walter Harrison, who caused us the most problems. Walter was a tough Yorkshireman and he almost singlehandedly thwarted every attempt by us to defeat his government. On one Friday we were plotting to lull him into a false sense of security by sending our people away from the House with instructions to return in time to vote, thus ambushing the government into an embarrassing defeat. Walter, as ever, was roaming around the corridors when he spotted one of our less assiduous Members walking through Members lobby. He became suspicious and set his whips to work to wheel in the payroll vote, the ministers and PPSs and other loyalists. The government scraped by once again.

No piece of legislation gave Walter Harrison more trouble than the Aircraft and Shipbuilding Industries Bill. It had a stormy passage through the Commons – passing its second reading with a majority of five and its third reading with an even smaller majority of three. The government's decision to introduce a guillotine motion, to curtail debate on the bill, was approved by the House by one vote and, on another occasion, they needed the Deputy Speaker's casting vote to overturn a House of Lords' amendment. The most controversial moment during the bill's passage occurred following a ruling by the Speaker of the Commons that the bill was 'hybrid'. A hybrid bill had been defined by a previous Speaker as 'a public bill which affects a particular private interest in a manner different from the private interest of other persons or bodies of the same category or class'. In the case of the Aircraft and Shipbuilding Industries Bill it was discovered by the opposition, and brilliantly argued in the House by the Member for Tiverton, Robin Maxwell-Hyslop, that the bill, by omitting a particular company from the list of those to be nationalized, treated that company in a different way from others 'of the same category or class'. This might appear to be a mere technicality, but in fact it involves a fundamental constitutional principle. The procedure for a hybrid bill allows private interests which regard themselves as the object of discrimination to petition parliament directly. The procedures for a public bill allow no such opportunity. The government, however, was determined to proceed with the bill and decided to ask the Commons to override its procedures and allow the bill to go ahead.

The government won by a majority of one, but it subsequently transpired that a Labour Member had been coerced into breaking his pair. Had he not done so, the motion would have been tied, the Speaker would have used his casting vote to reject the motion and to support his own ruling, and the bill would in practical terms have been lost. When the result was announced all hell broke loose. Labour backbenchers sang the Red Flag, and to everybody's astonishment Michael Heseltine leapt from the opposition front bench, seized the mace and offered it to the bewildered government ministers sitting opposite. Michael was a noticeable figure at the best of times, tall, with the shoulder-length blond hair that had earned him the nick-name 'Tarzan'. The incident itself was dramatic enough, but the story improved in the telling. Michael was alleged to have picked up the mace and stood in the centre of the chamber of the House of Commons whirling it around his head. The Speaker, George Thomas, suspended the sitting due to what were euphemistically described as 'scenes of grave disorder'. Michael apologized to the House the next day. Relations between government and opposition entered a phase of permafreeze as Mrs Thatcher suspended all pairing and other cooperation with the government. Four weeks later, a rerun of the debate was held. The government had done a deal with the fourteen Scottish and Welsh Nationalists who abstained and this time won by a majority of fourteen. Walter Harrison had saved his government and their legislation once again.

During the period from March 1974 to April 1976 the Labour Chancellor introduced no fewer than five Budgets. I served as the whip on four of the ensuing Finance Bills. There is always keen competition to serve on the Finance Bill Committee amongst Conservative backbenchers: there are usually about three applicants for every place. Once tax changes are announced in the Budget statement, they are usually implemented immediately under the Provisional Collection of Taxes Act to prevent avoidance and confusion. The executive is in effect implementing changes of which parliament has been informed but which it has not approved. For a Budget held in March or April the Finance Bill has to become law by 5 August of the same year or else any taxes collected would have to be handed back. For budgets held at any other time of the year (and under Labour Budgets and mini-Budgets took place regularly), the Finance Bill must become law within four months of the taxes coming into operation. So it is very important for the government to get its bill passed by the statutory date since theoretically it would face chaos if it didn't. In fact, since the opposition hopes to be the next government and accepts that it will face the same problem, the business managers on both sides agree that the government will get its bill by the due date. Having accepted that, the opposition sets out to make life as uncomfortable as possible and the committee stage is hard-fought and prolonged, with the committee often sitting through the night two or three times a week. The government lacked an overall majority in the House of Commons and, since parliamentary rules ensure that all committees reflect the balance of the House of Commons, Labour did not have a working majority on the committee either. So we were well equipped to harry the government. *The Sunday Times* political correspondent spent a few days listening to the debates and came to the conclusion that 'the Conservative party has an inexhaustible supply of members who can talk forever about money'. Once Margaret Thatcher became leader of the party, our team was led by John Nott and David Howell, but the star back-bench performers were Nigel Lawson, Peter Rees and Nicholas Ridley.

Nigel was elected to the House in February 1974, and arrived with a well-deserved reputation as an outstanding economic and financial commentator. A former editor of *The Spectator*, and political adviser to Sir Alec Douglas-Home when he was Prime Minister, he lost no time in establishing himself as a formidable and uncrushable parliamentary performer. Lawson became one of the gang of four, who briefed Mrs Thatcher for her twice-weekly jousts with Mr Wilson, and subsequently Mr Callaghan at Prime Minister's questions. The others were Norman Tebbit, Geoffrey Pattie and George Gardiner.

Nigel's main hobby was tripping up the Chancellor of the Exchequer, Denis Healey, who lacked his expertise and factual knowledge of economics, and who was frequently wrong-footed by the new backbencher. Nigel's skill coupled with his self-confidence could make him appear cocky almost to the point of arrogance. Those who worked with him quickly realized that in addition to his other qualities he had a sense of humour and an ability to coin epigrams which more than compensated for his justifiably high regard for himself. He was hugely hard-working and became a most valuable and popular member of the Finance Bill team. Nigel has a highly developed sense of the ridiculous and on occasion would reduce himself and the rest of the committee to a state of semi-helpless hysteria. His definition of the difference between a socialist moderate and a socialist extremist – 'An extremist is one who wants the socialist millennium tomorrow. A moderate wants it the day after his children finish their private education.' – is a classic Lawson epigram. It was clear to all who worked with him that he would one day be Chancellor of the Exchequer, but long before he was appointed in 1983, in opposition and as a junior Treasury minister he exercised enormous influence on the development of Conservative economic and monetary policy. As Energy Secretary from 1981–83, with the support of the Prime Minister, he persuaded the Treasury to fund the building-up of the huge fuel stocks which enabled us to face up to the challenge from Arthur Scargill and the National Union of Mineworkers in 1985, and to see the strike through to a satisfactory conclusion.

Peter Rees is a very eminent Queen's Counsel specializing in tax law. His ability to speak beautifully formulated sentences in committee at high speed on highly technical subjects at a second's notice was remarkable. He spoke in a rather flowery and somewhat dated English. I sometimes felt that the flow of words was self-replenishing and that, although talking perfect sense, Peter was scarcely aware of what he was saying. Once, when he was in the middle of a speech, he was interrupted by a Labour Member who made a rather inane remark. Peter dismissed this interruption with the comment, 'The honourable gentleman has just demonstrated why he has a well-deserved reputation as a pimple on the backside of parliament.' He then resumed his argument. The Labour Member was furious and came to see me with his whip. He threatened to raise the matter on the floor of the House the next day. I pointed out that this would ensure massive coverage for a remark which as of that moment had only been heard by a dozen people. By this time Peter had ended his speech and, once he had been convinced that he had actually made the remark, apologized in a most generous manner.

Like Nigel, Peter also had the ability to make a most telling point in a highly amusing way. His speech to the Finance Bill Standing

Committee in 1975, during a debate on the rate of VAT on imported furs, about his experience of yak-racing in the 'shadow of the Barroghil Pass in Chitral' in the central Asian uplands during his army service is a minor parliamentary classic. He became Chief Secretary to the Treasury with responsibility for getting Finance Bills through the House and paid a heavy price for his brilliance in opposition.

Nicholas Ridley had been a Member of Parliament since 1959 and had served in the Heath government for a short time. He was a convinced monetarist, shared many of Mrs Thatcher's convictions and was one of her closest friends. It was a surprise to many, including Nicholas, that he was not made a member of her front-bench team. When I asked her why this was so, she explained that she felt he was too valuable as a backbencher, with the ability to harry the government on a whole range of subjects, to be wasted in a restricted frontbench role. Nicholas used wit and ridicule with devastating effect and became famous for his Ten-Minute-Rule Bills, and his own personal amendments to Finance Bills. His Ghost-Workers (Abolition) Bill which highlighted the bizarre employment practices in Fleet Street, where Mickey Mouse and William Shakespeare regularly drew pay packets, underlined the need for reform in a highly effective way. On another occasion he tabled as an amendment to the Finance Bill a schedule covering about ten pages of the order paper. In the bill Labour gave the Inland Revenue the most far-reaching powers to break into the homes or offices of persons they suspected of nonpayment, seize papers, and question members of their family. Nicholas's new schedule was a reprint of the government's, but the words 'taxpayer' and 'inspector' had been transposed. His schedule gave the taxpayer the right to break into the Inspector of Taxes' home or office, seize his papers, and question members of his family. His amendment was rejected for being 'tendered in a spirit of mockery', but as a way of highlighting the injustice of the government's legislation, it was brilliantly effective. These are just two examples of a continuous series of initiatives taken by Nicholas which made him too valuable a backbencher in opposition to be promoted to the front bench. It was some slight consolation to me, following my resignation in 1983, that my place in Cabinet was taken by Nicholas, who thus received a belated but totally deserved promotion.

The Labour team on all the numerous Finance Bills between 1974 and 1979 was led by Joel Barnett and his great friend and ally Robert

Sheldon. In spite of extreme provocation they contrived to remain good-natured and polite, and to defend the indefensible. It was a matter of some satisfaction that although the government initially resisted our amendments at the time we moved them, many of them were accepted in subsequent Finance Bills. All the many amendments we tabled to the Capital Transfer Tax Bill were initially rejected, but some 200 were incorporated into subsequent acts. Wit and humour were part of our weaponry, but there was nothing frivolous about our opposition to the stream of tax changes made by the Labour government. At the end of two years of almost continuous sittings, both sides had developed a hearty respect for each other, and I believe the government side recognized that our opposition was always constructive.

After almost three years in the whips' office I felt it was time to move on and in October I told the Chief Whip that I would like to leave. He told me that Mrs Thatcher would be having a reshuffle of her front-bench team in mid-November and asked me to stay until then. On 19 November I was chairing a business meeting in my flat in Victoria when the telephone rang and I was told that Mrs Thatcher would like to see me in her office at the Commons at twelve noon. I adjourned the meeting and went to the House. Mrs Thatcher thanked me for my work in the whips' office and said she would like me to join Teddy Taylor to form a new Shadow Trade team. She asked me also to help Sally Oppenheim in opposing the government's prices and incomes legislation. She explained that she wanted Teddy in the Shadow Cabinet to provide a Scottish anti-devolution voice, to counter the pro-devolution view in Shadow Cabinet, and to give more balance to the discussion. Within four weeks Alick Buchanan-Smith resigned as Shadow Scottish Secretary following the Shadow Cabinet's decision to oppose devolution. Teddy was moved to take his place and John Nott joined the Shadow Cabinet as Trade Spokesman. We knew each other quite well from our work on the Finance Bills and worked together for the next four years in opposition and government.

After the regimented, almost regimental, and hectic time in the whips' office, life as a front-bench spokesman seemed incredibly leisurely. Trade, to me, had always been a fascinating area of government, dealing as it did not only with the promotion and financing of exports, but also with trade liberalization and resistance to protectionism. Civil aviation, shipping, company and market regulation, company law, tourism insurance, and many other aspects of commerce and the City combined to make it a most interesting department. It was not, however, a headline-grabbing department and parliamentary debates were rare. John and I spent a lot of time meeting representatives of various organizations and interest groups. One of our earliest meetings was with Freddie (later Sir Freddie) Laker. We went down to Gatwick by train and were ushered into the presence of the great man, who then launched into a half-hour-long harangue about governments and politicians. He was clearly out to intimidate us and when he had finished he said to John Nott, 'Well, have you any questions?' 'Yes,' said John, 'what time is the next train back to London? We didn't come here to listen to that kind of drivel, we came to learn about your airline, and if we're not going to, we might as well leave.' Freddie was not used to being spoken to in this way, and I waited for him to explode. To my surprise, after a moment's pause, his face broke into a broad grin, and he said, 'You and I are going to get on.'

John is a most polite person but, as Freddie Laker and, on another occasion, Robin Day discovered when he walked out of the studio in the middle of an interview, he could not stand gratuitous rudeness. He is also very stimulating and full of original ideas, but with one of the lowest boredom thresholds of anyone I have ever met. He was an excellent debater and often wound up debates for the opposition. An unusual feature of his speeches was that he enjoyed teasing Mrs Thatcher by referring to her in them. On one occasion, during a debate on prices, he talked about people appointed by the government to represent the consumer interest and argued that the views of what he called the 'statutory female aggravator' should not be exaggerated. The Labour Party was slow to catch on, but after he had repeated the remark, the Labour front bench started to point at Mrs Thatcher who was sitting alongside him. He pretended to be surprised and looked at where they were pointing. 'I realized that there was a possibility that some honourable Members might point in the direction of my right honourable friend the leader of the opposition, but she is one of the boys.' The whole House, including Mrs Thatcher, burst out laughing.

He could also be vicious in a very civilized way. John had been the last MP to be elected as a National Liberal and, perhaps as a result, he had a particular dislike for the Liberal Party and could be very cutting about them. He was particularly scathing about the Lib/Lab pact. During one debate he referred to a report in the *Western Daily News* which quoted the Liberal MP David Penhaligon as saying that the Liberal Party was in control of the government: 'We have never been anywhere near it since the 1920s. We have got power today like we never had it before.' John remarked that the Liberals had obtained responsibility but not power and that they had abandoned their principles. He argued: 'I hope that the Liberals enjoy their power, because it will be short-lived. The Prime Minister will not consult them on the timing of the election, nor on his manifesto. He will go to the country at the moment when the Labour Party can emerge from that election as a viable political party to fight again another day.' On another occasion, he taunted the Liberals by suggesting that David Steel, the Liberal leader, 'obviously prefers socialist ministers to his own supporters; and having fought several elections, we can all understand how he feels.'

About six weeks after I became an opposition spokesman, I received a note from the Chief Whip one Thursday afternoon to say that I would be opening the debate for the opposition on the following Monday, on a bill of which I had never previously heard, called the International Finance Trade and Aid Bill. Having obtained a copy of the bill I became even more alarmed. The bill was really three bills rolled into one. It adopted the new rules and quotas of the International Monetary Fund. It gave the Export Credit Guarantee Department the new right to offer buyer credit in foreign currencies, and it increased the borrowing limit of the Commonwealth Development Corporation. I had no detailed knowledge of any of the subjects and no access to any help other than the House of Commons library. I telephoned the library and asked them to pull together any useful material on the three subjects which covered three departments: Treasury, Trade and Foreign Office. I discovered that Sir Jeremy Morse, then Chairman of Lloyds Bank, had chaired the IMF Committee which had drawn up the new rules and quotas. I telephoned his office, explained my problem and asked if he could spare an hour the next day to see me. I also telephoned the head of the ECGD and of the Commonwealth Development Corporation. Each of them was incredibly helpful. By Thursday evening I had appointments arranged for the next day with all three of them, and the head of the ECGD had arranged for me to receive a detailed briefing from one of his bright young men, Malcolm Stephens, who subsequently became the head of the organization. By Friday evening I had a much clearer understanding of the bill and a mountain of briefing material to read over the weekend. On Monday morning I mapped out a speech, spent the morning writing it and on Monday afternoon at 4.15, made my first-ever speech from the dispatch box and proved to myself the truth of the old adage that in the land of the blind, the one-eyed man is king. Having had to do my own research and write my own speech, I was in some ways more comfortable with the subject than the ministers who were clearly working from scripts prepared by civil servants in three separate departments, each department having contributed a third. It was an interesting, educative and worthwhile introduction to front-bench life in opposition.

Early in March I took part in a short debate on shipping safety. A Labour backbencher, John Prescott, raised the subject of the storming of a ship, the *Globtik Venus*, by 'mercenaries' employed by the ship's owner to evict the crew, who, stirred up by the National Union of Seamen, were in dispute with the owner and had seized the ship. Prescott was almost incoherent with fury at the effrontery of the owner in making arrangements to repossess his own property. The words poured out of his mouth in a seemingly endless torrent with the odd verb making the occasional appearance and turning some of the flow into sentences. It was impossible to make sense of a lot of it, but the impression of authentic rage and class hatred was real enough. It was my first sight of a person of whom I was to see a great deal more in the years ahead.

The last two years of the parliament were dominated by two issues, the economy and devolution. In 1976 the government had been forced to seek the biggest loan in the history of the IMF in order to prop up an economy which was on the point of collapse. The IMF imposed the most stringent conditions including huge cuts in spending programmes, tax increases, and severe price, pay, and dividend controls. Nineteen seventy-seven was the year of the Budgets with no fewer than three being introduced over a period of only seven months. After a fourth Budget in April of the following year and following two major defeats on the Finance Bill, the Liberals announced that the Lib/Lab pact would end at the close of the parliamentary session. They clearly felt that the government was going down, and were determined not to go down with it. In June the government survived a motion of no confidence by five votes and after a further defeat on an outrageous bill to give additional rights to the already featherbedded dock workers, the House rose for the summer. We were all confident that an election would be held in the autumn, and in spite of all the problems the odds were still marginally on a Labour victory.

Over the summer, Conservative Central Office mounted a tremendously effective campaign, the linchpin of which was the famous Saatchi poster of a long dole queue under the slogan, 'Labour isn't working'. This and other factors, chief of which was his innate caution, persuaded the Prime Minister to soldier on. It was a huge error. I remember standing with Douglas Hurd in our offices in Old Palace Yard, packed up and ready to move out as all Members must on the day parliament is dissolved. We were listening to Jim Callaghan broadcasting his decision to the nation and were both convinced he had thrown away his best chance of retaining office. From that moment on he was in deep trouble.

As soon as parliament had reassembled a motion of no confidence was tabled and he was saved by the Ulster Unionists. His attempts to enforce a tough statutory pay policy with sanctions was rejected by parliament, caused outrage amongst the unions and ultimately led to the winter of discontent. Night after night pictures filled the television screens showing militant shop stewards deciding who would be allowed treatment in hospitals. Cancer patients were turned away by pickets. Cemeteries were closed and burials banned. Streets were piled with uncollected rubbish and running with rats. In the middle of all this a suntanned Prime Minister returned from a Summit meeting in Guadeloupe in mid-January and ruled out the declaration of a state of emergency. *The Sun* headlined their report, 'Crisis, What Crisis?' and Labour and Jim Callaghan's stock plummeted.

The issue which had united the minority parties around the Labour government was devolution – the legislation which would have created Welsh and Scottish assemblies and devolved power to them. The Liberals and the Scottish and Welsh Nationalists knew that a Conservative government would be opposed to such legislation and felt that their best bet was to prop up the Callaghan government until the assemblies were set up. The bill had occupied weeks on the floor of the House of Commons, and Michael Foot and Francis Pym led the front-bench teams. It was, however, their two young assistants, John Smith and Leon Brittan, who stole the limelight, did most of the donkey work, and in so doing made their parliamentary reputations. They had a great deal in common. Both are first-class advocates. Both had had successful careers as barristers and were Queen's Counsel. Each had the ability to master a complex brief quickly and was a skilled debater. They were so professional that I felt they could have swapped sides and continued to argue the other's case with equal conviction and brilliance.

Probably the most influential contributions to the debate on devolution were not from the front benches, but from two Labour backbenchers, Tam Dalyell and George Cunningham. Tam devised the West Lothian question which even today advocates of devolution have failed properly to answer. In essence Tam's argument was that if the Scots and Welsh had their own assembly, Scottish and Welsh MPs at Westminster would be able to vote and decide on policies in England on which they would have no say in their own constituencies in Scotland, since such decisions would be taken by the devolved assemblies in Edinburgh and Cardiff. Clearly, this arrangement would be very unfair. Between them, Tam and George Cunningham persuaded the House to accept an amendment which said that forty per cent of the electorate of Scotland, and in another bill, Wales, must vote Yes on a referendum before the government could proceed to create devolved assemblies for the two countries. It was the failure to achieve that forty per cent in March 1979 which so infuriated the Nationalists that they decided to commit electoral hara-kiri, and destroy themselves and the government at the same time.

For some time I had been negotiating the sale of my business to Losinger, Switzerland's leading civil engineering company. On 26 March I flew to Switzerland with my business partner and after a day's skiing with the Managing Director of Losinger in Grindelwald we drove to Basle. There we met the Chairman and other directors of the company. We had a very pleasant dinner together and arranged to meet the next morning at their offices. I had always understood that the Swiss conducted negotiations in a very formal manner and it came as a surprise to me when the Chairman handed me a pad and a pen. He told me that they wanted to buy the company, were satisfied with the proposed agreement and all that remained was to settle the price. He suggested that I wrote the sum I would accept on the pad he had given me. He would write the price he was prepared to pay on an identical pad, and we would then swop pads. This we did, and the figure I had put down was £100,000 more than he was offering. After a short discussion we tried again. I put down the same figure, he had increased his by £50,000. We agreed to split the difference. The whole process had taken about twenty minutes. We shook hands, and after a celebratory lunch we flew back to London.

The next day the government faced its third motion of no confidence in only four months. After an electrifying debate in which Margaret Thatcher demonstrated that she was more than a match for Jim Callaghan, the division was called. After twenty minutes the result was announced with an opposition whip reading the result, which meant that the government had been defeated, as it turned out, by just one vote: 311 to 310. It was the first time a government had been forced from office by a vote of the Commons since 1924. The Labour whips were shattered. They had been convinced that they would win and their secret weapon was an Irish Member Frank Maguire who had not previously voted but whom they had persuaded to come over for the occasion. From the moment he arrived he was accompanied everywhere by Walter Harrison or one of his fellow whips who spent the day buying him drinks and looking after him. By 10.0 p.m. he was paralytic and they wheeled him towards the division lobby. To their astonishment he refused to go in and announced that he had only come over to abstain in person! That personal abstention brought down a government.

It had been an extraordinary parliament. The Labour government, with a tiny overall majority which it quickly lost, had survived for four and a half years and had pushed through a very controversial legislative programme. A Prime Minister, Harold Wilson, had resigned and been replaced by the avuncular James Callaghan. A former Prime Minister had been beaten for the leadership of the Conservative Party against all the odds by Margaret Thatcher, who thus became the first woman leader of any political party in Britain. One of the most fascinating aspects of the whole parliament was the growing authority and self-confidence of Margaret Thatcher. Harold Wilson and James Callaghan always treated her with great politeness, but James Callaghan on occasions could appear to be patronizing. This came to an abrupt end when at Prime Minister's questions one day, he made the quip that Mrs Thatcher was 'a one-man band'. Without a moment's hesitation she replied, 'Is that not one more man than the government have got?'

I met Margaret very occasionally during this period. I did write a couple of speeches for her, but I found that I did not enjoy writing speeches for other people and I arranged with Airey Neave, who was then running her private office and who was a good friend of mine, not to be asked again. We met occasionally at the Economic Dining Club and on one occasion, because she had given her driver the evening off, I drove her and her security man back to Flood Street. After he had seen her into her home, I dropped him off at Victoria station. On the way to Victoria I asked him whether he liked working for her. His reply was interesting. 'I like her very much, we all do, and it helps you know. We have to be prepared to step between the would-be assassin and our charge and to put our lives on the line if necessary. My previous Labour boss was impossible. I sometimes think it will be one of ours who gets that bastard.'

She has always inspired that sort of affection and commitment amongst those who work for her, and she is always considerate and kind to her staff. She could be quite brutal in discussion with colleagues and her man-management left a lot to be desired in the latter years, but in these early years, she very skilfully united the party, changed its direction and involved dozens of backbenchers in policy groups, working up policies and new ideas for the manifesto. She also spent a lot of time in the House, meeting backbenchers formally in her office, or informally in the tea room, cafeteria or dining rooms. There was tremendous goodwill towards her in both the parliamentary party and in the party outside the House. There was also a feeling that the party was no longer dominated by a small group, but that she wanted to involve the optimum number of people in policy-making, to listen to the voices of those who had previously felt ignored and spurned.

During these years she developed great confidence and trust in Willie Whitelaw and their working relationship became the axle on which the Conservative Party wheel turned. In spite of all this there were many people who felt that Britain was not ready for a woman Prime Minister, and that having her as our leader would prove a disadvantage to us and provide our opponents with a substantial electoral bonus. Certainly many people in the Labour Party took this view which was why Labour chose to fight a presidential-style election campaign contrasting the reassuring, experienced, down-to-earth Uncle Jim Callaghan with the inexperienced, radical and challenging Margaret Thatcher.

One of Mrs Thatcher's most inspired moves was to bring back as Party Chairman Lord Thorneycroft, who had resigned in 1958 as Chancellor of the Exchequer from Harold Macmillan's government and who had done little politically since losing his seat in 1964. She had great confidence in his abilities to run Central Office and to organize the election campaign, and she valued his experience and political grasp. When she became leader she knew little about the workings of the party or the House for that matter. One day when I was talking to her she suddenly asked me, 'Cecil, what do the whips do ?' When I became Party Chairman I discovered that Central Office was just as much of a mystery to her as it was to the rest of the Party. With Peter Thorneycroft in Central Office, Willie in the House, Humphrey Atkins as Chief Whip, and Keith Joseph as her political mentor, she felt she had a central team covering all aspects of organization and policy. Airey Neave continued to run her own private office, but she brought in David Wolfson to organize the detailed workings of her office and to act as Secretary to the Shadow Cabinet. This role had been carried out by Chris Patten, the head of Research Department, who was rather unceremoniously bundled out to make way for David. From that time on they regarded each other with mutual suspicion, although Chris remained a valued member of her speech-writing team.

My friendship with Norman Tebbit continued to thrive. He had established a reputation as the scourge of Labour Prime Ministers. His chosen sphere of influence was Prime Minister's question time, and week after week he caused ructions in the House with abrasive questions, verging on the insulting. Brave and outspoken, he was scared of nobody, and on a number of occasions reduced Labour Members to such rage that they had to be restrained from physically attacking him. As a friend, I was becoming concerned that his 'bovver boy' image was obscuring his real abilities.

In January 1978 the Labour Party brought in a Civil Aviation Bill which amongst other things introduced a levy on passengers to pay for airport security arrangements. John Nott and I were involved in other legislation at the time, and I suggested that Norman should wind up the debate for the opposition and should take the bill through committee. There was a certain amount of ironic cheering when this was announced on the previous Thursday at the 1922 Committee and there was great curiosity in the House about how Norman would cope. I opened the debate, and he wound up. It was his first speech from the front bench and he made an excellent one, in the course of which he showed great knowledge of the subject and debating skill. Afterwards we had a drink together and celebrated the rebirth of our

Hemel Hempstead partnership and the beginning of his front-bench career.

For my part I had enjoyed the parliament. I found that the more I saw of parliament, the more I liked it. I still had little influence over events, but I now knew the people who had, and I saw them operating at close quarters. I felt that we would win the election and that if we did, I would have a reasonable chance of being included in the government, having been on the front bench for four and a half years. Above all, I had sold my business, and for the first time was owed money by the bank instead of owing money to it. I looked forward to the general election and the years after it with great anticipation.

8 Bosses and Buses

The day after his defeat in the no confidence debate, Jim Callaghan announced that the General Election would be held on 3 May. The next day Airey Neave was murdered when a bomb exploded underneath his car as he drove out of the car park of the House of Commons. Margaret Thatcher was devastated. Airey had played a major part in organizing her leadership victory and he had subsequently become one of her closest confidantes. Her reaction was typical, she became more determined than ever to win the election in Airey's memory and to take on the IRA.

In previous elections I had worked exclusively within my own constituency, but as a front-bench spokesman I was asked to set aside five days for visiting marginal constituencies in different parts of the country. The irony was that my own majority was only 2,228 and in most of the constituencies I went to we had bigger majorities than that. I found the experience very relaxing. I had never really enjoyed asking my constituents to vote for me. I found it much easier to ask other people's constituents to vote for them. It was also interesting to get an insight into the reaction of the electorate in different parts of the country and to compare the ways in which different people campaigned. For the first time I had a personal assistant to work with me for the duration of the election. He was a young barrister called Hartley Booth, who subsequently worked in the Number 10 Policy Unit and succeeded Margaret Thatcher at Finchley on her retirement. Fighting elections can be a nerve-wracking, introspective business and Hartley was a superb antidote to such feelings. One of the most memorable moments of the three-week campaign came on a journey down the M4 to the West Country. Hartley was driving along in the outside lane at a very high speed. He decided to switch on the windscreen de-mister. It had not been used for some time and there was moisture in the system. The windscreen became completely opaque and for a few seconds we were driving blind in the outside lane. Fortunately Hartley's grandfather, General Booth, had been the founder of the Salvation Army, and the Almighty decided to help us. Moments later the windscreen cleared.

Inside the constituency the campaign was running smoothly thanks to the efforts of my agent, Shelagh Ellis, and another excellent Chairman, Nora Spensley. The opinion polls which showed us in the lead throughout were confirmed by our own canvassing, and I felt sure, at all times, that we would win, and we did. We were elected with an overall majority of forty-three, and my own majority increased to 11,798.

The count took place at the Civic Centre in Borehamwood and was excruciatingly slow. It was not completed until 3.0 a.m. and after thanking various friends we arrived home at about 4.15. We slept in the next morning and then spent the day watching the remaining results coming through on the television. We marked the moment when Margaret Thatcher arrived at Downing Street by toasting her health in champagne.

The next day Ann and I went to Twickenham to watch the finals of the Middlesex Sevens with two old friends, Ann and Hugh Thomas. They were surprised that we turned up. They expected me to be sitting at home by the telephone, waiting for a call from Number 10. I explained with all modesty that although I hoped to become a member of the government I certainly did not expect to be a member of the Cabinet. I was sure that Saturday would be spent appointing the Cabinet, and that the other ministers would be appointed over the next few days after discussion with the newly appointed Cabinet ministers. Norman St John Stevas later described to me how he had spent that Saturday. He claimed that he had spent the day hovering near his telephone, thinking about his time in the Shadow Cabinet and Mrs Thatcher's declared intention of cutting public expenditure. The telephone rang, he picked it up, and a voice at the other end said, 'Mr St John Stevas, this is Number 10 Downing Street. Will you accept a reverse charge call from the Prime Minister?' It was not true, of course, but nobody would have been surprised if it had been.

The Cabinet, including Norman St John Stevas as leader of the House and Chancellor of the Duchy of Lancaster, was announced on Saturday evening and contained few surprises. All the former Shadow Cabinet were included except for Teddy Taylor, who had lost Glasgow Cathcart, Tom King and Sally Oppenheim. The biggest surprise was the appointment of Peter Walker as Minister for Agriculture. He had been dropped from the Shadow Cabinet four years earlier. Mrs Thatcher totally disagreed with his views on everything economic, but he was to serve in her Cabinet for ten years. It always seemed to me that she distrusted his views, but admired his competence and management and publicity skills. She also professed a great respect for his political shrewdness, but kept him well away from any of the major political decisions. Some of her friends argued that he was in Cabinet because he could cause less trouble inside than if he were on the back benches. I felt that she saw him in a far more positive light than that, but did not wholly trust him.

On the Sunday a hundred key workers from the constituency came to my home for a party before lunch. It was a way of saying thank you and of celebrating our victory. They all left by two o'clock and after a light lunch, I found myself unable to concentrate on the Sunday newspapers which I tried to read, or the television which I tried to watch. I knew that only seventeen miles away in Downing Street, decisions were being taken which could have a profound effect on my life and on the lives of my family and of my friends in politics, and I was anxious to know what they were. At about four o'clock I decided that I was not going to hear anything that day and that I had better go to my study and finish the audit of the accounts of the Achilles Club of which I had been the Honorary Auditor for some years. I had been working on them for only a few minutes when the telephone rang. It was Number 10, and the Prime Minister came on to the line. After a short chat about the result she said she would like me to join John Nott at the Department of Trade as Minister of State with special responsibility for trade policy and overseas trade. She also told me that Norman Tebbit would be joining the same department as Parliamentary Undersecretary for aviation and shipping. I was delighted with both pieces of news.

On the Monday, which was a Bank Holiday, I was attending a small celebration party in Potters Bar at the home of Eric and Joan Muddle. When the telephone rang it was a call for me. A very efficient-sounding person was at the other end of the telephone and introduced herself as Mrs Christine Bargery, my ministerial Private Secretary. She asked me if I would be going into the office that day and explained that even though it was a holiday the office was fully staffed and they were looking forward to meeting me. I arranged to go to the office in Victoria Street at three o'clock.

I found that my private office consisted of Christine Bargery, an Assistant Private Secretary and three other staff who looked after the diary and correspondence. I was shown around the office which had previously been occupied by Stanley Clinton-Davis and I realized that the people who were now working for me had only a few days before been loyally working for a Labour government. They appeared to make the switch without any difficulty and I was handed two very thick briefing books. One set out the issues covering the part of the department for which I was responsible, and the other covered general departmental issues. We were committed to abolishing the Price Commission and the Ministry of Prices and Consumer Affairs had been merged with the Department of Trade. Sally Oppenheim who had shadowed this portfolio in opposition came into the department as Minister of State and the team was completed by Reginald Eyre, a Birmingham solicitor who had responsibility for market regulation and company law.

We were to work together for the next twenty months until John Nott was transferred to defence in the first reshuffle in January 1981. He was pleasant to work with and determined that we should act together as a team and that the department should not operate as a series of isolated units. We had regular meetings of all ministers and the two PPSs, David Hunt who worked for John, and Michael Spicer, who came to work for Sally and agreed also to help me. John encouraged everybody to express their views about the subject under discussion and we took him at his word. He was one of a small group of ministers who breakfasted with the new Prime Minister very regularly during our first two years in office and was regarded throughout the government as a possible future Chancellor of the Exchequer. He was very keen to play a full part in Cabinet, and told me at our first meeting that he wanted me to be a virtually full-time Minister of Trade and to spend a great deal of my time travelling abroad promoting British exports and bilateral trade relations. He reserved for himself responsibility for Australia, New Zealand, Brazil, Nigeria, India, Korea, Japan and Nepal. Nepal was in fact the top of his list of priorities. He had served in the Gurkhas and had formed a tremendous attachment for them and their country and, although they were not a top priority as trading partners, there was no country in which he took more interest. He also told me that he did not like Communists and did not intend to visit any Communist country and that one of my first jobs would be to lead the British side of the

Anglo-Soviet Joint Commission the following October. His other bombshell was to tell me that I would be leading the British delegation to the fifth United Nations Conference on Trade and Development and would be leaving in three weeks for the Philippines.

We had our first question time on 21 May and I answered question two which had been tabled by Dennis Skinner. It was about Britain's trade deficit with the other EEC countries and Dennis Skinner, who has throughout the years remained consistent on this subject, said that the deficit provided evidence that we should leave the Community. I disagreed with him and explained that the deficit was caused by our low productivity and our lack of competitiveness, and that it was only by improving both that we could reduce the deficit.

I found question time a very odd experience. Having answered the first question one felt that one had done one's job. The next supplementary questioner was already speaking as one sat down from answering the first and if one was not very careful one could miss the second question. It took me a little time to get used to the apparently incessant stream of questions and from the first day I became convinced that once I had read the initial answer to the question there was no time to bother with the large briefing book which the department loves to give ministers: I had to brief myself before I went into the chamber. There was no time to look at it once I was there. I therefore gave up using the briefing book, a practice I was to follow for the rest of my ministerial career. One or two acquaintances on the other side of the House told me subsequently that it is quite intimidating for a minister not to appear to need the book since it gives the impression that the minister is totally comfortable with the subject, and confident of his ability to answer.

Four days later I was due to leave for Manila. I decided that it was a very long journey to make just to go to UNCTAD V and so the department arranged for me to go to Indonesia on my way out and to call in on Singapore and Malaysia on the way back for bilateral talks aimed at improving our trade. The day that I left for Manila was particularly hectic. I had to speak at a conference of building-equipment manufacturers at ten o'clock in the morning, then reply to an adjournment debate in the House on South Africa before leaving from Heathrow at about 4.0 p.m. Speeches had been written for me for both the conference and the adjournment debate and late the previous night I had read through them. The first was relatively easy. I had owned a business that manufactured building equipment, and I knew a fair amount about the subject and the prospects for the industry and rewrote it very quickly. The second, on South Africa, had been drafted by civil servants who clearly assumed that the new government would continue to pursue the Labour government's policy. I had a lot of papers to clear before I went abroad and my packing to do and there just was not time to rewrite the speech. I therefore telephoned the Duty Officer in the department asking him to arrange for the people who had written the speech to meet me in the department at eight o'clock the next morning. It was by then past midnight.

When I walked into my office the next morning both the officials were there. I explained to them what was wrong with the speech and where my ideas were different from those of our predecessors. We shared their detestation for apartheid but, unlike the previous government, which had argued that we should be reducing our investment in South Africa, we believed that the way to promote peaceful change was to promote economic growth and that in turn needed more foreign investment. I explained that when I was in South Africa three years earlier I had become convinced that the expansion of that economy, creating a demand for skilled labour which could not be met from the white population, was forcing changes in their despicable job-reservation laws. Helping those economic pressures to build up was the best way to ensure the changes we sought in South Africa's approach to its black citizens.

I then left to make my speech at the Royal Garden Hotel. By the time I arrived back a completely different speech on South Africa had been drafted to reflect my views and which had been cleared by the Foreign Office. The speech explained that the new government's policy was that 'civil trade with other countries should be determined by commercial considerations, not by the character of the governments of those countries'. To illustrate the point, the speech referred to the meetings which John Nott and I had had with delegates from fourteen countries 'representing a very wide spectrum of political systems of government' since we had been in office: 'The one thing that we have in common with all of them is that we trade with them and that economic relationship in no way implies approval or disapproval of those countries' policies, internal or external, or of their politics. I suggest that that is the context within which our trading relationship with South Africa is and should continue to be determined.'

The drafting of the South Africa speech provided me with my first evidence that top civil servants are extremely adaptable and capable of working at very high speed under pressure. I also realized something which again stayed with me during the whole of my ministerial career, which was that civil servants are advisers and implementers of the policy. They regard the making of it as entirely a matter for ministers. They are, however, very resilient and prepared to argue their case. For example, we were committed to the abolition of the Price Commission and, a few days after we had moved into the department, we had had a meeting with the Director of the Price Commission and his senior officials. They had just devoted six years of their lives to the Commission. They had seen a Prices Board started under the Wilson government, and then abolished by Ted Heath. They had only a year or so later been asked by the Heath government to create the Commission. The Labour Party had come to power and greatly strengthened it and here they were with a new government committed to abolishing it. They felt that the experience of previous years had proved that, whatever their initial views, governments of both colours eventually came to the conclusion that they needed such a body and they were genuinely trying not only to protect their creation, the Commission, but also to prevent us from making another mistake. They therefore suggested various ways in which we could modify its activities but retain it so that, if we needed it, it would be there to be used. We were adamant that it should go. We felt it had operated in a damaging and capricious way and had not succeeded in its objective of limiting price increases. It had at the very best deferred them for a short time but at a very high cost to industry and industrial investment.

In opposition we had worked on producing a competition policy which would prevent market manipulation and cartels and would allow industrialists to get on with the job which they know best of running their own businesses profitably and efficiently. We were determined, now that we were in government, to implement the policy. The arguments were heated and they went on for a couple of days, but John Nott, backed up by the rest of us, was adamant, and the officials finally accepted that the days of the Price Commission had come to an end. John Nott announced the abolition of price controls and the Price Commission in the Queen's Speech debate on 15 May. It was to me a wonderful example of what Enoch Powell once described in a speech as the 'inertia of the status quo'. Had we

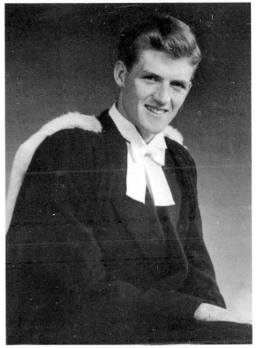

Schoolboy, aged 14

Graduating from Cambridge, 1955

Receiving Victor Ludorum from Mrs Timberlake, 1948

Training at Fenners, 1954

Mary 10, Emma 8 and Joanna 6 watching production of the *Northampton Chronicle and Echo*

Family skiing holiday, January 1970

Election Night, Northampton, June 1970

Below: European Parliamentary Ski Race, March 1972

Bottom: Arriving with Ann and the girls at the House of Commons to take my seat, December 1970

As Minister of Trade, chairing British side of Anglo-Soviet Joint Commission with Norman Lamont (right) and British Ambassador to the Soviet Union, Sir Curtis Keeble (left), Moscow, October 1979

Visit to Fiddler's Ferry power station, accompanying Vice Premier Yu Qiuli of China, 1979

Meeting President Videla of Argentina during trade visit, 8 August 1980

Above Right: Presenting English language laboratory to University of Cameroon, Yaoundé, 1981

Trade promotion visit to Saudi Arabia, 1981

Breakfast at the Old Vicarage with Ann and Joanna the day after becoming
Party Chairman, September 1981

As Chancellor of the Duchy of Lancaster accompanying the Queen on a visit
to the Duchy estates in Staffordshire, June 1982

Running in Battersea Park, September 1982

Below: Meeting with President Reagan, in the Cabinet Room at the White House, with the Chairman of the Norwegian Conservative Party, March 1983

Below Right: Celebrating election victory, Borehamwood, June 1987

Visit to Morecambe Bay gas platform as Energy Secretary, October 1987

Above Right: Landing in 'Hong Kong' in flight simulator as Transport Secretary, May 1990

With Mrs Thatcher, July 1991, at Jeffrey and Mary Archer's silver wedding party

not had the commitment to get rid of the Commission and the determination to see that commitment put into practice, then the arguments for maintaining what was there, but adjusting it slightly, might have prevailed.

The new government moved swiftly. Not only were price controls abolished, pay controls, dividend controls and exchange controls also went and a ban was announced on recruitment to the Civil Service. A huge government-wide exercise was put in hand to reduce the size and the scope of the Civil Service. In the Department of Trade each minister was asked to look at the areas for which he was responsible, to identify how savings of five, ten, fifteen or twenty per cent of the staff could be achieved and to pinpoint the functions that would need to be abandoned to make the necessary savings. I wondered how the Civil Service would react to being asked to identify how up to twenty per cent of them could be put out of a job. We all felt apprehensive about this and at the meeting of the ministers and the top civil servants of the department at which the findings were discussed, John Nott introduced the discussion by saying that he understood that the officials might resent the exercise. To my surprise one of the senior officials contradicted him and said that they had found the exercise very rewarding. He argued that taking a fresh look at their responsibilities had not only been interesting, but it had shown them that there was very large scope for savings and improvement.

The ideal civil servant always seems to me to be someone who sees life as a series of intellectual challenges. New governments give new challenges and bring a new excitement to their lives. Nevertheless, I am sure some of the changes we were proposing were resented, but that resentment was never shown.

There is one aspect of working with civil servants that I did find trying. No Civil Service job ever seems to be an end in itself. It is all part of the process of training for the next job. I lost track of the number of times over the years that I discussed personnel changes with senior civil servants and heard the expression: 'This move will be very good for his or her career development.' Career development seems to be the number one priority, ranking way above actually doing any particular job. This means that however good the person is at the job he or she has, they will only be there for a matter of time before they are moved on to the next, and probably totally unrelated, job. Bright young people are put in the minister's private office because it would be very good for them, and they are usually very good but they totally lack experience. Perhaps the best example I can give of this was after the 1983 election when I was merging the two departments of trade and industry and for a time the private offices of both my predecessors were combined. At this stage I had no fewer than four people with Oxbridge first-class honours degrees working as my Private Secretaries, and arranging an itinerary which took me from London to Carlisle and then down to Southampton involved a committee meeting of all these bright young people which took several hours. This compared with my experience in Central Office when Shirley Oxenbury, my outstanding personal assistant who headed up my much smaller private office, could draw on her experience to arrange a much more comprehensive itinerary in about half an hour.

Civil servants love to approach every challenge from first principles. Nevertheless I found them very stimulating to work with, very loyal and incredibly hard working. It was easy to caricature our drive to reduce the size of the Civil Service as hostility to civil servants, and there were undoubtedly members of the government who were initially antagonistic to the Civil Service, but most of us recognized that a government which is spending over £200,000 million needs a strong capable Civil Service with first-class leaders to adminster the spending of such a huge sum. We also felt that the increased size of the Civil Service reflected the different views of our government and the Labour government about the role of the state in our society. I touched on this in a speech to the European Management Forum in April 1980.

We have got to change the instinctive reflex in this country from 'What is the government going to do about it?' to 'What can I do about it?' Three decades of soaring taxation, increasing government intervention and subsidies, and proliferating controls have cumulatively reduced incentives and weakened independence and enterprise in Britain to the point where expectations of the state as prop, protector and universal provider have pervaded almost our entire society.

Our aim was to reduce the size of the Civil Service by reducing the role of the state, to ask fewer civil servants to do less, not fewer to do more.

I had never been to the Far East before and since I was the first minister in the government to travel in that direction since the election it was decided that I would go out on Concorde which had just started to fly from London to Singapore. The flight stopped in Bahrain before going on to Singapore, and when I got off the plane in Bahrain I was surprised to find our Ambassador and a member of the Bahrain government waiting on the tarmac to greet me. I was ushered into the VIP lounge and, although it was the middle of the night, we launched into discussions about the new government's policy and the general election result. Fortunately I had assiduously been reading the huge briefing books which had been prepared and knew a reasonable amount about Anglo-Bahrain trade.

We landed at Singapore at four o'clock in the morning and again I was surprised to find our High Commissioner and a member of the Singapore government waiting for me even though we were only stopping over for a couple of hours on our way to Indonesia. I had always had a very relaxed view about travelling and the formality involved in travelling as a minister took a certain amount of getting used to and I must say sometimes seemed rather unnecessary. However, I found that along with the unwelcome formality there were some bonuses. One never had to worry about passport, luggage, boarding passes, seat allocations, customs – all those things were taken care of – and every journey seemed to start and end in a VIP suite!

We stayed in Indonesia for four days before going on to Manila. During those days I had a series of meetings with various members of the Indonesian government at which we discussed bilateral issues affecting our two countries. I found these meetings very unsatisfactory. I was working from a prepared brief and the Indonesian minister would be doing the same, usually with a slightly less adequate brief. There was very little opportunity to get to know the person and one felt that the subjects raised could almost have been covered in correspondence and certainly by our Ambassador. But I found subsequently that having made contact with a number of ministers, who almost invariably made a return visit to Britain, one started to develop useful personal friendships, some of which continue to this day. I came to the conclusion that if I was going to make these visits, then I would prefer to make them more applied and specific and to bring with me businessmen who had the prospects of increasing their business with the country concerned. After this initial sortie overseas, I was always accompanied by a carefully chosen group whose company prospects could be boosted by ministerial support.

There were a number of amusing incidents during my visit to

Indonesia. I found, for instance, that our Ambassador in Indonesia lived in a fine house which had a small guest house halfway down the garden. To our mutual embarrassment, Christine Bargery and myself, who scarcely knew each other, were to be in this house alone and unaccompanied. At a rather grand reception which the Ambassador gave in my honour, he persisted in introducing me in the following manner: 'This is the minister and this is Mrs Bargery who is travelling with him.' After he had done this a few times I suggested he might introduce us a little differently since a number of eyebrows were already being raised.

I saw little of Indonesia, although on the Sunday we did travel to a small holiday bungalow which the embassy owned in the foothills about a hundred miles from Jakarta, and one got a glimpse of the countryside and of the scale of the problems which the government was trying to tackle in providing a reasonable standard of living for a huge and fast-growing population. It was an interesting introduction to the problems of the third world and of developing countries.

UNCTAD V had been going on for almost three weeks when I arrived in Manila. We had a deputation of about fifty attending the conference. The first minister I met was the Federal German Minister for Economic Affairs, Count Lambsdorff. His opening remarks were not promising: 'I have been here for three weeks now,' he said, 'and I still do not know why I am here.' The reason for his frustration quickly became apparent to me. The group of seventy-seven, the loose alliance of the developing countries, had been unable to agree on a common approach to the conference, or even on who their spokesmen should be, and the representatives of the developed countries were effectively sitting around waiting for the conference proper to begin once they had made up their minds. A large number of working groups had been set up and were beavering away, but very little progress had been made. Veterans of earlier conferences accepted that this was quite normal and that progress would only really be made within the last three days and most of it on the last day.

On my first day there I gave a press conference and found myself facing more than 500 journalists from all over the world. I had never given a press conference before. The journalists were bored out of their minds. They had been waiting for something to happen for four weeks and had had little to report. As a new minister in Mrs Thatcher's government I had a certain novelty value but I also faced a critical audience. Judith Hart, the Minister for Overseas Development in the Labour administration, had been expected to be the star of the conference and to arrive bearing promises of all sorts of additional aid and commitment. I arrived as a representative of a government which was very sceptical about the value of indiscriminate aid to third world countries and was committed to reducing our aid programme, but at the same time to increasing the opportunities for developing countries to expand their trade and to improving the prospects for investment by private companies. We planned to do this in two ways : by abolishing exchange controls, thus leaving companies free to invest where they would like and, secondly, by urging developing countries to improve investor protection so that people could invest both their money and their skills in the countries which so desperately needed both. It was a message which was only partially welcomed, but was distinctive.

My day seemed to consist of attending a series of ministerial meetings in the conference centre and also holding bilateral discussions with ministers from individual countries. I combined this with a number of calls on the Philippine ministers with whom I discussed ways of improving trade between our countries. One of the most interesting meetings I had was with the Argentinian Minister for Agriculture. He complained bitterly about the EEC's Common Agricultural Policy. Our membership of the Community had meant a huge reduction in Britain's trade with Argentina. They accepted with some reluctance that our markets would be closed to their products, but what they objected to was that we were ruining the markets which were open to them outside the EEC by dumping surplus EEC beef in those markets. His point was that Argentinian farmers were paying a very high price for the protectionism and the subsidies which were such a feature of the CAP then. They still are now, and even in 1992 we are putting at risk the world negotiations on trade liberalization because of continued reluctance to make our agricultural industry within the Community face up to the challenge of competition and to abandon subsidies and protectionism.

The conference was due to end at lunchtime on Saturday and was making little progress when I received an invitation to go and meet President Marcos. He had invited ministers from the USA, France, Japan, Germany and the UK to meet him. His aim was to urge us to make concessions so that the conference could be saved from being the disaster that it promised to be. We waited in an anteroom in his palace until he had finished lunch. As we sat there the Japanese minister took off his spectacles and a small screw which holds the arm to the frame fell out on to the very deeply piled carpet. We all got on our knees and started feeling gently with our fingers for this tiny screw. The Japanese minister found it himself, at which point Otto Lambsdorff quickly produced a Swiss Army penknife from his pocket and screwed the spectacles together. As he handed them back to the Japanese minister he said, 'That is the first useful thing I have done since I have been here.' Seconds later the President arrived. We were all laughing at the thought of what he would have seen had he arrived a couple of minutes earlier. Had he done so, he would have found us crawling around on our hands and knees on his carpet.

After the meeting with him, at which he did make the request which we had expected, I was asked to stay behind and was shown into another anteroom where the President's wife was waiting to see me. She wanted to talk about Mrs Thatcher and the general election. She was at that time the Governor of Manila and the Minister for Human Resources and clearly had ambitions to succeed her husband. She was very intrigued that a party led by a woman had been able to win our general election, and she wanted to discuss the campaign and also to know more about Mrs Thatcher. She, too, was anxious that the conference should be a success. The government had invested huge sums in staging it and needed a result which could be presented as some sort of triumph. In fact, after forty-eight frantic hours, worthwhile agreement was reached on a range of subjects, including an affirmation of the determination of all countries to resist protectionist pressures and a commitment to a programme of technology transfer from the developed world to the developing nations. The British delegation, brilliantly organized by a Deputy Secretary from the Department of Trade, William Knighton, played a major role in producing such agreement as there was.

The conference ended with a series of statements from ministers. I spoke for the British delegation, but the final moments were dominated by the Chinese minister who made a most violent attack on Russia and Russian imperialism.

On my way home I stopped off in Malaysia and Singapore. I found that on an individual basis one was able to reach agreement on a whole range of subjects on which at UNCTAD V, on a multilateral basis, there had seemed no possibility at all of agreement. During fourteen hectic days I had visited four countries, met ministers from about fifty countries and developed much clearer views on the need to remove barriers to trade and investment between developed and developing countries. It seemed to me that the discussion about relations between the latter had been dominated for far too long by a single figure – the UN target figure for official aid. The relationship is, and needs to be, a much more complex one than that. If the relationship is discussed simply in terms of aid then it becomes very patronizing indeed with the developed countries being the generous donors and the developing countries the hopefully grateful recipients. Trade flows between developed and developing countries are fifteen times larger than aid flows, and infinitely more important. Most developing countries want to sell as well as to buy. Their needs are enormous. The range of products they can offer is limited and they need access to our markets which is as unrestricted as possible. They also need investment and with the investment, almost more important than money, they need the transfer of technology and the marketing and management skills which developed countries have in profusion but which are in desperately short supply in the third world. They also need loans and access to finance at reasonable rates on generous terms. Our official aid compares not unfavourably with that of other countries, but in trade, investment and finance we compare more than favourably with most. I found it particularly repugnant that the Labour Party, which argued so passionately for increased aid, was under pressure from the trade unions, becoming increasingly restrictive and protectionist.

I found the argument that competition from poorer countries was unfair because their wage rates were so much lower than ours particularly obnoxious. The idea that poverty is an advantage also seemed to me very unattractive, and I attacked that thinking and continue to attack it wherever I find it. It is interesting that the European Community's Social Chapter is based very firmly on the notion that we must have identical conditions throughout the Community if we are to have fair competition. Markets work on the principle of comparative advantage, and an attempt to impose uniform standards on diverging economies can only lead to disaster and a decrease in competitiveness for the poor. If the Community were to succeed in imposing common internal standards it would be only a matter of time before those standards were used as an argument for discrimination against trade with other countries which have not adopted or cannot afford the Community standards.

Mrs Thatcher's arrival in government coincided with a world recession, in part triggered by high energy costs, but British industry faced particular domestic problems. Large sections of it, such as the steel industry and the motor industry, had only survived because of massive government support which quite clearly could not be continued indefinitely. British industry was already uncompetitive and its productivity compared very unfavourably with that of other countries. To all its other problems was added the problem of a very strong pound which made imports cheap and exports more expensive. Many people argued that the government should have cut interest rates and weakened the pound. I argued very strongly against this. The reason why the pound was strong was because the money markets believed for the first time in a long time that Britain had a government which was committed to sound money and not just paying lip service to the concept under instructions from the IMF. Although the government had not set interest rates which charged the borrower a real rate of interest, they did increase interest rates enough to reassure the markets that they meant what they said about sound money. Because people believed the government, the pound was very, very firm, but I have always felt that the critics ignored the simple fact that you cannot have policies which would produce partially sound money, you either believe in sound money or you do not. The government was seen to believe in it and the pound was strong. Had it taken the action our critics advocated, it would have been seen to be untrustworthy and the pound would have plummeted. The attempt to find a halfway house would have been disastrous. The markets either want to hold your currency or they do not. This did mean that if industry could not get help through a soggy exchange rate, then it increasingly looked to the government for protection against foreign imports and it was tempting to try to help. Certainly the minister who did intervene was seen by industry as an effective member of the government. The government that argued the case for the open trading system was received with less enthusiasm. I became very familiar with the argument about the uneven playing field and the fact that in Britain we were still playing cricket while the rest of the world was practising karate.

I understood the frustrations of British industry, but I was convinced that the way to improve our position was to root out other people's protectionism rather than emulate it. I set out the government's position in a series of speeches to different branches of indus-try and I found that after a time, although one did not get agreement, people did begin to recognize the validity of the arguments. All this had its lighter moments. The top civil servant in the Department of Trade responsible for trade policy was a rather unconventional character named Robin Gray. He told me that after we had been in the department about three months, the senior civil servants had a meeting to discuss the new ministers. Robin was always very out-spoken and one night over a drink he told me what he had said about me. He said, 'We are in a hell of a mess. We have a bloody idealist. He believes in the open trading system.' He said it with a smile and I took it as a compliment, which I think it was meant to be.

A few months later Margaret Thatcher came to visit the Depart-ment of Trade. She had decided to visit every Whitehall department to try to get a better understanding of the work of each department and to get the measure of the senior civil servants who worked in them. The first hour was spent with the Permanent Secretary, the Deputy Secretaries, of which there were five, and the ministers. The ministers sat on one side of the table, the officials on the other. She asked each of them in turn to give a description of what they and the part of the department they were responsible for did and what its immediate objectives were. After each had spoken I noticed that she was putting three dots under some names and a line under others. I came to the conclusion the line meant good and the three dots meant suspect. Robin lolled about on his chair. He was always studiously untidy and never wore a suit, and after his first intervention three very large dots appeared under his name. Subsequently a general discussion developed and she began to realize that she had made an error. By the end of the discussion Robin had two lines drawn under his name which I assumed meant outstanding. He subsequently travelled with her to the Far East on a prime-ministerial visit and she became a great admirer of his.

Some time after this he had been negotiating with the Spanish about quotas on British motorcars and a meeting was held in the Cabinet room at which about half a dozen people were present to discuss what then seemed to be a very important issue. Margaret Thatcher was not satisfied with the deal and, calling him by his first name, Robin, which was in itself unusual, she asked him whether he felt he could improve on what was on offer. I thought for one moment that he was going to address her as Margaret but, in the nick of time, he remembered and called her Prime Minister. He then said, 'Yes, I can improve the offer, but I want your authority to go back and reach agreement and if I can come back with that agreement I want to be sure you will accept it.' 'Of course, Robin,' she replied, 'if it is the best you can do, it is the best that can be done.' I could not help thinking that there would have been very few of her ministers in whom she would have had such confidence and that Robin had made great progress from the first minutes of their first meeting.

After a few weeks a pattern began to establish itself in my ministerial life. I spent roughly one week each month travelling to different countries all over the world, ranging from the Gulf to China, the German Democratic Republic to Argentina, Yugoslavia to Cameroon, Saudi Arabia to the United States. On all these visits I took with me a group of about six businessmen who either had interests in the country we visited and wished to expand them, or were seeking opportunities to win projects, or open up joint ventures with those countries. We found that the formula was very successful, that businessmen travelling with a minister could, in the space of a couple of days, actually meet the ministers and top officials whom they would otherwise have spent months trying to contact. I found the ministers in the countries I visited were much happier discussing specific possibilities for increasing trade or investment than exchanging generalities about the need for cooperation between developed and developing countries. From a purely domestic political point of view, businessmen saw for themselves that politicians did understand their problems and were prepared to work with them to improve their position. The cost to the government was miniscule, but I believe these visits generated great goodwill and business, and I believe that all my successors have continued to follow a similar pattern.

The country I was most pleased to leave was Iraq. My host had proved his loyalty to the President by shooting a number of fellow Cabinet colleagues who were accused of planning a coup against the President. It was a very sombre, unforthcoming person who met me at the airport on my arrival in Baghdad. For the next three days he never volunteered a single remark or opened a conversation or discussion. On the second day of my visit I asked him if he spoke any language other than his own. His reply was typical: 'No, do you?' I then explained that I was having French conversation lessons for two hours a week in my office in London with a young, attractive Frenchwoman who was engaged to an Englishman and was getting married shortly. He received this information with a nod. Two days later as we were driving out to the airport early in the morning, he finally started a conversation. Without any warning he suddenly asked me, 'What is the name of your French teacher?' He had clearly been thinking about this for a day or two. He subsequently came to Britain as my guest and when discreet enquiries were made about what he would like as a present, he told us he would like a new pistol. We arranged for him to receive one after his return to Baghdad.

I stayed in a state guest house in Baghdad which had huge television sets in each room and I occasionally got a chance to watch the local television stations. Saddam Hussein dominated every news bulletin. Each day he was seen greeting some foreign visitor or some senior Iraqi, but I noticed that each night a different aspect of Saddam Hussein was shown. One night he was walking into a fruit shop to discuss the price of oranges with the terrified shopkeeper. Another night he was sitting in his car without an escort waiting for the traffic lights to turn from red to green. I asked our Ambassador what the significance of this less than exciting news item was. He explained to me that no Iraqi minister ever waited for the traffic lights to turn from red to green. If a minister approached a road junction he did so with a number of outriders who stopped all the traffic so that he could go straight through the lights. This was extremely unpopular with the local people and Saddam Hussein was demonstrating that while his junior ministers might demand these privileges, he, as President, was quite happy to wait along with his fellow citizens. Whenever he appeared the same music was played in the background and one saw at first hand the brainwashing of the Iraqi people that was conducted on his behalf.

At the time, the Iraqis were seen as a bastion against the wild men who were coming to power in Iran. The country was potentially very rich. As Mesopotamia it had been one of the great grain-producing areas of the world and millions of people had enjoyed a high standard of living in what was then a fertile and pleasant land. One of the British projects which I visited was a project to irrigate thousands of hectares of what appeared to be desert with water from the Tigris and the Euphrates. It was astonishing just how fertile this apparently desert land became as a result of irrigation, and many hundreds of acres of tomatoes, and other fruit and vegetables grew in profusion. The country also had oil and gas and seemed at that time destined to prosper.

They were also keen to increase their civil trade with us. The occasion of my visit was in fact to open the British pavilion at the Baghdad Fair and British exports of non-military goods seemed to have good prospects. The Iraqis had no overseas debt and paid cash, but the regime even then was oppressive and brutal and I was very pleased when my visit came to an end.

The other visit which made a strong impression on me was my visit to Moscow in the autumn of 1979 to lead the British delegation to the eighth meeting of the British-Soviet Joint Commission. Relations between the two countries were not at all good and, symbolically, the day I arrived they had their first snow of the winter and the temperature was freezing. The political climate was, if anything, even cooler, and I spent three days meeting a succession of surly Russian ministers who told me that as long as Mrs Thatcher was our leader they did not want to increase their trade with us, and that in any case British goods were of inferior quality. For good measure they added that our country was always on strike and that they regarded Britain as the sick man of Europe. For three days during a visit to the Bolshoi, meetings of the Joint Commission and bilateral meetings with ministers, all at that time hard-line Communists, I and my colleagues fought back. Even at the airport on the day we were leaving, my Russian counterpart again started arguing that the west was doomed, Communism was infinitely superior to capitalism. After about two to three minutes of this I interrupted : 'You never give up do you? We are leaving in ten minutes time and I do not want to spend the last ten minutes arguing.' To my surprise and that of our Ambassador, Sir Curtis Keeble, he then said, 'Let me tell you a story. There was a scorpion standing by the side of a river when a camel came along and the scorpion asked the camel if he would carry him across the river. The camel said, "No, I will not carry you because you sting and you kill." "I won't kill you, you would be helping me to get across the river." The camel being a trusting beast said, "Come on," but when they got across the river, for no apparent reason the scorpion struck the camel with his sting. As the camel fell over into the river, the scorpion fell off its back, and just before it drowned the camel said, "Why did you do that?" The scorpion said, "I cannot help myself, it is my nature." ' The minister concluded this chilling story by saying, 'And I tell you that story against ourselves ; that is the way we are.'

I had always had low expectations of the USSR, but I was shocked by the drabness of the lives of the people, the appalling quality of the goods with which the shops were filled and the greyness of the city. I was also surprised at the privileges which ministers, members of the Politburo and visiting ministers enjoyed. At that time in all the main streets of Moscow there was a lane which was reserved for these privileged people, of which I found myself temporarily one. There was a policeman standing at each set of traffic lights and, if he saw a car approaching in this reserved lane, all traffic was stopped to allow it to take precedence. On the second day I said to my Private Secretary, 'Well, now I know the difference between a Communist and a free society. In a Communist society the reserved lanes are for the bosses, and in a free society like ours it is for the buses!'

The only colourful moment was a visit to the Bolshoi where we saw a magnificent production of *Boris Godunof* superbly sung. It was the most opulent and expensive-looking production I have ever seen. The contrast between the richness of the stage and the members of the audience was stark.

The most controversial visit I made was to Argentina and Chile. Although I had by this time visited the USSR, the GDR, Poland and Roumania without any complaint from anyone, the fact that I was going to Argentina and Chile caused an uproar amongst the left, and led to letters to me and to the Prime Minister from, amongst others, the TUC. I pointed out that trade in non-military goods with a country did not imply any sort of approval of its political system, but if we were to restrict our trade to western-style democracies there would be very few countries in the world with whom we could do business, certainly none in Eastern Europe, nor most of Africa, South America or many parts of the Far East. I accepted that the regimes in Argentina and Chile were repressive, but pointed out they were no more repressive than the hard-line Communist countries which I visited with the approval of the TUC. Both countries at the time had military governments which had total political control, but each of them was trying desperately to liberalize its economy, privatize its industries and reduce the barriers to trade. One saw in them this apparently conflicting desire to maintain tight political control while diffusing economic power. The economic supremo of Argentina, Dr Martinez de Hoz, was allowed to operate without military interference and was effectively Prime Minister. We believed that if he could produce economic success then he would become the next President. We were supporting him because we believed that by peaceful means he could supplant the military regime which had a half-hearted commitment to handing over power to a civilian government.

Chile was in a similar position. General Pinochet had total political control, but he had handed over the running of the economy to a group of Chicago-school economists who had transformed it. The economy was booming, barriers to trade had been removed and the Chilean people were allowed total economic freedom. Unfortunately after several years of great economic progress they tied their currency to the US dollar and paid a very heavy price. Both countries had strong connections with the UK, and in each country there were substantial bodies of British settlers who had been there for several generations, including in Argentina some relatives of my wife whose family had arrived there from Scotland more than a hundred years earlier.

In 1980 I went to Cameroon and Gabon. The Ambassador in Cameroon told me shortly after I arrived that Cameroon had the highest use per person of pharmaceuticals, pills and potions anywhere in the world, and within twenty-four hours I was to discover why. We went on from Cameroon to Gabon where we met, amongst others, President Bongo. Gabon is a tiny country with the highest per capita income in the whole of Africa because it has very substantial reserves of oil and gas. Unfortunately, in an attempt to impress his fellow heads of state, President Bongo had invested huge sums in creating a gigantic conference centre and residences for all his fellow heads of state and their staffs. This almost bankrupted the country. One could very rarely go wrong if one called the minister one was speaking to Mr Bongo. The Foreign Minister and the Finance Minister were his brothers. Other members of his family had other government offices. The leading dancer of the Gabon National Ballet was Miss Bongo, and the leading pop singer on Gabonese radio was Master Bongo. There were times when one felt that the country really was a small family business.

President Bongo was very tiny and extremely aware of being tiny and when we called on him in his impressive palace, which was also the headquarters of the national guard and the home of the national radio station, we waited in an anteroom alongside some very high doors. They were hydraulically operated and whipped back to reveal the President standing at a level about three steps above that of his guests. I had taken with me, amongst others, the Sales Director of

Landrover. I introduced him and later in the conversation the President said to him, 'If I ordered 1,000 Landrovers, when could you deliver them?', to which Jack Reardon replied, 'In about two months.' Landrover had just completed a huge modernization programme and had enormously increased their capacity. We explained this to the President. He then asked how long it would take for a further 1,000 to be converted into ambulances. Jack replied, 'Three months.' At this point the President picked up the telephone and spoke to his brother, the Finance Minister. 'I am going to order 2,000 Landrovers.' We could only hear one side of the conversation. 'Parliament? What has this to do with parliament? You order them and I will sort out parliament.' It was an impressive display of authority, but I am afraid the order never actually came through. We did, however, make a breakthrough and British suppliers received substantial orders for the second phase of the trans-Gabonese railway.

The next day we travelled on the railway for about a hundred miles through some of the most lush and beautiful forests in the world. We stopped at a small village and from there we flew to Dr Albert Schweitzer's settlement at Lambaréné. It was very moving to see the simple cottage in which this great doctor, musician and missionary had spent so much of his life.

One of the highlights of the visit took place on the second day. We had only recently opened an embassy in Gabon and the Ambassador had a small office and a very unpretentious, unreliable British car, on the front of which, when he rode in it, was a Union flag. We were driving down the road past the President's palace when the car broke down. The battery was absolutely flat and it would not restart. The Ambassador and I climbed out of the back and started pushing it, and eventually the driver was able to jump-start it. We were very relieved that the usual posse of journalists and photographers were not with us on this occasion. We thought it might set back the export of British cars which were already virtually non-existent in that part of the world.

During the two years I was Trade Minister I visited more than forty countries in many different parts of the world and learnt at first hand that although, as the slogan said, 'Exporting can be fun', it is always extremely hard work. I also shared the experience of many an export Sales Director who, on returning to the office after an extensive trip, is received with the comment, 'While you have been enjoying yourself, we have been working here.' On one occasion I met Mrs

Thatcher in the division lobby. I had been speaking that day at the World Economic Forum at Davos in Switzerland. I had originally hoped to have a weekend skiing before my speech, but it was not possible and I had arrived late the night before, wrote my speech overnight, spoke early the next morning and left immediately to get back to London for an important vote. The Prime Minister greeted me in the lobby with 'Hello, Cecil, I haven't seen you for some time; where have you been recently?' I said, 'I was in Switzerland this morning.' 'Not skiing, I hope?' and before I could answer she had moved off with the idea firmly in her mind that I had just had a weekend skiing, when in fact I had had the frustration of being in my favourite ski resort for a grand total of eleven hours during which I had barely glimpsed a mountain.

Another aspect of my job in the Department of Trade was that I attended most of the ministerial council meetings in Brussels at which trade issues were discussed. I voted for our membership of the European Economic Community and had campaigned very actively during the referendum about our membership. However, I found that close contact with the Community did nothing to increase one's enthusiasm for it. Trade was part of the agenda of the Foreign Affairs Council and the first aspect that I disliked was sitting around for hours waiting for the items on the agenda for which one was responsible to be reached. The ministerial lunches which were a feature of the meetings were conducted in French, and British representatives went into lunch with an interpreter who sat alongside. I found that there was a huge amount of wheeler-dealing. A leading official would have gone to Brussels a day or two early to attend meetings which were intended to prepare the ground for the ministerial meeting. Draft agreements for ministers to consider were already approved. They were littered with square brackets which contained the words about which the ministers would argue. It was nit-picking work and time after time agreement was only reached when we had arrived at the lowest common denominator.

I found the Community very protectionist and inward-looking, and attempts to reach an agreed mandate for world trade negotiations or renegotiations of the Multi-Fibre Arrangement were dominated by thoughts, not of liberalization, but of protecting national interests and nationalized industries. Even where the Community was prepared to remove barriers to trade internally, the attitude to barriers to trade with the rest of the world was that they must be maintained for as long as possible and as at high a level as possible. Time after time it was the British who argued the case for liberalization, the Germans who supported us, and the French who were in favour of liberalization as a principle but not on the particular occasion under discussion. The net result always seemed to be the same. The Germans finally let the French have their way, after explaining that this was an exception made in a particular case which must not be repeated. The fact that it would be repeated in another particular case at the next meeting was simply accepted.

The temptation to take part in the game was strong and on one occasion we sought the right to impose restrictions on the import of American synthetic fibres. The American industry had made huge inroads into part of our synthetic-fibre industry and there were some aspects of their success which were not fair. Their industry has access to deliberately low-priced energy, and there were restrictions placed on the export of the feedstock to other countries. The real reason for their success, however, was that the very strong pound made dollar imports cheap. Nevertheless, we went ahead and obtained quotas and were cheered by the industry. Within months the Americans in retaliation exercised their rights under the General Agreement on Tariffs and Trade and threatened to impose quotas on the import of British wool textiles into America. By this time the pound was easing against the dollar and American imports into Britain were slowing down. We gave the industry the choice whether we should renew the restrictions, even though they would provoke retaliation against the wool and textile industry, or whether we should drop them. The industry asked us to abandon the restrictions. It was an interesting experience, but it served no purpose at all. We were loudly cheered by the industry when we negotiated for restrictions to be imposed, but it was at the request of the industry that they were stopped. Incidentally, when the restrictions were imposed one of the biggest objectors to them was a subsidiary of the company that had been leading the demand for them.

It confirmed John Nott and myself in the view that this was an exercise that should not be repeated. Textiles and footwear were two of the industries which had a very hard time during the recession of the late Seventies and early Eighties, and one had enormous sympathy with them in their problems. As industries they had a superb record in the field of industrial relations and management, and the unions worked well together. The industry was virtually strike-free; nevertheless, they found it very hard to compete at the lower end of the market. They criticized the government for being too *laissez faire*, although at the time, under the Multi-Fibre Arrangement which was designed to control the growth of imports, I was administering more than 1,200 quotas with more than thirty countries covering a whole range of products. It was a slightly schizophrenic life. One spent a substantial part of one's time listening to the problems of those who worked in the industry at home and claimed that we were not helping them, and the other half listening to the complaints of ministers, especially from developing countries, who complained that the restrictions were preventing the development of their economy and the improvement of life for people whose standard of living was hugely lower than ours.

The Multi-Fibre Arrangement was introduced as a short-term measure but it is still with us. It is increasingly argued that the only thing that it has really achieved is to delay the necessary restructuring of our own industry and to put up the price to the customer of goods in our shops.

Although I was Minister for Trade I also took part in Commons debates on company law. Just before the election in 1979 the Labour Party had been pushing through the Companies Bill designed to reform our company law and to bring it into line with a number of Community directives. We had had a long and contentious committee discussion of the bill in the Commons and when the election was called we had almost completed consideration of this measure. With the election the bill fell and on the morning after the censure vote we met formally as a committee to put an end to our discussions. Following parliamentary tradition, the government spokesman thanked the committee Chairman and his officials and others who had worked on the bill. I replied for the opposition. I said with a certain amount of bravado that I hoped that the officials who had been drafting the bill and the amendments would note the reasons why we wished to amend the bill, and would make arrangements to draft those amendments because when we won the election we would be reintroducing the bill and amending it. Shortly after the election we reintroduced the bill. All the amendments which the Labour government, with the help of officials, had rejected had been written into the bill by the same officials and we spent several weeks in committee explaining to Stanley Clinton-Davies, who was leading for the opposition, and his colleagues why the arguments that they had put forward and were putting forward were wrong. The same officials who had drafted the speeches explaining why we were wrong were writing speeches a few weeks later explaining why we were right. It was a further example of the versatility of our civil service.

The bill was very complex and technical, but it did make some fundamental changes to the duties of directors and to the laws on insider-trading which were highly controversial. The Labour Party also attempted to reform the laws about company donations to political parties and this gave rise to some very interesting debates on the funding of political parties.

During February 1980 the Brandt Commission reported on relations between developed and developing countries. It was a highly prestigious commission on which the former Prime Minister, Edward Heath, had served and the government staged a debate in the House on the report on a motion proposed by Robert Rhodes James, the Member for Cambridge. I was asked to reply on behalf of the government and we held what was generally considered to be a most worthwhile and well-attended debate. Ted Heath took offence at the fact that the debate was being replied to by a trade minister outside the Cabinet and not a Foreign Office minister inside it. A further debate was held a few weeks later which was replied to by a Foreign Office minister who restated what I had said earlier. This satisfied Mr Heath.

In May 1980, as a result of the seizure of the American embassy in Iran, a decision was taken to impose sanctions on Iran. Douglas Hurd, who was then a Foreign Office minister, and I handled the bill on behalf of the government. It was the first time I had ever worked with Douglas Hurd and almost the first time that he had taken part in the committee stage of a bill, since the Foreign Office normally has little legislation to deal with. We took the bill through all its stages in the House of Commons in just over thirty-six hours. We had the second reading debate from seven o'clock to midnight on 12 May and the committee stage and third reading from 4.0 p.m. to 7.10 a.m. on the following day. I had never favoured sanctions as a political or economic weapon, but the behaviour of the new regime in Iran with whom it was impossible to discuss or negotiate left the west with sanctions as their only weapon. Tam Dalyell, the Member for West Lothian, decided to oppose the bill and did so brilliantly in a series of speeches covering some hours. Tam is unfailingly polite, very persistent and uncrushable.

Because my job took me abroad a great deal, I made very few appearances in the House of Commons during this period. I probably answered questions a dozen times and took part over the two years in a similar number of specialist debates. Company law, although an interesting subject, attracted very few parliamentary enthusiasts and the debates were always very low-key. The debates on textiles and the multilateral trade negotiations similarly had a relatively small but dedicated group of participants. Compared with most of my ministerial colleagues I appeared in the House very infrequently and was relatively detached from domestic politics. It was a strange preparation for my next job which was to be Chairman of the Conservative Party, wholly concerned with domestic politics.

9 A Very Straightforward Job

By July 1981, with unemployment rising, the economy in recession and bank rates soaring, the pressure on Mrs Thatcher to make the traditional U-Turn was growing. At the last meeting of Cabinet before the summer recess, at which the Cabinet discusses the government's spending plans for the next three years and commits itself to an agreed target, the Cabinet refused to endorse Geoffrey Howe's proposals. In *One of Us*, one of the best accounts of the Thatcher years, Hugo Young gives a detailed account of the meeting. Michael Heseltine, Peter Walker, Francis Pym, Sir Ian Gilmour, Lord Soames and Lord Hailsham all attacked the plans, but perhaps more significant for Mrs Thatcher was the hostility of John Biffen and John Nott, whose support she had counted on. By the end of a very acrimonious discussion only Keith Joseph, Leon Brittan and Geoffrey Howe had spoken in favour of the proposals. Mrs Thatcher therefore closed the meeting without reaching a decision.

At about the same time Lord Thorneycroft, the Party Chairman, held a meeting with the Sunday lobby (the political editors of the Sunday newspapers). He spoke very openly about the government's problems and when asked by one of those present whether he was a wet or a dry, he described himself as a 'rising damp'. The lobby assumed he was talking off the record, and no notes were taken. At the end of the meeting, one of the journalists asked whether the conversation had been on or off the record. To his astonishment Lord Thorneycroft said, 'On, of course.' The journalists all went round to a nearby pub and pieced together an agreed account of the meeting. The Sunday newspapers gave large coverage to the Chairman's apparent support for those opposed to the government's economic policy.

I spent a very considerable part of June and July that year in Saudi Arabia, Yugoslavia, Mexico, Peru and Colombia. I was, however, back in Britain for the last week of the parliamentary session and was walking through members' lobby one day when I was stopped by a group of four of the younger Members who had come into parliament in 1979. They asked me whether I had ever considered being the Party Chairman, and they told me that they had been sitting in the tea room discussing who should succeed Lord Thorneycroft and had decided that each of them would write a name on a piece of paper. They would then reveal the name to one another. They found to their astonishment they had all written down my name. I told them that I was very surprised by their choice and that I had never thought of myself as a possible Party Chairman. About three hours later I was walking through the division lobby when Ian Stewart, the Member for Hitchin who was then Geoffrey Howe's PPS, stopped me and asked me exactly the same question. I told him that until three hours previously I had not given the matter any thought and I then told him of my earlier meeting with colleagues. He advised me to start thinking about the possibility because people in high places were.

The whole House was buzzing with talk of a reshuffle. At these times colleagues spend hours drawing up their own lists of Cabinet changes and the whips spend a lot of time sounding out opinion. I gave the matter no further thought and went away in August on holiday with my family. When I came back to my office in the Department of Trade in early September I found the speculation was continuing and it became clear that there would be a reshuffle, probably on 14 September. On the morning of Sunday the thirteenth, Ann and I were having breakfast when the telephone rang. Ian Gow, the Prime Minister's PPS, was on the other end of the line and asked me if Ann and I would be free to join the Prime Minister for lunch at Chequers that day. I said that we were and he asked us to be there at about 12.15 p.m. I told my wife what had happened and said that while I had no idea what she was going to ask me to do, I was sure that Mrs Thatcher was not going to sack me because it would be the prelude to a very difficult lunch.

We arrived at Chequers at the appointed time and the first person I saw was Michael Jopling, the Chief Whip, who ran his finger across his throat while grinning at me and saying, 'You will enjoy life outside the government.' Willie Whitelaw was also there when Margaret Thatcher welcomed us and, after giving us a drink, she suggested that she and I should go into the White Parlour. She told me she was going to reshuffle the Cabinet and the rest of the government and that she wanted me to succeed Peter Thorneycroft as Party Chairman with a seat in the Cabinet as Paymaster General. 'The job is a very straightforward one; we just have to win the next general election together, and we know what will happen to both of us if we do not.' She said this with a smile. I said I would be very happy to accept and she then showed me the list of her proposed changes. Nigel Lawson was to go to the Department of Energy, Janet Young was to become the leader of the Lords and Norman Tebbit was to become Secretary of State for Employment. Ian Gilmour, Lord Soames and Mark Carlisle were to leave the Cabinet. She told me that there was some opposition to Norman's appointment, but she was determined to have him in that job and she hoped I would support her. I realized that my position had changed dramatically from being one of those who might have been discussed in a reshuffle to one of those who did the discussing.

She told me that the rest of the appointments would be made the next day and she swore me to secrecy until that time. The press read the changes correctly. Mrs Thatcher had chosen to break that disreputable convention in British politics which accepted that after two years a government would abandon the policies on which it had been elected and make the infamous U-Turn. She chose not to change the policies, but to change the Cabinet. The changes were rightly described by the *Daily Mail* as 'a clear indication that her economic policies go on'.

On the Monday I went into the Department of Trade and asked my Private Secretary to buy a couple of bottles of champagne and put them in the refrigerator. This caused a stir in the department. As the day wore on various Cabinet ministers were reported to have been summoned to Number 10 and Norman Tebbit, Nigel Lawson and Janet Young were also seen arriving and departing. Norman came in to see me immediately after he had been to see the Prime Minister and he and I went out to lunch together. By then he knew the full details of the reshuffle and we drank a glass of champagne to celebrate the fact that together we were joining the Privy Council and the Cabinet on the same day.

When I went back to the office I found my staff very puzzled indeed. I appeared to be very happy at the appointment of a number of friends, but those two bottles of champagne were still in the refrigerator and they clearly felt it was less and less likely that I would have anything to celebrate. At about four o'clock I called them into my office and told them that I would be leaving that day, that I would be the next Chairman of the Conservative Party and would join the Cabinet. They were delighted for me and the champagne was finally opened. I thanked them for their hard work over the previous two years and they, for their part, wished me well.

At about 4.30 p.m. the telephone rang and it was the press office from Central Office on the line asking me if I would do some television broadcasts and radio interviews since my appointment as Party Chairman was to be announced an hour before the other Cabinet changes, to separate the Party appointment from the government appointments. I told my Private Secretary to tell my driver that I would be leaving at 4.50 to go to the studios. My Private Secretary in the best 'Yes, minister' tradition then told me that he was very sorry, but I could not use a ministerial car for party business so I had to telephone Central Office and ask them to send a car. My government driver, John, was very surprised to see me walk out of the building a few minutes later and climb into a battered Citroën *deux-chevaux* driven by a secretary from the Central Office press office. She explained that Central Office was very hard up and that there had been a pay freeze for the previous eighteen months and, with a grin, she assured me that this was the most luxurious car that anyone in the office owned. After the interviews I was due to go to a reception at Number 10 and she offered to drive me there. Thinking that it would not give a very good impression if the press's first sight of the new Party Chairman was of me climbing out of a battered five-year-old French motorcar, I accepted her offer, but she agreed to drop me at the end of Downing Street so that I could walk up to Number 10.

Just before I went in to see the Prime Minister I telephoned my private office at the Department of Trade. I was astonished to hear the voice of my Private Secretary announcing, 'This is Peter Rees's office.' Peter had been named as my successor about ten minutes before and, so far as the Department of Trade was concerned, I was already only a memory.

On my arrival at Number 10, I was told that there had been a last-minute hitch. It had been pointed out to the Prime Minister that there would be too many Cabinet ministers if I joined the Cabinet since there is a limit to the number of paid Cabinet ministers who can be appointed. The initial announcement therefore said that I would be attending Cabinet but I would not be a member. I subsequently discussed this with the Prime Minister and said that since it would be clear to everyone that I would be devoting most of my time to organizing the next election campaign I felt it would not be wise to take a ministerial salary. This cleared the way for me to become a member of the Cabinet. I felt it was essential that the Chairman was seen to be a full member of the Cabinet and not just a visitor. I also felt it would give me more clout in Cabinet discussions if I was there as of right and not as a guest.

The Paymaster General, like other ministers, answers questions in the House once a month and at my very first question time, David Winnick, the Member for Walsall North, asked me whether I thought it wrong to be paid as a minister while I was in fact devoting a great deal of my time to the Conservative Party. I replied that it had already become clear that I would devote a substantial part of my time to Cabinet and to government, but I had decided not to take a ministerial salary in recognition of the partial validity of his point. For the next two years I only once had to answer questions in the House. My decision to take no salary had removed much of the political controversy from my job as Paymaster General.

The morning after my appointment was announced I went round to the Department of Trade to say goodbye to my private office and to a number of other officials with whom I had worked closely. I was collected by my driver in my ministerial car. The car belonged to the Department of Trade. The Paymaster General's department did not have a car. The Civil Service is very nervous about having anything to do with the party and this meant that a typical Whitehall debate was under way on whether I was a minister and or a party politician, and whether the government or the party should provide my transport. Someone volunteered the suggestion that I should have two cars and should switch them at an invisible line halfway between Central Office and the Cabinet room. While this was being sorted out I decided that I would walk round to Central Office. I had only been there a couple of times before and I was not quite sure where it was. I knew it was in Smith Square, but I did not know where in Smith Square. I walked along Gayfere Street and decided it was on the corner of the square which was diagonally opposite the point at which I had entered. I therefore crossed over to the middle of the square and started to walk round. There was a lot of building work going on and scaffolding was blocking the view of what turned out to be Central Office. When I walked past the scaffolding I saw a group of people staring towards the other end of the square. I realized that it was a reception committee for me but by then I had walked past them. They ignored me and continued to stare in the direction of the Embankment, clearly expecting a limousine to arrive bearing their new Chairman. I felt that it would give the press a wonderful story if the new Chairman did not even know where his new office was. I therefore walked round the square and as I approached the reception committee for a second time I gave a loud cough. Somebody looked in my direction and said to Lord Thorneycroft, 'That's him' and he walked towards me, a hand outstretched, saying, 'My dear Cecil, welcome to Central Office.' It was a strange arrival, but Peter Thorneycroft could not have made me more welcome and I spent the rest of the day meeting the key personnel in the building.

A few minutes after my arrival, the Cabinet office rang asking where my Cabinet papers should be delivered to. They said they could not be sent to Central Office and would like instructions. I sent a message back saying that as soon as they found me an office, they could send the papers to it. In the meantime they had better send them to me at Central Office. After a few days an office was found for me in the Privy Council building. I eventually had a small staff of three who processed the very substantial volume of Cabinet minutes and papers and prepared briefings for me. I was also allocated a ministerial car. It was agreed the car could wait outside to take me to ministerial meetings, but that the driver must in no circumstances enter Central Office. The car was never used on party business.

I knew very little about Central Office and what I found out was not encouraging. We had a very large overdraft. Very stringent economy measures had been put in hand by Peter Thorneycroft who had also imposed a recruitment and pay freeze. Morale was low. There was, however, one bit of encouraging news. Alistair McAlpine who was Treasurer and Deputy Chairman had, for reasons which I never discovered, fallen out with my predecessor and had not set foot in the office for twelve months. The day I arrived he came back and one of the great pleasures of the next two years was working with him to get the party's finances back in shape and to raise money to pay for the general election. Alistair is a most unusual person; short and unimposing in appearance, he has immense stature. As a fundraiser, bon viveur and conversationalist he is remarkable. His knowledge of an amazing range of subjects – from flowers and trees through to literature and music – is profound, but above all he is the most loyal and generous of friends with an enormous sense of fun. Within three months, by selling a building and raising interest-free loans, we had virtually eliminated the payment of bank interest which, when I arrived, was costing us almost £18,000 a week. Together we raised the money to pay a Christmas bonus to the staff and these two things combined to send Central Office off into 1982 in a much improved frame of mind.

Central Office is a small organization with a staff at the centre and in the regions of about 150. It had a budget at the time of about £5 million, all of which had to be raised by voluntary contributions. Central Office owes its allegiance to the leader of the Party and is in fact answerable to him or her. Along with the National Union of Conservative Associations and the Conservative parliamentary party it forms one of the legs of the three legged stool which describes itself as the Conservative Party. Shortly after I arrived at Central Office, we won a tax case in the High Court in which we proved conclusively that there is no such body as the Conservative Party. There are a number of constituent parts which qualify for the collective title, but there is no legal entity to which the name 'Conservative Party' can be attached. My official title was Chairman of the Party Organization but, with the consent of the National Union of Conservative Associations, the body that organizes the activities of the 650 independent Conservative Associations, this is shortened to Party Chairman, and the National Union and the parliamentary party accept the Chairman of the party organization as the Chairman of the non-existent party.

The next few weeks were quite stretching. Although I had been in parliament for eleven years and in the government for two, I had had relatively little experience of the media. I found the constant request for interviews by radio, television and newspapers a brand-new feature of my life, and the help of David Boddy in the press office during those first few weeks was invaluable. At the same time as I was being introduced to the public I was trying to get to know Central Office, setting up a small ministerial office in the Privy Council building, attending innumerable Cabinet committees and Cabinet meetings without the benefit of the departmental briefing which was available to other ministers, answering a large number of letters of congratulation and dealing with a greatly increased constituency post. Moreover, we had entered the party Conference season and three weeks after my appointment our own Conference was due to open in Blackpool. I had only made one four-minute speech to the party Conference more than a decade before. I recognized that, as a person who was almost totally unknown to the party, the impression made at the Conference would be of vital importance and I was anxious that the Conference, which would be the first test of my chairmanship, should be successful.

Willie Whitelaw said to me, on my appointment, that of all the jobs he had held the party chairmanship was the one he liked least, and that his time in Central Office had been six of the unhappiest months of his political life. I, for my part, found the first few days in Smith Square something of a culture shock after life in a government department, but I gradually began to enjoy and appreciate the informality and the ability to get things done speedily which are features of this much smaller organization. Michael Spicer, my PPS, had come with me from the Department of Trade into Central Office and I found him an invaluable ally.

Michael had already had a successful career as a computer specialist and had built up his own business and sold it. He is a very gifted person; a published novelist, a talented painter, and very competent, with an unfailing sense of humour. He is also extremely efficient and, given a job to do, does it very well. As a very young man he had fought two general elections against Emanuel Shinwell at Easington in County Durham. He had started Pressure for Economic and Social Toryism (PEST), which subsequently became the Tory Reform Group, and this earned him a reputation as a wet which stuck with him long after he had become very dry. In fact, PEST probably earned its left-wing label because it was youthful and anti-establishment rather than because of any particular policy proposals. It upset the party establishment by attacking Alec Douglas-Home's election to the leadership of the Conservative Party. Many of its publications and writings were actually rather market-orientated and it was always firmly opposed to the various botched attempts to introduce any form of incomes policy. However, I have no doubt that Michael's involvement in PEST made Mrs Thatcher suspicious of him, and I always felt that he would have been promoted into the government much earlier but for this connection. Initially he worked as my personal assistant, but three months after my appointment when I reorganized the management of Central Office, at my request he was made a Vice-Chairman of the Party with responsibility to me for the day-to-day operations of the office.

The party Conference came at a difficult time for us. We were languishing in the polls. The newly formed Alliance of the Social Democratic Party and the Liberals was riding high, and for a time we ran third in the polls behind Labour and the new Alliance. I arrived in Blackpool on the Sunday of the Conference and on the Monday I spoke to the annual meeting of the National Society of Conservative Agents, the party organizers, and in the afternoon at a press conference with the Chairman of the National Union, Russell Sanderson, later Lord Sanderson, and Edward du Cann, who was President of the National Union that year. It was the first time I had met the political journalists en masse and they gave us quite a hard time.

I spoke at the last session of the morning of the opening day of the Conference, and Margaret Thatcher and a number of Cabinet colleagues were there to support me. The hall was full and the audience was immensely receptive and friendly. I set out to achieve four basic objectives in my speech. The first was to establish a rapport with the party at the Conference and in the country. Unlike my predecessors I did not arrive in the job as a senior Cabinet minister. 'Cecil who?' was the most common remark made about me during my first days as Chairman. I decided to place my cards on the table and, after thanking Lord Thorneycroft, I spoke to the Conference about myself.

I do not bring to this job the vast experience of Peter Thorneycroft, but there are a number of things I would like Conference to know about me. I started my work in the party as a branch treasurer and subsequently became CPC Chairman, and then constituency Chairman. I know I have that in common with many of you here. I started and built up my own business, and I understand the problems and the difficulties faced by those who wish to do the same. I know that I have that in common with many of you here. I now have an overriding ambition – to be Chairman of the Conservative Party when we win the next election and to do all in my power to ensure that Margaret Thatcher returns to Number 10 for that second term of office which she so richly deserves and which the country so desperately needs. I know that I share that ambition with every single person in this place and with millions of people in the country.

My second aim was to launch a theme which we maintained right through to the election, that the Labour Party was an extreme socialist party and that the left wing was in total control.

First the Labour Party – and make no mistake about it, they will be the main opposition. At the end of their Conference they were committed to a series of measures which could turn the United Kingdom into exactly the sort of society which Poland is trying to cease to be. The flow of trade would be decided by the government; the direction of investment decided by the government; the investment of savings controlled by the government; in pensions, education, and health there would be one choice, Hobson's choice.

Wielding this enormous power would be a party dominated by Benn, with men such as Foot, Kinnock and Heffer available to act as moderating influences. That is the true measure of how far the Labour Party has moved to the left – that those three should appear as moderates in today's Labour Party.

I subsequently received a number of letters commenting on the speech. One was from Neil Kinnock who thanked me for mentioning him and pointed out that it never hurts an ambitious young Labour politician to be singled out for attack by the Chairman of the Conservative Party.

The third aim of my speech was to establish the Alliance of the Liberal Party and the SDP as a grouping of the left and not of the centre which was how the Liberals had always sought to represent themselves. I also wanted to show that their main role, whatever they claimed, would not be to form an Alliance government but to open the door to a Labour one.

Now, some facts about the SDP. They are a socialist party, as their own leaders have made clear. They do not wish to be mistaken for a centre party. 'I am not interested in the soggy centre,' said David Owen. 'We believe that a centre party would have no roots, no principles, no philosophy and no values', said Shirley Williams. 'We are not a centre party but are left of centre,' said William Rodgers.

I then pointed out that as individuals their leaders had

a one hundred per cent record of voting in favour of every nationalization measure, of every act extending trade-union privileges during their time in parliament. Collectively, their records as socialists are impeccable.

Every Labour victory since 1964 has been based on a large Liberal protest vote. A large Liberal vote has ensured a Labour victory. A vote for the Alliance would do exactly the same. Those tempted by the Alliance between the inexperienced and the discredited should remember this when the next election comes.

The final aim was to demonstrate that our economic policies would produce the right answer if we kept our nerve during the difficult economic conditions we were then facing. I recalled that, when I was Minister of Trade, I had spent a good deal of time abroad and time after time I had been asked whether the government would have the nerve to see its polices through. I promised the Conference that we had and that we would. I was particularly keen to dispel the claims of our critics that we were so obsessed with economic rhetoric that we had become a hard, uncaring and inflexible government. I pointed to the measures which had been taken to combat unemployment: 'Seven hundred thousand people helped by special employment measures at a cost of £1,000 million; 360,000 people in the youth opportunities programme, rising this year to 550,000.' I highlighted the help that the government was giving to small businesses:

which are going to be the main source of new jobs. Look at the things that the government are doing there – the business start-up scheme, the loan-guarantee scheme, cutting out over one million forms, raising the VAT threshold, getting rid of some of the planning restrictions that inhibit small business. Add to that the money invested in British Leyland, British Steel, British Shipbuilders, not just to save sound jobs in those companies, but in the thousands of small and medium-sized companies which depend upon them.

I ended with a call to the party to remain steadfast, and an assurance that we would win the next general election: 'It is my job, with your help, so to organize our affairs that that victory will be a certainty. I pledge myself to the Conference and to our Prime Minister to get on with that task. I call on each and every one of you here and every Conservative in the country to join us in this great adventure.'

At the end of the speech I received a prolonged standing ovation and Margaret Thatcher sitting beside me was delighted. The rest of the week passed in a whirl of press and television interviews and a round of social events and receptions, in the course of which I subsequently worked out that I had met more than 2,000 people.

The Conference was in a subdued mood. The party was not popular. A number of people were beginning to wonder whether the economic policies would deliver enough success to enable us to win the next election and the Conference showed its unhappiness by giving Willie Whitelaw, then Home Secretary and Deputy Leader, a very hard time in the law and order debate, by defeating a motion congratulating the government on the measures taken so far in assisting the police in maintaining law and order.

Ted Heath spoke critically of government policies in the economic debate and was booed at times during his speech. The mood of the Conference at this point was turning nasty and in a moment of inspiration the Chairman called Mr David Evans from St Albans to speak after Mr Heath. David, who was the Chairman and Managing Director of a cleaning company which had won the first local authority contract for refuse collection and street-cleansing services, started his speech by saying that his name was Evans, and that he emptied dustbins in Southend for a living. The Conference erupted with laughter and David carried on in a similar vein. The Chairman very wisely allowed him double the normal four minutes and, by the time he had finished, the Conference had recovered its good humour and he left the podium to thunderous applause and with the gratitude of the platform. He subsequently became Chairman of Luton Town Football Club, where he controversially banned all away supporters from his ground, and is now the Member of Parliament for Welwyn and Hatfield and continues in his rumbustious way in the Commons today.

Mrs Thatcher in her speech to Conference answered critics of the government's economic policies and pledged, 'I will not change just to court popularity. Indeed, if ever a Conservative government start to do what they know to be wrong because they are afraid to do what they are sure is right, then is the time for Tories to cry "Stop!" But you will never need to do that while I am Prime Minister.'

She was determined to hammer home the fact that whatever her predecessors had or had not done, she and her Cabinet were going to follow through the policies, especially the economic policies, on which they had been elected. At the traditional tea held in her hotel room after her speech, at which she thanked the police and all the people who had been running the Conference, she was pleased that a week which could have been difficult had gone off well and that the party showed no sign of losing its nerve even though its treatment of Willie Whitelaw indicated unease and concern about the recession.

I felt that the Conference had gone as well as could be expected in what were clearly difficult times. The most important speech after Mrs Thatcher's was the reply to the economic debate by Geoffrey Howe, then Chancellor of the Exchequer. The whole Cabinet had turned up on the platform to show its support for Geoffrey and as he got up to reply to the debate I was handed a note. It was from the Chief Superintendent of Police and he asked me to come down from the platform to have a word with him. I slipped out behind Geoffrey and met the policeman at the foot of the stairs. He told me that they had received two telephone warnings that a bomb had been placed in the hall under the platform and was due to go off at 3.30 p.m. It was then 3.15 p.m. He explained that in his opinion the telephone calls were hoaxes, but he made it clear to me that the decision about whether to empty the hall or not was mine and mine alone. He also told me that the whole hall had been checked at lunch time with meticulous care and that nothing had been found.

I decided to look under the platform, and a number of policemen joined me. There was nothing there except a fire bucket containing sand. This was emptied very gingerly and in the bottom we found a dead mouse. At this point I decided that it was a hoax and that we would not clear the hall, although stewards were instructed to continue a discreet search. I decided to go back on to the platform. I felt that, if I was wrong, life would not be worth living if the rest of the Cabinet had been destroyed. I also felt that I ought to show confidence in my own decision. I watched anxiously as the clock slowly moved to 3.30 p.m. Geoffrey finished about ten minutes later and it was with immense relief that I saw him and the Prime Minister and the rest of the Cabinet leave the platform unscathed.

During the Conference the Society of Conservative Agents has its annual dinner at which the Prime Minister is the guest of honour and to which the Chairman of the party is always invited. I sat next to the President of the society and, during the course of the dinner, he mentioned that for the first time the Conservative Party had less than 300 agents in the 622 constituencies in which we had had candidates at the previous general election. (Conservative candidates did not contest any of the twelve seats in Northern Ireland nor had we opposed the Speaker of the House of Commons, George Thomas, in his Cardiff West constituency.) In 1979 we had had more than 360 agents, but a substantial number had retired or changed jobs. I found this very worrying and on the following Monday I asked Tony Garner, then the head of organization, to come and see me to discuss this. He confirmed that it was true, and I decided that whatever it cost we must set in hand a recruitment programme to add at least eighty agents to our strength by the time of the next election. This was done, and although the agents were not due to finish their training until June 1983 we deployed them in the marginal constituencies for the local elections and they stayed for the general election which followed six weeks later.

I have always believed that a cadre of professional agents, properly trained, is an absolutely vital part of the party's election machinery and I am sure these newly recruited agents contributed substantially to our election victory in 1983.

On the Thursday following the party Conference we lost a by-election in the Croydon North West seat, made vacant by the sad death of Robert Taylor. This was a setback, but five weeks later we suffered a much bigger blow when Shirley Williams won the Crosby by-election for the SDP/Liberal Alliance with a majority of 5,289 compared with a Conservative majority of 19,272 at the general election in 1979. It was clear that the government was deeply unpopular and that we had a great deal of work to do if we were to be in a position to win the next general election.

I had always assumed that the Conservative Party had an established by-election team that could move into constituencies as and when a by-election arose. As Party Chairman I discovered to my surprise that there was no such team and that we put together a group of people on an ad hoc basis as and when by-elections arose. Fighting by-elections is a specialized business and it seemed pointless to me that we should reinvent the wheel on each occasion. I therefore asked Tony Garner to establish a team that could move into constituencies armed with printing and office equipment and all the other kit needed to fight a by-election. Tony Garrett was put in charge of the team and he still is. I saw him in 1991 at the by-election in Langbaurgh and he told me that this was the fortieth by-election that he had fought. I also found that in some of our apparently safer seats our organization was abysmal. At Crosby, for example, the organization was extremely run down. At Glasgow Hillhead, which we fought and lost a few months later, it was almost non-existent.

A routine was therefore established. Following the death of the local Member, a member of the Central Office by-election team would visit the constituency to report on its equipment, office staff and general resources, and with few exceptions, the report made very gloomy reading indeed.

I therefore decided to build up a clearer picture of the state of the party, constituency by constituency, and a survey was done of each association so that we could establish some basic facts about their offices, their organization, their membership and their money. We never did get a complete picture because a small number of constituencies, invariably the more prosperous ones, were convinced that this was another Central Office ruse to get control of their cash or their property and refused to give us the information we asked for. They were under no obligation to do so since they were independent bodies, as they pointed out very forcibly. However, we were able to gather enough information to make the exercise worthwhile and we used it to identify not only the critical marginal seats which we had to win to retain power, but also those which, through organizational weakness, had become vulnerable. Central Office agents and officers of the National Union were asked to go to these constituencies and, in detailed discussions with the local officers, pinpoint their needs, strengths and weaknesses. A detailed report was then made to the Head of Organization, Tony Garner, and the necessary action was taken. Angela Hooper, a very valuable Central Office organizer, was subsequently put in charge of the critical seats campaign. One hundred and three seats were classified as critical and at the time we identified them we had professional help in only forty of them. By the time of the general election that number had increased to ninety-nine, and we won ninety-eight of them.

The Crosby by-election marked a low point in our party's fortunes. We were trailing in the polls, the recession was reaching its deepest point and, in December, fourteen Conservative MPs abstained in two votes on the Chancellor's public spending proposals showing that the dissatisfaction felt in the country was also making itself felt inside the party in parliament.

On 15 December I announced a number of changes in the structure of the party organization. Michael Spicer was appointed a Vice-Chairman; a new marketing department was set up to be headed by Christopher Lawson; a new press and public relations department was set up to be headed by David Boddy, and Peter Cropper, then a Special Adviser to the Chancellor of the Exchequer, was appointed as head of the Conservative Research Department. Alan Howarth, who had been an invaluable help to Lord Thorneycroft and Director of the Conservative Research Department, resigned. I was sorry to see him go. I had told him that I wanted to be my own chief executive and asked him to become the full-time head of the Research Department, but he decided that it was time for him to leave. Shortly afterwards he was adopted as the candidate for Stratford-on-Avon and subsequently became a successful minister in the government.

Christopher Lawson had worked with Norman Tebbit and myself in Hemel Hempstead fifteen years earlier and had subsequently spent some years as a very senior executive in the Mars Corporation based in America. He had a first-class record as a marketing man and we were both ready for the inevitable headline, 'Man from Mars markets Tories', with which *The Guardian* duly obliged us. He was to take charge of all the publicity for which we paid. David Boddy, a very capable and popular young media man, was responsible for our unpaid publicity and for our relations with the press.

Peter Cropper was a highly organized, methodical person who brought to the Research Department, which at that time was a rather freewheeling organization, application and order, and the work rate improved dramatically. He had previously worked in the Research Department and felt that it had performed better when it had been distanced from Central Office and based in Old Queen Street. I felt that there was some validity to his argument and therefore, with the approval of the Prime Minister, appointed Lord Beloff as Chairman of a newly formed advisory board which would guarantee the department greater independence from Central Office. Peter would have preferred more freedom, and was at first sceptical about this proposal. He found, however, that the new arrangement gave him much of what he wanted and I retained control of the overall budget. The new governors, amongst other things, introduced a system of scholarships into the research department which attracted a number of extremely able people and raised the standards within the department.

We then had the team which was to fight the next election, with one exception. David Boddy had the opportunity to start a new magazine and to become the owner of a substantial block of shares. He came to see me early in 1983 to tell me that he would like to leave. It was a sad blow because he was a very important and congenial member of our group. Fortunately, the ideal replacement soon came to mind. I had lunched a few weeks earlier with Anthony Shrimsley who had been the Editor of the ill-fated *Now* magazine. He was, at that time, writing a regular column for the *Evening Standard* and I asked him if he had ever considered moving from the news-reporting side to the news-making side of journalism. I pointed out that I had no vacancy at the time, but if a vacancy did arise I would like to feel free to approach him. He said, without commitment, that he found the idea an interesting one. The day after David Boddy told me about his plans, I telephoned Tony and we reached agreement very quickly. I explained to the Prime Minister what had happened and that I wanted to offer the job to Anthony Shrimsley. She agreed immediately and David Boddy very kindly left earlier than he had intended so that Tony Shrimsley could have the optimum time to establish himself in Central Office before the election.

When I first approached Margaret Thatcher to tell her of my proposals for reorganization, she was horrified to hear that one or two people would be leaving and she argued that I should try to find jobs for them. She also argued against some of my proposals, but after I had defended and explained them to her she suddenly said, 'Well, it's your show,' and agreed that I could do what I wanted. This was a turning point in our relationship. After that she did not interfere overtly or covertly, at any stage up to and including the general election campaign, in the running of Central Office.

In spite of the loss of Hillhead in March 1982 we continued to make steady progress in the polls and on 31 March, for the first time since I had become Chairman, we took the lead over the other parties. We had gained about eight per cent in support compared with the previous December. Interest rates were being cut, the economy was beginning to grow. Economic confidence had been bolstered by Geoffrey Howe's budget. John Nott had announced that we were to buy Trident to replace Polaris as a nuclear deterrent and, as I set off on 1 April to drive to Cambridge to speak to a meeting and to carry out a programme for the rest of the day throughout the Eastern Area, things seemed set fair.

There had been increasing talk of a possible Argentinian invasion of the Falkland Islands and during the journey to Cambridge I heard on my car radio that this appeared to have happened. Because I was on party business I was driving my own car which did not have a telephone. When I arrived in Cambridge I was told that an emergency Cabinet meeting had been called, but by then it was too late for me to get back to it. I telephoned Number 10 and was told that there would be another meeting at 6.0 p.m. that evening and that it was essential that I got back to London for that. Throughout the rest of the day as I drove to different engagements I heard a series of broadcasts, including the one from a radio amateur in Port Stanley who described the Argentinian troop carriers rolling past his door.

This was followed by a broadcast of a statement made to the House by Humphrey Atkins in which he explained that the Foreign Office could give no information about what had happened and could not confirm that there had been an invasion. The government seemed incompetent and ill-informed and I drove back to London with a heavy heart for the six o'clock meeting.

The events of that Cabinet meeting have been fully reported and it is widely known that, with the exception of John Biffen, who bravely argued that we should try to negotiate our way round this difficulty, all agreed that the fleet should put to sea and that we should send to the South Atlantic whatever forces were necessary to drive the Argentinians out. It was pointed out that it would take at least eight weeks to assemble the necessary forces and to get them into position in the South Atlantic, and therefore a full-scale diplomatic offensive should be launched to persuade the Argentinians to leave peacefully. The sheer distance meant that diplomacy and force were not in this instance mutually exclusive, but that the one would buttress the other. After the Cabinet meeting I went with Michael Heseltine to the Stafford Hotel where we had dinner together. We both felt that unless we succeeded in ousting the Argentinians this incident could destroy the government.

The next morning the House of Commons met for an emergency debate which was broadcast to the nation. Margaret Thatcher opened the debate and struck a sombre, relatively uncontroversial note. Michael Foot, replying for the opposition, gave one of his most impressive performances and supported the decision to send the fleet. The debate was extremely tense. Edward du Cann, while supporting the government, voiced the unease of the back benches about how this had happened, and John Nott, in winding up, struck a partizan note which went down badly and alienated Members in all parts of the House. I was sitting on the front bench listening to the whole of the debate and, as the Prime Minister left at the end, she asked me to go with her and Willie Whitelaw and Francis Pym to her room.

The unease which had been hinted at during the debate was much more openly expressed at a meeting of the Conservative back-bench 1922 Committee which followed immediately after the end of the debate at which John Nott and Lord Carrington as Foreign Secretary had been invited to speak. Ian Gow, the Prime Minister's PPS, went to observe and to report back to us since none of us as members of the government was eligible to attend. He came back after about half an hour looking grim. He said that Peter Carrington had misjudged the mood of the meeting and had been savaged by a number of well-known 1922 protagonists. Peter, having spent his political life in the more polite House of Lords, did not know how to cope with our own side being rude to him. John Nott had done better but the back-bench committee was extremely angry. Immediately after the meeting, John Nott and Peter Carrington came to the Prime Minister's room in the Commons and gave us their version of events, which was very similar to Ian's account. John was badly shaken, both by his failure in the House and the only partially submerged hostility of the 1922 Committee, but Peter was shattered. After a brief discussion we parted and I went home to Hertfordshire.

I took no part in the events of the next day, but it was later reported to me that a series of meetings had been held between Willie Whitelaw, Peter Carrington and the Prime Minister. Peter Carrington wanted to resign because he felt that it was the honourable and correct thing to do. He also felt that the resignation would remove pressure from the government and enable it to focus on the future rather than spend its time defending the past. I was telephoned that evening by Margaret Thatcher. She asked me for my opinion. I said that I felt Peter would be a great loss because in my short time in Cabinet I had seen what a strong and influential character he was and what an important part he played in the government. However, I also felt that if he had decided to go, and we did decide to appoint some sort of Committee of Inquiry, then this would have the effect of closing off the discussion of events leading up to the invasion, which was clearly going to be very divisive and controversial, and would enable us to concentrate on the business of expelling the Argentinians from the islands supported by a united House of Commons.

From Saturday's debate it was clear that the House was united behind our forces and that any divisions were over the events which had led up to the invasion. Mrs Thatcher told me that Peter Carrington had decided under pressure to postpone making a decision that day and to see what the following day's newspapers had to say before he finally made up his mind. In the event, he decided to resign and Humphrey Atkins, his number two, and Richard Luce, the Foreign Minister with responsibility for South America, left with him.

Francis Pym became Foreign Secretary, John Biffen became leader of the House of Commons and Arthur Cockfield was brought into the government as Trade Secretary. I took over from Francis Pym as Chancellor of the Duchy of Lancaster. On the Tuesday, the Prime Minister announced she would be setting up a small sub-committee of Cabinet which would take responsibility for the day-to-day political direction of the Falklands campaign. Later that afternoon I received a memorandum confirming that a committee had been established and that its membership would consist of the Prime Minister, the Home Secretary (Willie Whitelaw), the Foreign Secretary (Francis Pym), the Defence Secretary (John Nott), and the Chancellor of the Duchy of Lancaster (myself). I was at the time the most junior member of the Cabinet and was very surprised to find myself included. The same group, plus Lord Carrington, had in fact worked together on the question of replacing the ageing Polaris and had recommended to Cabinet that we should purchase Trident.

John Nott told me that he had asked for my inclusion since he felt that he needed a contemporary to be a member of the committee to counterbalance the influence of the two ex-Chief Whips, Willie and Francis. Margaret Thatcher told me that she had wanted me on the committee so that I could deal with the media and put the government's case over on radio and television and to the party. Whatever the reason for my inclusion, I regarded it as a great honour and my membership of the Falklands War Cabinet was certainly one of the high points of my political career.

10 *That's a Hell of a Tough Lady*

My membership of the War Cabinet became controversial. James Callaghan, the former Labour Prime Minister, raised the matter in the House and suggested that the inclusion of the Conservative Party Chairman in the War Cabinet brought party politics into a matter which should be above them. He believed that my membership threatened the all-party consensus which had been reached over the invasion of the Falklands. The controversy was further increased by media reports that I had been added to the War Cabinet some weeks after its creation. In fact, I was a member of the War Cabinet from the start.

The membership of Cabinet committees and sub-committees was not then usually announced in public. The number of Cabinet committees has grown in the postwar period as the duties and responsibilities of government have increased. If there were no Cabinet committees, the full Cabinet would be in almost constant session. Cabinet would have to examine the minutiae of all policies and settle disputes between departments about particular aspects of policy. Ministers would have little time to run their departments or to perform their parliamentary duties. A system of Cabinet Committees allows small groups of ministers to examine policy in detail and to reach informed decisions.

Successive governments have taken the view that if the processes by which government reached decisions became publicly known, the collective responsibility of ministers would be weakened. Under Mrs Thatcher, the Cabinet committee system became rather more public than had previously been the case. She announced that she had set up an Overseas and Defence Committee (OD), an Economic Strategy Committee (E), a Home Affairs Committee (H) and a Legislation Committee (L). However, the membership of these committees was not announced.

The Falklands War Cabinet was a sub-committee of the Overseas and Defence Committee (OD–South Atlantic or ODSA). As usual, there was no announcement about its make-up and so journalists were forced to rely on their eyes and watch carefully which ministers went into Number 10 when the War Cabinet was thought to be meeting. Unfortunately for them, not all ministers find it convenient to enter Number 10 through the famous black front door. As Conservative Party Chairman, I was based at Central Office, but I had a ministerial office in the Cabinet office building in Whitehall to which all the top-secret War Cabinet papers were sent. Each day, before the War Cabinet met, I went to my ministerial office to read the papers and to receive briefing on the latest situation. I then went through the connecting door to Number 10 and after the meeting made the same trip in the reverse and handed all my papers to my Private Secretary. This meant that my papers never left the Number 10/Cabinet office complex and were therefore totally secure. It also meant that I was not seen entering or leaving through the front door of Number 10 as were all the other participants. The reason was one of pure practicality and not deception.

On 19 April I was speaking at a political dinner in the Carlton Club when I was handed a note saying that the Prime Minister had called an urgent meeting at Number 10. Since there were no papers to be read, I went straight to Downing Street and went in through the front door. I was astonished to find out later that my attendance was the main news item on radio and television news and became a lead newspaper story the next day. 'Party Chairman summoned to crisis meeting' was the gist of many of the headlines. This incident gave rise to the theory that I was added to ODSA at a later stage. In fact, I had been a member for almost two weeks by the time my presence was spotted.

I would not claim that my experience of South America was great at the time of my appointment to the War Cabinet. However, I had as Trade Minister in 1979–81 visited Argentina, Chile and Peru, and I was the only member of the War Cabinet actually to have met the leaders of these three countries. I also had family ties with Argentina. My wife's grandmother was Anglo-Argentine. Her family had settled in Argentina in the 1860s and owned and farmed substantial estates in different parts of the country. The men had returned to England to fight in the British forces in the two world wars this century and, in spite of living in South America for several generations, the family still speak English with a discernible Scottish accent. Since telephone communications were not cut off during the conflict, I did, from time to time, receive messages from my wife's relations during the conflict urging us to try to find a peaceful solution.

I will never forget the first meeting of ODSA on Tuesday 6 April. As Sir Terence Lewin, the Chief of the Defence Staff, introduced his team, I found myself hoping that these people were as good as they were going to need to be if military action proved to be necessary. Later, when we knew each other better, one of the service chiefs told me that they too looked at us and hoped that we would be capable of giving them the support they knew they were going to need. In practice, from the first meeting, a good working relationship was established. The politicians defined the objectives and set the parameters within which the military worked. If they wished to extend these parameters or to modify the rules of engagement, they made the case to us. I can only recall one occasion during the whole conflict when they asked us for permission to extend their sphere of activity and we asked them to think again and to bring the proposal back the next day if they still wished to pursue it. They decided not to.

One important moment came when the Prime Minister, having visited the command headquarters at Northwood, suggested that we should all go there the following Sunday morning, and then travel on to Chequers for lunch to be followed by an afternoon meeting of ODSA. The presentation at Northwood in which all three services participated was impressive, as was the quality of the people of all ranks who took part in it. I found the whole experience very reassuring, as did all my colleagues and from that time we developed a growing confidence in the services' ability to deliver. They for their part, having started with reservations about a group of politicians led by a woman Prime Minister, grew to trust us, and by the end of the conflict had built up a great admiration for Mrs Thatcher. Her handling of General Haig, the US Secretary of State, especially during his second visit to London and her refusal to play politics with the lives of our forces, even if it involved doing something as unwanted as sinking the *General Belgrano*, were particularly important moments in enhancing their perception of her. In my view they also saw their close contact with ministers from outside the Ministry of Defence as an opportunity to underline what they believed was the basic wrong-mindedness of John Nott's recent defence review.

As the stock of the military and the MOD rose, so the standing of the Foreign and Commonwealth Office sank. Ever since 1965 when the United Nations passed a resolution on the Falklands, calling on Britain and Argentina to negotiate to find a peaceful solution to the Falklands problem, the FCO had been trying intermittently to find an answer. A succession of junior FCO ministers, starting with Lord Chalfont in 1965 and carrying on through to Nicholas Ridley and Richard Luce in 1980 and 1982, had made efforts to solve the problem. The feeling in Whitehall was that the FCO wanted to be rid of the place, but on a number of occasions the House of Commons had frustrated them by insisting that the wishes of the islanders should be paramount, and in spite of all sorts of attempted bribes the islanders obdurately rejected all Argentinian approaches. The 1971 agreement which opened up air services between Argentina and the Falklands, and gave Falkland islanders travel, tax and educational privileges, produced no improvement. Nevertheless, the view persisted that the FCO was determined to find a way of releasing us from our obligations to the islanders and this made Mrs Thatcher extremely suspicious of their motives and advice.

I disliked what I saw as the pretentiousness of the FCO and, by their behaviour, some of the officials enhanced their department's rather undesirable reputation. I recall two incidents which illustrate the special view that some of them have of themselves and their department. The first was when I received a call from the Foreign Secretary's office saying that Lord Carrington, who was due to be the keynote speaker at the Young Conservative Conference in Harrogate on the Saturday, would only be arriving back on the Friday after a busy week and they wondered if he could withdraw. They realized that he was the most important speaker and would be missed. They had checked with Number 10 and found that the Prime Minister had a free Saturday. They wondered if I wouldn't mind asking her to stand in for him. I politely declined. The other incident also concerned Lord Carrington. He was due to make a visit to South America, and the idea was mooted that he should take a group of eight of our top businessmen with him and devote part of his visit to giving a boost to British exports. The FCO were horrified that their Secretary of State should have any contact with commerce, but they finally conceded, and this high-powered party left for South America. A couple of days later, news filtered back that the businessmen were being sidetracked by the officials who were determined that Lord Carrington should have the minimum to do with them. The point was then put to him. He immediately insisted that they become an integral part of his programme and the rest of the trip was an outstanding success. I might add that he was also unaware of the efforts of his officials to get Mrs Thatcher to act as a substitute for him.

Although Mrs Thatcher had a deep distrust of the FCO as an institution, she had a very high regard for individual members of it, especially Anthony Acland who became Permanent Secretary on the day the Argentinians invaded, our two Ambassadors in Washington and at the United Nations, Sir Nicholas Henderson and Sir Anthony Parsons, and Robert Wade-Gery, then Head of Foreign and Defence Liaison in the Cabinet office. Throughout the campaign, she maintained her ambivalent attitude to this group. She admired their skill, their intellectual athleticism and their achievements, but her ambivalence remained.

Anthony Parsons earned her undying gratitude and admiration when, against all the odds, he succeeded in persuading the United Nations to pass Resolution 502 demanding immediate Argentinian withdrawal from the Falklands. It is impossible to overestimate the boost which this gave to our cause at a time when the situation looked particularly grey and threatening and when the government was on the ropes.

Meetings of ODSA divided neatly into two distinct phases. The first, the diplomatic offensive and the search for a negotiated settlement, often gave rise to heated discussion. For, although we were all committed to achieving a diplomatic solution, the Prime Minister was determined to avoid what she called a sell-out. The second part passed off more smoothly as we discussed the arrangements for the military campaign and received reports on the progress of the fleet and the activities of the Argentinian command. As the task force neared the Falklands and the diplomatic initiatives faltered, the agenda for ODSA was switched so that we discussed the military campaign before we turned to discuss the fading diplomatic offensive.

Mrs Thatcher's decision to appoint Francis Pym as Foreign Secretary following Peter Carrington's resignation was hard for both of them and Francis asked for some time to think the matter over before he accepted her invitation. They did not find it easy to work together. She had found an excuse to move him from the job of Defence Secretary the previous year, because she did not think he would be tough enough to take on the service chiefs and to make the radical changes at the Ministry of Defence which she was seeking. He had become leader of the House of Commons and was extremely good at it. He was well liked throughout the House, and spoke very well in it. He was one of the earliest sceptics about the government's economic policies and used to make regular coded speeches in which he expressed his unhappiness about rising unemployment and called for a change of policy. After these speeches, reports would appear in the newspapers in which adjectives such as 'incandescent' were used to describe Mrs Thatcher's reaction to them. He and the Prime Minister were happy to see the minimum of each other, but his appointment as Foreign Secretary meant they would inevitably be working closely together. Neither of them, in my view, relished that prospect. Mrs Thatcher recognized, however, that Francis commanded the respect of the House of Commons and was the right man to rally and reassure the badly shaken Conservative parliamentary party and to unite the opposition behind the government's policies. To his credit, he achieved both these objectives and, by appearing both resolute and reasonable, played a key role in steadying the Commons at a difficult time. Privately, they found each other a trial, and were mutually suspicious of one another.

Almost the first decision which faced the War Cabinet was whether to encourage General Alexander Haig, the US Secretary of State, who had expressed a wish to mediate between Britain and Argentina. We were keen to meet him and were grateful for any help that he could give, but we were worried at suggestions that the American government might adopt a neutral approach and so were keen to stress that Haig was invited to come to London as a friend and ally rather than as a mediator.

On 7 April, the day before Haig's arrival in London, the War Cabinet met to discuss our approach to the meeting with him. We agreed that before negotiations with the Argentinians could start all Argentinian troops would have to have been withdrawn from the Falklands and British administration restored. Once these conditions were met, we would be prepared to discuss the future of the islands with Argentina although we would be guided by the wishes of the islanders, which clearly could not be determined whilst the Argentinians remained on the islands.

I did not attend the meeting with General Haig and so, after a very hectic few days, I was free to take a short break with Ann in Cornwall. On the Sunday, after a round of golf, I received a message from Number 10 calling me back to London for a meeting of the War

Cabinet that evening. An RAF jet would be waiting at nearby St Mawgan to fly John Nott and myself up to London. The War Cabinet met at 7.0 p.m. Haig, having returned from Buenos Aires where he had met the Argentinian junta, was to meet the Prime Minister and the Foreign and Defence Secretaries the next morning and we discussed the approach that should be taken.

The following afternoon, Monday 12 April, I had my first meeting with Haig. I was not encouraged. It was clear to me that he felt that we had bitten off more than we could chew. He was convinced that it was not possible for us to retake the islands by military means and that his job was to find a face-saving formula that would save the Americans from having to take sides on the question of sovereignty while making it clear that they deplored the Argentinian use of force. Even after the meeting on 8 April, Haig seemed to believe that, given time, we would accept that he was right and we were wrong about the military option.

During the meeting Haig outlined his proposals. He envisaged the withdrawal of all British and Argentine military forces within two weeks and their return to their normal operating areas, and the setting-up of a Special Commission comprising the US, Britain, Argentina and other observer countries. All laws would have to be submitted to, and ratified by, the Special Commission; the traditional administration, including the executive and the legislature, would be expanded to include Argentinian representation; and the flags of the US, Britain and Argentina would fly over the Special Commission headquarters. Travel, transport, communications and trade between Argentina and the Falklands should be reinstated; sanctions should be lifted within two weeks and there should be a commitment to negotiate the definitive status of the islands by 31 December 1992 consistent with the purposes and principles of the United Nations Charter.

Mrs Thatcher made it clear that we could not countenance halting the task force, at least until the Argentinians had withdrawn from the Falklands. Although Haig's proposals were not acceptable to us, I felt that the main achievement of the series of meetings on 12 April was to convince him that Mrs Thatcher and the rest of us, while preferring a diplomatic solution, would not buy peace regardless of price, and believed that we could and would win a military victory if it proved to be necessary.

The meeting was held in the Cabinet room at Number 10. As Mrs Thatcher forcibly pointed out to Haig when she reminded him that it was in that room that Chamberlain and his Cabinet had pursued their policy of appeasement towards Hitler, the Cabinet room has been the scene of many historic meetings. It is a long, narrow room with windows overlooking Number 10's garden on one side and in the centre of the opposite wall is a rather imposing fireplace. In the centre of the room is a long, thin, coffin-shaped table. The Prime Minister sits at the centre of the table with his or her back to the fireplace. At the meeting with Haig, the British side sat facing the garden with the Americans opposite. Haig and Mrs Thatcher did most of the talking with others coming in briefly from time to time. I felt that by the end of the day when we said goodbye to the Americans, Haig had accepted the British position but it was clear that Thomas Enders and General Vernon Walters, his two chief advisers, had not. Enders, the Undersecretary of State for Latin America, in particular looked more and more unhappy as the day went on. What he had seen as an exercise in persuading us to accept their proposals became instead an opportunity for us to make them realize that they were unlikely to find a compromise and were going to have to take sides. Since they were hardly likely to renege on the country their President regarded as his most reliable ally, and the Prime Minister whom he saw as a kindred spirit and friend, Mr Enders saw his South America policy about to go up in smoke and he did not like it.

As the negotiating positions became clearer, the possibility of a compromise between Britain and Argentina became more and more remote. With the benefit of hindsight, it is clear to me that there never was any real possibility of a negotiated settlement. For the Argentinians, the only thing that mattered was a recognition that sovereignty of the Falklands belonged to them. They were prepared to accept some formula that gave us time to acknowledge this gracefully, but only a little time. For us, Resolution 502 had to come first and any agreement had to recognize that the wishes of the islanders were to be paramount. Since the Argentinians were determined to have sovereignty and the islanders were more determined than ever not to become part of Argentina, the two positions were totally irreconcilable. At the end of our meeting with General Haig on 12 April I think that he recognized this. He left us, having accepted an impossible negotiating mandate which would be rejected in Buenos Aires and make his journey almost a waste of time.

The next morning I received a telephone call from Downing Street telling me that Haig had not left for Argentina but wanted further talks before he did. I was told later by an American official that on returning to his suite at the Churchill Hotel, Haig took off his jacket, threw it on to a chair and said, 'Somebody get me a stiff drink. That's a hell of a tough lady.' Enders and Co. got to work on him and convinced him that he must make a further effort to get Mrs Thatcher to modify her view. They suspected that the Foreign Office was urging on Francis Pym a slightly more conciliatory line than Mrs Thatcher's and felt that they should support him. In the end, Mrs Thatcher convinced Haig that she was not going to change her stated position and Haig flew back to America to report to the President.

I never believed that the Americans would betray us. I recognized that if they were to have any hope at all of acting as honest brokers, which was clearly their preferred role, then they had to appear to be even-handed. I never felt that they had the slightest chance of success, but equally, no harm was done to our military prospects by pursuing every diplomatic avenue. Because of the sheer distance, 8,500 miles from the UK to the Falklands, the main invasion force could not be in position for several weeks and diplomacy occupied centre stage. The arrival of the submarines and the task force, far from undermining the diplomatic effort, reinforced it, and at no stage did we need to ask the military to delay their efforts to enforce the exclusion zone or their preparations for invasion.

The next two weeks were dominated diplomatically by the American effort to find the elusive negotiated settlement and militarily by the recapture of South Georgia. After two days in Washington, Haig returned to Buenos Aires on 17 April with a new five-point peace plan. This involved withdrawal by both sides; a three-flag administration to last until December; restored communications with the mainland; talks in the New Year on a long-term settlement; and consultation to ascertain the islanders' views.

The proposals were unacceptable without modification to the Argentinians and, as modified by them, totally unacceptable to us. Another problem was emerging for Haig. It gradually became clear that Costa Mendez, the Argentinian Foreign Minister, spoke for nobody but himself, and that there was great difficulty in finding somebody with the authority to negotiate. Only decisions taken by the whole junta were binding on it and they were divided.

On the Thursday, 22 April, Francis Pym flew to Washington with our reaction to the Haig five-point plan and it was agreed that ODSA would meet again on the following Sunday at Chequers. I spent the Friday, St George's Day, standing in for Mrs Thatcher, who had been due to spend the day visiting Surrey County Council at Kingston and speaking to representatives of the eleven Surrey constituencies. After holding a surgery in one part of my constituency and attending the induction of a new vicar in another, I left early the next morning to drive to Harrogate where I was due to speak to the Yorkshire Area Conservatives. I arrived at about 12.30 and was asked to ring Number 10 immediately. I did, and was told that the Prime Minister had decided to hold a meeting of ODSA that afternoon, but that Willie Whitelaw could not get back from the West Country, where he was speaking, until six o'clock. 'Could I be back by then?' I said I could and it was decided by Eric Ward, our excellent Central Office agent in Yorkshire, to start the meeting early and to open it, rather than close it, with my speech. The meeting was quite full when I started to speak, but more people were arriving all the time and by the end the audience had doubled. Just as in Surrey the previous day, I found the audience tremendously welcoming and enthusiastic in support of our forces and the Prime Minister. Because it was essential that I be at Number 10 by six o'clock I was given a police escort to the motorway and instructed by the police to drive with headlights on at full speed. All the police forces en route to London had been warned and I was back in London less than two and a half hours after leaving Harrogate, without upsetting the police.

As we waited in the small anteroom outside the Cabinet room, Francis Pym came up to me and told me that he felt that Haig had worked up a set of proposals which were the best that could be hoped for and that he would be outlining them to the War Cabinet and would recommend their acceptance. Shortly afterwards, Mrs Thatcher and Willie Whitelaw came down from the study upstairs. I had noticed that such meetings always seemed to be held just before some really contentious issue was to be put before Cabinet. In the meeting Haig's plan, which had hardly changed from the one which he had presented to the War Cabinet, was put forward. After a heated discussion it was agreed that we should wait until the final package arrived so that we could take a more considered view.

One of the interesting features of the War Cabinet was that although John Nott had originally been concerned that Willie and Francis as ex-Chief Whips would gang up against him, in practice he and Francis worked well together and there were none of the expected schisms. We all wanted a negotiated settlement if it could be achieved on an acceptable basis, but we were all united in our support for military action if it proved necessary.

When we met at Chequers on Sunday, 25 April, we knew that the operation to recapture South Georgia would be under way. Two days earlier, during a reconnaissance landing, two helicopters had been lost but there had been no casualties. Later that day, news came through that the island had been recaptured and John Nott and the Prime Minister appeared outside Number 10 and made an announcement of the good news. Mrs Thatcher was irritated when what she considered to be grudging questions were aimed at John by journalists. 'Just rejoice at that news,' she said. Critics subsequently claimed she was glorifying in conflict. In fact, what she was delighted about was the recovery of British territory without the loss of a single British life, and with only one serious injury on the Argentinian side. The next day a tragic accident resulted in the death of an Argentinian soldier, but the recapture of the island was, thankfully, bloodless.

Two days later, on 27 April, at a meeting of the War Cabinet, two critical decisions were taken. The first was that the landing place for the invasion force should be San Carlos Bay. The second was that we should not react to the final American peace plan until we knew how the Argentinians had responded. They did not accept the proposal. Haig decided that he could do no more, and two days later President Reagan declared that the US would support Britain and would give 'material' aid, a promise which Caspar Weinberger and his defence department subsequently honoured in full.

The War Cabinet met at Chequers on Sunday morning, 2 May. Francis Pym was absent, having gone to Washington and New York to discuss the next diplomatic moves with Haig and Pérez de Cuellar, the Secretary-General of the UN. We faced a very serious decision. We had all been aware from the beginning that the preservation of our aircraft carriers was absolutely vital to the success of the operation. The main threat to them came from the Argentinian navy and in particular from the aircraft carrier, the *25 May* and the cruiser, the *General Belgrano*. We had discussed in general terms the damage which either of these ships could do, but that morning at Chequers we were told that the Royal Navy submarine, *HMS Conqueror*, had sighted the *General Belgrano* and Admiral Woodward, the task force commander, had requested permission to attack it. The Chief of the Defence Staff recommended that permission be given. Because this action would have been outside the rules of engagement previously set by the War Cabinet, we had to take the decision to vary them.

Much has been written about our motives in authorizing the attack. Some have argued that the decision to vary the rules was taken in Francis Pym's absence to spite his diplomatic efforts and, in particular, the peace plan produced by President Belaunde of Peru. The decision was taken on purely operational grounds. The cruiser was a threat to our carriers. Destruction of one of our carriers could have led to a huge loss of British lives and would have put an end to the operation. The Argentinians would have remained in possession of the islands. We had an opportunity to eliminate a very potent threat and we decided unanimously to take it. We all regretted the loss of Argentinian lives, but we felt that if we let the cruiser go and she subsequently sank a carrier, we would properly be vilified in Britain for deliberately putting British lives at risk, and causing the avoidable deaths of hundreds of British servicemen. It is interesting that the Captain of the *General Belgrano* subsequently confirmed that although he had withdrawn from the total exclusion zone, he was not planning to return to port but was awaiting further orders, and that his intentions were hostile and his aim was to sink a carrier.

General Galtieri used the sinking of the *General Belgrano* as his excuse for rejecting the Peruvian proposals, but the proposals themselves were a slightly varied version of the final Haig proposals which the junta had found totally unacceptable. No proposal which did not accept transfer of sovereignty to Argentina as inevitable commended itself at any stage to the junta, and the Peruvian proposal was no exception. One welcome result of the sinking was that the Argentinian navy stayed within the twelve-mile limit throughout the conflict. The naval threat to our carriers was eliminated.

The House did not sit on the Monday and the War Cabinet met twice on the Tuesday. At the morning meeting, we discussed at great length the unfavourable world reaction to the sinking of the *General Belgrano,* and the means of countering it. We decided to mount a full-scale diplomatic offensive to underline our commitment to finding a negotiated settlement. Nicholas Henderson, our Ambassador in Washington, was instructed to reopen discussions on the Peruvian peace plan. Our second meeting took place in the Prime Minister's room in the House of Commons. We had just begun when the door opened and in came Admiral Sir Henry Leach. He had some very bad news. *HMS Sheffield,* which had been acting as a 'picket' ship between the Argentine mainland and the task force had been hit by an Exocet missile and had been destroyed. This was the first mention I recall of the appallingly effective French-made Exocet missile which had been supplied to the Argentinians. *HMS Sheffield* had been positioned to act as a sort of sea-based early warning system in the absence of any land-based radar or airborne early warning system. It was on a high state of alert and ready to shoot down enemy aircraft and missiles. The loss was a major blow. We had also lost our first sea Harrier.

We were all shaken and I wondered how the Prime Minister would react. She was deeply shocked and insisted that the House be informed as soon as possible. She also decided that the full Cabinet should meet the next day to discuss the military situation and to decide on the Peruvian peace plan. The Cabinet agreed in principle to accept the plan. We were wasting our time: the Argentinians rejected the proposals for a second time. Nevertheless, the willingness of the British side to negotiate, combined with the sinking of *HMS Sheffield* and the intransigence of the Argentinians, moved world opinion back in our favour.

From then, until the surrender on 14 June, Britain retained the diplomatic initiative so that, by the time of the landing, the whole House of Commons, the Americans, our other allies, and the Secretary-General of the United Nations acknowledged that Britain had given the Argentinians enough opportunities to negotiate a settlement and it was their fault that we failed to achieve one.

On 14 May, Mrs Thatcher spoke at the Scottish Conservative Party Conference in Perth. Her speech was outstanding and clearly caught the mood of the conference. She told the audience that she hoped negotiations would succeed: 'I do not want one more life lost in the South Atlantic, whether Argentine or British, if it can be avoided,' but she stressed that there could be no settlement until the Argentinians left the Falklands. She told the conference: 'I should not be doing my duty if I did not warn you in the simplest and clearest terms that, for all our efforts, those of Secretary Haig and those of the Secretary-General of the United Nations, a negotiated settlement might prove unattainable.' She continued: 'Then we would have to turn to the only course left open to us, and that is why, as I have repeatedly said in the House of Commons, the government has done nothing in its attempt to find a diplomatic solution which forecloses any military action now or any military option in the future.' She finished her speech to a tremendous ovation. Once the cheering had died down she leant against the podium and talked very quietly and movingly of the dangers which lay ahead.

Francis Pym, who was due to speak to the conference the next day, was deeply upset by the tone struck by Mrs Thatcher and the mood of the conference. But he too caught its mood and made a very fine speech which was well received.

The final British offer was drawn up at a meeting at Chequers on Sunday 16 May. By that time the invasion fleet, which had left Ascension Island on 8 May, was only two days' sailing away from the rendezvous with the task force.

It was important that the diplomatic effort and the military plans be coordinated almost to the second. Since it had been made clear to us that, once troops arrived in the battle zone, they could only be held on board for a very short time, certainly not more than seventy-two hours, it was decided that they must begin to land by the following Friday. Forty-eight hours were needed from the time of the giving of the go-ahead to the actual landing. The landing could be stopped during that forty-eight hours if events so dictated, but it could not be completed in under that time. This meant that ideally the diplomatic efforts should be concluded by the Wednesday at the latest.

We were joined at Chequers by Henderson and Parsons who had flown in from the United States. We met for coffee at 9.30 a.m and at ten o'clock we moved upstairs into the Great Parlour. Our first job was to draw up the final British offer. For the first time, the FCO, reinforced by the two Ambassadors, and represented by Pym, Acland, Palliser, the former FCO Permanent Secretary who had been asked to head a Cabinet office 'communications group' by Mrs Thatcher, and Wade-Gery, had virtual parity of numbers with the military. They realized this was their last chance to impose themselves on the situation, and were determined to come away from the meeting with a set of proposals which had a chance of being accepted and would give Britain a good moral basis for action if rejected. As a result these proposals went, in my opinion, far too far. If they had been accepted by the Argentinians, they would have been hugely damaging to us. The main terms were the mutual withdrawal of forces, the timing and verification of which were laid down in meticulous detail; a UN administrator rather than a returning British Governor; the Falklands in the interim period would be governed in 'accordance with the laws and practices traditionally obtaining'; there would be three British and three Argentinian observers; further negotiations would be 'without prejudice' and would be completed 'with a sense of urgency' by the end of the year; South Georgia would be excluded.

We seemed to spend hours drafting each sentence. A drafting group of about fourteen was clearly far too big and it made for a heated and, at times, bad-tempered morning. In the event, the proposals achieved their desired end. They were accepted by the House of Commons and by world opinion as a fair basis for settlement. They were commended by Pérez de Cuellar, and rejected by the Argentinians. On the Wednesday evening, Pérez de Cuellar telephoned the Prime Minister to tell her that he could do no more. She thanked him profusely, too profusely as it turned out. He was so moved by her remarks that he decided he owed it to us to make one last effort. Since we had that morning anticipated the collapse of the negotiations and given Admiral Woodward the go-ahead for the landing, this presented us with a problem. We could stop the invasion process, but it might have been difficult to restart it in the military timescale available. We could not land, however, if the Secretary-General was still negotiating. A rather shamefaced Mrs Thatcher told us what had happened at the War Cabinet on Thursday morning. During the meeting, a message was received from her office confirming that Pérez de Cuellar had appeared on the steps of the UN and told the world's media that our very fair final offer had not been accepted and negotiations were over. The way was now clear for the military landing and we discussed what line to take with the media. They would clearly be asking what the next move would be and when it would be made. We decided to say that there would now be an intensification of military activity and a gradual escalation in the number of raids. We felt that if we could lull the Argentinians into a false sense of security and gain even a few hours' respite for our forces, it might be helpful.

During the course of the Falklands campaign I had gradually assumed a position as the main political spokesman for the War Cabinet. Francis Pym and John Nott had massive departmental responsibilities and little time to spare, Willie Whitelaw was also busy as Home Secretary, and although Central Office and Cabinet duties left me little time, I was clearly more available than the others. In addition to very regular interviews with the British media, I found there was huge international interest and I did dozens of interviews for overseas networks. On the night of 20 May I was due to do a live interview at 3.0 a.m. for one of the American networks and went to their offices near Regents Park. As I waited for the interview to begin, I was approached by a short dark American who asked me the inevitable question about the next step. He assured me that any answer I gave him would be treated in confidence. I gave him the standard answer and he charged off. I saw him go into the nearest office and pick up a telephone. I could hear him say, 'I have spoken to a member of the War Cabinet. There will be no invasion tonight, I am sure.' I found myself hoping that the Argentinians would draw the same conclusion from my carefully phrased answer. I found out later that the American was Carl Bernstein of Watergate fame. He had been sent to England to cover the campaign, but cut off from his life-support system of Washington contacts and trying to operate in a foreign country, he was having a very thin time.

Over the next few days as the bridgehead at San Carlos was being established, I watched with horror on the television screens dramatic and harrowing evidence of the destructiveness and sophistication of modern weaponry. Possibly the most memorable picture of the war was that of *HMS Antelope* exploding, the vessel silhouetted against a halo of brilliant light. The film of Argentinian planes roaring over San Carlos Bay pursued by missiles, disappearing over the skyline, and the inevitable explosion and flare of light a few moments later, all brought home to me the enormity of the venture on which we had embarked.

At a meeting of ODSA early in May, John Nott had explained that in view of the build-up of the Argentine forces, he had been advised that the landing force must be reinforced. 5 Infantry Brigade which, following reorganization at the beginning of the conflict, comprised the 1st Battalion Welsh Guards, the 2nd Battalion Scots Guards and the 1st/7th Duke of Edinburgh's Own Gurkha Rifles was the obvious choice for such a task and there was only one ship that could get the Brigade to the South Atlantic in the time available. It was the *QE2* and he requested permission to requisition her. There was something incongruous about the idea of a brigade of British troops going to war in the most luxurious ship in the British merchant fleet, but after satisfying ourselves that there was no alternative, we readily agreed. Only sixteen days after leaving Southampton, the QE2 arrived at South Georgia and 5 Brigade trans-shipped, landing at San Carlos three days later.

Although we had the support of most of the world community at the time of the landing, we realized that as the horrors unfolded, pressures for a ceasefire would grow. The worst of all worlds would be a ceasefire imposed on us halfway through the actual campaign. We would have suffered loss of men and equipment to, what might appear to the public, little purpose. We were anxious for a swift victory, so that we could put an end to casualties and prevent a bloody war of attrition.

I have been surprised at some of the subsequent comments of Admiral Woodward and Brigadier Thompson. At no stage did the politicians consider the loss of British lives a secondary factor, or seek to play politics with the campaign. At all times we accepted the advice of the Chiefs of Staff and if we shared their anxiety that the campaign should not become protracted, it was because of our deep concern that we should suffer the minimum of casualties and loss, and that such as we did suffer should not be in vain. This gave rise to a feeling of impatience as the days passed, the casualties grew and our troops stayed at San Carlos. The fact that Brigadier Thompson's commanding officer, Major-General Jeremy Moore, did not arrive until 30 May gave rise to some speculation that things might have been different had he been there from the beginning. In my view, Thompson was absolutely right to put military considerations first and last, and to let the politicians take any political pressure for a ceasefire which might be building up. Our final complete and unexpectedly sudden victory was the ultimate justification of Thompson's leadership and he emerged from the campaign with enormous credit and respect, and with the gratitude of us all. Any momentary doubts about him in the few days after the landing were totally erased by the success of the subsequent campaign.

The efforts of the troops and sailors in the South Atlantic won the admiration of the nation. I paid tribute to them, and to others, at the Conservative Women's Conference on 26 May: 'They have carried out their work with such professionalism that we are in danger of underestimating what they have achieved ... As long as any one of us here today lives we shall not forget these men. None of us here can ever repay our debt to them. All we can do is to repeat our sincere thanks.' I went on to pay tribute to 'three other sorts of hero' – the merchant seamen who had willingly sailed in the task force, the shipyard workers who were working night and day to finish ships which might have been needed for action, and the war correspondents who faced great physical danger 'armed only with microphones or pens'.

As the military campaign moved towards a conclusion, pressure grew at the United Nations in New York for a ceasefire and Resolution 505 urging Pérez de Cuellar to seek a settlement was passed. On 26 May, a few days later, a group of Argentinian military generals arrived in New York ready to surrender to the United Nations. On 3 June Mrs Thatcher was due to attend the western summit at Versailles. The US State Department and the British Foreign Office saw this as possibly the last opportunity to produce a negotiated ending to the conflict and Mrs Thatcher was expected to come under substantial pressure to accept a five-point peace plan to be produced by President Reagan. At the same time, the United Nations was debating a resolution sponsored by Panama and Spain calling for a ceasefire. The US, by mistake as it turned out, joined Britain in using their veto. Haig, having decided to order Mrs Kirkpatrick to use it, subsequently changed his mind, but could not contact Mrs Kirkpatrick, the US Ambassador to the UN, in time to prevent her carrying out his original instruction.

I was due to be interviewed by Brian Walden on LWT's *Weekend World* programme on the Sunday of the Versailles Conference. I had arranged to speak to Bernard Ingham, Mrs Thatcher's Press Secretary, and also to Francis Pym's Press Secretary before I left to do the programme. I was briefed by both of them about the latest position at Versailles and we agreed to speak again later that morning so that I would be aware of any last-minute developments.

During the interview, I made the government's position absolutely clear:

Cecil Parkinson: I believe that the public here share the view of the islanders that there can be no place for Argentina in those islands, in the future administration of them or in any share of the sovereignty of them.

Brian Walden: No place? So whatever Argentina says or does, whatever anybody else says or does on her behalf, as far as this government's concerned there is no place for Argentina, either in the administration of the islands or to have any share in sovereignty?

Cecil Parkinson: Mr Walden, I think that what has happened as a result of this invasion is that the Argentinians have made it almost impossible to imagine any accommodation with them about sovereignty. If they had behaved, if they'd kept the diplomatic options open, if they'd behaved well towards the Falklanders, pursued over a period of years a policy which reassured the Falklanders, then it might have been possible for us to reach an agreement with them, but I can't imagine any circumstances in which now the islanders are going willingly to see Argentina have a say, any sort of say, about their future, and I can't imagine the British people allowing a British government to come to any sort of accommodation of that kind.

The next morning, Francis spoke to me before the War Cabinet, saying that he was going to raise the matter of my interview at the meeting. He said that he had been unaware that I was going to do it. I pointed out to him that I had been briefed by his Press Secretary as well as the Prime Minister's. He was clearly taken by surprise. I am sure that some FCO people felt that the interview was part of a prime-ministerially prompted attempt to undermine their negotiations, but it was nothing of the kind. Afterwards, a number of the military came up to me and congratulated me on the interview. This further underlined the tension between the diplomats and the military, a tension incidentally mirrored on the other side of the Atlantic, in the US administration.

President Reagan came to London following the Versailles Summit and had breakfast at Number 10 with Mrs Thatcher. The War Cabinet was due to meet at 9.30 and, just before, he and she came down the staircase together. He was extremely relaxed and as we were introduced to him he launched into an entertaining but rather long story. The Prime Minister was clearly impatient to start the meeting and as soon as he had finished his story, and before he could start on another one, she took him firmly by the elbow and escorted him to his car.

The Versailles Conference effectively marked the end of the diplomatic effort. President Reagan, in his speech to both Houses of Parliament, made it clear that we had his total support in enforcing a military solution: 'On distant islands in the South Atlantic, young men are fighting for Britain and, yes, voices have been raised protesting their sacrifice for lumps of rock and earth so far away. But those young men are not fighting for mere real estate. They fight for a cause, for a belief that armed aggression must not be allowed to succeed.' One week later, after a brilliantly executed campaign, the Argentinians surrendered at Port Stanley.

President Reagan's address to parliament had another interesting result. It was the first time that I had seen a speaker use an Autocue. I had assumed that the two glass stands placed to either side of the President were bulletproof screens to protect him and so I was surprised, when I went to look at them, to see the text of his speech reflected in them. Having watched the President make his speech, without appearing once to look at his text, I had seen how effective the system could be. I wondered how Mrs Thatcher would take to it and so I persuaded Chris Lawson at Central Office to borrow one and arranged to have it set up at Number 10. We put a speech which Mrs Thatcher had made a few weeks before on to the Autocue and she started to read it. At first, I thought that she must have learnt the script by heart since she was not looking at her notes. However, it soon became clear that she was reading the speech – she had taken to the system like a duck to water. From then on, she used the Autocue system for almost every major speech.

ODSA continued to meet regularly for a few weeks after the surrender and then, following our meeting on 15 July, a memorandum arrived from the Cabinet Secretary announcing that ODSA was herewith disbanded and inviting me to sit on a new sub-committee to oversee the continuing arrangements for the future defence and development of the Falkland Islands. So ended the War Cabinet and with it the most extraordinary two and a half months of my political life.

Three events were held to mark the successful outcome of the campaign, a service in St Paul's, a dinner at Number 10 and a march past in the City followed by a lunch in the Guildhall. For me, the highlight was the dinner at Number 10. It was held in October, in the state dining room, on the evening before the victory parade. It was attended by the main participants in the campaign, civilian and military, and for the first time we met face to face Woodward, Thompson and a host of others whose names and faces were familiar, whose lives had been in our hands and in whose hands our political future had for a time rested. The dining room could only take about seventy people and wives could not be included. Mrs Thatcher was, therefore, the only lady present at the dinner although we met our wives at a reception at Number 10 after the dinner. I recently looked at a photograph which was taken before dinner and realized with surprise that had the Argentinians invaded a few months later the main participants would have been very different. Sir Terence Lewin, the Chief of the Defence Staff, Admiral Sir Henry Leach of the Navy, and Air Chief Marshall Sir Michael Beetham of the RAF all retired within months. Major-General Jeremy Moore also retired, as did Sir Anthony Parsons and Sir Nicholas Henderson. The Falklands campaign thus provided a fitting climax to a number of outstanding careers.

After the loyal toast, Sir Terence Lewin, the Chief of the Defence Staff, made a short speech in which he thanked the War Cabinet and, in particular, the Prime Minister for the support he and his colleagues had received. She, in turn, thanked him and his colleagues for their skill and courage. After these formalities were ended, Mrs Thatcher stood up and said with a smile, 'Gentlemen, shall we join the ladies?'

11 *In the Hands of the Electorate*

I found the role of non-departmental minister interesting and worthwhile. I was included by the Prime Minister in most of the major Cabinet committees and sub-committees and also on a number of ad hoc groups which were set up to look at particular subjects or deal with particular problems. Most members of those committees were ministers in charge of departments, and arrived at the meetings with a departmental brief setting out a line to take and argued a case from a particular department's point of view. The non-departmental minister can take a broader and more political view and can often be the decisive voice when a controversial issue is being discussed. There is a danger that departmental ministers can become blinkered, and need to be reminded of the overall commitments of the government and of the government's general approach.

I never asked to be put on any committee, but I found that the list of committees on which I served grew longer. The Prime Minister clearly found it useful to have a person with the broader view taking part in discussions. Although I found preparation for Cabinet committees and Cabinet meetings themselves very time-consuming, they were an excellent way of making sure that I was in touch with all the major initiatives in government. My close involvement in a wide range of policy areas gave rise to a new aspect of my work as Party Chairman.

After the Falklands, during which I appeared on innumerable television and radio programmes explaining the government's reasoning and actions, I found that I was increasingly contacted by the media to explain a wide range of policies, and departmental ministers accepted this. One became, in fact, the Cabinet all-rounder, and if the specialist minister was not available for some reason or did not want to appear, I appeared instead. This was a relatively new aspect of the Chairman's job, but it has now become established as an important part of the role.

Nevertheless, my main task was to prepare the organization to fight the general election and this was what I concentrated on. In the early summer of 1982, I called a meeting of all the departmental heads at Central Office and asked them to take stock of their departments, to assess what additional personnel and resources they would need to fight the campaign, and to work out where they would get them from at the minimum expense. I was very anxious not to see the permanent staff at Central Office hugely increased before the general election. Funds pour into Central Office ahead of a general election, but in the year or two afterwards people are less inclined to give. This means that if the permanent staff is built up ahead of the general election, as soon as it is over the funds necessary to sustain the organization are not available, nor is there a continued need for the enlarged staff.

Michael Spicer took charge of this exercise and it proved very worthwhile. Long before the end of the year we had a very clear idea of what we were going to need and plans were made to ensure that we met those needs. It became clear to us that the Central Office computer system was totally out of date, but we had no money to replace it. The Durbar Club, a group of Asian businessmen who supported the party, stepped in to help us. The Chairman and founder of the group, Narindar Saroop, persuaded his members to fund the purchase of a new computer system and this was in place some months before the election. It proved extremely useful and, amongst other things, was used to develop a direct mailing campaign to build up support and to raise money in a number of parliamentary constituencies which had been identified as in need of strengthening.

I asked Michael, in consultation with the departmental heads, to work out how we would use the space available in Central Office and where we would accommodate the additional people we were going to need. Our planning was put to the test on the day Mrs Thatcher decided to have the general election. Within a matter of hours additional people and equipment had been moved into Central Office; the building had been reorganized, and several hundred additional telephone lines had been installed. It was a brilliant piece of logistical planning, and Michael and his colleagues deserve great credit for it.

Chris Lawson revitalized and recast the Conservative Party's newspaper, *Newsline*, and built it up to a circulation of more than 150,000. He had established a good working relationship with Saatchi & Saatchi whom we had decided to reappoint as our advertising agency. He also, with Keith Britto, reorganized our private polls and, working with Tim Bell of Saatchi's, produced some excellent party political broadcasts. For some months before, we had been making our own broadcasts and it showed. They were very amateurish home movies, and I decided we should either stop having them, which was unthinkable, or find the money to produce worthwhile broadcasts. We decided to do the latter.

A recurring theme of all party Conferences and meetings was criticism of the party's attempts to get its message over, and Central Office was usually cast as the culprit. At this time David Boddy, who had not yet left, ran a press department of about three people, and it became clear to me that this small group alone could not change the public's attitude to the government. I therefore arranged to call on each government department and discuss with the Secretary of State, or the Senior Minister, ways of making sure that the government's case was put positively by its Press Officers who outnumbered my own by several hundred to one. I urged each departmental head to appoint a minister with special responsibility for making sure that good news about the department was given as much publicity as possible. I stressed that I did not want ministers to do Central Office's job and promote the party, but equally Central Office could not be expected to promote the government's case.

Chris Lawson and David Boddy set to work to draw up budgets for the election campaign and, in consultation with Saatchi & Saatchi, to discuss its style. There is a great deal of misunderstanding about the relationship between advertising agencies and the political parties they work for. My view was that it was the politicians' job to develop the policies and to decide the themes which would run throughout the campaign. The advertising agency's job was to give us the benefit of its expertise in putting our policies over. The agency took no part at all in the formulation of policy.

It was clear that the Prime Minister was going to be the focal point of our campaign and at a very early stage I set out to identify the team that would travel with her and work with her during the election. Roger Boaden had organized the 1979 tour and he took charge of drawing up a personal programme for her.

In November 1982 I asked the Prime Minister if she could set aside a day at Chequers early in the New Year at which we could report to her on the state of our election preparations and could take a preliminary view of the style of campaign we would wish to fight. We met at Chequers on Wednesday 5 January. Each of the directors gave a fifteen-minute presentation setting out their objectives and the state of their preparations. Each presentation was followed up by about half an hour's discussion. All went well until David Boddy made his presentation about the style of the campaign and our planned use of the media. He had produced an excellent paper in which he discussed how to use local radio and breakfast television. Since the 1979 campaign, local radio had become a very potent way of launching a story, not only to the local audience but to the national media networks and the newspapers. We also had at our disposal the new phenomenon of breakfast television and David had developed ideas about how we could take advantage of it. The Prime Minister was rather sceptical about it, and as David took us through his short paper he made the mistake of talking about 'your projected breakfast television appearances'. She grimaced at this and pointed out very icily that she had no plans to appear on breakfast television. This slightly unnerved David, for whom she had in fact a very high regard, but he recovered well.

The incident was not untypical and showed one of Mrs Thatcher's more infuriating characteristics. She could, on occasions, seize unreasonably on an unimportant, secondary point, and flog it to death while ignoring much more important and controversial issues. In addition, she did not seem on occasions to be aware of how intimidating she could appear to people who felt inhibited about arguing with a Prime Minister. She expected people to fight back and enjoyed an argument. What was combativeness to her was rudeness to a lot of people, particularly relatively junior people who worked for her.

The morning session was ended by Chris Lawson who outlined his plans for the use of polling and for taking stock regularly on a daily basis of any change in public opinion and its various shifts during the campaign.

The afternoon session was given over to Saatchi's who had done some extremely interesting in-depth research which clearly identified a number of perceptions and misperceptions about the party which would need to be strengthened or corrected either before or during the campaign itself. This was the first time I had seen Tim Bell in action on a major occasion with Mrs Thatcher present. She clearly had tremendous confidence in him and he showed that it was not misplaced.

The first part of his presentation consisted of a film which was an edited version of a number of group discussions which had been held in different parts of the country. The participants had been selected by an independent polling organization and were not political activists. They did not know on whose behalf the discussion was being held and it ranged over a wide number of subjects, covering all the parties, their leaders, political issues, economic issues and moral issues. It was like being the proverbial fly on the wall and not all of what was said was welcome, but most of it was. Unemployment was the biggest issue at the time, but there was no agreement about who was at fault and the government was only one of the culprits blamed. The unions and the Labour Party were both criticized. A strong thread of patriotism was revealed following the Falklands campaign, which was universally accepted as evidence that Britain mattered and needed strong defences. But time after time, the main subject of discussion was Margaret Thatcher. Many comments were positive and she was seen as far and away the best leader, but she was also regarded as a person who had little concern for individual people and was almost too tough and domineering. The overall conclusion about her was very positive and we felt we could build on her strengths and answer the criticisms. It was not easy to tell the Prime Minister face to face that the public thought she was uncaring and domineering, but Tim handled the whole presentation superbly and no punches were pulled.

He ended with a series of proposals for the campaign, including a set of proposed posters, most of which were rejected out of hand by the Prime Minister. I have sometimes suspected that Tim Bell deliberately produced designs she would not like before he produced the designs that he really wanted her to consider, expecting that she would reject a high percentage of what she was shown. At the end of the day, the Prime Minister was clearly well satisfied by what she had seen and heard, and we arranged to carry forward the work and to meet again at Easter.

Following this formal meeting I saw Mrs Thatcher regularly, but informally, quite often after a ten-o'clock vote in the House of Commons with Ian Gow the only other person present. At these meetings we would settle detailed arrangements over a glass of whisky before getting down to her favourite relaxation, discussing people and politics.

Ian Gow, her PPS from 1979 to 1983, was a person of enormous influence at that time. He had a tremendous capacity for hard work, and loved eating and drinking. He had a wide circle of friends and acquaintances inside and outside the House of Commons, and worked very hard at maintaining his contacts and promoting the interests of those he respected. Alan Clark, Nick Ridley, and John King, the Chairman of British Airways, all owed their positions, sometimes in the face of opposition, to Ian's influence with the Prime Minister, whom he admired enormously. His other great heroes were Winston Churchill and General de Gaulle, and he could recite at length and verbatim many of their great speeches. His working day started at 6.0 a.m. and he would rarely return to what he called 'the socialist republic of Lambeth' before midnight, quite often accompanied by two or three colleagues from the House. In the summer he enjoyed sitting in the small garden of his London house, drinking and chatting and, above all, laughing. He loved life, adored his wife and sons, and felt that working as closely as he did with a person whom he respected so much was a unique privilege. Mrs Thatcher, for her part, had a tremendous personal regard for Ian, and even after his resignation from her government over Northern Ireland policy, they continued to meet regularly and he continued to influence her thinking. She always intended to bring him back into the government at some stage and his murder in 1990 was a great blow to her. Some people, of whom I am one, believe that had he lived, she would have received the two votes she needed to win in the leadership election a few months later. He would have worked unceasingly for her and would have influenced the necessary votes and more. With his shining domed bald head, rather old-fashioned glasses, waistcoated suits, laced shoes and scholarly air, he deliberately gave the impression of being a rather passé family solicitor. He was, in fact, lively, in touch and immensely entertaining. The tributes paid to him on his death from all parts of the House were clear evidence of the pride the whole House placed in his membership of it.

In July 1982, I had raised with the Prime Minister the question of preparing our manifesto for the next election. She had always said that we would not have an election until the government had completed at least four years of its term. This meant that I had to make sure we were ready to fight from May 1983 onwards. She had already appointed Ferdinand Mount, a leading journalist, as head of the Policy Unit at Number 10, and her intention was that he would actually write the manifesto. I suggested to her that she should put Geoffrey Howe, the Chancellor of the Exchequer, in overall charge. I knew that he had been surprised not to be included in the War Cabinet, and felt that putting him in charge of producing the manifesto would demonstrate her confidence in him, and would enhance his already high standing in the party. At first, she was not enthusiastic, saying she did not want the dead hand of the Treasury on the manifesto. She later agreed, subject to me working with him, to make sure that politics did not take a back seat to economics.

At the last Cabinet before the 1982 summer recess, after the officials had left the room, she told the Cabinet this decision and added that we should all take advantage of our summer holiday since we might not get one in 1983, because it could be election year. Mrs Thatcher did not like holidays and often gave the impression that they were something that only lazy people took.

On the Friday before this Cabinet I had accompanied the Queen, in my role as Chancellor of the Duchy of Lancaster, to the Needwood estate, part of the Duchy estate in Staffordshire. The Duchy of Lancaster dates from 1265 when Henry III granted lands, forfeited by Simon de Montfort, Earl of Leicester, to his youngest son Edmund. The administrative functions of the Duchy date from 1351 when Edmund's grandson, Henry of Grosmont, was appointed Duke of Lancaster in recognition of 'astonishing deeds of prowess and feats of arms' and was given the rights and responsibilities of a Count Palatine within the County of Lancaster. Palatinate powers are royal powers which are given in franchise to an individual.

The first record of the office of Chancellor dates back to 1363 when he is described as a member of John of Gaunt's household. Today, although the Chancellor is appointed by the Prime Minister, he has a personal responsibility to the sovereign for the administration and management of the Duchy estates in Cheshire, Lincolnshire, Northamptonshire, North Yorkshire, Shropshire, and Staffordshire, as well as in the County Palatine (which after local government reorganization now includes Lancashire, Merseyside, and Greater Manchester). The Duchy also owns a number of properties in urban areas. The Chancellor is responsible for the appointment of all magistrates in the County Palatine and recommends to the Queen appointments for the office of High Sheriff in the county. The Duchy is also responsible for the upkeep of forty-two church livings as well as the administration of the Queen's Chapel of the Savoy, the Chapel of the Royal Victorian Order.

During lunch at Needwood, Her Majesty asked me where I was going for my holidays and asked me what sort of holiday Mrs Thatcher would be having. I explained my plans and said that I wasn't sure when the Prime Minister would be going away, but that it would only be for a few days because Mrs Thatcher did not believe in holidays. At the end of the day, after I had said goodbye to the Queen, who was flying back to London in one of the planes of the Queen's Flight, to my surprise she turned back to me. 'Mr Parkinson, they tell me you have influence with the Prime Minister. She must take a proper holiday and if you will speak to her about it so will I!' I said I would speak to her. I saw Mrs Thatcher the following Monday for lunch, and told her about my conversation with Her Majesty. I saw her again on the Wednesday before Cabinet. She had seen the Queen the previous evening. 'What on earth have you been saying to the Queen?' she asked. 'She told me that she hoped I would be having a proper holiday because she felt I deserved one.' She was touched that the Queen had shown such personal concern for her, but it didn't affect her attitude to holidays!

As an initial stage in preparing the party manifesto, Geoffrey decided to set up a number of policy groups to look at a range of problems, including housing, law and order, competition policy and the family. The groups were each to have about ten members, drawn from the back benches in parliament, academics and businessmen. They were to be chaired by a person appointed by Geoffrey and the Research Department would provide the secretariat. They were to report back by the end of January 1983. In addition, at a later stage, each departmental Cabinet minister was asked to prepare a 500-word summary of what his department's aims would be if he were to be in charge of that department in the next parliament. These reports and summaries were to provide the raw material from which Ferdie Mount would produce the first draft of the manifesto to be discussed at Number 11 with Geoffrey in the chair in early April. Ferdie did a superb job of putting all the disparate pieces into a coherent whole. Geoffrey and I decided that we would not show the document to the Prime Minister until we were satisfied with it and she finally saw it when it was in its third or fourth draft. On 9 April, a group including Nigel Lawson, David Howell, John Biffen, Norman Tebbit, Geoffrey, Ferdie and myself spent the whole day working through the draft page by page. Substantial changes were made and Ferdie then went away to revise and amend.

The final draft was approved by the Prime Minister at Chequers on the day before the election was announced. The manifesto contained a number of major new proposals for the reform of trade union law, local government and privatization, but it basically presented a continuation of policies which were being pursued, were working and were necessary. The real novelty of the manifesto was that a government which had been elected to pursue a set of policies and had actually done so was proposing to carry on the same policies if re-elected for a second term. The government offered the electorate continuity and consistency, which should have been unusual enough, but to a media brought up on a rich diet of spectacular policy U-turns and a continuing search for novelty, the manifesto was seen as anodyne.

By April 1983 our organization was in top gear, our finances were in better shape and the manifesto could be completed quickly. The one outstanding question was the date. In the autumn of 1982, Chris Lawson and I agreed that he would produce a huge diary for the remainder of our theoretical term of office up to the last possible date for a general election, 24 May 1984. Every event of political significance would be logged. At the time there were in theory about eighty available Thursdays, but by process of elimination we quickly reduced the number to seven or eight. There were two or three possible Thursdays in May/June 1983, September/October 1983 or March/April 1984. Because of the change in the method of registering school leavers for employment, we knew that the unemployment figures for August and September would be the worst for decades, and would make September difficult. The Liberals and Social Democrats were due to hold separate conferences in the first and third weeks of September, and would receive a substantial boost in the polls if we were to call an election after their conferences but before our own. If we waited until our own, then the election would be in November which is a little late, with the weather uncertain and the daylight hours fewer. I had begun early in 1983 to favour May or June of that year. I agreed with the Prime Minister that we would meet at Chequers on the Sunday after the local elections when we would be able to analyse the results and at that point would take a decision about a June election.

The local elections took place on Thursday 5 May and the results were very satisfactory with a net gain for us of 128 seats. As soon as the results were available our computer staff started the work of processing the data on a constituency-by-constituency basis. We had also commissioned independent polls taken on the Friday and Saturday with a sample of about 2,500 each, twice the usual number, so that we could analyse the results in more depth than is normally possible. Chris Lawson and Keith Britto were in charge of this operation, and on Sunday morning I drove to Central Office from my home in Hertfordshire to collect all the results and analysis. Chris and his team had worked all through the night on the Saturday and the results of their work and that of the polling organizations was finally ready at 10.0 a.m. Although there were some minor differences between them they gave a uniformly encouraging picture. I left for Chequers in a very cheerful frame of mind, but was brought down to earth sharply when I arrived at 11.30 a.m. to give the Prime Minister the information from Central Office. Before the others arrived for the twelve o'clock meeting, Mrs Thatcher left me in no doubt that she was not committed to a June election and would need a great deal of persuading. We had more than a year of our term left and, with the economy improving steadily, we were under no pressure to go early. With that, we joined the other Cabinet ministers plus various advisers and aides. Geoffrey Howe, Willie Whitelaw, Keith Joseph, Norman Tebbit, John Biffen, and the Chief Whip, Michael Jopling, had all been asked.

The number seven, (six Cabinet ministers, including me, plus the Chief Whip), gave rise to one of Denis Healey's best jokes. He quipped, 'This was not the Magnificent Seven riding out to do battle with the formidable enemy, this was the seven dwarfs trundling out to meet Snow White.'

I started the proceedings by taking the meeting through the full range of options and possible dates. I then went through the polls and local government results, on an area-by-area basis, and concentrated on the critical seats where the news was particularly encouraging. I then put some of the more general arguments in favour of going on 9 June. One point, which was developed later by Geoffrey Howe, particularly weighed with Mrs Thatcher. The election would be the first to be fought without exchange controls. The markets had been steady because we had been consistently ahead in the polls for several months. If we were to carry on and our lead were to decline, we could face damaging political and economic uncertainty leading to loss of confidence and a flight from the pound. After I had finished my presentation and answered various detailed questions, the Prime Minister held what she liked to call a second reading debate and each person expressed a view. It was clear that all present, with varying degrees of enthusiasm, favoured the ninth. We then adjourned for lunch with the Prime Minister looking troubled and under pressure.

After lunch we resumed our discussion, with Mrs Thatcher raising various arguments against calling an election, the chief of which was that the manifesto was not finished. I pointed out that it could be finished within a couple of hours, whereupon she decided that we would finish it there and then. We then spent about three hours going through the document, line by line. At various stages of this exercise the Cabinet ministers present found reasons for leaving and by the time we had finished at about 7.30 p.m., only Michael Jopling, Ian Gow and I were left. We then discussed a number of other problems such as her promise to President Reagan to attend the Williamsburg summit on 28 May. We felt that she could and should go.

At about 8.0 p.m., Mrs Thatcher was sitting staring into the fire and suddenly said, 'Even if I wanted to call an election, the Queen could hardly be available at such short notice.' Ian Gow slipped out of the room and came back ten minutes later to say that he had spoken to Buckingham Palace and the Queen could see Mrs Thatcher at twelve noon the next day. I am still not sure that the look she shot at him was one of gratitude. At this point she stood up, thanked us for our help, and said that she had taken no decision, would sleep on the matter and would tell us of her decision in the morning. Ian and Michael Jopling came back with me to my home in Hertfordshire and after a jovial supper, prepared by a surprised Ann, we were driven up to London together.

Early the next morning, I was telephoned and asked to go to Number 10 at 9.0 a.m. A brisk and untroubled Prime Minister told me she had decided to call an election on 9 June. She was holding a piece of paper which looked rather like a shopping list and was written in her own hand. It started, 'The Queen, the Speaker, the leader of the opposition ...' It was a list of the people she had to inform and she told me she had written it at about 5.30 that morning when she had finally taken her decision.

Parliament was dissolved on Friday 13 May and that night Mrs Thatcher launched our election campaign at the Scottish Conservative Conference in Perth. She concentrated her attack on the Labour Party which she branded as extremely left-wing and told the conference that at the election there was the 'chance to banish from our land the dark divisive clouds of Marxist socialism'. The extremism of the Labour Party was a continuing theme of our campaign, and the truth of the charge was underlined on the following Monday when Labour published its manifesto, *The New Hope for Britain*, which was described later by Gerald Kaufman as 'the longest suicide note in history'.

Labour and the Alliance published their manifestos and held their first press conferences on the same day. We decided to launch ours two days later and to hold our first press conference the following Friday. Since we were entitled to equal coverage on radio and television, we were able to upstage their formal press conferences with arranged events of our own choosing and to prepare meticulously our launch and opening press conference.

With the help of supporters, we had been able to modernize our conference rooms, and with good air conditioning and modern media facilities and furniture, the setting for our conferences was infinitely superior to that of our rivals. Behind the platform, the walls were covered with blue and grey drapes. A myth was created that we used the blue drapes for upbeat conferences and grey for the more sombre subjects. It was supposed to be part of our media-manipulating tactics. In fact, it depended on which our caretaker felt like using and he rang the changes as he thought fit.

We saw the press conference as our main opportunity to try and set the agenda for the day. The subject was chosen and the preparations were meticulous. The build-up began in the early hours of the morning between two and four o'clock when a member of the staff read all the day's papers and prepared a digest of them. At 5.0 a.m. Tony Shrimsley, now head of press and publicity, and Stephen Sherbourne, who briefed the Prime Minister, met and worked through the digest, deciding which subjects were likely to be raised at that morning's press conference. When the desk officers in the Research Department arrived at 6.30 a.m. they found on their desks the request for a one-page brief on the appropriate subject. Many of them had been prepared in advance but might need modifying, others had to be prepared from scratch. By the time I arrived for the 7.30

a.m. Chairman's meeting, which was attended by the key heads of department, all the briefing was ready.

My meeting began with a review of the polls and the fast-feedback report. This report was based on a selected cross section of fifty people from all over the country who at the end of each day telephoned in their reaction to the day's events, giving us their opinion on where we had scored or dropped a clanger and their view of the performance of our opponents. We found this an informative and useful pointer to our own performance and to our mistakes. After this, Tony Shrimsley summed up the previous day's media coverage, and his view of what subjects would be covered at the press conference, and of the action necessary to counter any unfavourable coverage or criticism. Stephen then produced the briefing and we worked through it to make sure we were satisfied with it. If it needed amending or improving this was done. By the time the Prime Minister arrived at 8.30 a.m. we were ready to provide an agreed, accurate and concise briefing.

We were joined for the Prime Minister's meeting by the Cabinet minister who would launch the chosen subject and our first task was to examine his draft press release. Once approved, it went away to be prepared for release, and we then followed a similar agenda to the one at the earlier meeting. At about 9.0 a.m. the person who had attended the Alliance press conference would give us a verbal report on it. The person from the Labour conference arrived about twenty minutes later and also reported. By 9.25, when we went down to the press conference, we were all fully briefed and ready to deal with anything the media could throw at us.

The first twenty minutes were devoted to the press release and questions were answered by the minister of the day, with the Prime Minister intervening very rarely. The second part of the session was devoted to questions to the Prime Minister and could cover any area of policy, or any other subject the huge gathering of journalists cared to raise. It was very testing for the Prime Minister, but thanks to years of preparing for the twice-weekly Prime Minister's questions in the House, plus our own briefing, she never failed to answer a question. Towards the end of the campaign, a group of journalists decided to try to trip her up by asking her an extremely technical question about social security, which we had not anticipated. She gave a superbly detailed answer and a short lecture about the social security system, and then produced the relevant act from her handbag. I asked her afterwards how she knew the answer. She pointed out that between 1961 and 1964 she had been Parliamentary Secretary in the Ministry of Pensions and had maintained a continuing interest.

About a month before the election was called, I had mapped out a draft programme for our press conferences, which would enable us to cover the areas of policy which we wanted to cover, in the order in which we would ideally like to discuss them. I recognized that we might have to change the subjects if events so dictated. In fact, we were able to stick to our chosen programme without change during the entire campaign. Our opponents never, at any stage, forced us off our agenda and on to ground of their choosing. This was in part a measure of their incompetence. I decided that we would raise as early as possible the subjects on which we were alleged to be vulnerable: unemployment, the Health Service, the economy, and caring. We raised each of these at least twice in the first few days, at the end of which the media wanted a change of subject and we were then able to focus attention on our strong areas: defence, housing, including the sale of council houses, trade-union reform, and privatization. By election day, we were seen, according to the polls, as the party with the best policies over the whole spectrum of issues, including jobs, the Health Service, and caring. We made substantial gains in the public mind in these areas during the campaign, and having started with a lead in the polls of fifteen per cent we ended with a lead of twenty-one per cent. Our well-thought-out, carefully costed, consistently and well-presented policies compared very favourably with those of our opponents who were deeply divided on some of the major issues and, in the case of the Labour Party, on most. Denis Healey and James Callaghan, for example, were presenting one defence policy; John Silkin and Michael Foot another. David Steel, David Owen and Roy Jenkins each gave different versions of the Alliance's taxation policy.

The leaders' campaigns presented a similar contrast. Margaret Thatcher left Smith Square each day after the press conference and, after a full and well-spent day in which the press and the media had every opportunity to get their stories for that evening's programme or for the next day's papers, and she had met large numbers of people and encouraged the optimum number of our supporters, she was back in Number 10 by 8.30 most evenings to work on her prime-ministerial papers and her next speeches. Michael Foot, on the other hand, would finish up late at night addressing a rally with the television news programmes having to transmit live whatever he happened to be saying to fill the time they had set aside for coverage of the Labour leader's campaign. Michael Foot's stamina and the personal effort he made were very impressive, but it was a criticism of Labour's organization that he had to make such an effort to make up for its inadequacy. He wasn't helped by the fact that Labour's General Secretary found it necessary one morning to reassure the world's press that Michael Foot was still the leader of the Labour Party.

The Alliance were so unhappy with Roy Jenkins' performance that ten days before polling day, after a weekend conference, they announced that David Steel was 'to take a very much more prominent role in the closing stages of the campaign'.

Divided on policy and unhappy with their leaders, our opponents became progressively less impressive and more shrill. We, for our part, kept to our programme, explained our record on policies and concentrated our main attack on Labour. The Alliance, partly on grounds of personal animosity, since all the SDP leaders were refugees from the Labour Party, spent most of their time attacking the opposition and not the government, as is usual at elections. We cast the Alliance as Labour's only hope of victory, pointing out that Labour governments had only ever been elected on the back of a large third-party vote, but other than that, we were happy to see our opponents fighting each other vigorously for second place.

The Saatchi & Saatchi team, led by Tim Bell, performed heroically during the period. Superb newspaper advertisements flowed endlessly from them and were a highlight of the campaign. Their first, headed 'Putting a cross in the Labour box is the same as signing this piece of paper' then listed fourteen hair-raising commitments which voters would be making if they voted Labour. It was drawn from the Labour manifesto and was scrupulously researched. It was, in an amusing way, a devastating indictment of Labour. They also produced the party election broadcasts for radio and television, and their work was of consistently high quality. They were also great fun to work with. Gordon Reece had returned from California for the duration of the campaign and gave Tim valuable help and support. Gordon is one of the very few people who can make one feel better just by being present. A former TV producer who worked closely with Mrs Thatcher from her early days as leader, he subsequently became Publicity Director at Central Office. After the 1979 general election, he went to America to earn some money, but never lost contact with the British political scene or the British media. Popular, jovial and kind, he is also immensely shrewd and experienced. He worked with Saatchi's on the party election broadcasts and with Mrs Thatcher on her television appearances and attended all key meetings. Gordon loves a glass of champagne and fine cigars and during the 1979 general election, a senior official at Central Office raised with our Treasurer, Alistair McAlpine, the cost of Gordon's champagne and cigars. 'What does your car run on?' asked Alistair in reply. 'Petrol,' said the puzzled official. 'Well, Gordon Reece runs on champagne and cigars, and he runs extremely well on them!'

The campaign had its lighter moments. When Labour published its manifesto, Alistair McAlpine gave them their biggest ever order for 1,000 copies. He did it for two reasons. First, he sent copies to our major supporters so that they would realize what they were in for if Labour won. Second, he felt that Labour might be incompetent or lucky enough not to get it into circulation, so we decided to do it for them.

One of our less successful posters was one where we offered a dozen bottles of claret (Roy Jenkins' favourite drink) to anyone who knew what the Alliance's policies were. Within hours of the posters appearing, a group of Alliance supporters carrying copies of their manifesto appeared outside Central Office demanding their prize.

On another occasion, Saatchi's asked permission to film inside a derelict hospital which had been closed. We wanted to make the point that although old hospitals were being closed, new ones were being opened and we already had the film of the new hospital about a mile away which had replaced it. The *Daily Mirror* then ran a story claiming that we had sent actors and actresses dressed as doctors, nurses and patients into the old hospital and had tarted it up to look like a new hospital in an attempt to mislead people. We pointed out that the reverse was true; for our purposes, the grimmer the empty hospital was the greater the contrast with the new one.

I had decided to be available at Central Office for the duration of the campaign, so that I could deal with any emerging events or stories which might call for an immediate response and without which might be damaging. We had set up a monitoring unit which recorded all radio and television broadcasts with any political content. As a result we were able to react quickly and nip trouble in the bud, or help a story to develop which was in our interest.

There were a number of such incidents. The first was the leak of a draft report from the Treasury Select Committee which implied that the government had followed the wrong economic policies and thus had contributed greatly and unnecessarily to the increase in unemployment. Since the Select Committee had a majority of Conservative members and was chaired by the Chairman of the 1922 Committee, Sir Edward du Cann, the report was potentially extremely embarrassing. I spoke immediately to Edward who assured me that this was a draft report prepared by officials and did not represent the views of the majority of the committee and would not be endorsed. I asked him if he would be prepared to issue a statement to that effect, and he said he would. We agreed to issue it for him. The story had broken on the early-morning BBC Radio 4 programme, *Today*. By the time of our news conference at 9.20 the du Cann statement had been issued, and the story was effectively dead.

On Wednesday 25 May the *Jewish Chronicle* revealed that our candidate in Stockton South, Thomas Finnegan, had once stood as a National Front candidate in the Midlands. He had subsequently moved to Stockton where he had abandoned his former views and become a much respected member of the local community. Having joined an engineering company as a junior manager, he had become the Managing Director and had turned it into a very successful business. He was a churchwarden, pillar of the local Rotary Club, and active in a host of local charities. He had been enthusiastically nominated for the candidates' list by people who had only known him after he had left the Midlands. He had not been asked about his membership of other political parties and had not volunteered the information. Keith Joseph, himself Jewish, was by coincidence due to go to Stockton to support him on the day the story appeared, and went ahead with his plans.

I asked Thomas Finnegan to come to London that day and met him at Central Office. He explained that he was ashamed of his National Front past and bitterly regretted both that he had once held racist views and that he had not told us about them. I decided that he should be given every opportunity to try to convince the public of the sincerity of his change of view. He appeared on a number of major radio and television programmes and came over well. For my part, I pointed out that many of the candidates Labour was fielding had been chosen because they still held extremist views, whereas Mr Finnegan knew that the fact he had once held racist views, even though he had long abandoned them, would disqualify him as a candidate for us. The story died very quickly.

Later in the campaign Denis Healey raised the Falklands, and in particular, the sinking of the *Belgrano*, accusing the Prime Minister of 'glorying in slaughter'. I was speaking at a meeting in my constituency when the news broke and immediately after the meeting spoke to Mrs Thatcher at Number 10. We agreed that she should stay out of it and that I would reply. I drafted a statement describing the remarks as 'the most contemptible of the campaign'. I then spoke to the Press Officer at Central Office who issued it. I also recorded a number of radio interviews from my car telephone on the way back into London so that our response went out with Healey's remarks.

The next day I was due to do the BBC television programme, *Question Time*, with Healey and Bill Rodgers from the National Exhibition Centre in Birmingham. Normally, the participants had dinner together before the programme, but I felt that it would feed public cynicism about politicians if, the day after remarks which I genuinely felt to be unacceptable, I was to be found having dinner with the person who made them. The first question was about the *Belgrano* and Denis Healey very wisely apologized for what he had said the night before.

The next question was about an advertisement which we had placed in the ethnic press showing a handsome, well-dressed black man, with the caption, 'to Labour he's black, to Conservatives he's British'. This had infuriated the Labour Party who regarded the ethnic vote as theirs. Our poster argued the case for equality of treatment and against positive discrimination. It was written by a black copywriter at Saatchi's and was extremely effective. The producer chose to spend nearly fifteen minutes of a fifty-minute programme on this subject having spent less on the *Belgrano*. I assume it was an attempt to redress the damage caused to Labour by the *Belgrano* issue, but it made for a very boring and repetitive programme. I had arranged to see the Prime Minister at Number 10 at 10.30 p.m. and to travel back to London by helicopter. Helicopters are not allowed into the Battersea Heliport after 10.30 p.m. so it was absolutely vital that I left the moment the programme finished. I had explained this to Robin Day, and had offered him a lift back to

London. My hurried departure was misunderstood and I was alleged the next day to have stormed off the set in a rage.

Question Time was recorded for transmission an hour or so later, and when I arrived at Number 10 I went up to the flat and into the sitting room where I found Mrs Thatcher talking to Ian Gow with Denis sitting at the far end of the room watching *Question Time* on the television. My picture was on the screen the moment I entered the room, and Denis, looking round, did a double take. 'How the hell do you manage to be here, when you're there?' he asked. Like many other people, until that moment, he had been convinced that *Question Time* was broadcast live.

We had planned to build up the tempo of our campaign and to dominate the week before the election. The Prime Minister was to address two huge rallies in the Midlands and the North and a youth rally at Wembley on the Sunday. In addition, she had three major television interviews, including one with Brian Walden, and as the government party had the final election broadcast on the Wednesday before polling, we had intended to accompany this with a massive newspaper advertising campaign, taking two pages in every national paper every day. Saatchi's had devised a superb three-page advertisement for all the Sunday papers, but I was uneasy about it. I felt that it would look as if we had money to burn, and would come back on us. I had decided not to run it and at the same time to cancel all newspaper advertising from the Sunday onwards. The news went down very badly with Tim, Alistair and Gordon who felt that I was taking an unnecessary risk. I felt I should put their arguments and my own to the Prime Minister, which was the reason for the Thursday-night meeting after *Question Time*. She accepted my advice and we saved ourselves about £1.5 million. Alistair had the last chilling word about the decision the next morning: 'If we win on Thursday, you'll be a hero, but if we lose by one, you should emigrate without delay.' In the event, we consolidated our position in the polls over the last week and had an average lead of about twenty per cent, with the seven polls on election day ranging from a sixteen to a twenty-three per cent lead for us.

On the day before polling day we had our final press conference and afterwards, over coffee, Mrs Thatcher suggested that we met at Number 10 the following day to discuss the next government. She asked me to think, in the meantime, about what job I would like to do in that government. She then left to make a final swing through the

Isle of Wight, Southampton and Portsmouth constituencies before concluding her campaign in Finchley that evening. I spent the evening in Hertsmere speaking at a crowded meeting in Potters Bar. After four exhausting but exhilarating weeks, we could do no more. We were all in the hands of the electorate.

12 The Big Decisions Are Taken Here

I spent the morning of election day touring all the committee rooms and polling stations in my constituency with Ann and my election agent, Mark Pendlington. We were clearly doing very well, and when I returned to London at lunch time I found that reports from constituencies in all parts of the country were equally encouraging. This should have been one of the happiest days of my life. We were going to have a huge electoral victory, after a very successful campaign. I personally was to record my largest ever majority in my own constituency. I was due to meet the Prime Minister at Number 10 at 4.30 p.m. for tea and she had asked me to think about what job I would like in her new Cabinet. There was, however, one large cloud on the horizon.

I had had a long term relationship with Sara Keays, who had been my secretary from 1971 to 1979 and who was back in the House of Commons as secretary to another Member, after working for a year in Brussels. We had spoken just before the campaign began when she told me that it was likely that she was pregnant. The news came as a shock to me. We met on a number of occasions over the next three weeks and Sara confirmed that she was pregnant. I decided on election day that I would tell the Prime Minister at our meeting that afternoon.

When I arrived at Number 10 I was shown up to her study. We discussed the campaign and the likely result for a few minutes and she asked me for my views about the next Cabinet. I said that I hoped that Nigel Lawson would be the Chancellor of the Exchequer. She said that he was her preferred choice. She then asked me what I would like to do and mentioned that she had a particular job in mind. I told her that I had a serious personal problem and that I was not sure I should be in her Cabinet at all. I explained what the problem was. She was immensely sympathetic, not at all censorious and said that she was sure that as sensible people we would sort it out. She

234

also pointed out that if I was not in the Cabinet when it was announced, when all the newspapers had been tipping me for a top job, every investigative journalist in the land would be given the task of finding out why, and the main news story would be that I was not in the Cabinet, not who was in it. We had to break off our meeting at this point because she was due to be interviewed by Bonnie Angelo, the head of the London bureau of *Time* magazine and she suggested that we should meet again for supper and carry on our discussion afterwards. This we did, and I suggested that a lower-profile job than the one she had in mind would give me a better chance of trying to find an answer to my problem. I had long felt that the Departments of Trade and Industry should be merged and, after further discussion, Secretary of State for a combined Department of Trade and Industry became a possibility. By the time I returned to Central Office later that evening we had more or less settled the Cabinet.

The Chairman traditionally holds a party at Central Office on election night and 1983 was no exception. People started to arrive at Smith Square from the time the polling stations closed at 10 p.m. I was joined there by Ann and my daughters, Mary, Emma and Jo, and by the time we left to be driven to Borehamwood for my own result, a crowd was gathering in Smith Square, and we left to a huge cheer. My own count was completed in record time, my majority was 14,870, an increase of 3,000 over the previous election. Because I was running the national campaign I had only been able to spend a limited amount of time in Hertsmere, but my excellent constituency organization, run superbly by Mark Pendlington and by Ann, had delivered this fine result. After expressing the traditional heartfelt thanks to all my workers, the police, the returning officer and his staff, and a few anodyne remarks about my opponents we returned to Central Office. There the party was really under way and we had a lot to celebrate. We were clearly set to win by a large majority. By the time the Prime Minister arrived at Central Office from Finchley we already had an overall majority, and as I greeted her outside Central Office, cheers echoed around the square. We went into the building and after a few minutes we were told that the huge crowd was calling for her. She went to the window in my office from where she and Denis waved to the crowd. She then asked me to join them at the window and I was delighted at the huge sea of smiling, cheering, waving people.

The next day, following a morning of television and radio interviews, we met at Number 10 for lunch. Ian Gow, Willie Whitelaw, Michael Jopling and I joined the Prime Minister and after lunch we got down to the business of confirming the new Cabinet. We were interrupted by a number of telephone calls from world leaders. One was from President Reagan, and the rest of us felt we should leave Mrs Thatcher to talk to him in private. We therefore went for a walk in the garden. Willie Whitelaw asked me if we could have a private word. He said very generously that the campaign had been a huge success and that he felt I should have one of the three top jobs, and added that he felt I could do any of them. I explained to him, without going into any details, that I had a huge personal problem, and this, in my opinion, made it necessary for me to decline. I also told him that I would explain the situation to him as soon as I felt I could. He was enormously kind, offered to help in any way he could and never breathed a word about our conversation. I have always been grateful to him for his understanding and his discretion at that time.

The new Cabinet was finally settled, Geoffrey went to the Foreign Office, Nigel to the Treasury, Leon to the Home Office. I was concerned that Norman would be bitterly disappointed at not moving from Employment. It had been intended that he should, but his proposed move was affected by my problems. Once again, our careers had become intertwined and a few months later, when I resigned, he succeeded me at the DTI, the job he really wanted.

The Cabinet was announced on Saturday evening. I had spent the afternoon at Number 10 and arrived home in the early evening. I was surprised to find a red box filled with briefing from the Department of Industry waiting for me in the hall. Apparently, at about five o'clock a driver in the standard grey suit had rung the doorbell and when my wife opened the door had asked if I was at home. Ann explained that I was at Number 10 and offered him a cup of tea. He declined politely, handed over the box and left. The trade box arrived the next day.

Two Permanent Secretaries, Sir Anthony Rawlinson and Sir Brian Hayes, had been appointed to the Departments of Trade and Industry only five or six weeks earlier, and each of them, when they moved to their new departments, had been assured that the two departments would not be merged. That decision had been changed and I was faced with the problem of having one merged department, but two fully fledged Permanent Secretaries. There was no suitable vacancy in Whitehall into which one of them could be moved and so the

Cabinet Secretary asked me if I would try to devise a means of employing them both. He suggested that we should set up an office of Corporate and Consumer Affairs as a department within a department along the lines of the Export Credit Guarantee Department, but this idea was scuppered when the Prime Minister refused to appoint a Minister of State to be the minister in charge of the proposed office. She felt that three were enough and Alex Fletcher, a very capable Undersecretary in the Scottish Office, joined the DTI to do the job. I felt that to be a senior Permanent Secretary working to a single Parliamentary Undersecretary would have made Anthony Rawlinson a laughing stock in Whitehall and beyond. I therefore abandoned the idea and invited both Sir Brian and Sir Anthony to come to my house on the Sunday afternoon to discuss the allocation of duties.

Ann was resting when they arrived, but an hour later she came into our drawing room to ask if we would like a cup of tea. I introduced her to our visitors, and I thought she looked surprised when she met Sir Brian Hayes. She explained to me that Sir Brian was the 'driver' who had delivered the red box and to whom she had offered the cup of tea the day before!

We decided that initially we would operate the department as two divisions, based on the previous departments headed up by their respective Permanent Secretaries. At my suggestion, aviation and shipping had been transferred from trade to transport, thus creating a fully fledged Department of Transport. Transport had previously been responsible only for road, rail and ports. The loss of these two divisions reduced substantially what had been the Department of Trade. It was clear that Brian Hayes would emerge as the ultimate head but for the period they had to work together the two Permanent Secretaries did so in a very civilized way.

The merged department had three Ministers of State, Paul Channon (Minister of Trade), Kenneth Baker (Minister for Industry and Information Technology), and Norman Lamont (Minister for Industry) and two Parliamentary Undersecretaries for industry, John Butcher and David Trippier, in addition to Alex Fletcher. Having settled their responsibilities, Sir Brian, Sir Anthony and I discussed the allocation of ministerial portfolios and by the time I met my colleagues the next day the shape of the department was pretty well settled.

The ministerial team was an extremely strong one, and I was

already personally friendly with all of them. At our first meeting we discussed the allocation of work. I was very keen that each minister should have clear responsibilities of his own and that the PUSSs should not be dogsbodies to the senior ministers. All were agreed about this. I then asked each minister to assume that he would be staying in his job for the next three years and to draw up a work programme setting out what he hoped to achieve during that period, bearing in mind our manifesto commitments. I asked them to break down that programme into three-monthly periods. I then saw each minister in turn and worked through the proposals. Once agreed, they were pulled together and became the department's corporate plan for the next three years. My intention was that every three months we should review achievements against the plan and could investigate any slippage or failure to meet a target. It was a simple but effective method of keeping control of the department while at the same time delegating to my colleagues to the optimum extent. I later followed the same policy in both the energy and transport departments.

I was enthusiastic about the merger and I explained my reasons in the debate on the Queen's Speech:

The arguments in favour of reuniting trade and industry were substantial. It is important that industry's dealings with the government should be kept as straightforward and simple as possible. The first benefit which I hope that industry will feel from the merger is a reduction in the duplication of effort and time spent in dealing with two government departments instead of one. It is important that government should speak to industry from a combined department with a single voice. I believe that the new department will be in an excellent position to stimulate competition in the British economy.

I had found from my time as Minister for Trade that the two departments approached most problems from a totally different point of view. The industry view was often interventionist and protectionist. Ministers were responsible for individual sectors and saw things from the point of view of those sectors almost regardless of the overall national interest. Trade traditionally took the view that it was the custodian of the GATT and the upholder of the open market wherever possible. It tried to ensure that we acted within the rules of the GATT and was sometimes regarded as almost unpatriotic when it argued the case that just because other people's imports were unwelcome this was not necessarily unfair.

A very good example of the difference in attitude between the two departments arose over the question of Brazilian footwear when I was Minister of Trade. The British Footwear Industry was facing enormous pressure from foreign imports. As an industry it had had an outstanding record in industrial relations with excellent cooperation between the unions and management. It was not a high-wage industry and the workers, recognizing the problems the industry faced, showed admirable restraint in their pay demands. Most shoe factories were also based in marginal seats, many of them Conservative-held. Unfortunately, despite some notable exceptions, the industry found it very difficult to compete on style and price with some countries, particularly Italy. Because we were fellow-members of the EEC we could not interfere with Italian imports. The industry therefore focused its discontent on Brazil. Brazil's exports to the UK were a tiny fraction of Italy's, but Brazil had high tariffs against imports of shoes into Brazil so the scene was set for the traditional argument about level playing-fields. Our tariffs were lower than theirs and this meant they had easier access to our markets than we had to theirs. The industry, backed by the Department of Industry, demanded action by the Department of Trade. We pointed out that we had a substantial surplus on our trade with Brazil overall and that if our imports from Brazil of raw materials, bought because we needed them, were eliminated, we had a huge surplus in our trade in manufactured goods. This cut no ice with the minister responsible for shoes, and I decided to arrange a meeting between the Brazilian Ambassador, the industry minister and myself. The industry minister put forward all his arguments about the pressure on the shoe industry, marginal seats and unequal tariffs and was very surprised that the Ambassador had heard them all before and was unconvinced. The Ambassador pointed out that in the year Brazil had exported seven million pounds worth of shoes to the UK, it had imported from the UK thirty-seven million pounds worth of mining equipment and that the balance of trade favoured the UK very heavily. He also pointed out that there had never been a trade in shoes from the UK to Brazil and that any Brazilians rich enough to be able to afford British shoes usually came to England to buy them. The industry minister was puzzled. He pointed out that he wasn't responsible for mining equipment but for shoes.

The concern in the Department of Trade about the merger was that industry, with its larger numbers, bigger budget and more immediate appeal to industry, would dominate the merged department and that trade's modified open-market approach would be swamped by its more interventionist counterpart. I think it was a relief to them that I had a trade background because it was clear that, within the new department, inter-departmental arguments would have to be resolved and, with me as Secretary of State, they were more likely to be resolved in trade's favour.

The next task was to agree the department's bids for the public expenditure round which had been interrupted by the general election and had to be settled as a matter of urgency. I was horrified to discover that our provisional bids exceeded the baseline set out in the previous year's public expenditure white paper by some £2,500 million. I asked each minister to review the bids submitted by his part of the department, and told them and the Permanent Secretaries that I intended to get back to baseline before submitting our final bid.

I had never liked the annual game of poker played between the Treasury and the spending departments, and was determined not to become involved. Traditionally departments inflated their bids, in the expectation that the Treasury would be its usual unreasonable self and would offer considerably less than the departments requested. Neither bid, nor counter offer, was genuinely related to need or available resources. It was a game with no losers except the taxpayer. The departments, by inflating their bids, usually settled for what they needed and sometimes more. The Treasury, and especially the Chief Secretary, got great credit for bringing about huge reductions from the original spending bids. I felt the whole process was an exhausting waste of time, and that if the spenders put in meaningful bids in the first place, and the Treasury behaved reasonably, the whole process would be a good deal shorter, much less acrimonious and would leave ministers free to concentrate on getting better value out of their current programmes rather than spending so much time arguing about next year's. When I put this case at a meeting of ministers and senior officials, it was regarded as heresy. We would be the laughing stock of Whitehall if we opted out of the game. Nevertheless, I insisted that we did go in at baseline, thus setting our own priorities, rather than having them imposed on us by the Treasury. We still ended the following year with an underspend, which suggests that I did not win a complete victory. The Treasury was also deeply suspicious of our motives in being so cooperative.

One of the first tasks I had to approach was the privatization of British Telecom. The bill to privatize British Telecom had lapsed because of the general election and had to be reintroduced as soon as possible. I had been unhappy about the original bill although I agreed that a toughly regulated private monopoly, with the opportunity for competition to develop, was infinitely to be preferred to a state-owned monopoly. I felt that more competition should have been introduced from the beginning. The problem was that the bill had been discussed exhaustively in the House in the previous parliament and there were acres of Hansard filled with arguments from government ministers, including Kenneth Baker, the Minister for Information Technology, who would be in charge of the bill again, setting out the case for not breaking it up – a case which the Cabinet had endorsed.

I explained my arguments for privatization to the House in the second reading debate:

We should proceed quickly to bring the new accountability to British Telecom by moving it into the private sector. That is one reason why I have decided against breaking up BT before offering it to the public. To do so would require a delay of many years in order to put British Telecom's accounts into a form that would make piecemeal disposals possible. The alleged advantages of that approach are greatly outweighed by the benefit of proceeding at once to improve BT's accountability. Enormous tactical problems must be faced. BT has developed as a single integrated network. To separate local services from trunk services, as has been proposed, would be immensely complex and costly. It would do more harm than good to the customer who, let us not forget, pays the bill in the end. I have also rejected the idea that British Telecom should be forbidden to sell apparatus and specialist services.

I did make a number of changes to the bill. It was made clear that all requirements placed by the act upon the Secretary of State and the Director-General of Telecommunications were statutory duties; an obligation was placed on BT to provide vitally important social services such as the 999 emergency services, public call boxes, ship-to-shore services and services in rural areas; and the bill also included provision to allow the government to pay grants towards the research and development of apparatus for the use of disabled people. I reached agreement with Sir George Jefferson, the Chairman of British Telecom, that BT, which was manufacturer, supplier and operator, should account for each of these functions separately so that if the Monopolies and Mergers Commission decided at some future date that BT should divest itself of one or more of these functions then the financial basis of the different parts would be clear. British Telecom faced competition in two of its businesses, those of manufacture and supply of equipment. Separate accounting would prevent cross-subsidization of those businesses by its main business, that of operator, where it had a monopoly.

It is easy to forget the state of British Telecom when we decided to privatize it and the achievements of George Jefferson in preparing it for privatization and taking it from a branch of the Civil Service into a business with ninety-five per cent of its employees as shareholders, and with millions of other shareholders either personally or through their pension funds and insurance policies. When he took over I understand there was only one qualified accountant among the 250,000 employees, that it had never produced a set of accounts which any auditor would sign without qualifying his report, and that it had no register of the properties it owned and therefore no knowledge of the value of them. I once suggested to him jokingly that since one of the most common sights in Britain at that time, from about 4 p.m. on any working day, was that of BT vans parked by the side of the road, the company's logo should consist of two BT vans parked in a layby. It is greatly to George's credit that he and his team rearranged this extraordinary organization and from it began to produce a modern, efficient and profitable telecommunications company. For my part, my experiences with BT made me determined, should I ever get another opportunity to privatize a state-owned monopoly, that I would not do so as a single regulated monopoly.

Perhaps the most satisfying reform that I initiated whilst at the DTI was the change to the way the Stock Exchange operated which subsequently led to the City's 'Big Bang.' In February 1979 Sir Gordon Borrie, the Director-General of the Office of Fair Trading had decided to start an action in the Restrictive Practices Court against the Stock Exchange and its rule book. The Restrictive Trade

Practices Act of 1976 is designed to outlaw cartels, monopolies, and a whole range of restrictive practices. The act, however, recognizes that there are restrictive practices which are in the public interest, and in addition to granting exemptions in the act, it is possible for bodies to register as acceptable restrictive practitioners. For instance, it is in everyone's interest that only qualified surgeons are entitled to operate and, more arguably, that only qualified lawyers should give legal advice. It was open to the Stock Exchange to seek to register on the grounds that it is essential that the nation's principal securities market should be properly regulated and governed, and that there should not be a proliferation of unreliable bucket-shop organizations. That the Stock Exchange was based on restrictive practices was unarguable, the question was whether they were acceptable and in the public interest as opposed to the interest of those operating the market. The Stock Exchange Council registered its rule book with the Director-General of Fair Trading in October 1977 and sought exemption from the act. The Labour government refused the request.

The Stock Exchange in the late 1970s was the quintessential City institution. It was run by a committee elected by the members. The members themselves were admitted by the committee. The committee's decision about an application for membership was final and there was no right of appeal. The organization was a perfect example of self-perpetuating oligarchy. The restrictions might have been acceptable for a London gentlemen's club, but they applied to the country's central securities market. Moreover, the committee also controlled access to the market and defined the terms on which those who traded in it could do so. Only the shares of companies acceptable to the committee could be quoted on the exchange. Anyone who wanted to buy or sell shares in those companies could do so only through a broker and then at a rate of commission fixed by the committee. In addition, the broker could only act as agent for the shareholder, the broker for his part had to buy or sell through a jobber who dealt only with the broker and never with the public. The jobber carried a stock of his selected shares and, having received an order, the broker would then negotiate a price with him. This system, known as single capacity, was criticized by some who claimed that it was a wonderful way for those working on the Stock Exchange to get two bites of the same cherry, the broker's bite and the jobber's. Others argued that single capacity was a worthwhile form of investor protection since the broker's role was clearly defined as that of agent for the investor. By separating his function from that of the market-maker, the investor had the assurance that he was not buying from, or selling to, the person who was advising him to buy or sell and that the price paid was being fixed independently.

Roy Hattersley, as Secretary of State for Prices and Consumer Protection, decided in February 1979 that the Stock Exchange should not be exempted from the provisions of the act and the way was then open for Sir Gordon Borrie to begin his action against the exchange. The aim was to force changes in its rule book and to bring an end to a number of what he regarded as unacceptable practices. There was no doubt that the Labour government relished taking on this bastion of City privilege and, to my mind, no doubt that changes were needed.

The Stock Exchange Council was lucky at that time to have as its Chairman Mr Nicholas Goodison, subsequently Sir Nicholas. He recognized the need for change and offered to undertake a review of its rules. He felt that by proceeding in this way, 'the government and the Bank of England would have more certain control of the outcome'. He was concerned, as I had been, that the court might strike down a number of the existing rules but was under no obligation to suggest what should replace them. A review of the kind he was suggesting would have ensured that destruction and replacement were considered simultaneously.

There was another reason for seeking change and that was far and away the most important. The City of London had established itself over a very long period as the leading financial centre of Europe and, along with Tokyo and New York, as one of the three great financial centres of the world. At the heart of this was a central securities market, run along the lines of a gentlemen's club and from which, by its own rules, all the world's major financial houses were excluded. Its members were dangerously underfunded and there had been recent evidence of this when the rules had been amended rather hurriedly to allow an overseas bank to inject much-needed capital into a struggling broking firm. I was concerned that our Stock Exchange would become a peripheral institution on the world financial scene and that it would be difficult for London to maintain its position as a world financial centre with a second-rate securities market at its heart. I was also concerned that at a time of great movement in the world's markets, the British Stock Exchange had been frozen into inactivity by the legal action. It was in fact being prevented from changing by a legal action designed to promote change.

Legal action seemed to be an expensive and protracted way of producing the necessary reforms and had the effect of freezing the Council of the Stock Exchange into its current position for an uncertain period. Before the 1979 election we had sought legal advice about how to bring the action to an end and produce the necessary changes by negotiation. We were advised that the only satisfactory way to end the action was to introduce primary legislation to exempt the Stock Exchange from the Restrictive Trade Practices Act. After the general election in 1979, I had discussed this possibility with John Nott, the Secretary of State for Trade, but his view was that after five years in opposition and with so much to be done, it would give the public a signal that we had our priorities wrong if one of our first acts was to appear to do the Stock Exchange a favour. I did not see it in the same way, but I accepted his decision. His successors, John Biffen and Arthur Cockfield, maintained the same position, although Arthur was reconsidering the matter. Four years later, when I became Secretary of State for Trade and Industry, I found that the case had not yet begun, but was due to get under way in the autumn. Substantial sums had already been spent, and the judge asked the parties to submit their pleadings by the beginning of October. This in itself would be a hugely expensive operation and would be followed by what promised to be a very long court hearing, at the end of which, if the government did not accept the outcome, we might have to legislate to overturn the findings.

Two weeks after the 1983 general election, I attended a meeting at Number 11 Downing Street with the new Chancellor and the retiring Governor of the Bank of England, Lord Richardson, and three officials. Lord Richardson told us that he, Geoffrey Howe as Chancellor, and Arthur Cockfield as Trade Secretary, had held preliminary discussions but that these had been interrupted by the general election. Although he would be retiring on 30 June he felt he should see whether we, as successors to Geoffrey and Arthur, wished to continue with discussions. I explained that I had been keen to bring the matter to an end for some time and Nigel Lawson was equally enthusiastic. The problem was that the judge was only prepared to adjourn the case if the government had made a statement in the House of Commons expressing its intention of introducing legislation. Since the House was due to rise within the next five weeks, we had little time to reach the necessary agreement. It was decided that I should approach Sir Gordon Borrie and Nicholas Goodison and explore the possibilities with them and that we would meet again as soon as possible. I saw Sir Gordon the next day and told him that I had it in mind to try to put an end to the action and to negotiate a settlement. He was not pleased and made it quite clear that, in his view, only primary legislation would relieve him of his duty under the act to continue the legal action.

I then invited Nicholas Goodison to come and see me. I collected Nicholas from the waiting room and we went to my office. I had arranged to see him alone and we came straight to the point. I explained that I was keen to put an end to the case and outlined my initial thinking. He replied that he was very pleased that we shared a common ambition to solve the dispute, but he made it clear to me that it would not be easy for him to deliver an acceptable agreement and that it would be for the Stock Exchange Council and not for him to take the ultimate decision. He expected his council to be divided on the issue. There were some members who believed that they would win the case in court and others who felt the action had gone on for so long that they might as well see it through.

There followed four weeks of frantic negotiation at the end of which a package of reforms had been agreed which substantially met the Office of Fair Trading's case, except in one very important respect. Minimum commissions were to be abolished by December 1986. New lay members would be brought on to the council to represent the interests of the users of the market and they would form the majority on a new independent appeal committee, to which anyone who was refused membership of the exchange would have a right of appeal. Lay members would also be in a majority on the appeals committee on disciplinary matters.

The one other major change sought by Sir Gordon Borrie had been the abolition of single capacity, the broker/jobber arrangement. Many people argued that this would not survive the abolition of fixed commissions since there would not be enough revenue to support the two separate professions. The government felt that although this might well prove to be the case, single capacity was a vital part of investor protection, and until other arrangements designed to protect the investor were in place the division between broker and jobber should be maintained. There was disagreement about this, not only between the OFT and the Stock Exchange, but between the government and the OFT. The negotiations were conducted in great secrecy and other than Nigel, Alex Fletcher and myself, no minister except for the Prime Minister was kept informed. Had we been unable to reach agreement, there would have been nothing to report. Were we to reach agreement then that would inevitably have to be reported to the Cabinet and to the House of Commons and to be endorsed by both of them. Sir Gordon had made it clear to me that unless he was relieved of his duty by legislation he would continue to pursue the case. He was advised that he had no discretion in the matter, and we accepted his position.

Having reached agreement in principle with the Stock Exchange, I arranged to take the matter to Cabinet on 26 July with the aim of making a statement to the House of Commons the following day. I spent the previous day in Brussels at a meeting of ministers responsible for the steel industry and, after a typical Euro-farce, had reached agreement about steel quotas which were themselves anathema to me at about four in the morning. After a couple of hours' sleep I flew back to attend Cabinet and before that to see Sir Gordon to tell him of my proposals. One or two of the newspapers had picked up hints of an agreement and there had been articles that morning critical of the government and, in particular, of me for interfering in the case. Sir Gordon was unhappy about the agreement, but accepted that parliament had the right to legislate to exempt the Stock Exchange from the act. Convincing Cabinet was a different matter. One or two senior colleagues, having read the critical articles based on partial leaks, were alarmed and a long discussion ensued. In the end it was agreed that we would go ahead and that I should make a statement subject to a further meeting in the Prime Minister's room in the House of Commons late that night, at which the final draft of my statement would be approved. The meeting was to be attended by a small group of the most senior ministers, but eventually almost all of the Cabinet seemed to be involved. Quintin Hailsham was particularly helpful in persuading some of the doubters. The final draft needed substantial rewriting to turn it back into English after the committee had collectively mangled it, but it did reflect the committee's views, so far as they were ascertainable.

The next day was extremely hectic. I saw my ministerial colleagues and told them of the agreement with the Stock Exchange. I then went to a long Cabinet meeting where we took a decision to buy a British weapon system instead of the American alternative. The

Treasury preferred the American system and the discussion was lively and long. I was due to speak to the political committee of the Carlton Club after lunch, and planned to spend the hour between lunch and the statement on final briefing. I mentioned this to my Private Secretary who pointed out that it was the department's day to answer questions in the House and this would occupy that hour. I therefore cancelled lunch but arrived afterwards to make the speech and went straight on to the House arriving just in time for questions. The statement followed and it was well received on our side of the House, but was widely criticized by the opposition.

The main burden of their criticism was that I was merely making cosmetic changes and that in the words of my shadow, Peter Archer, this was 'a deal between cronies in a smoke-filled room'. He described the concessions as 'minuscule'. It was interesting that when the House returned to the subject a few months later, when we debated the legislation arising as a result of my statement, the government was accused of promoting fundamental changes without being aware of the extent of them. The press were equally muddled. In September *The Times* argued that 'the deal with the Stock Exchange seems wholly at variance with the Conservative Party's professed aim to thrust a more competitive environment on to many areas of British life and business.' It went on to suggest that the agreement smacked 'of cosy corporatism'. In November I was astonished to read 'a government and party that believes in the virtues of a free market economy, and in wider share ownership as a barrier to corporatism should have no doubt that the right course is the one set by Mr Parkinson on 27 July.' Only a heavyweight newspaper could thunder out two totally opposing points of view within a few weeks. *The Times*, like the Labour Party, criticized the agreement without understanding it the first time. Subsequent events provided incontrovertible evidence that the changes promoted by the agreement with the Stock Exchange were fundamental. This was no accident and followed in many ways the pattern set some years earlier by the New York Stock Exchange. The abolition of minimum commissions triggered innumerable changes and, before December 1984, the Stock Exchange Council decided to get rid of single capacity as I had always expected and hoped they might.

In 1990 Sir Gordon Borrie sent me a copy of an article from *The Independent on Sunday* headed 'My biggest mistake'. He was kind enough to admit that he had been wrong to oppose the agreement with Sir Nicholas Goodison and that it would have been a mistake to continue with the case. There are still those connected with the Stock Exchange who look back nostalgically to the good old days. However, most recognize that change was inevitable and that in the end it was promoted more speedily and effectively by the agreement of 27 July, even though four years were lost through an unnecessary, expensive and inconclusive court action.

The House rose two days later and a week after that I left for a holiday with Ann in the Bahamas. We were joined by our two elder daughters, Mary and Emma, and during that holiday, after discussions stretching over several days, we decided that we wanted to stay together as a family. I arranged to see Sara Keays after our return to England and to tell her that I had decided to remain with Ann and the family. Following negotiations between our solicitors a statement was issued on 5 October. That evening I was due to speak at the annual dinner of the Energy Industries Council at the Grosvenor House Hotel. It was a large gathering – there were about 1,500 people present. I arrived late at the dinner, straight from a meeting with my solicitor, and I was called out of the meal two or three times to consider some last minute changes to the text and, after my speech at about 11.0 p.m. to approve the final draft. My own solicitor felt that, in view of the lateness of the hour, the statement should be issued the next day, but Sara Keays' solicitors were adamant that it should be issued that night. The following statement was therefore issued to the Press Association.

To bring to an end rumour concerning Miss Sara Keays and myself and to prevent further harassment of Miss Keays and her family, I wish, with her consent, to make the following statement.

I have had a relationship with Miss Keays over a number of years. She is expecting a child due to be born in January, of whom I am the father. I am of course making provision for the mother and child.

During our relationship, I told Miss Keays of my wish to marry her. Despite my having given Miss Keays that assurance, my wife, who has been a source of great strength to me, and I decided to stay together and to keep our family together.

I regret the distress which I have caused to Miss Keays, to her family and to my own family.

Both Miss Keays and I wish it to be known that neither of us nor any member of our respective families will be prepared to answer any questions from the press about this statement.

The next morning we awoke to find a crowd of journalists and photographers milling around our house in Moreton Terrace and we had our first experience of the British press in the grip of collective hysteria. Just before I left for the office, I received a telephone call from a friend who was the editor of a popular daily newspaper. He advised me not to say a word, not even good morning, to his 'jackals' or to anyone else's. I suggested that if he felt like that, perhaps he could take his away. He replied that as long as other people's were there he could not move his!

Ann and I decided that, so far as it was possible, we would carry on with business as usual and after two hectic days in the department, we drove to Eastbourne where I was due to speak at a political dinner for Ian Gow and to stay with Ian and Jane for the weekend. The media were present en masse outside the hotel, but the dinner was a private one and the audience of about 200 was friendly and enthusiastic.

The Conservative Conference was to take place in Blackpool the following week and at the end of it I had planned to visit America and Japan. It was to be my first major visit abroad as Secretary of State and I had a very full programme including speeches in Washington, New York, Los Angeles and Tokyo. While I was away the government's expenditure plans would be finalized. Except for a few important decisions on the nationalized industries, I had reached agreement with the Treasury and I wanted to tie up any loose ends before I went away. I had resigned as Chairman of the party in September and John Gummer had taken my place. There was, therefore, no need for me to go to Blackpool until I was due to speak on the Thursday. I spent the week in London working in the department and, since all the political journalists were in Blackpool, I was able to get on with my work without interruption or harassment. I had one public commitment before the Thursday. Some weeks earlier I had accepted an invitation to do a live interview on the Monday for the BBC television programme, *Panorama*, on the state of the British economy and the government's economic policies. I considered withdrawing from the interview, but having pointed out the last sentence of my statement to the producer, I decided to go ahead with the broadcast. When I arrived at the studios I was greeted by the producer, and I asked if I could see Fred Emery who was to do the interview. I stressed that I had agreed to do an interview on economic policy and not my personal life, and that I could and would add nothing to my statement. Fred argued that if the matter was not raised, it would look as if the BBC had been gagged. We therefore agreed that for the first five minutes of the fifty-minute programme, Fred would ask his questions, but I made it clear that I would not go beyond the statement. I also stressed that if these questions continued for more than five minutes I would walk out. After five minutes and two seconds Fred brought the interview to a close, and the programme moved on with a brief film about the country's economic prospects following which I was interviewed about the government's economic policies.

On the Wednesday evening, I had my final ministerial meeting at 6.0 p.m. during which we agreed the external financing limit of the British Steel Corporation with the Chairman, Bob Haslam. After he left, Michael Portillo, who had joined me as Special Adviser after the general election, and I started working on my Conference Speech. It went extremely well and at about ten o'clock we agreed to adjourn and to finish it in the car on our way to Blackpool the next day. We drove up the next morning. I had had a very constructive week. The *Panorama* interview had been well received, and by the time we arrived in Blackpool I was confident we had prepared an excellent speech.

The peaceful working days in London had been misleading. When we arrived at the hotel there was chaos. Hundreds of journalists, and radio and television crews packed the drive and the entrance to the hotel. With the help of the security guards we were able to get to the lift and from there to Alistair McAlpine's suite. He had arranged a buffet lunch and had invited a dozen or so close friends. They were very encouraging, but their tales of skulduggery and of the contrast between the public posture and the private words of a few of my colleagues were not. The Prime Minister and the overwhelming majority were, however, totally on my side. The Bishop of Bath and Wells had given a radio interview to the BBC which was interpreted as a call for my resignation, and the BBC was referring to this on every possible occasion and using it to build up the tension for the afternoon's events. The Bishop subsequently wrote to me, explaining that he had not wished to give the interview, that the BBC had urged on him that it was his duty to do so, and that he hoped that nothing he had said had in any way influenced my decision. It seemed to me to be a very good example of the BBC's news-making as opposed to news-reporting abilities.

The scenes inside the Conference hall were extraordinary. I was cheered as I walked in. The speech was received with tremendous enthusiasm and it ended to roars of approval. I started by referring to my time as Party Chairman: 'I am here today as Secretary of State for Trade and Industry. But before that I had two very happy years as Chairman of the Party organization. There are literally hundreds of people to whom I owe my thanks, but this is not the time to mention individuals. But may I just thank all my colleagues and friends for their support during that period. My wife, Ann, joins me in these thanks and I add my thanks to her.' I then went on to outline a vision of a share-owning democracy. I pointed out that Mrs Thatcher's first government had encouraged home ownership: 'Now we must launch our second drive to make Britain a democracy in which people not only own their own homes, but have a stake in the business in which they work. First, home ownership: now job and company ownership. This is the second great barrier against social-ism. We have transformed the attitude to home ownership. Now we must transform the attitude to private enterprise.'

As Chairman, I had engineered standing ovations for speakers. This normally involved the platform rising as one as the speaker finished, and the audience taking the hint. On this occasion, the platform group remained in their seats while the audience stood and cheered.

I had tea with the Prime Minister afterwards. She felt that the speech and in fact the week had gone well. I had one outstanding departmental matter to clear up and that was the question of funding for a new Rolls-Royce engine. We settled the figure at £80 million and I telephoned Peter Rees, the Chief Secretary, and confirmed this with him. This meant that my department had reached a complete agreement with the Treasury. We had eliminated huge sums from our provisional bids and were back to baseline as I had set out to be.

Later that evening, after dinner with Sir Larry Lamb, at that time the editor of the *Daily Express*, and Lady Lamb, I went to a reception organized by Alistair McAlpine. As I left to go to bed I was told that Sara Keays had issued a statement to *The Times*. This I felt sure meant that my visit to America would be dominated by stories of my pregnant former mistress and that I would be unable to do the job that I was going there to do – to promote trade and the case for Britain. I decided that I had become a liability to the government and that I should resign. I saw the Prime Minister late that night and told her of my decision. She asked me to sleep on it. I saw her again the next morning and confirmed that I wished to go. She agreed. This harrowing incident ended on a note of high farce. The police had arranged for Ann and I to get away quietly before the news broke, but, alas, the person who had parked my car when we arrived the day before had mislaid the keys and after a frantic search we were unable to find them. Alistair insisted that we borrow his car but by this time the press had been alerted and we left as we had arrived – surrounded by a mob of wild media representatives.

I remember very little about that day and the two days that followed. Our house in Northaw was again under siege from the press, and Ann and the girls were wonderfully comforting about the future. Ann and I decided to go away to a friend's house in Portugal and another friend loaned us his plane to get there. Saturday and Sunday were spent making the necessary arrangements and we left early on Monday morning, flying from Luton.

Saturday evening was miserable and wet and I felt sorry for the press who were standing around outside to absolutely no purpose since none of us was leaving the house. I suggested to them through the police that they might like to shelter in the garage. They accepted the offer with enthusiasm and I sent out a couple of bottles of whisky which they drank with alacrity.

On the Sunday morning, a deputation from the sixty or so journalists came to the front door. They suggested that if we would take a short walk through the village during which they would take their photographs and their film, then they would go away and leave us in peace for the rest of the day. The police, who were concerned that someone might get hurt in the narrow road outside our house, recommended that we agree. This incident had a funny result. I received about half a dozen letters asking where I had bought the bomber jacket I was wearing in the photographs.

It was a relief to get away from England and to rediscover privacy. For the next few weeks we played golf, swam, read and talked about our future lives. Having just been re-elected as an MP I was committed to the House of Commons for at least the next four years and I obviously had to shape my new life around that. We received messages from home and my secretary told me that thousands of letters were pouring in from all over the country and from different parts of the world. They were overwhelmingly supportive and when Mary, Emma and Jo came to join us they brought a number of these letters with them.

The British press finally found us at the end of the second week. We were playing golf some miles from where we were staying, on a lovely course at Quinta de Lagos. We were just about to putt when three cars filled with journalists and photographers drove up a little cart track by the side of the green. We said good morning and carried on with the game. At the next tee Ann hit an excellent long drive, and one of the photographers congratulated her. She said with a smile, 'Perhaps I am stronger than I look.' Next day, under the huge banner headline, ' "I am a very strong lady," says Ann Parkinson', an entire story was built around her seven words.

I dreaded my return to England. I have always been a workaholic and I hated the prospect of being underemployed. I need not have worried. Awaiting me on my return were more than 16,000 letters, all but a handful friendly and sympathetic. In addition, there were dozens of invitations from Conservative Associations, universities and Young Conservative branches inviting me to speak at annual dinners, annual meetings, business lunches and fund-raising events. It was as if the party in myriad ways was encouraging me to stay in politics by making it difficult for me to leave. One of the first letters was from the constituency Chairman of my colleague, Peter Tapsell, urging me to honour a previous commitment to be the guest speaker at their annual dinner the following week, and telling me that his Association had unanimously passed a resolution of support at their executive meeting a few days before. I found that replying to the thousands of letters and invitations kept me fully occupied for several weeks and, by the time I had finished, my diary for the ensuing months was becoming uncomfortably full. I made my first speech from the back benches for nearly ten years in November in a debate on the Stock Exchange reforms which I had initiated the previous July.

It was frustrating to be out of government for the next four years, but the time passed surprisingly quickly. In addition to my political work I joined the boards of a number of companies as a non-executive director and thoroughly enjoyed my reintroduction to the business world where I had previously spent many happy years. During this time I had a number of offers of full-time jobs which would have involved leaving the Commons. The most interesting was an invitation to join the board of a very large company with a view to becoming its Chairman. It was an exciting prospect and I decided to discuss it with my old boss, Michael Heseltine. He asked me whether the biggest decision taken over the previous year by any company in which I was involved would have been important enough to be included in the agenda for Cabinet. He then said, 'The big decisions are taken here, and if you want to influence them, you have to be here.' Some years later when I was back in Cabinet and he was out, he never wavered in his determination to return even though he knew he would have to bring down the Prime Minister to get back.

Each year in August, when the press had little else to write about, the question of my return to the government was taken off the shelf, dusted down and set running. In 1985 after a particularly severe bout of speculation, the Prime Minister telephoned me and told me that she wanted me to rejoin the government, but her closest advisers felt it should wait until after the next general election. She wanted to see what the electorate had to say.

It was a relief to me when the general election was called in June 1987. After four weeks of campaigning, in which I visited fifty constituencies as well as working in my own, I was re-elected as MP for Hertsmere with a record majority of 18,106. The excellent result in Hertsmere opened up the way for my return.

Norman Tebbit had invited us to the traditional election night party. Ann and I had decided to wait in the crowd outside Central Office and to see Margaret Thatcher's return from her count. Having seen all this from the inside in 1983 we wanted to see it from the outside in 1987. By the time she arrived, we had already achieved an overall majority and the crowd was ecstatic. As we stood at the back we recognized the burly figure of Charles Price, then US Ambassador to the UK, who was a golfing friend of mine, and we invited him to join us at the party inside. He was concerned not to appear to be interfering in British politics, but we pointed out to him that we had already won and he could be the first member of the diplomatic corps to greet the newly elected PM if he came in with us. He was delighted to have the excuse and as we walked in we were greeted with tremendous cheers. The one sad note of the evening was struck by Norman. He took me into a small office near his own, which was crowded, and told me that he was leaving the government. He had presided over a difficult but successful campaign, but he felt he must have more time available for his wife, Margaret, who had been appallingly injured in the Brighton bombing three years earlier. I understood his reasons and sympathized with them, but I had been looking forward to working with him again and his departure undoubtedly weakened the whole government. It seemed a sad reward for all his efforts.

On the Saturday morning I went for a long run in the woods opposite my home, and on my return, Ann told me that I had been asked to meet the Prime Minister at Number 10 at 2.15 that afternoon. It was clear that I was to rejoin the Cabinet, but in what capacity I would discover later.

13 Megavars and Motorways

I arrived at Number 10 at about 2.15 p.m. having driven myself up from Northaw. The policeman at the door smiled and welcomed me back, as did the doorkeeper and other members of the staff. I chatted to Charles Powell, one of the Prime Minister's Private Secretaries, for a few minutes before being shown into her study on the first floor. Norman Fowler was just leaving. Mrs Thatcher congratulated me on my increased majority and we then talked briefly about Norman Tebbit's decision not to join the Cabinet. Although they had had an unhappy election campaign, albeit a successful one, she felt that he would be sorely missed. She then said that she would like me to become Secretary of State for Energy. The main task was to prepare the electricity supply industry for privatization. She also urged me to keep a careful eye on Arthur Scargill, and above all to make sure that coal stocks were maintained at a high enough level to see off the National Union of Mineworkers if he brought them out on strike again. She was sure that he would try.

I left after about half an hour and was told by one of her staff that I should report to Buckingham Palace at 4.0 p.m. for a meeting of the Privy Council at which we would be sworn in as ministers and collect our seals of office. We were quite a large group, and after the meeting Willie Whitelaw invited us back to his London home where we were given a glass of champagne and drank to the health of the Prime Minister and to the success of the new government.

The Department of Energy was numerically one of the smallest in Whitehall and had been one of the pioneers of privatization under Nigel Lawson and, later, Peter Walker. The British National Oil Corporation, Amersham International and British Gas had already been privatized. The department still retained responsibility for the licensing and regulation of the offshore oil industry and controlled British Coal and the Atomic Energy Authority. Its biggest responsibility, however, was the electricity supply industry which employed nearly 250,000 people and had a virtual monopoly of the supply and distribution of electricity in England and Wales. It was a huge and complex industry, dominated by large but responsible trade unions whose leaders were unanimous in their opposition to privatization, and whose members, should they feel inclined, could bring the country to a grinding halt and make our towns and cities uninhabitable in a matter of days if not hours.

Peter Morrison, an Old Etonian, whose bluffness conceals great shrewdness and determination, was appointed Minister of State and took responsibility for oil, gas, offshore supplies and energy efficiency. Michael Spicer became Parliamentary Secretary and was responsible for coal, electricity, nuclear power and renewable sources of energy. Michael was disappointed not to have been promoted and came reluctantly. I asked Michael Fallon to be my Parliamentary Private Secretary. I had first met him when he was our candidate at the Darlington by-election in 1983. At the time he was a rather aloof character, clearly very clever, and the combination of these two qualities could make him appear superior and arrogant. I went back to Darlington during the 1987 general election where we both spoke to a well-attended meeting at a school in the town, and I was impressed with the warmth and friendliness with which he greeted people and was greeted by them. I felt that the House of Commons was misjudging him and that I would enjoy working with him. The whips were opposed to the idea, but I nevertheless went ahead and appointed him. He proved to be an excellent PPS and eighteen months later he was asked to join the whips' office. They, too, had quite clearly changed their minds about him.

The department, which had been re-created during the miners' dispute in 1974 with Lord Carrington in charge, dealt with a vital area of the economy and had always attracted staff of a very high calibre. Although the Conservative election manifesto had pledged to 'bring forward proposals for privatizing the electricity industry', only a little work had been done on possible methods before the election. However, Peter Gregson, the Permanent Secretary, had, in the event of a Conservative victory at the general election, put together the team of civil servants who would work on the project. That team was to be led by John Guinness, one of the two Deputy Secretaries working in the department. He had been involved in a number of other privatizations, notably British Gas. Following that financially successful privatization he had been offered a number of jobs in the City but had turned them down, even though the salary on offer was several times that paid to him by the government. A member of the Guinness banking family, as opposed to the brewing company, wealthy and intelligent, he brought to his work an independence of mind and an originality of thought that were unusual in Whitehall. After I left the department he became its Permanent Secretary and early in 1992, following John Major's decision to abolish the department, he finally left the Civil Service to become Chairman of British Nuclear Fuels. Working with him was a team of Assistant Secretaries, including Willie Rickett and Geoff Dart, who were quite outstanding.

I was totally committed to the privatization programme and was keen to oversee the return of the electricity industry to the private sector. Whatever the aims of the 1945 Labour government, the nationalization process which they had started, and which successive governments had continued right up until 1979, had proved to be a disaster. The collective losses of the nationalized industries since the mid-1940s amounted to over £40,000 million. In one year British Airways lost £564 million and in 1979, when we took office, British Steel was losing £3 million every day and was the most inefficient steel industry in Europe. Those industries which were profitable, such as the gas and electricity industries, produced a very low rate of return on the capital employed. Investment in the nationalized industries was low since ministers had to argue with the Treasury for extra resources and were competing against the much more politically appealing areas of health, pensions and education for limited funds. Prices were set for political purposes and, in the case of gas, industrial users were asked to pay higher prices than domestic consumers.

The nationalized industries were trade-union dominated and chronically overmanned; the customer was at the bottom of their list of priorities. All too often it appeared that industries were being run for the benefit of the workforce and that the customer was merely a necessary evil. Managers were not free to manage. The plain fact was that government took a view about the numbers of people who should be employed and about where plants should be located, not for the benefit of the industry but to bring jobs to a particular region. However keen ministers were not to interfere in the running of the nationalized industries, they invariably found themselves doing so. The inevitable result was demoralized management and poor performance, both financially and operationally. Nationalization was bad for the taxpayer, bad for the employee who had low wages to go with his security of employment, and bad for the customer who suffered high prices and poor performance.

Although I had no firm ideas about the privatization of electricity, I was determined that we would not follow the pattern set by British Telecom and British Gas and take it to the market as a highly regulated monopoly. I wanted to introduce competition where possible and regulation where it was not. One of the options on which the department had done some work was one they called the 'two-track solution'. Under this there would have been two joint companies. The Central Electricity Generating Board would have been the producer of all electricity with a duty to allow in new producers over a long period of time. Because this company would have been so dominant, all the twelve area boards which distributed the CEGB's electricity would have become subsidiaries of a holding company, which in theory would have been strong enough to stand up to the CEGB. The great attraction of this solution was its simplicity. The Electricity Council, the coordinating body which under the existing structure brought together the two sides of the industry, would have become the holding company for the area boards. There would be the minimum of disruption, jobs for everybody, and the two companies would have been easy to sell. It seemed to me to be a classic Whitehall solution, with the interests of the producer and the employees paramount and those of the customer and the public a distinctly secondary consideration. I made it clear from the beginning that I found this a very unattractive option and that I wanted the approach reversed, with future decisions about the supply of electricity to be driven by the needs of the customer not by the arbitrary decision of the supplier.

At the heart of the existing system was a statutory obligation to supply electricity, which had been imposed by parliament on the CEGB. This meant that the CEGB was the ultimate arbiter of what capacity should be maintained – how many power stations, of what type and at what cost. The CEGB, often as a result of political pressure, had a rather unenviable record of building the wrong type of power stations at the wrong time. Nowhere was this failure more apparent than in the nuclear field where, partly as a result of political pressure, Britain had decided to develop its own technology for power stations. The theory was that having developed the finest technology we would dominate the world nuclear scene. Britain would have the advantage at home of cheap electricity and would export dozens of power stations to countries all over the world to the benefit of the British manufacturing industry.

In practice, we incurred the heavy cost of uniqueness and only ever exported two power stations. The first generation, the Magnox stations, performed well but the electricity produced proved to be more expensive than was ever imagined. The next generation, the AGRs (advanced gas-cooled reactors) were an even bigger dis-appointment. Eight were built, but the technology was constantly being changed with the result that each power station was effectively a prototype with all the expense and the technical problems that a new technology inevitably involves. Only the last two to be built, Torness and Heysham II, were of a similar design. In contrast, even the chauvinistic French realized that it was far too expensive to develop their own technology and opted for the American West-inghouse PWRs (pressurized-water reactors). They used these as the basis for building a series of identical power stations which they became ever more expert at constructing.

At a meeting with Lord Marshall, the Chairman of the CEGB, shortly after my appointment, he started the conversation by saying that since none of his AGR power stations had produced any elec-tricity for the previous three months he would have to put up his prices. This struck me, with my private-sector industrial background, as extremely odd. In the private sector if a company does not perform it makes a loss. In the public sector, it simply puts up its prices to cover the cost of its own inefficiency or the non-performance of its power stations. In the absence of competition, the electricity industry was free to pass on whatever costs it incurred and to add to those costs whatever margin it required to produce the desired profit. If the resulting charge turned out to be politically unacceptable then, in consultation with the minister, a politically acceptable price increase would be agreed, and if the resulting profit was too low then the taxpayer as owner had to accept a lower rate of return on the money invested on his behalf in the industry. The last Labour government in its 1978 white paper on the nationalized industries had recognized that if money was invested in state-controlled industries and did not produce a reasonable rate of return then this represented a misapplication of funds. It decreed that monies invested should produce a rate of return of at least five per cent over the rate of inflation. The electricity supply industry had been set a different target. It was charged to produce an average rate over a given period. This gave ministers and the industry room for manoeuvre. The biggest charges would be made after elections, the smallest before. For example, the industry's target over the three years 1985–86 to 1987–88 was to produce an average rate of return of 2.75 per cent. In the first year of that period it had produced 2.63 per cent, in the second 3.17 per cent, which meant that in the third, which happened to be election year, it needed to produce only 2.45 per cent. This meant that in election year no price increase proved to be necessary. As a system for concealing true costs and giving scope for price manipulation it was superb; as a way of producing electricity efficiently, giving accountability to the public and promoting productivity within the industry it was disastrous.

It became clear to me that this would be the most difficult privatization of them all. As a result of the pricing policy, the profits of the previous year were unacceptably low. Because too many power stations had been built some years earlier the industry had had surplus capacity. This was now being used up and the industry faced the need for a substantial investment programme. The first generation of nuclear stations was approaching the end of its useful life and would need to be replaced. The industry was geared to the notion that whatever the cost the consumer would have to pay, or alternatively the owner would uncomplainingly accept a low rate of return on his investment. In November 1987 after several months of fact-finding I announced new financial targets for the industry. I realized that I would be accused of fattening the industry up for privatization, and John Prescott, the Labour spokesman, made the allegation immediately after I had made my statement. But I remain convinced that even had we had no plans for privatization the rate of return would have had to be improved for the reasons I set out in my statement:

... although in the recent past the electricity supply industry has had surplus capacity, that position is now changing. On current forecasts, the Central Electricity Generating Board envisages that at least 13GW of new capacity will be needed to meet demand by the end of the century. The industry also needs to modernize its transmission and distribution system if it is to maintain secure and economical supplies into the next century.

At a time of surplus capacity, it is possible to meet extra demand by using that surplus at relatively little extra cost. In the past, this has been reflected in a low rate of return. It took account of the fact that some of the industry's assets were under-used ... When new capacity has to be built to meet additional demand, the costs of meeting that extra demand rise. It must be right that the rate of return should rise to a level closer to that which nationalized industries are required to earn on new investment as a whole ... The government have therefore agreed that the industry's overall target on current cost assets should be 3.75 per cent in 1988–89 and 4.75 per cent in 1989–90.

In addition to these structural problems were the personalities involved and, in particular, the redoubtable figure of Lord Marshall. One of the benefits of the job was the opportunity of getting to know him and of working with him. A brilliant physicist, the former head of the Atomic Energy Authority and a Whitehall warrior of the very front rank, he had earned the undying gratitude of Margaret Thatcher for keeping the electricity industry producing to full capacity during the 1984–85 miners' strike. She had made him a peer and always referred to him, almost reverentially, as 'Dear Walter'. It became clear to me at an early stage that any fundamental change in the structure of the industry would involve major changes in the CEGB, and Walter left me in no doubt that he would resist any such changes. Whitehall was mindful of the fact that in the privatization of the gas industry, Sir Denis Rooke, the Chairman of British Gas, had contrived to keep his industry intact and take it to the market as a monolith, and thus in their terms 'beat' Peter Walker, the then Energy Secretary, and it was waiting to see whether Walter would 'beat' me or vice versa. I never thought in those terms and my difficulty was enhanced by the fact that I developed a great liking and respect for him. I met him within days of my appointment and over the next few weeks we had regular meetings. He treated them as a series of seminars at which I was the pupil and he was the teacher. Hours passed during which I was schooled in such subjects as the working of the national grid, reactive power and megavars. The message was clear from day one and was repeated in one subtle form after another: 'Don't interfere with the CEGB.'

After about a month of meetings with people from all parts of the industry, I realized that we could continue chatting about the problem indefinitely without coming to any conclusions. I therefore told the privatization team that I wanted them to work on a range of options, starting at one extreme with the privatization of the monolith, through to the break-up of the CEGB into five companies plus a nuclear company to be owned jointly by the five and with the grid transferred to a separate company, whose ownership could be decided later. I also asked that technical, accounting, legal, banking and broking advisers should be appointed to make sure that each option was examined from these different perspectives. I was determined that our proposals should be practicable, that the chosen structure should be operationally and financially sound and that the industry must be saleable.

I then asked the Prime Minister if she would set aside a day when we could make a presentation of the range of options to her and a group of colleagues. The meeting was arranged for 14 September at Chequers and it was agreed that Nigel Lawson, the Chancellor of the Exchequer, David Young, the Secretary of State for Trade and Industry, Malcolm Rifkind, the Secretary of State for Scotland, and Norman Lamont, the Financial Secretary to the Treasury, should be the ministers present, in addition to the Prime Minister, Michael Spicer and myself. This was a vital meeting for us and I decided that Willie Rickett should make the presentation.

Over the next two months an immense amount of work was done and in early September we ran through the proposed presentation on a number of occasions until I was satisfied that it was succinct, interesting and informative. I was anxious that we should emerge from the meeting with clear answers to a number of specific questions. I wanted the whole picture to be presented before the discussion began rather than embarking on a piecemeal discussion of individual sentences or ideas. I therefore saw the Prime Minister before the rest of the party arrived and asked her to ask those present if they would not interrupt but would save their questions until after the presentation. When she made this request at the beginning of the meeting everyone around the table looked at her. They were all convinced that she was the one person present who might find it difficult to remain silent.

A number of decisions were taken that day. First of all, it was agreed that we would not privatize the industry as a monolith and that no further work should be done on that option. Second, it was decided that the nuclear industry should be included in the package. I appreciated, as did everyone present, that this would be the most difficult part of the whole process, but the decision was clear – it must be done. My question to those present was, 'Do we have to have nuclear?' and the answer was, 'Yes'. Third, it was agreed that the new generation of PWRs to replace the ageing magnox stations must proceed. Fourth, we decided that we should aim to have the industry privatized by the summer of 1991, the likely date of the next general election. We considered whether we could privatize the distribution companies in the current parliament and the CEGB in the next. The reason for this was that the time constraint effectively governed the extent to which the industry could be restructured. To create, for instance, five generating companies plus a grid company and a nuclear company from the CEGB would mean that we would be trying to sell to the public newly created companies which would have no profit record and which would have difficulty in making forecasts about the future. It would be hard to find a self-respecting group of directors or advisers to put their names to a prospectus for sale. There was a further difficulty. The industry would in future be based on contracts placed by the area boards with the generating companies. With twelve area boards, dealing with five generators and a nuclear company plus the two Scottish companies who would be free to compete in England and Wales, the permutations were almost infinite. The area boards, who had previously taken what supplies they needed from the CEGB and paid the price the CEGB asked, would now have to make their own assessment of their need. They would have a choice of suppliers and would have to agree prices with those suppliers. The more diverse we made the structure of the industry the longer the time needed before it could be sold to the public. The shorter the time available before the sale, the less radical the changes could be. Finally, it was agreed that if there was a conflict between introducing competition into the industry and getting the best price for it then competition should take precedence over price. Nigel Lawson, as a former Energy Secretary, was particularly insistent on this and throughout the whole process I found his advice and support invaluable. Our agreed aim was to produce a more competitive and efficient electricity supply industry operating in the private sector.

It was an excellent meeting at the end of which it was agreed that we would intensify the work on the remaining options, bearing in mind the decisions taken, and would meet again early in the New Year to make a final recommendation. The target was to produce a white paper in February 1988 and a bill in the new session of parliament beginning in November 1988.

The Conservative Conference was held in Blackpool that year and I was due to speak on the Wednesday in reply to a debate on electricity privatization. I was in no position to announce detailed plans, but I wanted to indicate the way in which we were approaching the subject. I decided to talk about the need for competition and about making the industry more responsive to the customer. The East Midlands Electricity Board had been experimenting with a scheme of paying compensation to its customers if it failed to perform. I asked John Derrick, who had joined me as Special Adviser, to find out more about it. We became convinced that it was sound and that it should be extended as a right to all domestic customers. I felt that for far too long we had talked about customer protection, which to me always conveyed a rather patronizing picture of the poor inadequate consumer looking to the politician for protection. The concept of customer rights had a much more positive ring about it. The individual would be given rights to assert against the big battalions and there was no bigger battalion than the electricity industry. I like to think that this approach, announced at Blackpool in 1987, was the precursor of John Major's Citizen's Charter of 1991.

It was an extraordinary experience to walk once again on to the platform at Blackpool to reply to a debate. As I went into the Winter Gardens my mind flew back to that fateful Thursday four years earlier and I wondered just how the audience would react. I took my seat as the platform was being re-organized following the previous debate. To my astonishment the whole audience rose and cheered. Norman Tebbit who was sitting next to me was delighted and as we sat down after acknowledging the applause, said with a grin, 'It'll be awful if they don't cheer when you've made the speech.' We need not have worried. The pledge that the industry would not be sold off as 'one vast monopolistic corporation' and that competition would be introduced was well received. My promise that 'when we privatize electricity, service to the customer will be the top priority' also proved to be popular. At the end the audience rose again, and Norman's earlier tease remained a joke.

Work on the remaining options intensified and while this was going on I continued with a round of meetings with a wide variety of people who had views about how the privatization should be carried out. I was keen to keep the trade unions informed and to have their views, and so I saw their representatives on a regular basis and encouraged them to feel they were involved in developing the policy. They found themselves in a strange position. They were opposed to privatization, but they accepted that it was going to happen and they wanted to safeguard the interests of their members and to make sure that they got a fair allocation of shares. This was the first privatization where trade union leaders argued about the size of the shareholding their members should have. In every other privatization the trade union leaders had advised their members not to accept a shareholding. They were also concerned that the national negotiating machinery would not survive privatization and they were worried by what they saw as the fragmentation of the industry. They much preferred national wage bargaining with one monolithic organization and they were not alone in preferring the monolith. Many of the private sector suppliers were happy making cosy deals with a single customer, and rather feared the prospect of having to compete for business and to negotiate with a range of customers.

One of our biggest concerns centred around the national grid. If we were to open up the market at all, I felt sure that we had to take the ownership away from the CEGB. If the companies generating the electricity owned the means of distributing it then competitors would be reluctant to emerge. The odds would be stacked against them. The CEGB argued that, unless there was common ownership of power stations and grid, the system would not work and the security of supply would be threatened. They subsequently modified their argument following meetings with our technical advisers and instead suggested that it would be possible to separate ownership but only at the most enormous cost. After further discussions it became clear that not only was it possible but that the cost was easily bearable. Our advisers were doing precisely the job for which they had been appointed.

The other overriding concern centred around the nuclear programme. I wanted to be sure that the sums set aside for decommissioning the Magnox power stations were adequate and so, after a series of meetings with the auditors of the CEGB, I increased the provisions by £700 million in the next financial year. Our financial advisers assured us that if provisions on the same scale continued to be made up to the date of flotation then enough money would have been set aside to cover future costs and the balance sheet would be viable. The provision of £700 million in a single year should be set against the fact that the accumulated provisions for decommissioning over the previous thirty years had only been around £1,600 million. The claim that the question of decommissioning only started to be addressed at a later stage is simply untrue.

In October 1987 a hurricane struck the South East of England. The first I knew of it was when my telephone rang early in the morning. It was Lord Marshall calling to tell me of the night's events and that electricity supplies over the whole of the South East of England were disrupted. We agreed to meet at the National Grid Control Centre to take stock of the situation three-quarters of an hour later. As I drove through London the scene was of devastation with trees and lampposts strewn across roads and pavements. However, because most of the London electricity distribution system is underground, very little damage had been done to London's electricity supply. I had visited the National Grid Control Centre once before and been impressed by the efficiency and smooth working of the system. That morning it was particularly impressive and the CEGB was soon ready to offer electricity to the area boards. Unfortunately, the real damage had been done to the local distribution networks and not to the national grid, and so the local companies were unable to accept the offer of electricity since they had no means of getting it to their customers.

The way that the industry coped with the crisis was subsequently hailed as evidence of the need to maintain control of the grid and the power stations under the same ownership. In fact, the lesson to be drawn from the hurricane was that the area boards cooperated superbly with one another, and large numbers of technical staff from the areas which were not affected were drafted into the regions which were. It was an example of how individual area boards could cooperate with each other, not of the necessity for a national grid.

What was remarkable about the aftermath of the hurricane was that, despite the huge amount of damage done to the local distribution systems and the fact that millions of people were denied supplies of electricity, some of them for several days, very few complaints were received. This was because the industry made a major effort to explain itself and to tell people what they were doing and when relief was likely to be available. People could see with their own eyes the huge damage that had been done. It was a remarkable performance and I was pleased to be able to pay tribute to the workforce and management in the House of Commons at the next Department of Energy question time.

After I had been shown around the Control Centre, Lord Marshall and I went upstairs for a cup of coffee. He said that he had given me his ideas for the future of the industry, but that I had given him no indication of my approach or of what decisions I was likely to make. I decided that this was a suitable time to tell him of my very preliminary ideas and of my ambition to separate the grid and subdivide the CEGB, and of my commitment to the nuclear programme and my determination to find ways of maintaining it and financing the new generation of power stations. He listened with great care and was clearly disappointed, but I stressed that I had taken no decisions and that this was just the way that my thoughts were developing. As usual our conversation was extremely amicable, and he promised to go away and think about my ideas and to let me have his considered view as soon as possible.

As I examined the various options for privatization, I became more and more convinced that we would need to get away from the Department, taking with us all the key officials, ministers and advisers, and discuss each option in depth without interruption. We therefore arranged to go to a conference centre, Nuneham Court near Oxford, for the weekend beginning 21 November. We contrived to keep the meeting secret until a day or two before when the press, and in particular the CEGB, learned of the meeting. In spite of a major effort on their parts, they never did find out where it was being held and we were not disturbed. A senior official was put in charge of explaining each of the four remaining options and each one was discussed in detail and in depth with all our advisers present. One official, responsible for producing the option which would break the CEGB into seven different companies, introduced her presentation by showing a picture of Saint Jude, the patron saint of lost causes. This was not because this was an undesirable option, but because there was a growing feeling that it could not be implemented in the time available.

On the Saturday evening Peter Gregson, the Permanent Secretary, asked if we could meet for a drink before dinner. He told me that the day before he had had a visit from Lord Marshall who had told him that if any attempt was made to break up the CEGB the whole board would resign. Lord Marshall had also seen the Cabinet Secretary, and the CEGB's Company Secretary had been to see the Prime Minister's Principal Private Secretary to pass on the same message. I felt that we couldn't allow that sort of threat to influence our decision, and so I told Peter that we would carry on with our meeting ignoring the threat and that over the next few weeks we would have to identify a number of people who could form a board to replace the former board should the threat be carried out. Over the next fortnight, I therefore invited various people to give me their views on privatization and on the future of the electricity industry. I don't think that any of them realized that my invitation was a pretext and that my real purpose was to select a replacement board.

By the end of the weekend meeting, I was sure that the most practical option was the one which eventually became the basis of the white paper. However, the overwhelming majority including me agreed that had the time been available a more diverse structure would have been desirable. I did in fact ask that the possibility of an exploding share be investigated. This would have meant that one share would have been sold covering all the generators, but within that company five companies, plus the separate nuclear company, would have been established. At a subsequent date, when the five companies had had the time to establish themselves, the share would have been subdivided into five shares with the nuclear company jointly owned by the five companies. We were advised that this was not practical. We subsequently investigated it as a way of floating the twelve distribution companies, but again decided to have twelve separate flotations.

Following the meeting, intensive work was carried out on the preferred option, although work on the other options continued until the meeting in January at Number 10 with the group that had met at Chequers the previous September. At all stages, as our proposals developed I discussed them fully with Professor Brian Griffiths and his team at the Number 10 Policy Unit. I wanted them to understand both the proposals and the rationale behind them. They were very helpful and came forward with a number of suggestions which we were able to incorporate. This also had the advantage of ensuring that when the Prime Minister discussed the proposals with them they would be supportive.

After a thorough discussion, the meeting at Number 10 in January accepted my proposals for the structure of the privatized electricity industry. It was agreed to float the area boards as twelve separate companies and to transfer the ownership of the grid from the CEGB to a new national grid company owned by the twelve area boards. We accepted the advice of our bankers and brokers that the nuclear industry could be privatized and that the new generation of PWRs could be funded in the private sector provided that the company which included them also had a substantial holding in conventional power stations. It was therefore agreed to subdivide the CEGB into two new generating companies. One company, PowerGen, would own some thirty per cent of the CEGB's existing non-nuclear capacity. The second company, National Power, would comprise the remainder of the CEGB's generating capacity, including the nuclear power stations.

In addition to the two generators, which would compete with each other, plans were discussed to strengthen the interconnector, which allows the transmission of electricity between Scotland and England, so that the two Scottish boards would be free to compete in the English market. British Nuclear Fuels, which generated more electricity than it needed for its own uses, would also be free to enter into contracts with the area boards. And the area boards themselves would be given the right to generate up to fifteen per cent of their own requirements. We realized from the very beginning that it would take time to create a market in electricity in which area boards could shop to buy their supplies. Since nobody, other than the CEGB, had built and operated a commercial power station in Britain for almost fifty years, some people questioned whether any private sector companies would want to enter the market. We felt that the area boards which had been at the mercy of the monopoly supplier would, given the ownership of the grid and the urge to diversify their sources, be keen either to build their own power stations, or to go into joint ventures with private suppliers. In fact, within a year of the proposals being announced, some twenty new suppliers were in negotiation with the area boards and all the signs are that a diverse market will develop.

What I found interesting was that from day one there was more competition in the supply of electricity than there will be for decades in the supply of telecommunications services and gas. It was not as much as we would have wished but it was a start. Given the fact that we were determined to get the industry into the private sector within the lifetime of one parliament, the structure was the most competitive that could have been implemented. The development of the national grid, not just as a common carrier but as a market-maker, is the most significant innovation of any privatization. Since privatization, electricity prices are now quoted on a half-hourly basis and it is not fanciful to imagine a market in electricity futures developing and the job of power broker being created. In spite of subsequent criticism, notably by the House of Commons Energy Select Committee, taking full advantage of hindsight to criticize what has been a success, the electricity industry remains the most competitive of any of the industries so far privatized. For my part, I found it difficult to take the Select Committee seriously. Their criticism of Malcolm Rifkind and myself was included in the text of their report on the deciding vote of a new committee member who knew nothing about the privatization and had heard none of the evidence.

Such an incident is all too typical of the way in which Select Committees operate. As a new Member of Parliament in the early 1970s, I had been sceptical about their worth, and over the years, particularly as a minister, I have not seen any evidence to make me alter my opinion. The present Select Committee system was introduced by Norman St John Stevas as leader of the House of Commons in 1979. At best they are a pathetic attempt to copy the committee system of the US Congress, but their fatal flaw is that they can be no better than the quality of the people available to serve on them. In the United States, where current members of Congress are barred from being members of the Administration, Congressmen make a career of committee membership and of examining the activities of the Administration. In this country the executive is drawn from both Houses of Parliament and it is the ambition of the overwhelming majority of MPs to become members of the government, an ambition which a substantial proportion of them achieve. The most able members of the governing party are either in the government, hope to be in the government or have been in the government. They are by their nature loyalists and reluctant to criticize.

Conservative members of Select Committees in the parliament elected in 1992 include a substantial number of such people, but among the rest are people who had ambitions to be in the government but have found those ambitions unfilled. They are clearly potential critics of those who did get into the government. They are hardly objective would-be controllers of the administration. As for the opposition members of Select Committees, although they talk about representing parliament and overseeing the executive, in fact, almost without exception, they see their role as being to criticize whatever the government has done. The whole aim of the opposition on Select Committees is to try to inveigle one or two Conservative MPs to join with them in their criticisms so that they can produce an unfavourable report which will inevitably be headlined in the press as 'Conservative-controlled committee slams government'.

In my experience of dealing with Select Committees, I found that very few MPs were properly briefed, and many asked questions which had been prepared for them by the committee Clerk or advisers and which they clearly did not understand. It often seemed to me that the committee system existed to promote a dialogue between its team of specialist advisers and the department. Members were a channel for others' views and not a fount of considered advice, criticism or knowledge. Committee reports are often drafted by the committee Clerk, and on a number of occasions, both as a PPS and a minister, I was told by a member of a Select Committee that the first time he saw the committee's final report was when it was published. Far from enhancing the authority of parliament most Select Committees, by their inadequacy, lower parliament in the eyes of officials and ministers. The inadequacy of their members' knowledge and the subservience to their advisers makes them anything but intimidating.

In their first report on electricity privatization, the House of Commons Energy Select Committee described the government's proposals as 'spatchcock legislation'. When they launched their report at a press conference, the committee Chairman was asked what he meant by 'spatchcock'. He did not know, nor did any member of his committee, and so it was left to the Clerk to explain the meaning of a key section of a report which the whole committee had signed. I do not believe that the Energy Select Committee in the last parliament was any worse, or any better, than other Select Committees. But such a performance hardly encourages ministers to take the strictures of Select Committees to heart.

I always realized that my decision to privatize nuclear power stations would be controversial. Although privately financed utility companies elsewhere in the world successfully generate nuclear electricity, many people doubted that it was possible to privatize our existing nuclear stations. However, the Department of Energy's advisers were convinced that nuclear stations could be sold and certainly evidence from overseas appeared to support that view. One of the most successful utility companies in America, Duke Power, generates substantial proportions of electricity from its seven privately funded nuclear reactors. VEBA in Germany and Tractebel in Belgium have each funded, built and now operate successfully six PWRs, and our financial advisers were confident that, so long as the company with nuclear stations also owned conventional stations, it would be floatable.

What also became clear from the process of preparing the nuclear stations for privatization was that the costs which had previously been given for producing nuclear electricity were hopelessly optimistic. I had never defended the nuclear industry on the grounds of price. The days when the country had been told that electricity from nuclear power stations would be so cheap that it would not be worth the cost of metering had long past. To my mind the importance of nuclear power had been demonstrated during the year-long miners' strike which had begun in March 1984. Diversity of supply of electricity is a crucial part of the security of supply. Coal, gas and oil are finite sources of fuel which by definition will become more scarce and therefore more expensive. This convinced me and my predecessors that a nuclear component must be maintained in electricity supply.

I had outlined my thinking in a speech to the Chartered Institute of Building in February 1988. I had been speaking about the importance of energy conservation, but argued that this could only be one part of a far-sighted energy strategy:

We must also draw on other forms of energy. The fact is that known reserves of fossil fuels will have run out by the end of the next century. Conservation is important – but it will only postpone the day of reckoning for future generations. And those generations would not forgive us if we recklessly, and selfishly, failed to provide them with alternatives. That is why the government is determined that Britain will have other forms of energy at its disposal. Among them is a strong nuclear power industry. There has been some talk lately that nuclear isn't 'economically viable'. But when you look at this argument, it seems to rest on the immediate merits of nuclear at a time when fossil fuel prices have hit a low and supplies are secure. There is no point just waiting for the next fossil fuel crisis before we start thinking about alternatives – we have to be prepared. We cannot ignore nuclear while the going is good, and then expect it to be there when we really need it.

The Labour Party criticized my decision to continue to support the development of nuclear power and to include the nuclear stations in the privatization plans, and alleged that as a result electricity users would pay an additional 'nuclear tax'. The argument was spurious since the cost of nuclear power was already included in consumers' bills. Under our plans the cost of nuclear would be isolated. Each area board would be placed under an obligation to buy a proportion of nuclear-produced electricity, which would be purchased at the going price for conventionally produced electricity. If the price of producing nuclear electricity was higher than the price of conventional electricity, the additional cost would be spread across all users. We called this the non-fossil-fuel levy, it was not a 'nuclear tax'. It was simply a way of identifying existing costs and of making sure that they were borne equally by all users. The existence of the levy didn't increase or in any way affect the cost of nuclear electricity. What it did was identify the cost and spread it evenly. Time after time I pointed out to Labour spokesmen that under the old system costs were hidden and unfairly allocated, and that heavy industrial users, who could negotiate advantageous prices with the CEGB, made no contribution to the cost of nuclear. Although all electricity users benefited from the security of supply which nuclear stations guaranteed, it was largely the domestic user who bore the brunt of the cost of the nuclear power stations. Under the new system the costs would be identified and spread across all users. Needless to say, the Labour Party never grasped this fundamental point.

The irony of all this was that privatization was criticized for revealing a problem which had been concealed under the previous nationalized structure. Privatization did not cause the problem, it uncovered an existing problem and forced the industry and the government to face up to it and to deal with it. One of the great advantages of privatization was that the system became transparent and the possibility of fudging just disappeared.

I had got the idea for the non-fossil-fuel levy and the non-fossil-fuel obligation in rather unlikely circumstances. I had gone up to Orkney to inaugurate the biggest wind generator in the world, a structure higher than St Paul's with a sail over sixty meters across. In the party was an American who told me that he operated the biggest commercial wind farm in the world in California. He explained that the electricity he produced was more expensive than electricity generated by conventional methods, but told me that the California state legislature had imposed a duty on the utility companies to buy his electricity at a price which gave him a fair return on his investment. The legislature had taken the view that encouraging renewable sources of energy was desirable and had therefore given him a right to sell. It seemed to me that precisely the same arguments could be applied to our nuclear industry and so we included in the bill an obligation to buy electricity from nuclear and renewable sources. Not only has this protected nuclear, it has also given rise to a huge increase in the number of renewable projects, many of which are now coming to commercial fruition.

I was disappointed that after I left the Department of Energy, the European Commission insisted that the non-fossil-fuel obligation should expire in 1998. It seemed to me that they misunderstood our proposal. Our aim was not to create a subsidized sector, but to encourage the development of non-fossil-fuel sources of electricity supply. The ending of the obligation in 1998 will deter potential investors from backing renewable projects since they are highly capital-intensive and no investor can hope even to recoup his investment by 1998. Renewable technologies have a vital contribution to make in meeting the concerns of those alarmed at the prospects of increases in acid rain and the threat to the environment from the greenhouse effect. To conduct an argument about the desirability of nuclear and renewable energy purely on the basis of price is short-sighted and blinkered.

I saw Lord Marshall early in February and told him of the proposals which I intended to put to Cabinet. I had promised him previously that I would arrange for him to see the Prime Minister so that he would have a chance to put arguments against the proposals if he so wished and so, soon after the Downing Street meeting, we went to see Mrs Thatcher at Number 10. The press got wind of the meeting and *The Times* was not alone in predicting 'a political storm'. Mrs Thatcher listened very sympathetically to Walter's arguments and clearly would have preferred us to come forward with mutually agreed proposals, but in my view that was wishful thinking, the gap between us was unbridgeable. The meeting concluded without firm agreement. The next morning, the Prime Minister's Private Secretary telephoned to say that she would like to see me at Chequers the following day. After a long discussion, the Prime Minister agreed that we should go ahead with the preparation of a white paper based upon my proposals. I asked her whether she wished to see Walter Marshall again so that he could have another opportunity to put his objections to her, but she said that she did not think that it would be necessary.

It was agreed that the white paper should be produced on 25 February and that I should make a statement to the House on that day. My statement was well received on the Conservative benches and I outlined the rationale behind the plans:

In adopting my proposals, I have adopted six principles. Decisions about the supply of electricity should be driven by the needs of the customers. Competition is the best guarantee of customers' interests. Regulation should be designed to promote competition, oversee prices and protect the customers' interests in the areas where natural monopoly will remain. Security and safety of supply must be maintained. Customers should be given new rights, not just safeguards. All who work in the industry should be offered a direct stake in their future, new career opportunities and the freedom to manage their commercial affairs without interference from Government.

Following my statement a succession of Conservative members rose to support my plans. I was particularly pleased to have the support of David Howell, a former Secretary of State for Energy and now a very influential backbencher.

Far too often government proposals leak out into the newspapers in the weeks before their publication, so I was delighted that the contents of the white paper remained secret throughout the preparation of our plans. On the day before it was to be presented to parliament I arranged to outline my proposals to the leaders of the industry. By coincidence, most of them were attending a conference at Harrogate including all but two of the area board Chairmen, and so, on my way to speak at a conference in Edinburgh, I stopped off at Leeds/Bradford airport and met them at the headquarters of the Yorkshire Electricity Board. They were delighted that the boards were to be floated as independent companies, pledged total support for the proposals and expressed a determination to make them work. Jim Smith, the Chairman of Eastern Electricity, had emerged as the spokesman for the Chairmen, and throughout the period when the plans were being developed, during the passage of the bill and the implementation of the proposals, played a key role. On my return to London I saw Lord Marshall and the two area Chairmen who had been unable to be at the meeting in Yorkshire and told them of my plans.

That evening a party was being held at Number 10 to say goodbye to two members of the Policy Unit who had been very involved in the privatization plans, and I dropped in for a few minutes before going on to a dinner in the House of Commons at which I was due to speak. As I was leaving, Max Wilkinson, the energy correspondent of the *Financial Times*, who had followed the whole privatization process very carefully, approached me and asked me when we would be producing the white paper. At that time he did not seem to know either the timing or the contents and I subsequently confirmed with him that that was the case. I told him that the white paper would be coming out soon and he seemed satisfied with this information. However, between 8.30 p.m. when I saw him and the time when the late editions of the *Financial Times* went to press he discovered our main proposals. It was infuriating that we'd got so near to publication date without any leaks, only to fall at the last fence and to see our plans in the *Financial Times* on the morning of the white paper's publication.

Once the white paper had been published, the next step was to press on with the preparation of the bill which would enable the plans to go ahead. Geoff Dart was put in charge of its preparation. Once published, it had a relatively uneventful passage through the House due, in the main, to an informal agreement between Michael Spicer and Tony Blair, who had replaced John Prescott as Shadow Energy Secretary. One feature of the bill's passage through the Commons was that, although it was a major and controversial piece of legislation, we managed to get it through the House without the use of a guillotine motion. We agreed an informal timetable with the opposition which left plenty of time for full discussion, and the legislation was duly delivered on time.

As the bill entered its final parliamentary stages, I received disturbing news from the CEGB's auditors. As a result of discussions between the CEGB and British Nuclear Fuels it had become clear that the provisions for nuclear reprocessing and decommissioning, about which I had sought and received assurances earlier, were inadequate. That was bad enough, but what was even worse was that nobody was prepared to put a figure to the amount by which they were inadequate. A general estimate of between £8 billion and £13 billion was the best that could be offered. There was a precedent for this last-minute discovery of underprovision. The privatization of water had revealed a hopeless underprovision for the costs of repairing the existing infrastructure, and so the government had handed back to the industry a substantial part of the proceeds of the privatization. Similar action was not possible in the electricity industry since nobody was prepared to sign up to an agreed figure – the costs were simply too conjectural. I did put a number of proposals to the Treasury but in the end I had to decide to withdraw the Magnox stations from the privatization. It was agreed that I should make a statement to the House of Commons the following Monday when we would be discussing Lords amendments to the Electricity Bill which affected nuclear power.

In my statement on Monday, 24 July, I told the House that as a result of preparing for privatization it had been discovered that the cost of reprocessing and waste treatment of spent Magnox nuclear fuel would be much greater than had been expected and that as a result it had been decided to withdraw the Magnox stations from the privatization of electricity. I pointed out that the Magnox stations were drawing to the end of their lives: 'One is already closed, and most of the others are due to close within the next few years. Most of these costs therefore relate to the past, to electricity already generated and paid for. Future customers will be bearing the full cost of the electricity they consume. It would not be right to burden them also with costs arising from the past.' I explained that the same arguments did not apply to the advanced gas-cooled reactor stations, which had many years of operation ahead, and that they would still be included in the privatization. I firmly believed that, freed from the costs of reprocessing the fuel and decommissioning the Magnox stations, there was no reason why the rest of the nuclear power stations could not have been successfully privatized.

It was not an easy statement to make. There were a number of people on both sides of the House whose hostility to the nuclear industry, or to the privatization proposals, meant that they were eager to make the most of this change of policy. The statement's reception was not helped by the fact that Mrs Thatcher had decided to reshuffle her Cabinet. I had been summoned to Number 10 at 9.30 a.m. where Mrs Thatcher had told me that she wanted me to become Secretary of State for Transport. She felt that, since the Electricity Bill was due for royal assent the next day and the argument had been won, the privatization was now, in her words, a matter for the 'bankers, accountants and solicitors' and that I should move to a new department. Transport had moved up the scale of political concern and Mrs Thatcher was keen to ensure that the government's case was effectively put across. So, by the time I made my statement at, according to Hansard, 4.21 p.m., I knew that I would be moving and rumours of the reshuffle were already circulating around Westminster.

I was not the only member of the Department of Energy to leave at this time. On the same day as the reshuffle Peter Gregson, the Permanent Secretary, moved to the Department of Trade and Industry. Only days earlier the Chief Information Officer had left the department to join the Metropolitan Police and one of his deputies, who had been very closely involved in the privatization process, left to join one of the new generating companies. I have often felt that some of the government's apparent inability to explain the reasoning behind electricity privatization since that time can be explained, at least in part, by these departures.

Although privatisation of electricity dominated my time at the Department of Energy, it was my announcement of another privatization which most pleased the 1988 Conservative Party Conference. On our way down to Brighton, Michael Fallon and I had sat in the back of my car rewriting my Conference speech. Although the government's plans for electricity privatization were to be the centrepiece of the speech, I had won agreement from my colleagues to announce that the coal industry would be privatized and I was keen to find the right words to make the announcement. After much discussion Michael and I finally coined the phrase 'the ultimate privatization'. When I spoke to the Conference I said that I recognized the desire within the party to see the coal industry privatized and pledged that, 'Coal will be privatized. By the next parliament, we shall be ready for this, the ultimate privatization.' At these words the Conference erupted and my speech was interrupted for a long time by the cheers of the audience.

The coal industry and the abuse of their economic power by the miners had dominated the 1970–74 parliament culminating in the downfall of the Heath government. The miners ruled the roost and successive governments pandered to them. The coal industry was a law unto itself and governments handled it with kid gloves. Arthur Scargill, the President of the National Union of Mineworkers, had tried to bring the Thatcher government down and had been forced to a humiliating climb-down in 1985. What was ultimate about the proposed privatization of coal was that it would mark the end of the political power of the National Union of Mineworkers and would make the coal industry what it should always have been, another important industry, no more and no less important than many others. I developed the thought towards the end of my speech:

Just think, Mr Chairman, miners in Britain will be shareholders with a stake in their own industry. Mr Scargill – if he is not in Cuba – will be sitting down to negotiate with the managers of private companies. From the days when the miners' leaders thought they owned the government – to the day when every miner owns part of his own mine.

That's the change, that's the British revolution.

Arguments were put to me almost from the moment I arrived at the department that we should privatize the coal industry before electricity. I was not convinced by the arguments. We had not proposed this in our election manifesto and could therefore have been open to the charge that we had no mandate. But, much more importantly, it was obvious that the reorganization of the electricity industry, and the breaking of British Coal's monopoly as a coal supplier, would fundamentally change the shape of the industry. I did not see how the government could sell an industry to the public knowing that it was going to break its monopoly in the near future and unsure of the impact that this would have upon it. Anyone buying a share in British Coal before the privatization of electricity would have been doing so against a most uncertain background and would have had a right to feel aggrieved if the industry was suddenly altered by the new structure of its major customer. Nevertheless, I was determined that the industry should go into the private sector and was delighted when I was authorized to make that commitment, a commitment that is now in the process of being honoured. I had made it clear in my speech that privatization of the coal industry would be for the next parliament but, before I left the department, I ensured that work was started on the industry's future structure in the private sector.

It is sometimes argued that Mr Scargill was right in predicting the number of pits that would be closed in the years ahead. By his behaviour, and their repeated demonstration of their willingness to abuse their economic and political power, Mr Scargill and the National Union of Mineworkers made his predictions a self-fulfilling prophecy. He proved in 1985 that no government could allow itself to be at the mercy of an industry and a trade union which would use its economic power for political purposes. He underlined, in a way which made the contraction of the industry inevitable, his belief that it was his duty to bring down a Conservative government whatever the views of the electorate. I have never understood the argument that Britain somehow owes a great debt to the mining industry. The industry was given a privileged position and it abused the privilege.

Inevitably electricity privatization and the modernization of the coal industry dominated parliamentary discussion of energy matters, but other major decisions were taken and crises resolved. I will never forget the horrific Piper Alpha tragedy which resulted in the loss of 167 lives. Thanks to the dedicated work of Lord Cullen, the Scottish judge who accepted my invitation to chair the public enquiry which was to take up most of the next three years of his life and who came forward with a comprehensive range of suggestions for improving North Sea safety, future generations of workers in the North Sea will be better protected. Difficult decisions about the future of the fast-breeder reactor at Dounreay, fusion and further successful rounds of licensing for exploration in the North Sea all combined to make two years of very satisfying and worthwhile work in the department for my colleagues and me.

I would have preferred to stay and finish the privatization. I had decided not to fight another general election, and it would have been a very fitting end to a Thatcherite ministerial career, after having contributed to increasing the amount of the nation's energy supplies in private hands from forty per cent in 1979 to eighty-seven per cent by the end of the parliament and, having announced the privatization of British Coal which accounted for the other thirteen per cent, to have concluded my work by abolishing the department. So it was with some reluctance that I moved on to the Department of Transport. I received a large number of letters after I left the Department of Energy and one which I appreciated above all others was from Lord Marshall. He wrote a typically warm and friendly letter, and I was particularly pleased that he expressed his support for the privatization of the electricity industry: 'You have now seen us through to a new privatized world and, of course, I am delighted at that. I am happy to acknowledge that the decisions you made in the last few weeks have gone a long way to meeting my original concerns, so hopefully we can work with your successor to pull off a successful flotation.'

There was a lighter side to my change of job. The Department of Energy was due to move into a new building opposite Buckingham Palace since the lease on our old offices in Millbank had expired and the landlord wanted us to leave. We too were anxious to get out of offices that were daily becoming more uninhabitable. The decision to leave had been taken before I arrived, and the new building chosen. Thanks to the government-owned Property Services Agency's inimitable inefficiency in overseeing the modifications and fitting-out of the building, it was proving to be very expensive. Inevitably I was criticized for this although I had no control over the PSA's activities. Nonetheless, I had been looking forward to the consolation of a nice office in the new building. Needless to say the best offices were going to the senior civil servants on security grounds. Ministers were promoted to a rather inferior floor above the leading officials on the excuse that the higher floor was more secure. Sir Humphrey, once again, proved to be the winner.

The reshuffle took place about two weeks before the department was due to move into the new offices. On my arrival at the Department of Transport, I found Paul Channon's office in a very rundown state. It was explained to me that some years before, Paul, as a very junior minister, had had his office redecorated and that a journalist had got hold of the story and made a fuss about it. Paul had vowed never again to spend money on any office he occupied. He had, however, made the office habitable and concealed its innate unattractiveness by bringing in some beautiful paintings, including a Canaletto or two. Some while later, I asked him if it was true that he had had Canalettos in his office. He replied with a smile 'It is true, but they were not very good Canalettos.' No other member of the government was in a position to make such a statement!

The Department of Transport had over a very short period become a high-profile department. The transfer of responsibility for aviation and shipping, which I had promoted in 1983, had turned the department from a small organization concerned exclusively with domestic transport into a fully fledged department of transportation with a substantial international dimension.

My predecessor, Paul Channon, who was a deservedly popular minister, had been desperately unlucky during his term of office. Three appalling tragedies, at King's Cross underground station, on British Rail at Clapham Junction and the terrorist bombing of a Pan Am flight over Lockerbie had occurred. He had also inherited the aftermath of the *Herald of Free Enterprise* disaster at Zeebrugge. As a result of the sustained economic growth during the 1980s, the whole of our transport infrastructure was under pressure. The roads system was chronically overloaded, the London underground was almost dangerously overcrowded and every weekend air traffic control problems caused tens of thousands of holiday-makers to be delayed at our airports. The whole system was creaking. The public was angry and the Treasury was obstructive. The poor old Department of Transport was in the middle, taking criticism from all sides. To the public it was failing to provide the necessary infrastructure and to the Treasury it was another government department seeking to be profligate. Paul Channon summed up his predicament well when he told me soon after my appointment that the Secretary of State for Transport is the only person in the country who apologizes to his guests if they arrive late.

In spite of all the difficulties he faced Paul Channon had succeeded in coping with the disasters and setting in motion proposals for tackling the long-term problems. A white paper, 'Roads for Prosperity', outlining an ambitious and necessary set of plans for improving our road network, had been approved by Cabinet, studies into London's long-term traffic problems were in hand, British Rail was planning its biggest investment programme for thirty years and work was under way on the fast link to connect the Channel Tunnel to London and beyond. Unfortunately, although these plans were being developed, the Treasury had not committed itself in any way to their funding. In fact, the Treasury was very determined not to fund a number of them and was especially set against increasing investment in the London underground.

On my appointment, certain newspapers pointed out that I had had a reputation for submitting low budgets in the Department of Energy and of being a staunch ally of the Prime Minister in her belief in a tight monetary policy. They wondered how I would reconcile this with the requirements of my new department where I was bound to demand increases in expenditure. I didn't find this the problem that some of the commentators did. I had devoted quite a lot of my ministerial time to measures to improve the supply side of the economy, and it seemed to me that improvement in our transport system was an absolutely essential part of improving the supply side. I was determined that any money I could negotiate should go into investment and not into subsidy, and was convinced that wherever possible we should carry on with a programme of privatization and the introduction of private capital.

I found a department that had felt under siege waiting nervously for the next disaster and the next bout of criticism, but I was fortunate to have an excellent team of ministers and was particularly lucky to find Michael Portillo already installed as the Minister for Public Transport and my number two. Michael and I had worked together in different capacities on three occasions in the past. First of all, when I was trade spokesman and he was working in the Conservative

Research Department as the desk officer responsible for trade; secondly, as Party Chairman when he acted as unofficial special adviser and worked with me on a number of major speeches; and thirdly, as my official Special Adviser in the Department of Trade and Industry after the 1983 general election. I had a very high regard for him as a person and for his ability. He is a man of great principle and stands by those principles. Two incidents particularly spring to mind. The first was when I told him that I was not prepared to proceed with one of his pet schemes for improving traffic flow in the King's Cross area of London. I had doubts about the scheme which, in my view, had limited prospects of improving the traffic situation and was hugely unpopular. I explained my reasons for coming to this conclusion. His reply was: 'We weren't elected to be popular, we were elected to find answers to problems.' The second occasion came later, the night before Mrs Thatcher resigned, when Michael twice led small groups of ministers and backbenchers to see Mrs Thatcher to urge her not to resign. By that time she was pretty well decided and many Conservative members were already working out where the balance of advantage to them lay in the choice of a successor. Michael believed that she was the right person to continue as Prime Minister and, unlike some of his more calculating colleagues, made his views absolutely clear. He is a deservedly popular minister and I have no wish to blight his prospects by making predictions about his future other than to say that it will be a bright one.

Robert Atkins joined the department with me. He had acquired a reputation in Whitehall for being able but idle, and after a spell in the Department of Trade and Industry in something of a non-job many thought that he was lucky to survive. He was extremely suspicious of me and felt that I would wish to get rid of him. He took over from Peter Bottomley as the Minister for Roads and Traffic which is an important job and he did it extremely well. Robert is no ideologue but an extremely effective political operator, and his period in transport certainly changed people's perception of him, to his and the government's benefit.

Patrick McLoughlin was given his first ministerial job as Minister for Aviation and Shipping and one of the pleasures of my time in the Department was to see him develop in confidence and become an established minister. I had first met him when I was Chairman of the party and he was a leading figure in the Young Conservatives, and I had always admired his plain-speaking and his clear ideas.

Elizabeth Buchanan had been Paul Channon's Political Adviser and with his resignation her job came to an end, but Michael Portillo suggested to me that she was quite outstanding and that I should interview her with a view to taking her on as my adviser. In addition to Michael, a number of other people urged me to reappoint her and having met her I decided to do so. She was a great success, trusted within the department and she had very good connections with the media which stood the department in good stead. She worked very closely with Gill Samuel, the Director of Information at the department and one of the best in Whitehall. Elizabeth and Gill made a formidable team and my nickname for them, the gorgons, was soon in common use throughout the department.

I had been due to go on holiday at the end of July 1989, but I decided to delay it so that I could spend a week looking at different parts of my new responsibilities – the railways, the Channel Tunnel, air traffic control, coastguards and roads. During this week I was due to visit British Rail and on the morning of the visit a train was derailed between Paddington and Reading because vandals had placed an obstruction on the line. Fortunately nobody was killed but I was shocked that anyone could see anything entertaining in putting the lives of hundreds of people at risk, and I made a very strong statement in which I pointed out the incident was very serious and that the investigation into its cause could easily have turned into a murder hunt: 'Had it turned into murder, then the people who did it would have gone to jail for a very, very long time.' British Rail was grateful for this strong stance since, for the first time in some years, it was seen as the victim and not the villain, and the public rallied to its side.

The week was not without other incident. Since I was trying to cram a great deal into a short time, I had arranged to fly down to the Channel Tunnel by helicopter rather than travel by road or rail. A very large number of press, television and radio representatives had travelled down earlier by train to report on my visit. Unfortunately, the helicopter was grounded by bad conditions and it looked as if we would not be able leave Battersea heliport. Eventually, the weather lifted for a moment and we were halfway down the Thames when the door on my side of the helicopter flew open. Fortunately, I was wearing a safety belt, but the incident served to convince us all that the fates were not on our side and we were forced to return to Battersea. Needless to say, the press had something of a field day as a result of my non-arrival.

I went on holiday a week late and, having been away for a week, was awakened one Sunday morning by Michael Portillo with the news that a pleasure boat, the *Marchioness*, had collided with a cargo vessel on the Thames and that many young people, who had been enjoying a birthday party on the river, had been killed. I decided at once to put an end to my holiday and to return to London and take charge of the government's handling of this awful tragedy. Eighteen hours later I was back in London and within hours we were able to introduce a package of measures designed to tighten the rules on passenger safety on the Thames. The department's Marine Accident Investigation Branch immediately mounted a detailed enquiry into the tragedy. They quickly produced an interim report containing a number of proposals, some of which required a change in legislation, but after meetings with the Thames pleasure-boat operators, the Port of London Authority and others, it was agreed that the changes would be observed voluntarily until we could give them the full force of law.

Some of the relatives of those who died demanded a public inquiry into the tragedy. I had great sympathy for their arguments, but felt it was important for independent experts to look at this terrible accident coolly rather than in a blaze of publicity and with all the emotion that surrounds a public inquiry. The Marine Accident Investigation Branch had recently been physically separated from the rest of the department to underline its independence and I had every confidence that it would do a thorough job. Its equivalent in the aviation field, the Air Accident Investigation Branch, has established a worldwide reputation for thoroughness and integrity. Our aim was for the Marine Accident Investigation Branch to achieve a similar reputation.

In September I was interviewed on BBC television's *Panorama* programme about the future for British Rail and I made it clear that I felt that 'privatization may be the best way forward' although I stressed that 'whether and how best it could be done remain decisions for the future'. Paul Channon had very guardedly mentioned the possibility of privatization at the previous year's party Conference and I had no choice but to mention the subject again in my speech in 1989. However, the Prime Minister was anxious not to raise the temperature on the subject and asked me to play down the possibility.

I made it clear to her that in my view privatization was the best way forward and that it was something to which we should commit ourselves, but I accepted that it might be wiser to do so later. In my speech, I acknowledged that Paul Channon had said that privatization might be the way ahead and told the audience that work on the subject was making good progress, but I again stressed that decisions on privatization were for the future. The next day's newspapers made it clear that the press felt that my remarks were a watering-down of those made by Paul the year before, and this was hailed as a change of government policy. I was pleased that, by the time of the next party Conference in 1990, I was authorized to commit the government to the privatization of British Rail, a commitment underlined by the Prime Minister in her closing speech to the Conference.

A few days after I had been appointed to the department, I had met Enoch Powell who suggested that he would like to come and talk to me about transport. We had a very interesting chat, during the course of which he crystallized in his remarks an idea which I had been developing. He said that one should never underestimate the ability of the public to make sensible choices provided that they are given a sensible range of options. From this conversation, I developed the concept of the balanced transport policy. I became convinced that we needed to improve the whole of our transport arrangements – better railways, better underground and mass transit systems, better airports and means of access to them, better air traffic control, better ports with better access and better roads.

I made the balanced transport policy the theme of my 1989 Conference speech, telling the audience of the commitment of the team of ministers at the Department of Transport: 'to give the customer the best and safest transport service. To achieve a balance between public transport and the road user. To achieve a balance between transport and the environment. To give our nation a transport system fit for the Nineties and beyond.' I contrasted this approach with Labour's 'unbalanced policy' which would discriminate against the car owner in favour of state-monopoly transport. Labour's policy, I told the Conference, was 'to order people to leave their cars at home and take the state-run train or bus. And that is the policy of totalitarian socialism.' Conservatives believed: 'People must be free to make choices. Not bludgeoned, bullied or bribed. We live in a free society and Labour shouldn't forget it.'

One of the heaviest crosses that any Transport Secretary in this period had to bear was the opposition spokesman on transport, John Prescott. A few days after my appointment he asked if he could come and see me. I was warned against seeing him since it was predicted that he would come, make a series of half-thought-out proposals, bang the table, leave the department and then hold a press conference at which he would criticize the government, me and all associated with transport policy. I decided to ignore the advice; he came to see me alone and we had a very worthwhile talk about transport problems. We were both the sons of railwaymen and both had had a lifelong interest in trains. I enjoyed our talk and hoped that the fact that he didn't hold a press conference, and that our talks remained confidential, might signal the beginning of a new era. My optimism was ill-founded and after that first meeting I never again had a rational discussion with him about transport. He was passionately devoted to subsidies and was genuinely convinced that every accident, whether it was the Lockerbie air disaster or the Clapham train tragedy, stemmed from cuts in government expenditure. No matter how often I explained that Lockerbie was caused by a terrorist bomb and Clapham by the modernization of the signalling system which was wrongly carried out, he maintained his argument that government cuts were the cause of all our difficulties. No matter how often I pointed out to him that the Conservative government had invested far more in public transport than any Labour government had in the previous thirty years, he persisted in talking about cuts.

I attacked Labour's obsession with Conservative cuts at the 1989 party Conference:

Mr Chairman, I want to begin by putting an end to a myth. I'm fed up with reading it and today I'm nailing it. Far from investing in transport, the last Labour government, in hock to the IMF and the unions, allowed the nation's infrastructure to crumble and decay. Labour began with promises and ended in bankruptcy. They'd like you to forget it. They'd like it, but we won't allow you to. They damaged our infrastructure and we are putting it right.

I contrasted Labour's record with that of the Conservative government's since 1979: 'Nine hundred miles of new roads have been built. Three thousand four hundred new coaches are now running on our railways. Over 400 miles of railway line have been electrified. That's what Conservative governments have been doing.'

My immediate priority on my arrival at the Department of Transport was to negotiate a reasonable financial settlement with the Treasury for the ensuing financial year and the Public Expenditure Survey period. An old friend, Norman Lamont, had been appointed Chief Secretary to the Treasury and, although I expected no favours from him and received none, I knew him to be fair-minded and fully aware of the pressures on the transport system. After a period of tough negotiation, and in spite of predictions in the newspapers that I was to be 'steamrollered' by the Treasury, I negotiated an increase of £1.8 billion for investment in the new road and rail programme. The increased funding brought total public spending on roads and public transport to £13 billion during the next three years which represented a quantum jump from the £8 billion spent over the previous three years. Public spending on new and expanded motor-ways and trunk roads was planned to increase by about £900 million in real terms to £5,700 million. British Rail's investment programme, which was already the highest for thirty years, was to be increased by more than £600 million to £3,700 million by 1993. Investment in London Regional Transport was to be increased by fifty per cent to £1,700 million over the next three years. It was a very satisfactory settlement which enabled us to make a start on implementing the plans laid out in 'Roads for Prosperity', and improving both British Rail and the London underground. There was also a substantial programme for improving our air traffic control system.

No mention was made in the autumn statement of the extension of the Jubilee Line from Green Park into Docklands and the East End of London. This was because negotiations were under way with the Treasury and with Olympia & York, the developers of Canary Wharf, about the contribution they might make to the proposed extension. A bill had to be lodged in parliament by mid-November if we were to avoid a further year's delay in beginning this desperately needed project. An argument had been under way for months and little progress was being made, so I decided to invite Paul Reichmann, the head of Olympia & York, to meet me to see if we could negotiate an agreement. After very hard bargaining, we agreed that Olympia & York would contribute a figure of £400 million to the cost of the railway. The Treasury argued that this was not enough and so I once again invited Mr Reichmann to visit me to see if he could improve the offer and, after further tough negotiating, we were able to improve the terms but not the sum. The Treasury were still unhappy and so I decided to settle the matter once and for all and arranged to meet

Mr Reichmann early in the morning of 15 November, the day on which the autumn statement was to be announced, and to see Norman Lamont at noon on the same day. I also arranged to see the Prime Minister that evening at Number 10. At the first meeting Mr Reichmann repeated his terms and made it clear that it was his final offer. I then went to see Norman Lamont and we agreed to settle the matter at Number 10. We met at 8.0 p.m. as arranged and at the end of the meeting it was agreed that we would go ahead with the Jubilee Line extension on the terms negotiated. I made the announcement the next day.

It is sometimes argued that the Jubilee Line extension will only serve Docklands and so is rather a luxury. But in fact it takes a much-needed line south of the Thames, crossing over to Canary Wharf and then back under the river to the Greenwich peninsula, thus connecting the whole of that part of London to the underground system for the very first time. The line then carries on to the East End where the service is desperately needed. A year later, I won a similar argument about the need for the East-West crossrail and agreed with London Transport that we would protect the route of a proposed Chelsea-Hackney line so that it couldn't be blocked by any future development.

In addition to the biggest-ever investment programme to modernize the existing London underground system with improved stations, trains and signalling systems which will lead to a substantially better service in the years ahead, I was able to gain approval for the first two underground lines to be authorized in London for twenty years. Alongside this, the Docklands Light Railway extension to Beckton was authorized and the plan to take the railway to Lewisham was developed.

South London has always been less well served by the underground than London north of the Thames. The reason is that north of the Thames the substructure consists of heavy clay which is easy to tunnel, whilst south of the river there is a preponderance of gravel. A look at the underground map of London shows very clearly how this has affected the development of the system. The Jubilee Line extension into Greenwich and the Lewisham extension of the Docklands Light Railway represent a much-needed increase in the public transport infrastructure south of the Thames.

One of the most serious problems facing me on my arrival at the Department of Transport was how to improve the flow of traffic in London. Nicholas Ridley, one of my predecessors as Transport Secretary, had set up four assessment studies in 1984 to examine options for new road-building and improvements to existing arrangements. Most of the plans for new roads had predictably met with heavy opposition and, since they included a considerable amount of tunnelling, they were also financially unrealistic. Even if we had been prepared to accept the schemes in principle and ignore the public opposition, the Treasury would never have agreed to fund them. My proposals were more modest but more realistic.

In March 1990, I unveiled plans for a number of road improvement schemes costing £250 million and announced that consideration would be given to various new public transport projects, including the Chelsea-Hackney underground line, the East-West crossrail and the extension of the Docklands Light Railway to Lewisham. At the end of 1989 I had published a consultation document, 'Traffic in London', which contained plans to improve the management of traffic in the capital. Among the ideas contained in the document were the establishment of a 300-mile priority 'red route' system aimed at speeding up London's traffic, and the appointment of a traffic director for London who would coordinate its introduction. On those roads which are designated as red routes, stringent parking controls have now been introduced and heavy fines are imposed if the free flow of traffic is interrupted by parked or waiting vehicles. The first red routes have been an outstanding success and although their introduction has been controversial they are already making a substantial contribution to improving London's traffic flow. A survey in January 1992 on the first red route on the A1 found that journey times had improved and the number of accidents had dropped.

The 'Traffic in London' package was criticized by some for failing to consider the case for road pricing. Road pricing means that road users have to pay for driving on a particular road. Its advocates argue that charging drivers an economic rate for using road space will combat congestion, particularly in large cities, since, if the price is set at a high enough level, people will be priced off the roads. I had some sympathy for this view and, ironically, the week before I moved to the Department of Transport, Paul Channon had written to Cabinet colleagues asking for approval to prepare and publish a discussion document on the subject. I wrote a very enthusiastic letter back saying that I thought it was essential and what is more that it should be a very detailed study with a view to it being implemented.

I little thought that I would be moving to the Department of Transport only a few days later and would receive my own memorandum when it arrived. I did take proposals to Cabinet for a consultation document. However, by then, as I had studied the matter more closely, I had become far less certain that road pricing was the answer to London's traffic problems. But I still felt that it had a superficial attraction and that what we needed was a really detailed and well-informed discussion about it. It is interesting that, with the exception of Norway and Singapore, road pricing has been abandoned in every country in which it has been tried. In Norway, road pricing and tolling have not been introduced as a way of controlling traffic but as a method of raising revenue to fund the building of new roads. In Hong Kong it was abandoned on libertarian grounds because the sophisticated monitoring system enabled the police to know too much about where everyone was. But, in spite of the international precedents, I felt that this was a subject that should be discussed so that people could understand its advantages and disadvantages. Unfortunately, only two colleagues in Cabinet supported me and they didn't include any of my successors as Transport Secretary.

I have always been an enthusiast for pricing mechanisms, but as I studied the case for road pricing, I became convinced that in order to price people off the roads you needed to be able to price them on to something else. The underground system was already overloaded, and although we were planning to improve them, the South East commuter services were at that time overcrowded and badly in need of the investment package which we were introducing. It simply was not possible to price people on to the trains or on to the underground, as both systems were already overflowing. The only under-used part of the public transport system was the bus service, which had been going down in popularity since the buses moved too slowly through London's traffic. Although I was tackling this with the introduction of red routes, I did not believe that it would be possible for the buses to take up the strain imposed by pricing car drivers off the roads.

The dilemma that I faced as a one-time supporter of road pricing was that pricing could not be introduced until there were other adequate means of getting people to and from work. Road pricing could be introduced once the new underground lines were built, the commuter services improved, the fast link from Paddington to Heathrow built, and good train services to Stansted and Gatwick introduced, but by the time these improvements had been made the need for road pricing would have disappeared. All the evidence suggested that people did not want to drive into London. The number of people using private cars to come into London had fallen, and the number of people coming in by train had risen by twenty-five per cent. I was sure that once the infrastructure was in place to allow people to make sensible decisions they would choose not to drive into work and so the problems to which road pricing might be the answer would diminish.

I had one other serious doubt about road pricing. If it was to work effectively and really reduce the numbers using London's roads, then charges would have had to have been very high. Adding £1 to the price of driving in London would make little or no difference to car numbers. Small price rises are never successful in persuading people to change their habits. An extra twenty pence on the price of cigarettes has very little effect on the numbers who smoke. I have similar doubts about European Community proposals for a carbon tax which would add only about five pence to the price of petrol. As a tax it will produce additional revenues, but as a means of discouraging consumption of fuel it will have only a minimal impact. Much more severe price rises would be necessary if consumption levels were to be radically cut.

A myth had been created by our opponents that Conservative governments are hostile to the railway system and to British Rail. We had demonstrated our hostility in a most peculiar way by regularly and consistently increasing the amount of money made available for investment. But the fact that we had reduced British Rail's operating subsidy and were planning to reduce it further was hailed by our critics as evidence of our distaste for railways. The fact was that the railways had benefited from the improved performance of the economy. The increase in people commuting into London by rail had given rise to very substantial increases in revenue and, on top of that, the steadily increasing investment programme had produced improvements in productivity and costs. Such money as was available was going more and more into investment rather than into indiscriminate subsidy and that investment, coupled with improved performance, was benefiting the passengers and the staff of British Rail. When we set targets for further reducing the subsidy, we coupled them with a huge increase in investment. We did not just tell British Rail to reduce its subsidy, we provided it with the means of reducing its costs, improving its services and attracting more passengers. This contrasted with the Labour GLC's treatment of the London underground in the early 1980s when, under Ken Livingstone's leadership, they devoted huge resources to subsidizing fares as a result of which they had had no money left for investment and so attracted more and more people on to an ever worsening system.

The Chairman of British Rail, Sir Bob Reid, was approaching retirement and the search was on for his successor. Headhunters had been appointed who had sounded out a number of people as to whether they would like to be considered for the job. I wasn't particularly impressed with the list which had been drawn up and one day I saw in my diary that I was due to meet another Bob Reid, the Chief Executive of Shell UK, who I had got to know during my time at the Department of Energy. He wanted to tell me about the outcome of the Monopoly and Mergers Commission investigation into retail petrol sales which had been set up during my time at the Department of Energy. When we had finished our conversation about petrol, I asked him what he was going to do when he left Shell and whether he would be interested in taking over from his namesake at British Rail. Bob Reid had a very high reputation in the oil industry, he had successfully managed huge investment programmes on behalf of Shell and had an excellent reputation in man-management. To my delight he said that he could well be interested, but that he would like to think it over for a few days. After one or two more meetings we reached agreement that he would join BR, initially as a non-executive Chairman and on his retirement from Shell as full-time Chairman. There were a number of jokes about Bob Reid taking over from Bob Reid, but in my opinion one very fine man succeeded another. The first Bob Reid, the existing Chairman, had done a superb job for British Rail. His reputation had been unfairly dented by the series of mindless one-day strikes that had taken place in the early part of 1989, but I was determined that that should not obscure a very fine record of service to British Rail and of improvement in its services. The other Bob Reid, the new Chairman, had lost an arm in an accident as a child and had overcome this handicap to the extent that he became the Chief Executive of a huge company and one of the best one-arm golfers in the country with a single-figure handicap. He wasn't coy about his disability and shared my amusement when I told him that I had been asked by a colleague in parliament whether it was true that the new Chairman intended to run British Rail single-handedly.

*   *   *

One of the biggest issues facing British Rail was the question of the fast link from the Channel Tunnel to London and beyond. The Channel Tunnel Act ruled out any possibility of public subsidy for the fast link. The rationale behind this was that the Channel Tunnel would be in competition with ferries, lorries, and air services, none of which were subsidized, and it should therefore compete with them without subsidy. This prohibition was, at least at first, enthusiastically backed by the Labour Party, mainly at the behest of the shipping trade union, which sponsored John Prescott. Proposals had been invited from a number of consortia who wished to be involved in the fast link and eventually Eurorail was selected as British Rail's proposed partner. The consortium undertook to come back to the government within a few months with a viable proposal, but when it eventually arrived it was anything but viable. The government had recognized that the proposed service would help relieve congestion on the commuter network in the South East and I had always been prepared to consider making a contribution to the cost of the fast link, not as a subsidy to that link, but as a means of improving passenger services for those living in the South East. Nevertheless, the consortium's demands were quite unacceptable. They asked for a cash grant payable at the beginning of the project of £500 million, for a loan of £1000 million on which interest would be accrued but not payable until the year 2010, this loan and the accumulated interest were to rank behind other creditors in the event of the fast link failing as a business venture, and finally £400 million of the expenditure, notably at the proposed terminal at King's Cross which had previously been regarded as part of the project, was to be undertaken by British Rail outside the project. Eurorail quite properly felt that this was a high-risk venture and that a higher than normal rate of return must be available to the investor, but it seemed to me that the taxpayer was to be left with a major part of the risk. Eurorail had done an excellent job in identifying cost savings and I was very impressed by their work, but the proposals were so far removed from what I had hoped for as to be unacceptable and, of course, funding of this kind would have been illegal under the act. However, although parliament had passed the law prohibiting subsidy, members did not feel inhibited from criticizing the government for observing the law which they had passed.

I made a statement to the House announcing my decision. I confirmed the line of route from Dover to the North Downs to remove uncertainty from those whose properties had been threatened and to entitle them to compensation. I also confirmed that the London terminus would be at King's Cross and I asked British Rail to come back to me within an agreed time with proposals for taking the line from the North Downs through to King's Cross.

Many people contrasted the behaviour of the British government in the matter of the Channel Tunnel with that of the French, to our disadvantage. But those arguments ignored a number of important and relevant factors. First, north east France is a deeply deprived region with high unemployment and a declining industrial base in steel, textiles and coal. The French government saw the fast link from Paris as a huge regional regeneration project. On the other side of the tunnel, Kent is one of Britain's most prosperous and beautiful counties. With its environment already under great pressure, the last thing it needed was regeneration. With an articulate population represented in parliament by a very able group of Conservative members, it was quite clear that the new rail link would be unpopular. To make the scheme at all acceptable, almost half of the length from London to Dover would have to be in tunnel. This would have meant driving tunnels at huge cost, not only through Kent, but through the uncertain ground of south London. Whereas the Mayors of towns in France were threatening to lie down and obstruct the track if it didn't go near their town, Mayors in Britain were threatening to do the same if it did. Moreover, the fast link was never part of the original proposal for the Channel Tunnel. Quite naturally Sir Alistair Morton and his colleagues at Eurotunnel, the Anglo-French consortium which was building the tunnel, desperately wanted a fast link because it would greatly improve the commercial prospects of their tunnel, but they did not raise their money on the basis that there would be one.

Transport must be one of the most devotee-ridden areas of government policy. Everybody has views about it, everybody has their pet answer to the problems and all of them seem to involve other people changing. Railway enthusiasts have no time for roads, and road enthusiasts are highly critical of railways. Environmentalists seem to be opposed to most forms of transport and the heritage bodies, whilst seeking to encourage large numbers of people to visit lovely homes, or places of great natural beauty or special scientific interest, criticize the government for making arrangements for people to get to them.

It is the motor car which provokes the most criticism. From the way people talk about cars, one can sometimes form the impression that they are issued to people by the government and that it is the government's fault that more people want to own them. All too often the green lobbyist wants the government to limit the prospect of motorcar ownership except, of course, for him and his friends. Although the number of cars in Britain has increased dramatically as the country has become more prosperous, we still have fewer cars per thousand members of the population than in other major western countries. In 1989 there were 653 cars per 1,000 of the population in the United States, 480 in West Germany, 410 in France and 366 in the UK. Even today, one-third of families in Britain have no access to a private car, and therefore we have every reason to expect that as Britain becomes still more prosperous it will follow a well-established pattern and the number of cars will increase. It is easy for those who have cars to criticize but I can see no reason why the government should take action to deprive people of the opportunity of car ownership.

The environmental lobby was particularly hostile to the roads programme, even though we pointed out that the most uselessly polluting phenomenon is the traffic jam where carbon dioxide is pushed into the atmosphere to no purpose at all, and that bypasses, which take heavy traffic from towns and villages, produce an improvement in the quality of life for local residents. The environmentalists simply refused to accept the need for a roads programme. I sometimes feel that the environmental lobby means the countryside when it talks about the environment and finds it hard to accept that an improvement in our urban environment can be just as important as an improvement to our countryside. I also found that the environmentalists, because they feel that their motives are beyond reproach, are prepared to resort to any sort of misleading argument as a means of achieving their end. For example, National Heritage published an assessment of the likely damage to archeological sites from new road schemes. The plan was nothing more than guesswork, it took the roads programme, assumed that the roads would be designed in the most environmentally damaging way, making detours if necessary so that we could destroy sites of archeological interest, and then on the basis of this totally warped projection came up with an equally bogus number of sites that would be destroyed. This was all too typical of the work of the well-intentioned but ill-informed. Nevertheless, we believed that the economic and environmental benefits of 'Roads for Prosperity' justified that programme. It was never a substitute for investment in rail and public transport, it was intended to be implemented alongside programmes for investment in the rest of our transport infrastructure.

In speech after speech I answered those who criticized the fact that eighty-six per cent of all our freight travels by road and the same proportion of journeys cover less than fifty miles from door to door. Many people argued that this traffic could be transferred from the roads to the railways. But, in fact, even if rail freight were hugely increased it would make very little impact on overall freight movements. It has been estimated that a one hundred per cent increase in rail freight would reduce road freight by less than ten per cent. Moreover, there are a very large number of freight movements which are simply unsuitable for transfer to rail. By making this argument I immediately found myself classified as anti-rail or pro-road, but all I was trying to do was bring facts to the attention of the public.

In what was to prove to be my final speech to a party Conference I summed up the transport problems facing the country and our approach to solving them:

Over the last eleven years our economy has grown at a record rate. The country has become more prosperous. More people now travel. There are more goods to be moved. Some people talk as if it is a sign of failure that we have over five million more vehicles on the road; that eighty million more tonnes of freight is moving through our ports; that the number of people using our airports is growing at six per cent a year every year; that the number of people using our railways has increased by twenty per cent in the last five years. These are not signs of failure, but of success and progress. Only the closed-minded can pretend that it's bad news that more people can afford to travel. What was once the province of the few is now open to the majority. This isn't evidence of decadence or decline. It's evidence of the spreading of wealth, the sharing of privilege. Privilege shouldn't be the preserve of the few but something to be enjoyed by the overwhelming majority. That's the way that we Conservatives attack privilege.

In transport our challenge is to meet the aspirations of the people. To meet the needs of business in the new era of the single market. It is a challenge we will meet.

And we shall do it with a balanced transport policy. We're for giving people a choice and for high standards of service. And it's to give that choice and that service that we are are investing more now than for decades – right across the spectrum of our transport system.

This was not an idle claim. During my time in the department the public expenditure programme was doubled from £8 billion to nearly £16 billion for the three years ending in 1993–4. New underground lines for London had been approved, a new air traffic control system was being developed and the 'Roads for Prosperity' programme was under way. When I left the department in November 1990 it had just embarked upon its largest legislative programme for many years. Four major new bills were planned for the parliamentary session. These would radically reform road traffic law and introduce tough new measures for bad driving; ease congestion in London by establishing the red routes, appoint a traffic director for London and introduce tough new parking controls; make public utilities more responsible for street works and improve the speed and quality of their repairs; allow for the building of privately funded roads; provide for the privatization of trust ports; and enable the design and building of a privately funded second road crossing of the Severn estuary. There were also plans to privatize municipal airports and bus services. It had been a productive time.

One of the difficulties with a department like Transport is that plans take a long time to come to fruition. A new Transport Secretary inherits his predecessor's successes and his failures. Any plans or projects which a new Secretary of State initiates will almost certainly be completed after he has left the department. My own contribution as Transport Secretary will, for example, almost certainly be forgotten by the time that the East-West crossrail opens in London at the beginning of the next decade. But that is the reality of the job. I had moved to the Department of Transport reluctantly, but after seventeen fruitful months I was sorry to leave.

Epilogue

Margaret Thatcher did not invent the principles or policies which she carried out in government. Successive Conservative manifestoes, most explicitly of all Ted Heath's 1970 election manifesto, outlined a belief in less government, lower taxes and sound money. Mrs Thatcher's invaluable contribution was to prove that these ideas could in fact work. For years Conservative politicians had paid lip service to a set of policies, but had assumed that the public would not support their implementation. Mrs Thatcher demonstrated the practicality of the policies and by single-mindedly sticking to them she ensured their success.

Without Mrs Thatcher, John Major could not have won the 1992 general election. The election on 9 April was the most searching test of the changes which Mrs Thatcher had brought about since 1979. John Major's remarkable victory was proof of their fundamental nature and of her significance.

The policies which collectively have come to be known as 'Thatcherism' – trade union reform, the sale of council housing, tax reform, privatization and the changes in health and education – had one thing in common. They were all designed to promote choice, to tackle the power of the big battalions and to reduce the role of the bureaucracy in the everyday lives of ordinary people. The trade unions were given back to their members. Council houses were sold at discounted prices to their occupants. Reductions in the rate of income tax allowed people to choose how to spend their own money. The privatization of state-owned industries gave shares to the workforce and took power away from the politicians and trade union leaders who had dominated the nationalized industries. The health service reforms made the patient the focus of the health care system. Individual hospitals became more responsive to the needs of local communities and were no longer just a cog in a national and anonymous health bureaucracy. In education, parents and teachers were given the opportunity to work together and to bypass local education apparatchiks.

Mrs Thatcher was much criticized for remarking that 'there is no such thing as society', yet the vision that she outlined and the thread that ran through her policies were much more warm-hearted and ambitious in concept than a socialist ideal of society. Mrs Thatcher's view was much closer to that of Jonathan Swift who wrote, 'I have ever hated all nations, professions and communities, and all my love is towards individuals ... But principally I hate and detest that animal called man; although I heartily love John, Peter, Thomas, and so forth'. To her, the challenge for government was to devise policies which would benefit not an amorphous entity called society but all individual men and women.

Under Mrs Thatcher, the ideal of a property-owning democracy, which had been a theme of successive Conservative leaders, became a reality. Two-thirds of families in the United Kingdom now live in a home which they own. This means that not only are two-thirds of families property-owners, they are capital-owners as well. As a result, in the hands of future generations parental homes will translate themselves into family capital. As a result of the privatization programme, the number of individuals owning shares has increased from 3.5 million in 1979 to 11 million today.

These fundamental changes have led to a fundamental shift in attitudes.

It is a shift which even the Labour Party has been forced to recognize. In launching a review of policy following the party's 1987 general election defeat, Neil Kinnock recognized the problem facing his party. He told the 1987 Labour Conference that: 'if this movement pretends, for instance, that a few million more people owning a few shares each will not make any difference to their perception of their economic welfare then this movement will be fooling itself ... and the result of it is that our policies are going to have to take account of that reality, and of a number of others.' In what is probably the most-remembered passage of his speech he went on to quote Ron Todd, the then leader of the Transport and General Workers' Union: 'Ron Todd made the point with deadly accuracy just a couple of months ago when he asked, "What do you say to a docker who earns £400 a week, owns his house, a new car, a microwave and a video, as well as a small place near Marbella? You do not say," said Ron, "let me take you out of your misery, brother."'

The policy review led Labour to abandon its defence policy and embrace the European Community. It accepted, albeit half-heartedly, the free market and committed itself to the anti-inflationary discipline of the Exchange Rate Mechanism. The party began to move away from the trade union block vote and accepted many of the Conservative trade union reforms. Even on tax, although its proposals proved fatally damaging to its 1992 election campaign, Labour dared not suggest a top rate higher than fifty per cent. It recognized that a return to rates of eighty-three per cent on earnings and ninety-eight per cent on investment income, of which it had been so proud when in government, were simply unacceptable.

One would have thought that the coincidence of Labour's real attempt to accommodate themselves to a changed world and a deep and lasting recession would have been the basis for a Labour victory. But it did not happen. Although Labour might have changed its policies, the public's perception of the party had not altered. Even the watered-down socialism of Neil Kinnock was too red for the British people.

Labour's failure in 1992, like its defeat in 1987, came in spite of undoubtedly running the slickest general election campaign. Following its disastrous election in 1983, the Labour Party had learnt the techniques of campaigning which the Conservatives had pioneered in this country in 1979 and 1983. But in 1992 slickness and over-production produced a backlash. Labour's rally at Sheffield gave the electorate the impression that the party thought the election was won. What the party managers thought was a display of confidence appeared to the voters as a demonstration of arrogance.

When the Conservative campaign faltered John Major read the mood of the electorate brilliantly and his inspired antidote was to turn away from the skills of the Party's Media advisers and to get out his soapbox. A plain-speaking Prime Minister on a soapbox cut the spin doctors and the campaign managers down to size.

The 1992 general election campaign was fought at a difficult time for the Conservative Party. The fact that the party won with a good working majority clearly illustrates the fundamental nature of the changes which Mrs Thatcher brought about. In 1992 anything that smacked of socialism was clearly not wanted by a substantial majority of the people. It is the Conservative Party which is the party of opportunity. It is the Conservative Party which has elected as its last three leaders a carpenter's son, a small-shopkeeper's daughter and the son of a small-businessman and acrobat. It is the Conservative Party which, in spite of Neil Kinnock's efforts, represents the aspirations of the British people. The Labour Party, far from being, as Harold Wilson once described it, the 'natural party of government', is now addressing itself to an ever-shrinking band of the under-privileged, a band which it is the fundamental aim of our party to ensure continues to become smaller. Labour now attracts the support of an increasingly bizarre bunch of deeply unattractive well-to-do socialists in the arts and professions, to whom the public reacts at best as figures of fun and at worst with a profound distaste.

Internationally, Mrs Thatcher can claim to have brought Britain back to the centre of the world stage. In the European Community, she demanded and won reform of the EC budget, began the process of reform of the Common Agricultural Policy and pushed the Community towards completing the single market. Her ideas and vision live on. Not only will she continue to speak out on the future direction of Europe, but John Major in his totally different but equally effective way is just as determined to ensure that Britain will not become a province of a federal Europe. His negotiations at Maastricht gave Mrs Thatcher's supporters a great deal more to cheer about than the Euro-fanatics in the Conservative, Labour and Liberal Democrat Parties.

Perhaps her greatest international achievement came outside the Community. It is fashionable in certain quarters to ridicule Mrs Thatcher's contribution to the downfall of Communism, but it is accepted almost as a truism in Russia and the former Soviet empire. It was she who, together with President Reagan and other leaders, did so much to convince the Soviet Union that the arms race was unwinnable. Without the determination, to which Mrs Thatcher contributed more than her share, of the Nato countries during the 1980s to spend whatever was necessary to maintain the west's defences, the Soviet Union would not have collapsed. A cruel and extended experiment with the Communist system ended with its ignominious disintegration when its leaders finally realized that, whereas the west could maintain and increase military spending without damaging the standard of living of its people, the Soviet Union could not.

For my part I still marvel at the fact that a young man from Carnforth, who set out as a schoolboy to promote socialism, should have ended his career working for its destruction; that the son of a railwayman should have committed a Conservative government to the privatization of the railways; that the son of a 'Bevin boy' should have committed a Conservative government to the privatization of the coal industry; that a former Treasurer of the Labour League of Youth in a small northern town should have become the Chairman of the Conservative Party; that a person who had spent a substantial part of his working life in the City of London, and who had wondered at its autocratic and exclusive nature, should have had the opportunity to open up the Stock Exchange; that someone who in an early stage of his life was a pacifist should have served in a War Cabinet.

Like John Major and Margaret Thatcher, having enjoyed enormous opportunities in a free and ever more open society, I still retain a burning ambition to see those opportunities and that openness further extended – it is the collective ambition of the Conservative Party and it is this ambition which presents such a formidable problem for our opponents in the years ahead.

Index

The following abbreviations have been used:
AP: Ann Parkinson; CP: Cecil Parkinson;
MT: Margaret Thatcher

Achilles Club 71, 78, 148
Acland, Anthony 197, 206
AGRs (advanced gas-cooled reactors) 261
Aircraft and Shipbuilding Industries Bill
    131–132
Allason, James 93–94, 96, 107, 108
Alliance, SDP/Liberal 181–182, 225, 226,
    227, 228
Anderson, Reverend 58
Angelo, Bonnie 235
Angus, (Sir) Michael 95
Antelope, HMS 208
Archer, Peter (Lord) 248
Argentina 157, 165–166, 189–190, 194–211
Ashdown, Paddy 42
Ashridge College 79
Atkins, Humphrey 119, 121, 129, 190, 191
Atkins, Robert 11, 285
Atkinson, Norman 60
Attlee, Clement 11, 60–61

Baker, Kenneth 7, 20, 28, 36, 38, 46, 104,
    237, 241
Baker, Mary 7
Bargery, Christine 148–149, 156
Barlow, Sir Robert 82, 83
Barnes, John 102
Barnett, Joel (Lord) 135
Bath and Wells, Bishop of 251–252
Beetham, Air Chief Marshall Sir Michael
    213
Belaunde, Terry President 204
Bell, (Sir) Tim 216, 217–218, 228, 232
Beloff, Lord (Max) 188
Bennett, Nicholas 24
Berkeley, Humphry 31
Bernstein, Carl 208
Bevan, Aneurin 61–62
Biffen, John 72, 114, 173, 190, 192, 222,
    223, 245
Blair, Tony 278
Blue Chip Club 11–12, 20
Boaden, Roger 216

Boddy, David 179, 187, 188–189, 216,
    217
Bongo, President 166–167
Booth, Hartley 146–147
Borrie, Sir Gordon 242, 243, 244, 246,
    247, 248
Bradbury, Reg 90
Bradshaw, John 102
Branch, Philip 100
Brandt Commission 171
British Airways 259
British Coal 124, 257, 281, 282
British Gas 257, 258, 260, 263
British Nuclear Fuels 259, 271, 278
British Rail 284, 286, 287–288, 290, 294,
    295–296, 296–297
British Steel 183, 251, 259
British Telecom 241–242, 260
Brittan, (Sir) Leon 140, 173, 236
Britto, Keith 216, 223
Brooke, Peter 38, 46
Brown, Michael 24
Buchanan, Elizabeth 2, 32, 49, 286
Buchanan-Smith, Alick 136
Butcher, John 24, 237
Butler, Adam 119
Butler, Sir Robin 2–3
Butterfill, John 24

Cabinet committees 193–194, 214
Callaghan, James 14, 72, 124, 130, 133,
    140, 142, 143, 146, 193, 227
Cambridge 62, 63–64, 65–77
Cambridge Union Society 64, 71–72
Cambridge University Conservative
    Association (CUCA) 64
Canary Wharf 290–291
Carlisle, Mark (Lord Carlisle) 11, 175
Carmichael, Keith 30, 46, 127
Carnforth 51–55, 57, 60, 304
Carr, Robert 125, 126
Carrington, Lord 8, 44, 190–191, 192, 196,
    197, 258
Castle, Barbara (Lady Castle) 61, 109
Central Electricity Generating Board
    (CEGB) 260, 261–263, 265, 267, 268–
    271, 275, 278

Chamberlain, Neville 52, 54
Chambers, Drew 82, 83–84
Channel Tunnel 284, 296, 297
Channon, Paul 237, 283, 284, 286, 287, 288, 293, 296, 297
Chelsea-Hackney line 291, 292
Chope, Christopher 1, 2, 12, 31
Churchill, Sir Winston 61, 65, 71, 99
Clapham rail crash 283, 289
Clark, Alan 34, 219
Clarke, Kenneth 2, 20, 45, 129
Clinton-Davis, Stanley (Lord) 149, 171
coal industry (privatization) 119, 280–282
Cockfield, Lord (Arthur) 192, 245
Cocks, Michael (Lord Cocks) 131
Common Agricultural Policy 157, 304
Community Charge 27–28, 39
Concorde 117–118, 154
Conservative Party
    Central Office 176, 177, 180, 186–189, 215–216, 223, 229–231
    election manifestos: 1955 9; 1970 122, 301; 1983 59, 219–220
    leadership election rules 31–32
    Party Conferences: 1981 179–180, 181–186; 1983 250; 1987 265, 266; 1988 280–281, 288; 1989 15; 1990 5, 15, 27, 299–300
    Conservative Research Department 187–188, 221, 225
    National Union of Conservative Associations 179, 181
    Society of Conservative Agents 181, 185
Cope, (Sir) John 102
Corrin, Jack 102
Crofts, Joan 98–99
Cropper, Peter 187, 188
Crosby by election 16, 57, 186, 187
Croydon North West by election 186
Cullen, Lord 282
Culver, John 73, 74–75
Cunningham, George 141
Currie, Edwina 29

Dalyell, Tam 141, 171
Dart, Geoff 259, 278
Day, Robin 41, 137, 231
de Cuellar, Perez 207, 210
de Hoz, Martinez 165
Defence, Ministry of 195, 197
Derby Aviation 92
Derrick, John 266
Devolution 130, 140–141
Devlin, Bernadette 111
Dixon, Piers 99
Docklands Light Railway 291–292
Douglas-Home, Sir Alec (Lord Home) 31, 94, 126, 133, 180

Doyle, John 96
de Cann, Edward 181, 190, 230
Duchy of Lancaster 220–221
Dunkley, Ken 96
Durbar Club, The 215

East/West crossrail 291, 292
East Midlands Electricity Board 266
Eastbourne by election 16, 27
Economic and Monetary Union 15–16, 17
Economic Dining Club 124–125, 143
Eden, Anthony (Lord Avon) 10
Eden, John (Lord Eden) 102, 108
Edinburgh Festival 62
Electricity Council 260
electricity supply industry, privatization 119, 257–280
Elizabeth II 221
Elliot, Sir Walter 98
Ellis, Shelagh 147
Emery, Fred 251
Emmanuel College, Cambridge 56, 59, 63–64, 65–77
Enders, Thomas 200, 201
European Commission 5, 18, 276
European Community 14–17, 21, 39, 103, 109–110, 122, 124, 304; CP's views on: 103, 110, 168–169
European Defence and Security Conference (Paris) 22, 26
European Monetary System 13; Exchange Rate Mechanism 13–14, 16–17, 303
Evans, David 184
exchange controls 153, 157, 223–224
Eyre, (Sir) Reginald 149

Falkland Islands 189–213, 214
Falklands War Cabinet (ODSA) 192–213, 305
Fallon, Michael 258, 280
Farrer, Bert 60
Favell, Tony 24
Finnegan, Thomas 230–231
Fisher, Moorton 92
Fitt, Gerry (Lord) 111
Fletcher, Alex 237, 247
Foot, Michael 110, 140, 182, 190, 227–228
Foreign and Commonwealth Office 195–196, 201, 211
Forsyth, Michael 12
Fowler, (Sir) Norman 19, 257
Furbank, Peter 66

Gaiger, Charlie 82
Galtieri, General Leopoldo 204
Gander, Fred 55

Gardiner, (Sir) George 133
Garel-Jones, Tristan 11, 33
Garner, Tony 185, 186, 187
Garrett, Tony 186
General Agreement on Tarrifs and Trade (GATT) 17, 169, 238
General Belgrano 195, 203–204, 231
Ghost Workers (Abolition) Bill 135
Gibb, Nick 30
Gibbs, Jim 74
Gilmour, Sir Ian 11, 173, 175
Glasgow Hillhead by election 186, 189
Goodison, (Sir) Nicholas 244, 246, 249
Gould, Bryan 67
Gow, Ian 6, 39, 174, 190–191, 218, 219, 224, 232, 236, 250
Gow, Jane 6, 250
Gray, Robin 161–162
Greater London Council (GLC) 123, 295
Gregson, Sir Peter 258, 269, 279–280
Griffiths, Professor Brian (Lord) 270
Guinness, John 258
Gummer, John 250

Haig, General Alexander 195, 198–201, 202, 203, 205
Hailsham, Lord (Quintin) 104, 173, 247
Hampson, Keith 25
Hargreaves & Mason 86
Harrison, Walter 131–132, 142
Harrocks, Gyde, 101
Hart, Billy 90–91
Hart, Judith (Lady Hart) 157
Haslam, Robert (Lord) 251
Hattersley, Roy 67, 244
Hayes, Sir Brian 236–237
Healey, Denis (Lord) 23, 127, 133, 223, 227, 231
Heath, (Sir) Edward 44, 48, 96, 97, 100, 107, 109–110, 119–120, 121, 122, 125, 126, 127, 128, 152, 171, 184, 301
Heath Government 10, 12, 112–113, 135, 280
Heffer, Eric 109, 110, 182
Henderson, Sir Nicholas 197, 204, 206, 213
Heseltine, Anne 117–118
Heseltine, Michael 3, 4, 5–6, 8, 21–22, 24–25, leadership campaign 25–49, 86, 95, 102, 114–115, 115–118, 132, 173, 190, 255
Hickmet, Richard 15
Hoblyn, John 80
Hogg, Douglas 11
Hood, Tommy 100
Hooper, Angela 187
Hordern, (Sir) Peter 114

Horner, Arthur 55
House of Citizenship 79
Howard, Michael 45
Howarth, Alan 24, 187–188
Howarth, Gerald 24
Howe, Elspeth (Lady) 15, 24, 113
Howe, Sir Geoffrey (Lord) 8, 11, 12–21, 23–24, 30, 39, 113, 173, 174, 184–185, 189, 220, 221–222, 223–224, 236, 245
Howell, David 127, 133, 222, 277
Hunt, David 11, 12, 45, 149
Hurd, Douglas 4, 6, 7, 11, 12, 15, 22, 23, 33, 35, 36, 43, 44–45, 46, 48, 49, 95, 140, 171
Hussein, Saddam 163
Hyatt, Leslie 93

Industrial Relations Bill 67, 109, 125
Ingham, (Sir) Bernard 15, 210–211
International Finance Trade and Aid Bill 138
International Monetary Fund 9, 17, 139, 160
IRA 6, 146

Jarvis, Frank (AP's grandfather) 90, 92
Jarvis, Tony (AP's father) 81, 90
Jefferson, Sir George 242
Jellicoe, Lord 118
Jenkins, Roy (Lord) 227, 228, 229
Jenkins, Simon 35
Jones, Robert 24
Jopling, Michael 26, 174, 223, 224, 236
Joseph, Sir Keith (Lord) 8, 11, 12, 59, 125, 126, 144, 173, 223, 230

Kahn, Herman 99
Kaufman, Gerald 225
Kavanagh, Trevor 1
Keays, Sara 40, 234–235, 249–250, 252
Keeble, Sir Curtis 164
Kennedy, Teddy 74–75
King, Lord (John) 219
King, Tom 45, 76, 147
Kings Cross tragedy 285
Kinnock, Neil 31, 41, 42–43, 182, 302, 303, 304
Kitson, (Sir) Timothy 113–114, 122, 128
Knighton, William 158

Labour Government 9, 11, 41, 56–57, 65, 96, 243–244, 259, 261
Labour League of Youth 60, 305
Labour Party 42, 93, 114, 159, 181–182, 225–226, 228; election manifesto 1983 225, 229
Laker, Sir Freddie 137
Lamb, Sir Larry 252

Lambsdorff, Count Otto 156, 158
Lamont, Norman 28, 33, 34, 35, 45, 48, 127, 237, 264, 290–291
Lancaster 51, 62
Lancaster Royal Grammar School 56–58, 62
Lawson, (Sir) Christopher 95, 187, 188, 212, 215–216, 217, 222, 223
Lawson, Nigel (Lord) 11, 13–14, 15, 16, 17, 19, 28, 39, 45, 95, 127, 129, 133–134, 175, 222, 234, 236, 245, 247, 257, 264, 265
Leach, Sir Henry 204, 212
Leavis, F R 63, 66–67, 75
Lees, Dodo 61
Leigh, Sir Geoffrey 30
Lewin, Sir Terence 195, 212–213
Lib/Lab pact 130, 139
Liberal Democrats 16
Liberal Party 48, 125, 130, 137–138, 139, 140, 222
Lilley, Peter 12, 45
Livingstone, Ken 295
Lockerbie bomb 283, 289
London Underground 290, 291–292
Longstone, Roy 106
Luce, (Sir) Richard 191, 196
Luton Airways 92

MacGregor, John 20, 34, 36, 46, 127, 129
Mackay of Clashfern, Lord 2, 3
Mackie, Bob 80–81
Mackley, Bob 73
Maclean, Fitzroy 60, 61
Macleod, Eve (Lady Macleod) 104, 106
Macleod, Iain 72, 104, 105, 111–112
Macmillan, Harold (Earl Stockton) 10, 143
Macve, John 69
Magnox nuclear power stations 261, 264, 267, 278–279
Maguire, Frank 142
Major, John 3–4, 5, 14, 15, 22, 23, 33, 35, 36, 42, 43, 44–45, 46, 47, 48, 49, 50, 301, 303, 305
Marchioness 287
Marcos, President 157–158
Marine Accident investigation Branch 287
Marsh, Alan 81
Marshall, Lord (Walter) 261, 263, 268–269, 276, 277, 282
Mates, Michael 25
Maude, Francis 12, 48
Maudling, Reginald 95, 104, 11
Maurice, Spencer 92, 93
Maxwell-Hyslop, (Sir) Robin 131
McAlpine, Alistair (Lord) 38, 178, 229, 232, 251, 252, 253

McCagg, Louis 73
McLoughlin, Patrick 285–286
McManus, Frank 111
Mellish, Bob (Lord) 131
Mendez, Costa 201
Mercer, Canon 55
Merchant Taylor's School, Crosby 57
Metal Box Company 76, 78–84, 88
Mildmay, Sir Walter 72
Miller, Perry 2
miners strike 1973 111
    1984–85 263, 274, 280, 281
Mineworkers, National Union of 143, 257, 280, 281
Molyneaux, James 111
Moore, John (Lord) 26, 36
Moore, Major-General Jeremy 209, 213
Morris-Adams, Richard 102
Morrison, Herbert 72
Morrison, (Sir) Peter 27, 36, 258
Morse, Sir Jeremy 138
Morton, Sir Alistair 297
Mount, Ferdinand 220, 221–222
Muddle, Eric 148
Muddle, Joan 148
Multi-Fibre Arrangement 170

Nabarro, Gerald 108
National Coal Board (see also British Coal) 124
National Front 105, 230
National Heritage 298
nationalization 259–260
National Power 271
Neave, Airey 116, 117, 127, 128, 142, 144, 146
Newton, Tony 33, 100, 127
Nicholson, Emma 28
1992 Committee 144, 190–191
No Turning Back Group 12, 24
non-fossil-fuel levy 274–276
Northampton Town FC 101
Nott, (Sir) John 14–15, 133, 136–138, 144, 148, 149–150, 151, 152, 153, 169, 173, 189, 190–191, 192, 195, 199, 202, 203, 207, 208, 245
Number 10 Policy Unit 220, 270, 277

Odgers, Freddie 67–68
Office of Fair Trading 242, 246
Onslow, Cranley 31, 36, 48, 115, 118
Oppenheim, Sally (Lady) 110, 136, 147, 149
Orme, Stan 109
Orr, Willie 111
overseas aid 159
Owen, David (Lord) 14, 182, 227
Oxbridge athletics 69–70

Oxenbury, Shirley (Dame) 154

Packer, Reverend J W 58
Paget, Reginald 99, 100, 101, 103
Paisley, Ian 111
Palliser, Sir Michael 206
Parkinson, Ann (Lady) 1, 30, 79–80, 81,
    92–93, 97, 100, 101, 104, 106, 107, 113–
    114, 124, 174, 198, 224, 234, 235, 236,
    237, 249, 250, 252, 253, 254, 255, 256
Parkinson, Annie (grandmother) 52
Parkinson, Bridget (Betty) (mother) 52,
    53, 54
Parkinson, Cecil (Lord)
    Leadership Election: hears that MT is
    to resign 1; supports MT 2; assesses
    MT's support in Cabinet 7, 22; joins
    Cabinet 11; legislative programme
    1990–91 18–19; role in campaign 26;
    backs MT in Walden interview 27;
    decides to leave Cabinet and Commons
    30, 40–41; votes for MT 31; reaction to
    election 32–34, 36–37; reasons for MT's
    defeat 38–39; views on 3 candidates 43–
    45; backs Major 45, 47; final meeting
    with MT as PM 47–48;
        Early Years: family 52–53; earliest
    memories 53–54; wartime memories
    53–54; at School 55–56, 56–59; interest
    in Church 58–59; national service 59,
    63; Early Politics: joins Labour Party 55,
    58, 60, 62; 1950 General Election 60–
    61; 1951 General Election 61; attends
    Labour Party Conference 61–62; begins
    to doubt Socialism 64, 71
        Cambridge: post-war Cambridge 65;
    studies 66–67; runs for Cambridge 70–
    71, 76; decides to enter industry 68, 76;
        Family and Business: joins Metal Box
    78–84; meets Ann Jarvis 79, proposes
    81, married 92; considers emigrating to
    Canada 82–83; joins West Wake Price
    83–84, qualifies as accountant and
    becomes Partner 88–89; starts own
    business 89–90; sells business 141–142;
        Political career: joins Conservative
    Party 92–98; works with Norman
    Tebbit 94–98; looks for seat-Truro 98–
    99, selected for Northampton, fights
    1970 General Election 99–103; Enfield
    West by election 104–106; meets MT
    106; enters Commons 107; maiden
    speech 111–112; PPS to Michael
    Heseltine 114–118; appointed whip 119–
    120, 129–131; Feb 1974 election 123–
    124; MT appoints as Trade spokesman
    136–139; relations with MT 142–143;

friendship with Norman Tebbit 144–
145; 1979 election campaign 146–148;
    Minister of Trade: appointed 148–
150; working with civil servants 151–
152, 153–154; Visits: Philippines 150,
156–158, Singapore 155, 158, Bahrain
155, Indonesia 155–156, Malaysia 158,
the Gulf 162, GDR 162, Argentina 162,
165–166, Yugoslavia 162, 173,
Cameroon 162, 166, Saudi Arabia 162,
173, USA 162, Iraq 162–164, Soviet
Union 164–165, Chile 165–166, 194,
Gabon 166–167, Mexico 173, Peru 173,
Columbia 173;
    Party Chairman: appointed 174–175;
Central Office 176–181, 185–189; 1981
Party Conference 181–183; and MT 189;
discusses election strategy with MT
216–218; 1983 election called 222–224;
campaign discussed 225–233;
Falklands War: joins war cabinet 189–
92; family ties to Argentina 194–195;
view of FCO 195–197; assumes role as
Government spokesman 207–208;
speaks to Conservative Women's
Conference 209–210; Falklands Dinner
212;
    DTI Secretary: appointed 235;
merging departments 237–240; stock
exchange reform 242–248; Keays
statement 249–250; 1983 Conference
252; resignation 253;
    Energy Secretary: appointed 257; sets
financial targets for electricity industry
261–263; working with Lord Marshall
263, 269; privatization options 263–
265; Party Conference 1988 265–266;
nuclear power 273–275; withdraws
Magnox stations 278–279; coal industry
119, 280–282;
    Transport Secretary: appointed 279,
283; attitude to public spending 284;
balanced transport policy 288; 'red
routes' 292
Parkinson, Daniel (grandfather) 52
Parkinson, Emma (daughter) 93, 102, 235,
    249, 254
Parkinson, Joanna (daughter) 96, 102, 235,
    254
Parkinson, Mary (daughter) 93, 102, 235,
    249, 254
Parkinson, Norma (sister) 53
Parkinson, Sydney (father) 52, 53, 54, 83
Parkinson Hart Securities 90–91
Parris, Matthew 23
Parsons, Sir Anthony 197, 206, 213
Paterson, Ben 95

Patten, Chris 11, 27, 33, 45, 144
Patten, John 11
Pattie, (Sir) Geoffrey 133
Pendlington, Mark 234, 235
Penhaligon, David 138
Peters, Douglas 58
Piper Alpha 282
Poole, John 102
Porter, Sir George 75
Portillo, Michael 12, 27, 251, 284–285, 286, 287
Powell, (Sir) Charles 19, 38, 257
Powell, Enoch 95, 110, 114, 121, 124–125, 152, 288
PowerGen 271
Prescott, John 46–7, 139, 262, 278, 289, 296
Pressure for Economic and Social Toryism (PEST) 180
PWRs (pressurised-water reactors) 261, 264, 270, 273
Price, Charles 255
Price Commission 149, 152
Prior, James (Lord) 8
Property Services Agency 283
public expenditure round (PES) 240–241, 290–291
Pym, Francis (Lord) 8, 44, 106, 107, 140, 173, 190, 192, 197, 201–202, 203–204, 206, 207, 210–211

Quinton, Sir John 87

Rawlinson, Sir Anthony 235–236
Reagan, President Ronald 26, 200, 203, 210, 211, 212, 224, 236
Reardon, Jack 167
Reece, (Sir) Gordon 228–229, 232
Rees, Peter (Lord) 127, 133, 134–135, 176, 252
Reichmann, Paul 290–291
Reid, Sir Robert B 295
Reid, Sir Robert P 295–296
Renton, Tim 36
Restrictive Trade Practices Act 1976 242–243, 245
Rhodes-James, (Sir) Robert 171
Richardson, Lord 245
Rickett, Willie 259, 264
Ridley, Nicholas (Lord) 5, 11, 19, 124, 127, 133, 135, 196, 219, 292
Rifkind, Malcolm 33, 45, 264, 272
road pricing 292–294
Roads for Prosperity 284, 290, 300
Robertson, David 29
Rodgers, William (Lord) 182, 231
Rooke, Sir Denis 263

Royal Air Force (RAF) 63
Ryder, Richard 34

Saatchi and Saatchi 140, 216, 217, 228, 229, 231, 232
Samuel, Gill 286
Sanderson, Russell (Lord) 181
Saroop, Narindar 215
Sawter, David 95
Scargill, Arthur 134, 257, 280–281
Scottish Conservative Party Conference 205, 225
Scottish National Party 130, 140
Seamen, National Union of 139, 296
Select Committees
    Energy 271–272, 273; Science and Technology 116–117; Treasury 230; CP's views on 272–273
Sharples, Richard 98
Sheffield, HMS 204–205
Sheldon, Robert 135–136
Sheppard, Sir John 66–67
Sherbourne, Stephen 225–226
Shrimsley, Tony 188–189, 225–226
Silkin, John 227
Simons, Tony 105, 123
Skinner, Dennis 42, 150
Slater, Arthur (AP's step-father) 81, 83
Slater, Barbara (AP's mother) 81
Smith, David 94, 96, 98
Smith, Jim 277
Smith, John 140
Soames, Lord 8, 11, 173, 175
Social Democratic Party 181, 182, 186, 222, 225, 228
sound money 9, 10, 11, 160
South Africa 150
Speed, Jeffrey 104, 105
Spensley, Nora 147
Spicer, Michael 149, 180, 187, 215, 258, 264, 278
St John Stevas, Norman (Lord St John of Fawsley) 147, 272
Steel, (Sir) David 130, 138, 227, 228
Stephens, Malcolm 138
Stewart, Allan 24
Stewart, Ian 174
Stock Exchange 87, 242, 243, 244, 246, 247, 248, 249, 254
Stock Exchange Council 243, 246
Stone, John 88
student loans 59
Swift, Jonathan 302

Tapsell, (Sir) Peter 254
Taylor, Robert 186
Taylor, (Sir) Teddy 136, 147

Tebbit, Margaret (Lady) 97, 256
Tebbit, Norman (Lord) 1, 11, 36, 37, 94, 97, 98, 103, 108, 133, 145, 148, 175, 188, 222, 223, 236, 255–256, 257, 266
Thatcher, Carol 127–128
Thatcher, (Sir) Denis 7, 38, 106, 128, 232, 235
Thatcher, Margaret (Lady Thatcher) (see also references to MT under Parkinson, Cecil)
Resigns as leader 1, 38, 50; announces resignation 2–4, 39; position in Cabinet 5, 9, 10–11, 12, 173; supports John Major 6; 1990 Conference 6; Cabinet appointments 7–8, 11, 19–20, 147–148, 174–175, 234–236; and Geoffrey Howe 12–21; attitude to ERM 14, 16, 17; attends Rome Summit 17–18; agrees to bring forward date of leadership election 22; in Paris 22; speaks at Mansion House 23; listens to G Howe's resignation speech 23–24; style of campaign 25–38; attitude towards elections 26–27; reaction to first ballot 32–37; meets Cabinet 37; speaks in no confidence debate 41–43; urges friends to support Major 47; role in Oct 1974 election 125–126; leads Conservative team on Finance Bill 126–127; stands against Heath 127–128; growing confidence of 142–144; Airey Neave's death 146; and Peter Walker 147–148; at 1981 Party Conference 184; during Falklands war 190–213; and General Haig 199–201; view of FCO 197; and Francis Pym 197–198; speaks to Scottish Tory Conference 205–206; and Tim Bell 217–218; and Ian Gow 218; decides to call 1983 election 222–224; election campaign 226–227; regard for Lord Marshall 263, 276; Other references: 46–50, 59, 106, 124–125, 132, 133, 137, 160, 161–162, 164, 167–168, 173, 181, 186, 215, 232–233, 234–235, 257, 279, 288, 301–305
Thomas, Ann 147
Thomas, George 132, 185
Thomas, Hugh 147
Thomas, Peter 106
Thompson, Brigadier Julian 209, 212
Thorneycroft, Lord 10, 11, 143, 144, 173, 174, 178, 181, 187
Thorpe, Jeremy 48, 125
Timberlake, R R 56, 61
Timoshenko, Marshal 55
Todd, Ron 302
Tombs, Lord 32
Tompkins, Fred 101

Tory Reform Group 5, 180
Trades Union Congress 165
Traffic in London 292
Treasury, The 240–241, 290–291
Trippier, (Sir) David 237
Truman, President Harry 7
Turnbull, Andrew 38

'U-turn' 10, 113, 173, 175
Ufford, Charlie 73–74
UNCTAD V 150, 156–158
unemployment 9, 10, 41, 218
United Nations 197, 199, 205, 206, 210; Resolution 502 197, 200; Resolution 505 210

Waddington, David (Lord) 46
Wade-Gery, Robert 197, 206
Wakeham, John (Lord) 36, 37, 46
Waldegrave, William 11, 20, 28, 33, 45, 59
Walden, Brian 17, 23, 26–27, 43, 67, 210–211, 232
Walder, David 129
Walker, Peter (Lord) 8, 19, 125, 148, 173, 257, 263
Walters, General Vernon 200
Ward, Eric 202
Weatherill, (Jack) Bernard (Lord) 107, 121
Weinberger, Caspar 203
Welbourne, Edward 59, 63, 65–66
Welsh Nationalists 130, 140
West, Mike 86, 93, 96
West Wake Price and Co 83–89
Whewell, William 58
whips, role of 120–121
Whitelaw, William (Lord) 6, 8–9, 11, 34, 143, 144, 174, 180, 183–184, 190, 191, 192, 202, 207, 223, 236, 257
Whittingdale, John 32
Wilberforce, Lord 113, 114
Wilkinson, Max 277–278
Williams, Shirley 57, 182, 186
Wilson, Geoffrey 98
Wilson, Harold (Lord) 61, 103, 108, 125, 130, 142, 304
Winnick, David 177
Wolfson, David 144
Woodward, Admiral Sir John 203, 207, 209, 212
Woof, Robert 62

Yew, Lee Kuan 118
Young, Lady (Janet) 11, 175
Young, Lord (David) 11, 264
Young, Hugo 173
Young Conservatives 5, 196, 286
Younger, George 25, 37